THE FUTURE OF AIR TRAFFIC CONTROL
HUMAN OPERATORS AND AUTOMATION

Christopher D. Wickens, Anne S. Mavor,
Raja Parasuraman, and James P. McGee, editors

Panel on Human Factors in Air Traffic Control Automation

Commission on Behavioral and Social Sciences and Education
National Research Council

NATIONAL ACADEMY PRESS
Washington, D.C. 1998

NATIONAL ACADEMY PRESS • 2101 Constitution Avenue, NW • Washington, DC 20418

NOTICE: The project that is the subject of this report was approved by the Governing Board of the National Research Council, whose members are drawn from the councils of the National Academy of Sciences, the National Academy of Engineering, and the Institute of Medicine. The members of the committee responsible for the report were chosen for their special competences and with regard for appropriate balance.

This report has been reviewed by a group other than the authors according to procedures approved by a Report Review Committee consisting of members of the National Academy of Sciences, the National Academy of Engineering, and the Institute of Medicine.

This study was supported by Grant No. 94-G-042 between the National Academy of Sciences and the U.S. Department of Transportation. Any opinions, findings, conclusions, or recommendations expressed in this publication are those of the author(s) and do not necessarily reflect the view of the organizations or agencies that provided support for this project.

Library of Congress Cataloging-in-Publication Data

The future of air traffic control : human operators and automation /
    Panel on Human Factors in Air Traffic Control Automation, Commission
    on Behavioral and Social Sciences and Education, National Research
    Council ; Christopher D. Wickens ... [et al.], eds.
       p. cm.
    Includes bibliographical references (p.   ) and index.
    ISBN 0-309-06412-0
    1. Air traffic control—Automation. 2. Aeronautics—Human
    factors. I. Wickens, Christopher D. II. National Research Council
    (U.S.). Panel on Human Factors in Air Traffic Control Automation.
    TL725.3.T7F88   1998
    387.7′40426—dc21   97-45303

Additional copies of this report are available from:

National Academy Press
2101 Constitution Avenue, NW, Lock Box 285
Washington, DC 20055
Call 800-624-6242 or 202-334-3313 (in the Washington Metropolitan Area).

This report is also available online at **http://www.nap.edu**

Printed in the United States of America

COMMITTEE ON HUMAN FACTORS

WILLIAM B. ROUSE (*Chair*), Enterprise Support Systems, Norcross, GA
TERRY CONNOLLY, Department of Management and Policy, College of
    Business and Public Administration, University of Arizona, Tucson
COLIN G. DRURY, Industrial Engineering Department, University of Buffalo
WILLIAM C. HOWELL, American Psychological Association Science
    Directorate, Washington, DC
DANIEL R. ILGEN, Department of Psychology and Department of
    Management, Michigan State University
BONNIE E. JOHN, Human-Computer Interaction Institute, Carnegie Mellon
    University
TOM B. LEAMON, Liberty Mutual Research Center, Hopkinton, MA
DAVID C. NAGEL, AT&T Laboratories, Basking Ridge, NJ
KARLENE H. ROBERTS, Haas School of Business, University of California,
    Berkeley
BENJAMIN SCHNEIDER, Department of Psychology, University of
    Maryland
LAWRENCE W. STARK, School of Optometry, University of California,
    Berkeley
EARL L. WIENER, Department of Management Science, University of Miami
GREG L. ZACHARIAS, Charles River Analytics, Cambridge, MA

ANNE S. MAVOR, *Study Director*
JERRY S. KIDD, *Senior Adviser*
SUSAN R. McCUTCHEN, *Senior Project Assistant*

Contents

Preface

This report is the work of the Panel on Human Factors in Air Traffic Control Automation, which was established in fall 1994 at the request of the Federal Aviation Administration (FAA). The panel was appointed to conduct a two-phase study of the human factors aspects of the nation's air traffic control system, of the national airspace system of which it is a part, and of proposed future automation issues in terms of the human's role in the system. The impetus for the study grew out of a concern by members of the Subcommittee on Aviation of the House Public Works and Transportation Committee, then chaired by Congressman Oberstar, that efforts to modernize and further automate the air traffic control system should not compromise safety by marginalizing the human controller's ability to effectively monitor the process, intervene as spot failures in the software or environmental disturbances require, or assume manual control if the automation becomes untrustworthy. Panel members represent expertise in human factors, decision making, cognitive psychology, organization structure and culture, training and simulation, system design, controller operations, and pilot operations. The primary focus of the study is the relationship between humans and the tools provided to assist in accomplishment of system tasks.

The first phase of the panel's work focused on the current air traffic control system and its development and operation within the national airspace system from a human factors perspective. The specific purposes of the first phase were to understand the complexities of the current system that automation is intended to address, characterize the manner in which some levels of automation have already been implemented, and provide a baseline of human factors knowledge as it relates to the functions of the air traffic controller in the system and the organizational context within which these functions are performed. The results of the panel's deliberations for the first phase were reported in *Flight to the Future: Human Factors in Air Traffic Control*.

The second phase has assessed future automation alternatives and the role of the human operator in ensuring safety and efficiency in the air traffic control system. In the second phase we examined the human factors aspects of automation both for the general development of new systems and for specific, key subsystems at various stages of testing and implementation. A critical focus of the second phase has been the interaction between the automation and the controller on the ground and the automation and the pilot in the cockpit.

This report provides the results of the panel's deliberations during the second phase. The first part of the report discusses fundamental human factors issues pertaining to automation of air traffic control functions and reviews several emerging technologies that may support automation of future air traffic control functions. The second part of the report reviews current and future initiatives and programs that automate functions for surveillance, communication, flight information, immediate conflict avoidance, strategic long-range planning, training, and maintenance. The third part of the report discusses the integration of research and development as well as human factors issues with respect to the free flight initiative, and also presents the panel's vision of the evolution of automation in the national airspace system in the next decade. The final chapter presents the panel's key conclusions and recommendations. Research results available after August 1997 were not reviewed by the panel for this report.

We direct this report to a broad audience, including those interested in the air traffic control system and its operation and policy as well as those interested in general issues of aviation psychology research and air safety. We direct the attention of our policy-making readers to the Summary and Chapter 10, which present our conclusions and recommendations; to the introduction to Part II, which provides an overview of the trend toward automation in the national airspace system; and to Part III, which presents discussions of management issues, program development issues, free flight, and a future vision.

Many individuals have made contributions to the panel's thinking and to various sections of this report by serving as presenters, advisors, and liaisons to useful sources of information; all of these individuals provided us with valuable information. A list of contributors and their affiliations is presented in Appendix B. A few people played a more direct role in the coordination of information used in the preparation of this volume, and they deserve special mention. We extend our gratitude to several individuals in the Federal Aviation Administration: to Mark Hofmann and to Maureen Pettitt for their consistent support of the panel's activities; to David Cherry for helpful and timely responses to numerous requests from the panel for documentation and technical information, and for arranging visits to FAA facilities and discussions with subject-matter experts; and to Michael McAnulty for providing and for coordinating presentations to the panel at the FAA Technical Center. We are especially grateful to Neil Planzer, director, Air Traffic System Requirements Service at the Federal Aviation Administration, for his continued interest in and guidance to the panel.

We would also like to extend our thanks to Brian Hilburn, at the National Aerospace Laboratory (NLR) in the Netherlands, for contributing to the section on interactive planning and for providing materials on European developments in air traffic control automation; and to Jonathan Taylor, at the Massachusetts Institute of Technology, for contributing to the section on the global positioning system.

This report is the collective product of the entire panel, and each member took an active role in drafting sections of chapters, leading discussions, and/or reading and commenting on successive drafts. The first part of the report, which discusses automation issues and principles, as well as emerging technological resources, reflects significant contributions by Raja Parasuraman, Thomas Sheridan, Tora Bikson, Robert Helmreich, Todd LaPorte, Marvin Cohen, and David Hopkin. The second part, which reviews current and envisioned automation initiatives for air traffic control, reflects significant contributions by Paul Stager, Earl Wiener, Charles Aalfs, Richard Stone, Joseph Pitts, James Danaher, Laurence Young, and Diane Damos.

Staff at the National Research Council made important contributions to our work in many ways. As study director, Anne S. Mavor managed the overall course of the study, ensured that the work was done carefully and well, and made intellectual contributions that can be found in every chapter of the report. James P. McGee worked closely with the study director on all aspects of the study, taking particular responsibility for drafting descriptions of a number of the systems presented in Part II as well as the material on integration of research and development. Jerry Kidd contributed insights across many areas of the report and drafted sections that address conflict avoidance technologies and the application of research methodologies. We would also like to express our appreciation to Alexandra Wigdor, director of the Division on Education, Labor, and Human Performance, for her valuable insight, guidance, and support; to Susan McCutchen, the panel's senior project assistant, who was indispensable in organizing meetings, arranging travel, compiling agenda materials, managing the exchange of documentation across the panel, and preparing the final manuscript; and to Christine McShane, who edited and significantly improved the report.

Christopher D. Wickens, *Chair*
Panel on Human Factors in
Air Traffic Control Automation

THE FUTURE OF AIR TRAFFIC CONTROL
HUMAN OPERATORS AND AUTOMATION

Summary

The nation's air traffic control system is responsible for managing a complex mixture of air traffic from commercial, general, corporate, and military aviation. Despite the strong safety record achieved over the last several decades, the system does suffer occasional serious disruption, often the result of outdated and failed equipment. When equipment failures occur, the safety of passengers and airplanes depends entirely on the skills of controllers and pilots.

Pressures to increase the number of flights that can be moved through the national airspace system safely and efficiently have led to proposals to provide more reliable and powerful equipment and at the same time increase the level of automation in air traffic control facilities—that is, to use advances in technology to take over tasks that are currently performed by humans. Such proposals have raised concern that automation may compromise the safety of the system by marginalizing the human controller's ability to provide the necessary backup when disruptions occur.

A second concern revolves around current planning toward a concept in which pilots, airline dispatchers, and managers assume more authority for air traffic control. This concept, referred to as *free flight*, has many implications for the controller's performance that parallel the implications of high levels of automation.

The Panel on Human Factors in Air Traffic Control Automation was convened at the request of the Federal Aviation Administration (FAA) to study the air traffic control system, the national airspace system, and future automation alternatives from a human factors perspective. The central premise of the analysis is that considerations of public safety require that the air traffic control system continue to be designed so that the human controller can intervene successfully as spot failures in the software or environmental disturbances require or can even assume manual control when the automation fails. The panel's first phase, which focused on the current system and its development, led to recommendations regarding safety and efficiency, system management, personnel selection and training, the development of an integrated approach to human factors, and system design considerations of human strengths and vulnerabilities. These recommendations and their supporting analyses are presented in *Flight to the Future: Human Factors in Air Traffic Control*, the panel's Phase I report. This second phase assesses future automation alternatives and the role of the human operator in ensuring safety and efficiency in the air traffic control system. Along with this assessment, the panel has included a human factors analysis of free flight focusing on its implications for the performance of air traffic controllers.

The panel concludes that current system needs and the availability of various technologies provide adequate justification to continue the development and implementation of some forms of air traffic control automation, but we strongly argue that this continuation should be driven by the philosophy of human-centered automation, which we characterize as follows:

> The choice of what to automate should be guided by the need to compensate for human vulnerabilities and exploit human strengths. The development of the automated tools should proceed with the active involvement of both users and trained human factors practitioners. The evaluation of such tools should be carried out with human-in-the-loop simulation and careful experimental design. The introduction of these tools into the workplace should proceed gradually, with adequate attention to training, to facility differences, and to user requirements. The operational experience from initial introduction should be very carefully monitored, with mechanisms in place to respond rapidly to the lessons learned from the experiences.

The complete set of the panel's conclusions and recommendations, presented in Chapter 10, covers (1) the general topics of locus of authority, levels of automation, recovery from failure and degradation, teamwork, and cross-cultural issues; (2) issues related to the design, development, and testing of specific systems; (3) free flight; and (4) the role of human factors in the process of introducing automation. In this summary, we present the most important recommendations, on levels of automation, system recovery from failure, locus of authority as it relates to automation and free flight, and the process of introducing automation.

LEVELS OF AUTOMATION

In the Phase I report, the panel identified a 10-level scale of automation relating to decision and action selection. At the extreme of total manual operation, a particular function is continuously performed by the human operator, with no machine control. At the other extreme of total automation, all aspects of the function (including its monitoring) are delegated to a machine, so that only the end product and not its operation is made available to the human operator. In between these two extremes lie different degrees of participation in the function by the human and by automation.

In this report we propose two additional scales, one representing levels of automation that can be applied to the dimension of information acquisition and integration (referred to as information automation) and another that is related to the dimension of action implementation. The level of information automation is determined by the presence or absence of computer functions enabling filtering, information distribution, information transformation, confidence estimates, integrity checks, and flexible information based on requests from users. Systems that possess all of these features have high levels of information automation. The dimension of action implementation is treated in this context as a dichotomous scale providing either manual or automatic implementation.

- **The panel recommends that automation efforts focus on reliable, high-level automation applications for information acquisition, integration, and presentation and for aiding controller decision making in order to support all system functions. Especially important in the near future is the development of decision aids for conflict resolution and maintaining separation. These aids should be directed primarily toward ensuring proper spacing between aircraft in preparation for the final stages of approach to landing and toward en route flight path efficiency improvement.**
- **The panel recommends implementation of high levels of automation of decision and action selection for system tasks involving relatively little uncertainty and risk. However, for system tasks associated with greater uncertainty and risk, automation of decision and action selection should not proceed beyond the level of suggesting a preferred decision/action alternative. Any consideration for automation at or above this level must be designed to prevent: loss of vigilance, loss of situation awareness, degradation of operational skills, and degradation of teamwork and communication. Such designs should also ensure the capabilities to overcome or counteract complacency, recover from failure, and provide a means of conflict resolution if loss of separation occurs.**

RECOVERY

A central issue is the potential influence of automation on the ability to efficiently and effectively recover from emergency situations. Automation may increase capacity, but it will also increase traffic density and may increase airspace complexity by inducing changes in traffic flow from standard air routes. We predict that increases in traffic complexity and density will reduce the controller's situation awareness. We also anticipate that manual skills will degrade for most functions that one might automate, given the nearly universal findings that there is some forgetting and skill decay with disuse (although the magnitude of such a decline in air traffic control is not well known). As a result, controllers are likely to react more slowly to emergencies if they require use of those manual skills during the recovery from a degraded state. Furthermore, it is anticipated that automation will introduce new procedures for recovery and that these procedures will also require training and practice. Developing training for emergency skills is a difficult problem because it requires preparation for an open-ended set of circumstances, many of which may never occur.

Linking the two human performance elements of change in situation awareness and skill degradation makes it possible to predict the change in *recovery response time*—that is, the time required to respond appropriately to unexpected failure situations and intervene with manual control skills or alternative automated functionality. It is assumed that the less skilled controller, responding appropriately to a situation of which he has less awareness, will do so more slowly. Specifically, we predict that recovery response time will be greatly modulated by individual differences, characteristics of the team environment, the complexity of the airspace (number of response options), and the familiarity of procedures necessary to cope with a degraded system. All important safety consequences of system or component failures are related to the margin by which available time exceeds the recovery response time. In order to effectively predict recovery under a variety of conditions, it is necessary to develop models based on recovery scenarios that are based on human performance data concerning responses to low-probability events under different levels of skill degradation and lowered situation awareness.

• **The panel recommends investing sufficient resources in studies of human response to low-probability emergencies; actively pursuing failure modes/fault tree analysis, particularly to identify situations in which two or more coordinating agents receive information inputs that are incongruous or contradictory; and involving human factors specialists in the development and testing of system recovery procedures.**

• **The panel recommends the development of models, for given designs and procedures, to examine the implications of recovery in a high-density, unstructured airspace created by increased capabilities of ground-based automation or free flight.**

• **The panel recommends the development of airspace safety models that can predict the likelihood of midair collisions, as a function of frequency** and parameters of near-midair collisions[1] and losses of separation,[2] for varying standards of traffic separation. To do this, models should be developed that are sensitive to loss of situation awareness and the possible degradation of skills that may result from moving controllers to progressively higher levels of automation of decision and action selection.

• The panel recommends that air traffic control subject-matter experts collaborate with specialists in the behavioral sciences to model individual and team responses to emergency situations and to populate the models with data to be collected in studies of human response time to low-probability emergencies. Policy makers should be made aware that choosing median response times to model these situations can have very different implications from those based on worst-case (longest) response times; these kinds of modeling choices must be carefully made and justified.

• The panel recommends that system functionality should be designed so that failure recovery will not depend on skills that are likely to degrade.

LOCUS OF AUTHORITY

Future airspace projections dictate a need for increases in capacity without sacrificing safety. Two alternative vehicles for accomplishing these goals have been proposed: a free flight scenario and a scenario involving ground-based authority; both presume automation. Any action or technology that moves to reduce pilot constraints on maneuvering is a move in the direction of free flight. There is, however, an important distinction between *strategic free flight*, in which route planning by the pilot in collaboration with the dispatcher is done in a manner that is unconstrained by air traffic control (i.e., free scheduling and free routing), and *tactical free flight*, in which the pilot is empowered to make flight path changes and conflict avoidance maneuvers without consulting the ground controller. There is of course a continuum of levels between strategic and tactical maneuvering. At least four different programs already involve some aspects of free flight: standard visual flight rules, the expanded national route program, the conflict resolution advisories of the traffic alert and collision avoidance system (TCAS), and the oceanic in-trail climb procedure.

---

[1]Incidents associated with the operation of an aircraft in which a possibility of a collision occurs as a result of proximity of less than 500 feet to another aircraft, or a report is received from a pilot or flight crew member stating that a collision hazard existed between two or more aircraft.

[2]Loss of separation is a condition in which the prevailing standards for separation are violated.

A large number of issues must be addressed and resolved before determining if expanded concepts of free flight are feasible in an airspace whose regulators and users are committed to safety as a primary goal. It can be argued that any radical change to an already safe system will have at least the possibility of compromising safety. Unfortunately, given the complexity of the free flight concept, accurate assessment and prediction of its safety benefits may not be achievable for several years after its implementation.

The versions of free flight that assume high levels of airborne authority have the predicted ability to greatly increase airspace flexibility and hence to potentially increase capacity as well. However, a large number of uncertainties are associated with safety. These include uncertainties as to how pilot-to-pilot negotiations will be resolved in worst-case scenarios; problems relating to controllers' maintaining awareness of the tactical situation in an airspace made more complex and dense by the implementation of free flight; the workload impact of both increasing decision load in the cockpit and increasing monitoring load on the ground; and issues regarding possible confusion in the residence of authority among air traffic controllers, pilots, and airline operations personnel.

In considering these issues, the panel concludes that the residence of authority should be as unambiguous as possible to minimize opportunity for confusion between perceived and actual authority. For the foreseeable future, both actual and perceived authority should reside consistently and unambiguously on the ground. The justification is that authority on the ground is centralized, whereas authority in the air in a free flight regime is of necessity distributed among multiple aircraft, dispatchers, and controllers, and its residence would vary over time. Distributing authority flexibly across these agents is an invitation for ambiguity, which in turn compromises safety.

The structural consistency of the airspace should be preserved. A major component of the controller's mental model of the airspace is associated with the enduring characteristics of a particular sector. Therefore, although air routes can and should be substantially modified from their current structure in order to improve efficiency, these modifications, once in place, should be relatively enduring in order to maintain safety. Air routes should not be altered on a flight-by-flight basis. Although more alternative routes may allow far greater flight path efficiency than in the current airspace, for example, by taking advantage of prevailing winds, there should be a fixed database of what these direct routes are, and an expectation that pilots will adhere to them (subject to controllers' granting of pilots' requests), in this way preserving consistency in the structure of the airspace.

   • **A ground-based scenario consistent with formulated plans of the Federal Aviation Administration can increase efficiency without radical changes in authority structure from the current system (e.g., the expanded national route program). The panel therefore recommends the development and** fielding of current and proposed automation tools for ground-based air traffic control, following the guidelines specified in this report regarding the selection of levels of automation. We also recommend the vigorous pursuit of projections of how various tools will operate in concert.

• Because free flight design concepts that assume a high level of airborne authority over control of aircraft flight paths have more uncertainties than design options involving ground-based authority with increased automation, the panel recommends extreme caution before existing levels of free flight are further expanded to greater levels of pilot authority for separation. Furthermore, we recommend the conduct of extensive human-in-the-loop simulation studies and validation of human performance models before decisions are made regarding the further implementation of free flight; this is needed to obtain reliable prediction of the safety implications of worst-case scenarios. We also recommend heavy reliance on scenario walk-throughs and focus group sessions with controllers, pilots, traffic managers, and airline dispatchers.

INTRODUCING AUTOMATION

The introduction of automation, whether incremental or comprehensive, involves some interference with an ongoing process that cannot be disrupted. Consequently, careful planning is required so that the transition can be made with minimal interruption. These issues are discussed in detail in the panel's Phase I report.

Despite the FAA's past efforts to foster greater human factors involvement in the development and implementation of advanced air traffic control systems, the agency's success record has been mixed at best. However, a recently completed, independent study (by the Human Factors Subcommittee of the FAA's Research, Engineering, and Development Advisory Council) examined the current FAA organizational structure, staffing, and operating practices as they relate to human factors support activities, making recommendations for improving the effectiveness of this function. These recommendations appear to be well founded and offer the potential for better integration of human factors activities in the development of advanced automation technologies.

• The panel recommends that senior Federal Aviation Administration management should reexamine the results of the study by the Human Factors Subcommittee of the FAA's Research, Engineering, and Development Advisory Council, with a view toward implementing those recommendations that appear most likely to achieve more active, continued, and effective involvement of both users and trained human factors practitioners in the development and implementation of advanced air traffic control systems. All aspects of human-centered automation should be considered in fielding new automated systems.

• The Federal Aviation Administration should continue to support integrated product teams with well-trained human factors specialists assigned to the teams. Both users and human factors specialists should be involved at the early stages to help define the functionality of the proposed automation system. These specialists should be responsible to report to human factors management within the Federal Aviation Administration as well as to project managers.

• The Federal Aviation Administration should continue to work toward an infrastructure in which some human factors training is provided to personnel and program managers at all levels of the organization (and contract teams).

• The Federal Aviation Administration should ensure that adequate funding is provided for needed human factors work at all stages of system development and field evaluations both before and after systems acquisition.

• During the development of each automation function, system developers should consider possible interactions with other automation functions (under development or already existing), tools, and task requirements that form (or will form) the operational context into which the specific automation feature will be introduced.

PART I

Automation Issues
and Emerging Technologies

This book provides a rationale, based on a human factors perspective, for making decisions about (1) the extent to which automation should be applied to the performance of national airspace system functions and (2) the issues to consider and the methods to apply during design and introduction of systems that incorporate automation to maximize the safety, efficiency, usability, and acceptance of systems that incorporate automation. The discussion and analysis is divided into three parts: Part I introduces definitions, concepts, and promising emerging technologies; Part II analyzes key automation initiatives; and Part III discusses research and development for the national airspace and presents conclusions and recommendations. A glossary of aviation and related acronyms appears in Appendix A.

Part I contains two chapters. The first chapter begins by examining the rationale for pursuing automation, presenting the panel's characterization of human-centered automation, and exploring levels of automation in three dimensions: information acquisition, decision and action selection, and action implementation. The discussion then turns to issues of system performance, human performance, adaptive automation, and design and management influences. These discussions provide a basis for the analytic framework for current and proposed systems used in Part II.

The second chapter reviews some advances in hardware and software that may offer opportunities for automating a greater range of information-processing, decision-making, and control functions. The emerging technologies reviewed include visualization, intelligent decision aiding, and computer-supported cooperative work.

9

1

Automation Issues in
Air Traffic Management

The pressures for automation of the air traffic control system originate from three primary sources: the needs for improved safety, and efficiency (which may include flexibility, potential cost savings, and reductions in staffing); the availability of the technology; and the desire to support the controller.

Even given the current very low accident rate in commercial and private aviation, the need remains to strive for even greater safety levels: this is a clearly articulated implication of the "zero accident" philosophy of the Federal Aviation Administration (FAA) and of current research programs of the National Aeronautics and Space Administration (NASA). Naturally, solutions for improved air traffic safety do not need to be found only in automation; changing procedures, improving training and selection of staff, and introducing technological modernization programs that do not involve automation per se, may be alternative ways of approaching the goal. Yet increased automation is one viable approach in the array of possibilities, as reflected in the myriad of systems described in Section II.

The need for improvement is perhaps more strongly driven by the desire to improve efficiency without sacrificing current levels of safety. Efficiency pressures are particularly strong from the commercial air carriers, which operate with very thin profit margins, and for which relatively short delays can translate into very large financial losses. For them it is desirable to substantially increase the existing capacity of the airspace (including its runways) and to minimize disruptions that can be caused by poor weather, inadequate air traffic control equipment, and inefficient air routes. The forecast for the increasing traffic demands over the next several decades exacerbates these pressures. Of course, as with safety, so with efficiency: advanced air traffic control automation is not the only solution. In particular, the concept of *free flight* (RTCA,[1] 1995a, 1995b; Planzer and Jenny, 1995) is a solution that allocates greater responsibility for flight path choice and traffic separation to pilots (i.e., between human elements), rather than necessarily allocating more responsibility to automation. Automation is viewed as a viable alternative solution to solve the demands for increased efficiency. Furthermore, it should be noted that free flight does depend to some extent on advanced automation and also that, from the controller's point of view, the perceived loss of authority whether it is lost to pilots (via free flight) or to automation, may have equivalent human factors implications for design of the controller's workstation.

It is, of course, the case that automation is made possible by the existence of technology. It is also true that, in some domains, automation is driven by the availability of technology; the thinking is, "the automated tools are developed, so they should be used." Developments in sensor technology and artificial intelligence have enabled computers to become better sensors and pattern recognizers, as well as better decision makers, optimizers, and problem solvers. The extent to which computer skills reach or exceed human capabilities in these endeavors is subject to debate and is certainly quite dependent on context. However, we reject the position that the availability of computer technology should be a reason for automation in and of itself. It should be considered only if such technology has the capability of supporting legitimate system or human operator needs.

Automation has the capability both to compensate for human vulnerabilities and to better support and exploit human strengths. In the Phase I report, we noted controller vulnerabilities (typical of the vulnerabilities of skilled operators in other systems) in the following areas:

1. Monitoring for and detection of unexpected low-frequency events,
2. Expectancy-driven perceptual processing,
3. Extrapolation of complex four-dimensional trajectories, and
4. Use of working memory to either carry out complex cognitive problem solving or to temporarily retain information.

In contrast to these vulnerabilities, when controllers are provided with accurate and enduring (i.e., visual rather than auditory) information, they can be very effective at solving problems, and if such problem solving demands creativity or access to knowledge from more distantly related domains, their problem-solving

---

[1]Prior to 1991, when its name was formally changed, the RTCA was known as the Radio Technical Commission for Aeronautics.

ability can clearly exceed that of automation. Furthermore, to the extent that accurate and enduring information is shared among multiple operators (i.e., other controllers, dispatchers, and pilots), their collaborative skills in problem solving and negotiation represent important human strengths to be preserved. In many respects, the automated capabilities of data storage, presentation, and communications can facilitate these strengths.

As we discuss further in the following pages, current system needs and the availability of some technology provide adequate justification to continue the development and implementation of some forms of air traffic control automation. But we strongly argue that this continuation should be driven by the philosophy of *human-centered automation*, which we characterize as follows:

> The choice of what to automate should be guided by the need to compensate for human vulnerabilities and to exploit human strengths. The development of the automated tools should proceed with the active involvement of both users and trained human factors practitioners. The evaluation of such tools should be carried out with human-in-the-loop simulation and careful experimental design. The introduction of these tools into the workplace should proceed gradually, with adequate attention given to user training, to facility differences, and to user requirements. The operational experience from initial introduction should be very carefully monitored, with mechanisms in place to respond rapidly to the lessons learned from the experiences.

In this report, we provide examples of good and bad practices in the implementation of human-centered design.

LEVELS OF AUTOMATION

The term *automation* has been defined in a number of ways in the technical literature. It is defined by some as any introduction of computer technology where it did not exist before. Other definitions restrict the term to computer systems that possess some degree of autonomy. In the Phase I report we defined automation as: *"a device or system that accomplishes (partially or fully) a function that was previously carried out (partially or fully) by a human operator."* We retain that definition in this volume.

For some in the general public the introduction of automation is synonymous with job elimination and worker displacement. In fact, in popular writing, this view leads to concerns that automation is something to be wary or even fearful of. While we acknowledge that automation can have negative, neutral, or even positive implications for job security and worker morale, these issues are not the focus of this report. Rather we use this definition to introduce and evaluate the relationships between individual and system performance on one hand and the design of the kinds of automation that have been proposed to support air traffic controllers, pilots, and other human operators in the safe and efficient management of the national airspace on the other.

In the Phase I report we noted that automation does not refer to a single either-or entity. Rather, forms of automation can be considered to vary across a continuum of levels. The notion of levels of automation has been proposed by several authors (Billings, 1996a, 1996b; Parasuraman et al., 1990; Sheridan, 1980). In the Phase I report, we identified a 10-level scale, that can be thought of as representing low to high levels of automation (Table 1.1). In this report we expand on that scale in three important directions: (1) differentiating the automation of decision and action selection from the automation of information acquisition; (2) specifying an upper bound on automation of decision and action selection in terms of task complexity and risk; and (3) identifying a third dimension, related to the automation of action implementation.

First, in our view, the original scale best represents the range of automation for decision and action selection. A parallel scale, to be described, can be applied to the information automation. These scales reflect qualitative, relative levels of automation and are not intended to be dimensional, ordinal representations.

Acquisition of information can be considered a separate process from action selection. In both human and machine systems, there are (1) sensors that may vary in their sophistication and adaptability and (2) effectors (actuators) that have feedback control attached to do precise mechanical work according to plan. Eyes, radars, and information networks are examples of sensors, whereas hands and numerically controlled industrial robots are examples of effectors. We recognize that information acquisition and action selection can and do interact through feedback loops and iteration in both human and machine systems. Nevertheless, it is convenient to consider automation of information acquisition and action selection separately in human-machine systems.

Second, we suggest that specifications for the upper bounds on automation of decision and action selection are contingent on the level of task uncertainty. Finally, we propose a third scale that in this context is dichotomous, related to the automation of action implementation, applicable at the lower levels of automa-

TABLE 1.1 Levels of Automation

Scale of Levels of Automation of Decision and Control Action

HIGH	10.	The computer decides everything and acts autonomously, ignoring the human.
	9.	informs the human only if it, the computer, decides to
	8.	informs the human only if asked, or
	7.	executes automatically, then necessarily informs the human, and
	6.	allows the human a restricted time to veto before automatic execution, or
	5.	executes that suggestion if the human approves, or
	4.	suggests one alternative, and
	3.	narrows the selection down to a few, or
	2.	The computer offers a complete set of decision/action alternatives, or
LOW	1.	The computer offers no assistance: the human must take all decisions and actions.

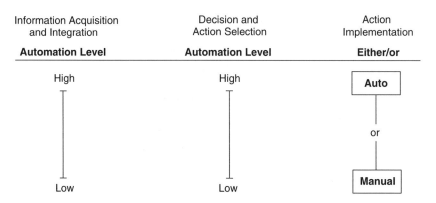

FIGURE 1.1   Three-scale model of levels of automation.

tion of decision and action selection. The overall structure of this model is shown in Figure 1.1, and the components of the model are described in more detail as follows.

Information Acquisition

Computer-based automation can apply to any or all of at least six relatively independent features involving operations performed on raw data:

1. *Filtering.* Filtering involves selecting certain items of information for recommended operator viewing (e.g., a pair of aircraft that would be inferred to be most relevant for conflict avoidance or a set of aircraft within or about to enter a sector). Filtering may be accomplished by guiding the operator to view that information (e.g., highlighting relevant items while graying out less relevant or irrelevant items; Wickens and Yeh, 1996); total filtering may be accomplished by suppressing the display of irrelevant items. Automation devices may vary extensively in terms of how broadly or narrowly they are tuned.

2. *Information Distribution.* Higher levels of automation may flexibly provide more relevant information to specific users, filtering or suppressing the delivery of that same information for whom it is judged to be irrelevant.

3. *Transformations.* Transformations involve operations in which the automation functionality either integrates data (e.g., computing estimated time to contact on the basis of data on position, heading, and velocity from a pair of aircraft) or otherwise performs a mathematical or logical operation on the data (e.g., converting time-to-contact into a priority score). Higher levels of automation transform and integrate raw data into a format that is more compatible with user needs (Vicente and Rasmussen, 1992; Wickens and Carswell, 1995).

4. *Confidence Estimates.* Confidence estimates may be applied at higher

levels of automation, when the automated system can express graded levels of certainty or uncertainty regarding the quality of the information it provides (e.g., confidence in resolution and reliability of radar position estimates).

5. *Integrity Checks.* Ensuring the reliability of sensors by connecting and comparing various sensor sources.

6. *User Request Enabling.* User request enabling involves the automation's understanding specific user requests for information to be displayed. If such requests can be understood only if they are expressed in restricted syntax (e.g., a precisely ordered string of specific words or keystrokes), it is a lower level of automation. If requests can be understood in less restricted syntax (e.g., natural language), it is a higher level of automation.

The level of automation in information acquisition and integration, represented on the left scale of Figure 1.1, can be characterized by the extent to which a system possesses high levels on each of the six features. A system with the highest level of automation would have high levels on all six features.

Decision and Action Selection and Action Implementation

Higher levels of automation of decision and action selection define progressively fewer degrees of freedom for humans to select from a wide variety of actions (Table 1.1 and the middle scale of Figure 1.1). At levels 2 to 4 on the scale, systems can be developed that allow the operator to execute the advised or recommended action manually (e.g., speaking a clearance) or via automation (e.g., relaying a suggested clearance via data link by a single computer input response). The manual option is not available at the higher levels for automation of decision and action selection. Hence, the dichotomous action implementation scale applies only to the lower levels of automation of decision and action selection.

Finally, we note that control actions can be taken in circumstances that have more or less uncertainty or risk in their consequences, as a result of more or less uncertainty in the environment. For example, the consequences of an automated decision to hand off an aircraft to another controller are easily predictable and of relatively low risk. In contrast, the consequences of an automation-transmitted clearance or instruction delivered to an aircraft are less certain; for example, the pilot may be unable to comply or may follow the instruction incorrectly. We make the important distinction between lower-level decision actions in the former case (low uncertainty) and higher-level decision actions in the latter case (high uncertainty and risk). Tasks with higher levels of uncertainty should be constrained to lower levels of automation of decision and action selection.

The concluding chapter of the Phase I report examined the characteristics of automation in the current national airspace system. Several aspects of human interaction with automation were examined, both generally and in the specific context of air traffic management. In this chapter, we discuss system reliability and recovery.

SYSTEM PERFORMANCE

System Reliability

Automation is rarely a human factors concern unless it fails or functions in an unintended manner that requires the human operator to become involved. Therefore, of utmost importance for understanding the human factors consequences of automation are the tools for predicting the reliability (inverse of failure rate) of automated systems. We consider below some of the strengths and limitations of reliability analysis (Adams, 1982; Dougherty, 1990).

Analysis Techniques

Reliability analysis, and its closely related methodology of probabilistic risk assessment, have been used to determine the probability of major system failure for nuclear power plants, and similar applications may be forthcoming for air traffic control systems. There are several popular techniques that are used together.

One is fault tree analysis (Kirwan and Ainsworth, 1992), wherein one works backward from the "top event," the failure of some high-level function, and what major systems must have failed in order for this failure to occur. This is usually expressed in terms of a fault tree, a graphical diagram of systems with *ands* and *ors* on the links connecting the second-level subsystems to the top-level system representation. For example, radar fails if any of the following fails: the radar antennas and drives, *or* the computers that process the radar signals, *or* the radar displays, *or* the air traffic controller's attention to the displays. This amounts to four nodes connected by *or* links to the node representing failure of the radar function. At a second level, for example, computer failure occurs if both the primary *and* the backup computers fail. Each computer, in turn, can experience a software failure *or* a hardware failure *or* a power failure *or* failure because of an operator error. In this way, one builds up a tree that branches downward from the top event according to the *and-/or-gate* logic of both machine and human elements interacting. The analysis can be carried downward to any level of detail. By putting probabilities on the events, one can study their effects on the top event. As may be realized by the above example, system components depending on *and-gate* inputs are far more robust to failures (and hence reliable) than those depending on *or-gate* inputs.

Another popular technique is event tree analysis (Kirwan and Ainsworth, 1992). Starting from some malfunction, the analyst considers what conditions may lead to other possible (and probably more serious) malfunctions, and from the latter malfunction what conditions may produce further malfunctions. Again, probabilities may be assigned to study the relative effects on producing the most serious (downstream) malfunctions.

Such techniques can provide two sorts of outputs (there are others, such as cause-consequence diagrams, safety-state Markov diagrams, etc.; Idaho National Engineering Laboratory, 1997). On one hand, they may produce what appear to be "hard numbers" indicating the overall system reliability (e.g., .997). For reasons we describe below, such numbers must be treated with extreme caution. On the other hand, reliability analysis may allow one to infer the most critical functions of the human operator relative to the machinery. In one such study performed in the nuclear safety context, Hall et al. (1981) showed the insights that can be gained without even knowing precisely the probabilities for human error. They simply assumed human error rates (for given machine error rates) and performed the probability analysis repeatedly with different multipliers on the human error rate. The computer, after all, can do this easily once the fault tree or event tree structure is programmed in. The authors were able to discover the circumstances for which human error made a big difference, and when it did not. Finally, it should be noted that the very process of carrying out reliability analysis can act as a sort of audit trail, to ensure that the consequences of various improbable but not impossible events are considered.

Although reliability analysis is a potentially valuable tool for understanding the sensitivity of system performance to human error (human "failure"), as we noted above, one must use great caution in trusting the absolute numbers that may be produced, for example, using these numbers as targets for system design, as was done with the advanced automation system (AAS). There are at least four reasons for such caution, two of which we discuss briefly, and two in greater depth. In the first place, any such number (i.e., r = .997) is an estimate of a mean. But what must be considered in addition is the estimate of the variability around that mean, to determine best-case and worst-case situations. Variance estimates tend to be very large relative to the mean for probabilities that are very close to 0 or 1.0. And with large variance estimates (uncertainty of the mean), the mean value itself has less meaning.

A second problem with reliability analysis pertains to unforeseen events. It seems to be a given that things can fail in the world, failures that the analysts have no way of predicting. For example, it is doubtful that any reliability analyst would have been able to project, in advance, the likelihood that a construction worker would sever the power supply to the New York TRACON with a backhoe loader, let alone have provided a reliable estimate of the probability of such an event's occurring.

The two further concerns related to the hard numbers of reliability analysis are the extreme difficulties of making reliability estimates of two critical components in future air traffic control automation: the human and the software. Because of their importance, each of these is dealt with in some detail.

Human Reliability Analysis

Investigators in the nuclear power industry have proposed that engineering reliability analysis can be extended to incorporate the human component (Swain, 1990; Miller and Swain, 1987). If feasible, such extension would be extremely valuable in air traffic control, given the potential for two kinds of human error to contribute to the loss of system reliability: errors in actual operation (e.g., a communications misunderstanding, an overlooked altitude deviation) and errors in system set-up or maintenance. Some researchers have pointed out the difficulty of applying human reliability analysis (to derive hard numbers, as opposed to doing the sort of sensitivity analysis described above [Adams, 1982; Wreathall, 1990]). The fundamental difficulties of this technique revolve around the estimation of the component reliabilities and their aggregation through traditional analysis techniques. For example, it is very hard to get meaningful estimates of human error rates, because human error is so context driven (e.g., by fatigue, stress, expertise level) and because the source of cognitive errors remains poorly understood. Although this work has progressed, massive data collection efforts will be necessary in the area of air traffic control, in order to form even partially reliable estimates of these rates.

A second criticism concerns the general assumptions of independence that underlie the components in an event or fault tree. Events at levels above (in a fault tree) or below (in an event tree) are assumed to be independent, yet human operators show two sorts of dependencies that are difficult to predict or quantify (Adams, 1982). For one thing, there are possible dependencies between two human components. For example, the developmental controller may be reluctant to call into question an error that he or she noticed that was committed by a more senior, full-performance-level controller at the same console. For another thing, there are poorly understood dependencies between human and system reliabilities, related to trust calibration, which we discuss later in this chapter. For example, a controller may increase his or her own level of vigilance to compensate for an automated component that is known to be unreliable; alternatively, in the face of frustration with the system, a controller may become stressed or confused and show decreased reliability.

Software Reliability Analysis

Hardware reliability is generally a function of manufacturing failures or the wearing out of components. With sophisticated testing, it is possible to predict how reliable a piece of hardware will be according to measures such as mean time between failures. Measuring software reliability, however, is a much more difficult problem. For the most part, software systems need to fail in real situations, in order to discover bugs. Generally, many uses are required before a piece of software is considered reliable. According to Parnas et al. (1990), failures in software are the result of unpredictable input sequences. Predicting failure rate is based on the probability of encountering an input sequence that will cause the system to fail. Trustworthiness is defined by the extent to which a catastrophic failure or error may occur; software is trusted to the extent that the probability of a serious flaw is low. Testing for trustworthiness is difficult because the number of states and possible input sequences is so large that the probability of an error's escaping attention is high.

For example, the loss of the Airbus A330 in Toulouse in June 1994 (Dornheim, 1995) was attributed to autoflight logic behavior changing dramatically under unanticipated circumstances. In the altitude capture mode, the software creates a table of vertical speed versus time to achieve smooth level-off. This is a fixed table based on the conditions at the time the mode is activated. In this case, due to the timing of events involving a simulated engine failure, the automation continued to operate as though full power from both engines was available. The result was steep pitchup and loss of air speed—the aircraft went out of control and crashed.

There are a number of factors that contribute to the difficulty of designing highly reliable software. First is complexity. Even with small software systems, it is common to find that a programmer requires a year of working with the program before he or she can be trusted to make improvements on his or her own. Second is sensitivity to error. In manufacturing, hardware products are designed within certain acceptable tolerances for error; it is possible to have small errors with small consequences. In software, however, tolerance is not a useful concept because trivial clerical errors can have major consequences.

Third, it is difficult to test software adequately. Since mathematical functions implemented by software are not continuous, it is necessary to perform an extremely large number of tests. In continuous function systems, testing is based on interpolation between two points—devices that function well on two close points are assumed to function well at all points in between. This assumption is not possible for software, and because of the large number of states it is not possible to do enough testing to ensure that the software is correct. If there is a good model of operating conditions, then software reliability can be predicted using mathematical models. Generally, good models of operating conditions are not available until after the software is developed.

Some steps can be taken to reduce the probability of errors in software. Among them is conducting independent validation using researchers and testing personnel who were not involved in development. Another is to ensure that the software is well documented and structured for review. Reviews should cover the following questions:

- Are the correct functions included?
- Is the software maintainable?
- For each module, are the algorithms and data structures consistent with the specified behavior?
- Are codes consistent with algorithms and data structures?
- Are the tests adequate?

Yet another step is to develop professional standards for software engineers that include an agreed-upon set of skills and knowledge.

Recently, the capacity maturity model (CMM) for software has been proposed as a framework for encouraging effective software development. This model covers practices of planning, engineering, and managing software development and maintenance. It is intended to improve the ability of organizations to meet goals for cost, schedule, functionality, and product quality. The model includes five levels of achieving a mature software process. Organizations at the highest level can be characterized as continuously improving the range of their process capability and thereby improving the performance of their projects. Innovations that use the best software engineering practices are identified and transferred throughout the organization. In addition, these organizations use data on the effectiveness of software to perform cost-benefit analyses of new technologies as well as proposed changes to the software development process.

Conclusion

Although the concerns described above collectively suggest extreme caution in trusting the mean numbers that emerge from a reliability analysis conducted on complex human-machine systems like air traffic control, we wish to reiterate the importance of such analyses in two contexts. First, merely carrying out the analysis can provide the designer with a better understanding of the relationships between components and can reveal sources of possible failures for which safeguards can be built. Second, appropriate use of the tools can provide good sensitivity analyses of the importance (in some conditions) or nonimportance (in others) of human failure.

System Failure and Recovery

Less than perfect reliability means that automation-related system failures can degrade system performance. Later in this chapter we consider the human performance issues associated with the response to such failures and automation-related anomalies in general. Here we address the broader issue of failure recovery from a system-wide perspective. We first consider some of the generic properties of failure modes that affect system recovery and then provide the framework for a model of failure recovery—that is, the capability of the team of human controllers to recover and restore safety to an airspace within which some aspect of computer automation has failed.

We distinguish here between system failures and human operator (i.e., controllers) failures or errors. The latter are addressed later in this chapter and in the Phase I report. System failures are often due to failures or errors of the humans involved with other aspects of the air traffic control system. They include system designers, whose design fails to anticipate certain characteristics of operations; those involved in fabrication, test, and certification; and system maintainers (discussed in Chapter 7). Personnel at any of these levels can be responsible for a "failure event" imposed on air traffic control staff controlling live traffic. It is the nature of such an event that concerns us here. We also use the term system failure to include relatively catastrophic failures of aircraft handling because of mechanical damage or undesirable pilot behavior.

System failures can differ in their severity, their time course, their complexity, and the existing conditions at the time of the failure.

1. Severity differences relate to the system safety consequences. For example, a failed light on a console can be easily noticed and replaced, with minimal impact on safe traffic handling. A failed radar display will have a more serious impact, and a failed power supply to an entire facility will have consequences that are still more serious. As we detail below, the potential seriousness of failures is related to existing conditions.

2. In terms of time courses, failures may be abrupt (catastrophic), intermittent, or gradual. Abrupt failures, like a power outage, are to some extent more serious because they allow the operator little time to prepare for intervention. At the same time, they do have the advantage of being more noticeable, whereas gradual failures may degrade system capabilities in ways that are not noticeable—e.g., the gradual loss of resolution of a sensor, like a radar. Intermittent failures are also inherently difficult to diagnose because of the difficulty in confirming the diagnosis.

3. Complexity refers to single versus multiple component failures. The latter may be common mode failures (such as the loss of power, which will cause several components to fail simultaneously, or the overload on computer capacity), or they may be independent mode failures, when two things go wrong independently, creating a very difficult diagnostic chore (Sanderson and Martagh, 1989). Independent mode failures are extremely rare, as classical reliability analysis will point out, but are not inconceivable, and their rarity itself presents a particular challenge for diagnosis by the operator who does not expect them.

4. Existing conditions refer to the conditions that exist when a failure occurs. These will readily affect the ease of recovery and, hence indirectly, the severity of the consequence. For example, failure of radar will be far more severe in a saturated airspace during a peak rush period than in an empty one at 3:00 a.m. We address this issue in discussing failure recovery.

A model framework of air traffic control failure recovery is provided in Figure 1.2. At the left of the figure is presented the vector of possible air traffic control automation functionalities *1–i*, discussed in Chapters 3-6 of this report. Because automation is not a single entity, its consequences will vary greatly, depending on what is automated (e.g., information acquisition or control action). Next to the right in the figure is a set of variables, assumed to be influenced by the introduction of automation (the list is not exhaustive and does not incorporate organizational issues, like job satisfaction and morale). Associated with each variable is a sign (or set of signs) indicating the extent to which the introduction of automation is likely to increase or decrease the variable in question. These variables are described in the next sections.

Capacity

One motivation for introducing automation at this time is increasing airspace capacity and traffic flow efficiency. It is therefore likely that any automation tool that is introduced will increase (+) capacity.

Traffic Density

Automation may or may not increase traffic density. For example, automation that can reduce the local bunching of aircraft at certain times and places will serve to increase capacity, leaving overall density unaffected. Therefore, two possible effects (+ and 0) may be associated with density.

Complexity

Automation will probably increase the complexity of the airspace, to the extent that it induces changes in traffic flow that depart from the standard air routes and provides flight trajectories that are more tailored to the capabilities of individual aircraft and less consistent from day to day.

Situation Awareness and Workload

Automation is often assumed to reduce the human operator's situation awareness (Endsley, 1996a). However, this is not a foregone conclusion because of differences in the nature of automation and its relation to workload. For example, as we propose in the framework presented in Figure 1.2, automation of information integration in the cockpit can provide information in a manner that is more readily interpretable and hence may improve situation awareness and human response to system failures. In the context of information integration in air traffic management, four-dimensional flight path projections may serve this purpose. Correspondingly, automation may sometimes serve to reduce workload to man-

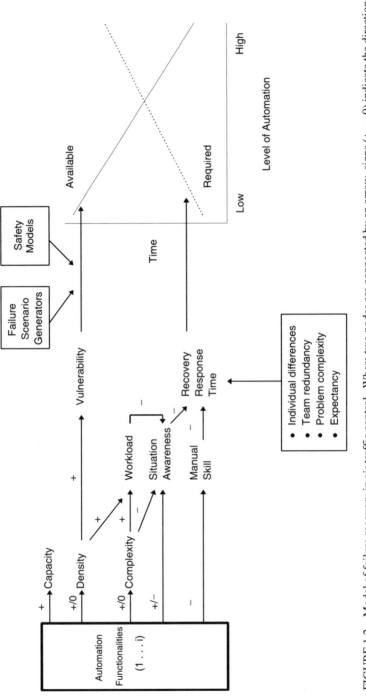

FIGURE 1.2 Model of failure recovery in air traffic control. Where two nodes are connected by an arrow, signs (+, −, 0) indicate the direction of effect on the variable depicted in the right node, caused by an increase in the variable depicted in the left node.

ageable levels, such that the controller has more cognitive resources available to maintain situation awareness. This is the reasoning behind the close link with workload presented in Figure 1.2. However, the figure reflects the assumption that the increasing (+) influence of automation on traffic complexity and density will impose a decrease (–) on situation awareness. The effect of increasing traffic complexity on situation awareness will be direct. The effect of traffic density will be mediated by the effect of density on workload. Higher monitoring workload caused by higher traffic density will be likely to degrade situation awareness.

Skill Degradation

There is little doubt that automation of most functions eventually degrades the manual skills for most functions one might automate, given the nearly universal findings of forgetting and skill decay with disuse reported in the behavioral literature (Wickens, 1992), although the magnitude of decline in air traffic control skills with disuse is not well known. For example, suppose predictive functions are automated, enabling controllers to more easily envision future conflicts (discussed in Chapter 6). Although the controllers' ability to mentally extrapolate trajectories may eventually decay, their ability to solve conflict problems may actually benefit from this better perceptual information, leading possibly to a net gain in overall control ability.

Recovery Response Time

Linking the two human performance elements, situation awareness change and skill degradation, makes it possible to predict the change in *recovery response time*, that is, the time required to respond to unexpected failure situations and possibly intervene with manual control skills. It is assumed that a less skilled controller (one with degraded skills), responding appropriately to a situation of which he has less awareness, will do so more slowly. This outcome variable is labeled recovery response time (we acknowledge that it could also incorporate the accuracy, efficiency, or appropriateness of the response). Such a time function is a special case of more general workload models in which workload is defined in terms of the ratio of time required to time available (Kirwan and Ainsworth, 1992). As an example, in a current air traffic control scenario, when a transgression of one aircraft into the path of another on a parallel runway approach occurs (discussed in Chapter 5), the ratio of the time required to respond to the time available has a critical bearing on traffic safety.

A plausible, but hypothetical function relating recovery response time to the level of automation, mediated by the variables in the middle of the figure, is shown by the dashed line in the graph to the right of the figure, increasing as the level of automation increases. It may also be predicted that recovery response time will be greatly modulated by individual skill differences, by the redundant characteristics of the team environment, by the complexity of the problem, and by the degree to which the failure is expected.

At the top of the figure, we see that failures will be generated probabilistically and may be predicted by failure models, or failure scenario generators, which take into account the reliability of the equipment, of the design, of operators in the system, of weather forecasting, and of the robustness (fault tolerance) of the system. When a failure does occur, its effect on system safety will be directly modulated by the vulnerability of the system, which itself should be directly related to the density. If aircraft are more closely spaced, there is far less time available to respond appropriately with a safe solution, and fewer solutions are available. In the extreme case, if aircraft are too closely spaced, no solutions are available. The solid line of the graph reflects the increasing vulnerability of the system, resulting from the density-increasing influences of higher automation levels in terms of the time available to respond to a failure. Thus, the graph overlays the two critical time variables against each other: the time required to ensure safe separation of aircraft, given a degraded air traffic control system (a range that could include best case, worst case, median estimates, etc.) and the time available for a controller team to intervene and safely recover from the failure, both as functions of the automation-induced changes in the intervening process variables.

We may plausibly argue that the all-important safety consequences of auto-mation are related to the margin by which time available exceeds the recovery response time. There are a number of possible sources of data that may begin to provide some quantitative input to the otherwise qualitative model of influences shown in the figure. For example, work by Odoni et al. (1997) on synthesizing and summarizing models appears to be the best source of information on model-ing how capacity and density changes, envisioned by automated products, will influence vulnerability. Work conducted at Sandia Laboratory for the Nuclear Regulatory Commission may prove fruitful in generating possible failure sce-narios (Swain and Guttman, 1983). Airspace safety models need to be developed that can predict the likelihood of actual midair collisions, as a function of the likelihood and parameters of near-midair collisions and losses of separation and of decreases in traffic separation. The foundations for such a model could be provided by data such as that shown in Figure 1.3.

Turning to the human component, promising developments are taking place under the auspices of NASA's advanced air transportation technology program, in terms of developing models of pilots' response time to conflict situations (Corker et al., 1997), and pilots' generation of errors when working with automa-tion (Riley et al., 1996). However, models are needed that are sensitive to loss of situation awareness induced by removing operators from the control loop (as well as the compensatory gains that can be achieved by appropriate workload reduc-tions and better display of information). The data of Endsley and Kiris (1995), as

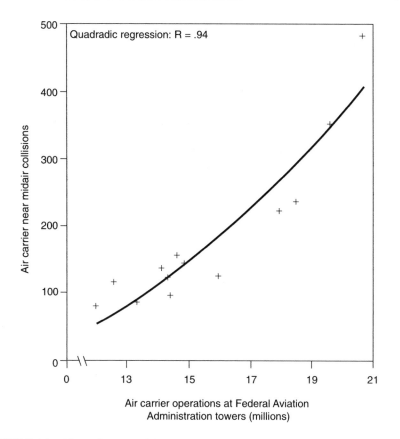

FIGURE 1.3   Air carrier near-midair collisions, 1975-1987. Source: Office of Technology Assessment (1988).

well as those provided by Endsley and Rodgers (1996) in an analysis of operational errors in air traffic control, provide prototypes of the kinds of data collection necessary to begin to validate this critical relation.

Rose (1989) has provided one good model of skill degradation that occurs with disuse, which is an important starting point for understanding the nature of skill loss and the frequency of training (or human-in-the-loop) interventions that should be imposed to retain skill levels. Finally, air traffic control subject-matter experts must work with behavioral scientists to begin to model individual and team response times to emergency (i.e., unexpected) situations (Wickens and Huey, 1993). The models should include data collected in studies of human response time to low-probability emergencies. Policy makers should be made aware that choosing median response times to model these situations can have very different implications from those based on worst-case (longest) response times (Riley et al., 1996); these kinds of modeling choices must be carefully made and justified.

HUMAN PERFORMANCE

Understanding whether responses to failures in future air traffic management systems can be effectively managed requires an examination of human performance, both individual and team, in relation to automation failures and anomalies. At the same time, an understanding is required of how controllers and other human operators use automation under both normal and emergency conditions. The human performance aspects of interaction with automated systems were considered in some detail in the concluding chapter of the Phase I report. Here we review and summarize the major features of that analysis with reference to current and future air traffic management systems.

Several studies have shown that well-designed automation can enhance human operator and hence system performance. Examples in air traffic management include automated handoffs between airspace sectors and display aids for aircraft sequencing at airports with converging runways. At the same time, many observations of the performance of automation in real systems have identified a series of problems with human interaction with automation, with potentially serious consequences for system safety. These observations have been bolstered by a growing body of research that includes laboratory experiments, simulator studies, field studies, and conceptual analyses (Bainbridge, 1983; Billings, 1996a, 1996b; Parasuraman and Mouloua, 1996; Parasuraman and Riley, 1997; Sarter and Woods, 1995b; Wickens, 1994; Wiener, 1988; Wiener and Curry, 1980). Many of these, although not all, relate to human response when automation fails, either through failure of the system itself or failure to cope with conditions and inputs. Automation problems also have arisen, not as a result of specific failures of automation per se, but because of the behavior of automation in the larger, more complex, distributed human-machine system into which the device is introduced (Woods, 1996). Here we consider specific categories of human performance limitations that surface when humans interact with automation.

Figure 1.4 presents a general framework for examining human performance issues discussed in this section by illustrating relationships between three major elements of human interaction with dynamic systems—*trust, situation awareness,* and *mental models*—as well as factors that can affect these elements. It is not intended to represent a model of the cognitive processes that underlie the elements illustrated. Generally speaking, the controller's mental model of an automated function and the system in which it is embedded reflects his or her understanding of the processes by which automation carries out its functions ("How does it work?"). The controller's mental model is affected by the complexity of the system and by the effectiveness with which information about system functioning, status, and performance are displayed. The controller's men-

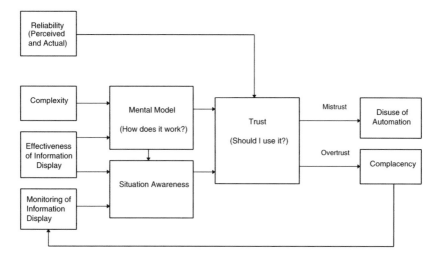

FIGURE 1.4   Framework for examining human performance issues.

tal model affects his or her awareness of the current and predicted state of the situation that is being monitored. Situation awareness is also affected by the degree of effectiveness of both the information display and the controller's monitoring strategy.

A key driver of the human operator's trust of the automation ("Should I use it?") is the reliability or unreliability of the system being monitored. The controller's perception of reliability or unreliability may differ from the actual reliability of the system. The degree of correspondence between actual and perceived reliability may change over time; the software in new systems is often complex, not completely tested, and, therefore, may fail or degrade in ways that may surprise the controller. The controller's trust is also affected by expectations that are based on the controller's mental model and by the controller's situation awareness. Mistrust can lead to disuse of the automation. Overtrust can lead to complacency, which can lead, in turn, to poor monitoring by the controller. Poor monitoring will have a negative effect on the controller's situation awareness.

Trust

Trust is an important factor in the use of automated systems by human controllers (Lee and Moray, 1992; Muir, 1988; Parasuraman and Riley, 1997; Sheridan, 1988). Although the term *trust* in common usage has broader emotional connotations, we restrict its treatment here to human performance. For example, automation that is highly but not perfectly reliable may be trusted to the point that the controller believes that it is no longer necessary to monitor its behavior, so that if and when a failure occurs, it is not detected. Conversely, an automated tool that is highly accurate and useful may nevertheless not be used if the controller believes that it is untrustworthy.

Attributes of Trust

Trust has multiple determinants and varies over time. Clearly, one factor influencing trust is automation reliability, but other factors are also important. Below is a listing of the characteristics of the most relevant determining factors:

1. *Reliability* refers to the repeated, consistent functioning of automation. It should also be noted that some automation technology may be reliably harmful, always performing as it was designed but designed poorly in terms of human or other factors; see the discussion of designer and management errors later in this chapter.

2. *Robustness* of the automation refers to the demonstrated or promised ability to perform under a variety of circumstances. It should be noted that the automation may be able to do a variety of things, some of which need not or should not be done.

3. *Familiarity* means that the system employs procedures, terms, and cultural norms that are familiar, friendly, and natural to the trusting person. But familiarity may lead the human operator to certain pitfalls.

4. *Understandability* refers to the sense that the human supervisor or observer can form a mental model and predict future system behavior. But ease of understanding parts of an automated system may lead to overconfidence in the controller's understanding of other aspects.

5. *Explication of intention* means that the system explicitly displays or says that it will act in a particular way—as contrasted to its future actions having to be predicted from a model. But knowing the computer's intention may also create a sense of overconfidence and a willingness to outwit the system and take inappropriate chances.

6. *Usefulness* refers to the utility of the system to the trusting person in a formal theoretical sense. However, automation may be useful, but for unsafe purposes.

7. *Dependence* of the trusting person on the automation could be measured either by observing the controller's consistency of use, or by using a subjective rating scale, or both. But overdependence may be fatal if the system fails.

Overtrust and Complacency in Failure Detection

If automation works correctly most of the time, the circumstances in which the human will need to intervene because automation has failed are few in number. We can liken this process to a vigilance monitoring task with exceedingly rare events (Parasuraman, 1987). Many research studies have shown that, if events are rare, human monitors will relax their threshold for event detection, causing the infrequent events that do occur to be more likely to be missed, or at least delayed in detection (Parasuraman, 1986; Warm, 1984). Thus, we may imagine a scenario in which a highly reliable automated conflict probe carries out its task so accurately that a controller fails to effectively oversee its operations. If an automation failure does occur, the conflict may be missed by the controller or delayed in its detection. Parasuraman et al. (1993) showed that, when automation of a task is highly and consistently reliable, detection of system failures is poorer than when the same task is performed manually. This "complacency" effect is greatest when the controller is engaged in multiple tasks and less apparent when only a single task has to be performed (Parasuraman et al., 1993; Thackray and Touchstone, 1989). One of the ironies of complacency in detection is that, the more reliable the automation happens to be, the rarer "events" will be and hence the more likely the human monitor will be to fail to detect the failure (Bainbridge, 1983).

Numerous aviation incidents over the past two decades have involved problems of monitoring of automated systems as one of, if not *the* major cause of, the incident. Although poor monitoring can have multiple determinants, operator overreliance on automation to make decisions and carry out actions is thought to be a contributing factor. Even skilled subject-matter experts sometimes have misplaced trust in diagnostic expert systems (Will, 1991) and other forms of computer technology (Weick, 1988). Analyses of ASRS (aviation safety reporting system) reports have provided evidence of monitoring failures linked to excessive trust in, or overreliance on, automated systems (Mosier et al., 1994; Singh et al., 1993). Although most of these systems have involved flight deck rather than air traffic management automation, it is worthwhile noting that such problems may also arise in air traffic management as automation increases in level and complexity.

Many automated devices are equipped with self-monitoring software, such that discrete and attention-getting alerts will call attention to system failures. However, it is also true that some systems fail "gracefully" in ways such that the initial conditions are not easily detectable. This may characterize, for example, the gradual loss of precision of a sensor or of an automated system that uses sensor information for control, which becomes slowly more inaccurate because of the hidden failure of the sensor. An accident involving a cruise ship that ran aground off Nantucket island represents an example of a such a problem. The navigational system (based on the global positioning system) failed "silently" because of a sensor problem and slowly took the ship off the intended course. The ship's crew did not monitor other sources of position information that would have indicated that they had drifted off course (National Transportation Safety Board, 1997a).

Overtrust and Complacency in Situation Awareness

There is by now fairly compelling evidence that people are less aware of the changes of state made by other agents than when they make those changes themselves. Such a conclusion draws from basic research (Slameca and Graf, 1978), applied laboratory simulations (Endsley and Kiris, 1995; Sarter and Woods, 1995a), and interpretations of aircraft accidents (Dornheim, 1995; Sarter and Woods, 1995b; Strauch, 1997).

On the flight deck, then, accident and incident analyses have revealed cases in which higher automation levels have led to a loss in situation awareness, which in turn has led to pilot error. In air traffic management, the connection is slightly less direct. However, recent research by Isaac (1997) has revealed the causal link between automation (automated updating of flight strips) and loss of situation awareness in response to radar failure. Endsley and Rodgers (1996), through examination of operational error data preserved on the SATORI system, have linked operational errors to the loss of situation awareness.

It is important to emphasize that simply providing direct displays of what the automation is doing may be necessary, but it is not sufficient to preserve adequate levels of situation awareness, which would enable rapid and effective response to system failure. Execution of active choices seems to be required to facilitate memory for the system state. There is clearly much truth in the ancient Chinese proverb: *"Inform* me and I forget but show me how to *do* and I remember."

Mistrust

Both complacency and reduced situation awareness concern controllers who trust automation more than they should. Operators may also trust automation less than they should. This may occur first because of a general tendency of operators to want to "do things the way we always do." For example, many controllers were initially distrustful of automatic handoffs, but as their workload-reducing benefits were better appreciated over time, the new automation was accepted. This problem can be relatively easily remedied through advance briefing and subsequent training procedures.

More problematic is when distrust is a result of an experience with unreliable automation. Following the introduction of both the ground proximity warning system and the traffic alert and collision avoidance system (TCAS) in the cockpit, pilots experienced unacceptable numbers of false alarms, the result of bugs in the system that had not been fully worked out (Klass, 1997). In both cases, there was an initial and potentially dangerous tendency to trust the system less than would be warranted, perhaps ignoring legitimate collision alarms.

Mistrust of automated warning systems can become prevalent because of the false alarm problem (Parasuraman and Riley, 1997). What should the false alarm rate be and how can it be reduced? Technologies exist for system engineers to design sensitive warning systems that are highly accurate in detecting hazardous conditions (wake vortex modeling, ground proximity, wind shear, collision course, etc.). These systems are set with a decision threshold (Swets, 1992) that minimizes the chance of a missed warning while keeping the device's false alarm rate below some low value. Because the cost of a missed event (e.g., a serious loss of separation or a collision) is phenomenally high, air traffic management alerting systems such as the conflict alert are set with decision thresholds that minimize misses.

Setting the decision threshold for a particular device's false alarm rate may be insufficient by itself for ensuring high alarm reliability and controller trust in the system (Getty et al., 1995; Parasuraman et al., 1997). Alarm reliability is also determined by the base rate of the a priori probability of the hazardous event. If the base rate is low, as it often is for many real events, then the posterior odds of a true alarm can be quite low even for very sensitive warning systems. Parasuraman et al. (1997) carried out a signal detection theory/Bayesian analysis that illustrates the problem and provides guidelines for alarm design. For example, the decision threshold can be set so that a warning system can detect hazardous conditions with a near-perfect hit rate of .999 (i.e., that it misses only 1 of every 1,000 hazardous events) while having a relatively low false alarm rate of .059. Nevertheless, application of Bayes' theorem shows that the controller could find that the posterior probability (or posterior odds) of a true alarm with such a system can be quite low. When the a priori probability (base rate) is low, say .001, only 1 in 59 alarms that the system emits represents a true hazardous condition (posterior probability = .0168).

Consistently true alarm response occurs only when the a priori probability of the hazardous event is relatively high. There is no guarantee that this will be the case in many real systems. Thus, designers of automated alerting systems must take into account not only the decision threshold at which these systems are set (Kuchar and Hansman, 1995; Swets, 1992) but also the a priori probabilities of the condition to be detected (Parasuraman et al., 1997). Only then will operators tend to trust and use the system. In addition, a possible effective strategy to avoid operator mistrust is to inform users of the inevitable occurrence of device false alarms when base rates are low.

Finally, with other types of automation, the consequence of failure-induced mistrust may be less severe. For example, a pilot who does not trust the autopilot may simply fly the aircraft manually more frequently. The primary cost might then simply be an unnecessary increase of workload or lack of precision on the flight path. Similarly, a controller who finds the conflict probe automation untrustworthy may resolve a traffic conflict successfully using manual procedures, but at the cost of extra mental workload. In either case, the system performance-enhancing intention of the automation is defeated.

Calibration of Trust

As the preceding shows, either excessive trust of or excessive mistrust of automation on the part of controllers can lead to problems. The former can lead to complacency and reduced situation awareness, the latter to disuse or under-utilization. This suggests the need for the calibration of trust to an appropriate level between these two extremes. Lee and Moray (1992, 1994) have shown that such optimization requires assessment of the human operator's confidence in his or her manual performance skills. Appropriate calibration of trust also requires that the controller has a good understanding of the characteristics and behavior of the automation. This understanding is captured by the controller's mental model of the automation.

Mental Models

A mental model is an abstract representation of the functional relations that are carried out by an automated system or machine. The model reflects the operator's understanding of the system as developed through past experience (Moray, 1997). A mental model is also thought to be the basis by which the operator predicts and expects the future behavior of the system. A mental model can also refer to a conscious Gedanken (thought) experiment that is "run" in a mental simulation of some (typically physical) relation between conceptually identifiable variables. This can be done to test "what would happen if" (in a hypothetical process) or "what will happen" (in an observed ongoing actual process). It is implied that a person can "use" the mental model to predict some outputs, given some inputs. Given two aircraft having specified positions and velocities, a controller presumably has a mental model capable of predicting whether they will collide.

When automation is introduced into real system contexts, experience has shown that in many cases it fails. Often it fails or is perceived to have failed because operators do not understand sufficiently well how the system really works (their mental models are wrong or incomplete), and they feel that to be safe they should continue with many of the steps previously used with the old system. But this gets them into trouble. An operator who does not understand the new system is likely to feel safe doing things the old way and does not do what is expected, thus causing failure downstream or at least jeopardizing proper system functioning.

The solution can be: (a) better training, particularly at the cognitive level of understanding the algorithms and logic underlying the automation, rather than just the operating skill level, and including failure possibilities and (b) having operators participate in the decision to acquire the automation, as well as its installation and test, so that they "own it" (share mental models and other assumptions with the designers and managers) and are not alienated by its introduction.

One of the causes of mistrust of automation results when operators do not understand the basis of the automation algorithms. A poor mental model of the automation may have the consequence that the operator sees the automation acting in a way different from what would be expected, or perhaps even doing things that were not expected at all. Mental models may also be shared among teams of operators, as we discuss below.

Mode Errors

A large body of research has now demonstrated that, when a human operator's mental model of automation does not match its actual functionality and behavior, new error forms emerge. New error forms have been most well documented and studied with respect to flight deck automation, and the flight management system in particular. Several studies have shown that experienced pilots have an incomplete mental model of the flight management system, particularly of its behavior in unusual circumstances (Sarter and Woods, 1995b). This has led to a number of incidents in which pilots took erroneous actions based on their belief that the flight management system was in one mode, whereas it was in fact in another (Vakil et al., 1995). Such confusions have been labeled mode errors (Reason, 1990), in which an operator fails to realize the mode setting of an automated device. In this case, the operator may perform an action that is appropriate for a different mode (and observe an unexpected system response, or no response at all). The crash of an Airbus 320 aircraft at Strasbourg, France, occurred when the crew apparently confused the vertical speed and flight path angle modes (Ministère de l'équipement, des transports et du tourisme, 1993). Another form of mode error occurs when the system itself responds to external inputs in a manner that is unexpected by the operator.

Because air traffic management automation has been limited in scope to date, examples of mode errors or automation surprises have not frequently been reported, although Sarter and Woods (1997) have reported mode errors in the air traffic control voice switching and control system (VSCS). Because new and proposed air traffic management automation systems will increase in complexity, authority, and autonomy in the future, it is worthwhile to keep in mind the lessons regarding mode errors that have been learned from studies of cockpit automation.

Skill Degradation

Given that automation is reliable, understandable (in terms of a mental model), and appropriately calibrated in trust, controllers will be able to use air traffic management automated systems effectively. However, effective automation raises the additional issue of possible skill degradation, which was considered earlier in this chapter in the context of human response to system failure. The question arises: even if automation that addresses all the human performance concerns raised previously is designed and fielded, will safety be affected because the controller skills used before automation was introduced will have degraded?

There is no doubt that full automation of a function eventually will lead to manual skill decay because of forgetting and lack of recent practice (Rose, 1989; Wickens, 1992). An engineer who has to trade in his electronic calculator for a slide rule will undoubtedly find it tough going when trying to carry out a complex calculation. The question is, to what extent does this phenomenon apply to air traffic management automation, and if so, what are its safety consequences? To better understand this issue, it is instructive to distinguish between situations in which any skill degradation from disuse may or may not have consequences for system safety.

With the level of automation in the current air traffic management system, skill loss is unlikely to generate safety concerns. Most air traffic management automation to date has involved automation of input data functions (Hopkin, 1995). Controllers may be less skilled in such data acquisition procedures than they once were, but the loss of this skill does not adversely affect the system. In fact, because of their workload-reducing characteristics, systems such as automated handoffs and better integrated radar pictures have improved efficiency and safety.

In contrast, however, safety concerns should be considered for future air traffic management automation, because these systems are likely to involve automation of decision-making and active control functions. For example, the CTAS (center TRACON automation system) that is currently undergoing field trials will provide controllers with resolution advisories (discussed in Chapter 6). If controllers find these advisories to be effective in controlling the airspace and come to rely on them, their own skill in resolving aircraft conflicts may become degraded. Design functionality should act as a countermeasure and not require the use of degraded skills. Research is urgently needed to examine the issue of skill degradation for automation of high-level cognitive functions.

If evidence of skill degradation is found, what countermeasures are available? Intermittent manual performance of the automated task is one possibility. Parasuraman, Mouloua, and Molloy (1996) showed that a temporary return to manual control of an automated task benefited subsequent monitoring of the task, even when the task was returned to automation control. In recurrent check rides with automated aircraft, pilots are required to demonstrate hand flying capabilities. Given that these monitoring benefits reflect enhanced attention to and awareness of the task, the results suggest that they would also be manifested in improved retention of manual skills. Rose (1989) also proposed a model of the skill degradation that occurs with disuse and provided guidelines for the frequency of training (or human-in-the-loop) interventions that should be imposed to retain skill levels. An alternative possibility is to pursue design alternatives that will not rely on those skills that may be degraded, given a system failure.

Cognitive Skills Needed

Automation may affect system performance not only because controller skills may degrade, but because new skills may be required, ones that controllers may not be adequately trained for. Do future air traffic management automated systems require different cognitive skills on the part of controllers for the maintenance of efficiency and safety?

In the current system, the primary job of the controller is to ensure safe separation among the aircraft in his or her sector, as efficiently as possible. To accomplish this job, the controller uses weather reports, voice communication with pilots and controllers, flight strips describing the history and projected future of each flight, and a plan view (radar) display that provides data on the current altitude, speed, destination, and track of all aircraft in the sector. According to Ammerman et al. (1987), there are nine cognitive-perceptual ability categories needed by controllers in the current system: higher-order intellectual factors of spatial, verbal, and numerical reasoning; perceptual speed factors of coding and selective attention; short- and long-term memory; time sharing; and manual dexterity.

As proposed automation is introduced, it is anticipated that the job of the controller will shift from tactical control among pairs of aircraft in one sector to strategic control of the flow of aircraft across multiple sectors (Della Rocco et al., 1991). Current development and testing efforts suggest that the automation will perform such functions as identifying potential conflicts 20 minutes or more before they occur, automatically sequencing aircraft for arrival at airports, and providing electronic communication of data between the aircraft and the ground using data link. Several displays may be involved and much of the data will be presented a graphic format (Ei-feldt, 1991). These prospective aids should make it possible for controllers in one sector to anticipate conflicts down the line and make adjustments, thus solving potential problems long before they occur.

Essentially, as automation is introduced, it is expected that there will be less voice communication, fewer tactical problems needing the controller's attention, a shift from textual to graphic information, and an extended time frame for making decisions. However, it is also expected that, in severe weather conditions, emergency situations, or instances of automation failure, the controller will be able to take over and manually separate traffic.

Manning and Broach (1992) asked controllers who had reviewed operational requirements for future automation to assess the cognitive skills and abilities needed. These controllers agreed that coding, defined as the ability to translate and interpret data, would be extremely important as the controller becomes involved in strategic conflict resolution. Numerical reasoning was rated as less relevant in future systems, because it was assumed that the displays would be graphic and the numerical computations would be accomplished by the equipment. Skills and abilities related to verbal and spatial reasoning and to selective attention received mixed ratings, although all agreed that some level of these skills and abilities would be needed, particularly when the controller would be asked to assume control from the automation.

The general conclusion from the work of Manning and Broach (1992), as well as from analyses of proposed automation in AERA 2 and AERA 3 (Reierson et al., 1990), is that controllers will continue to need the same cognitive skills and abilities as they do in today's system, but the relative importance of these skills and abilities will change as automation is introduced. The controller in a more highly automated system may need more cognitive skills and abilities. That is, there will be the requirement for more strategic planning, for understanding the automation and monitoring its performance, and for stepping in and assuming manual control as needed. An important concern, echoed throughout this volume, is the need to maintain skills and abilities in the critical manual (as opposed to supervisory) control functions that may be performed infrequently. Dana Broach (personal communication, Federal Aviation Administration Civil Aeromedical Institute, 1997) has indicated that the Federal Aviation Administration is currently developing a methodology to be used in more precisely defining the cognitive tasks and related skill and ability requirements as various pieces of automation are introduced. Once in place, this methodology should be central to identifying possible shifts in both establishing selection requirements and designing training programs.

ADAPTIVE AUTOMATION

The human performance vulnerabilities that have been discussed thus far may be characteristic of fixed or *static* automation. For example, difficulties in situation awareness, monitoring, maintenance of manual skills, etc., may arise because with static automation the human operator is excluded from exercising these functions for long periods of time. If an automated system always carries out a high-level function, there will be little incentive for the human operator to be aware of or monitor the inputs to the function and may consequently not be able to execute the function well manually if he or she is required to do so at some time in the future. Given these possibilities, it is worthwhile considering the performance characteristics of an alternative approach to automation: *adaptive* automation, in which the allocation of function between humans and computer systems is flexible rather than fixed.

Long-term fixed (or nonadaptive) automation will generally not be problematic for data-gathering and data integration functions in air traffic management because they support but do not replace the controller's decision-making activities (Hopkin, 1995). Also, fixed automation is necessary, by definition, for functions that cannot be carried out efficiently or in a timely manner by the human operator, as in certain nuclear power plant operations (Sheridan, 1992). Aside from these two cases, however, problems could arise if automation of controller decision-making functions—what Hopkin (1995) calls computer assistance—is implemented in such a way that the computer always carries out decisions A and B, and the controller deals with all other decisions. Even this may not be problematic if computer decision making is 100 percent reliable, for then there is little reason for the controller to monitor the computer's inputs, be aware of the details of the traffic pattern that led to the decision, or even, following several years of experience with such a system, know how to carry out that decision manually. As noted in previous sections, however, software reliability for decision-making and planning functions is not ensured, so that long-term, fixed automation of such functions could expose the system to human performance vulnerabilities.

Under adaptive automation, the division of labor between human operator and computer systems is flexible rather than fixed. Sometimes a given function may be executed by the human, at other times by automation, and at still others by both the human and the computer. Adaptive automation may involve either *task allocation*, in which case a given task is performed either by the human or the automation in its entirety, or *partitioning*, in which case the task is divided into subtasks, some of which are performed by the human and others by the automation. Task allocation or partitioning may be carried out by an intelligent system on the basis of a model of the operator and of the tasks that must be performed (Rouse, 1988). This defines adaptive automation or adaptive aiding. For example, a workload inference algorithm could be used to allocate tasks to the human or to automation so as to keep operator workload within a narrow range (Hancock and Chignell, 1989; Wickens, 1992). Figure 1.5 provides a schematic of how this could be achieved within a closed-loop adaptive system (Wickens, 1992).

An alternative to having an intelligent system invoke changes in task allocation or partitioning is to leave this responsibility to the human operator. This approach defines *adaptable* automation (Billings and Woods, 1994; Hilburn, 1996). Except where noted, the more generic term *adaptive* is used here to refer to both cases. Nevertheless, there are significant and fundamental differences between adaptive (machine-directed) and adaptable (human-centered) systems in terms of such criteria as feasibility, ease of communication, user acceptance, etc. Billings and Woods (1994) have also argued that systems with adaptive automation may be more, not less, susceptible to human performance vulnerabilities if they are implemented in such a way that operators are unaware of the states and state changes of the adaptive system. They advocate adaptable automation, in which users can tailor the level and type of automation according to their current needs. Depending on the function that is automated and situation-specific factors (e.g., time pressure, risk, etc.), either adaptive or adaptable automation may be

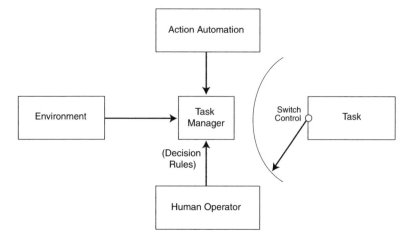

FIGURE 1.5   Closed-loop adaptive system.

appropriate. Provision of feedback about high-level states of the system at any point in time is a design principle that should be followed for both approaches to automation. These and other parameters of adaptable automation should be examined with respect to operational concepts of air traffic management.

In theory, adaptive systems may be less vulnerable to some of the human performance problems associated with static automation (Hancock and Chignell, 1989; Parasuraman et al., 1990; Scerbo, 1996; Wickens, 1992; but see Billings and Woods, 1994). The research that has been done to date suggests that there may be both benefits and costs of adaptive automation. Benefits have been reported with respect to one human performance vulnerability, monitoring. For example, a task may be automated for long periods of time with no human intervention. Under such conditions of static automation, operator detection of automation malfunctions can be inefficient if the human operator is engaged in other manual tasks (Molloy and Parasuraman, 1996; Parasuraman et al., 1993). The problem does not go away, and may even be exacerbated, with highly reliable automation (Parasuraman, Mouloua, Molloy, and Hilburn, 1996).

Given automation-induced monitoring inefficiency, how might it be ameliorated? One possibility is adaptive task allocation, or reallocating a formerly automated task to the human operator. Given that an in-the-loop monitor performs better than one who is out of the loop (Parasuraman et al., 1993; Wickens and Kessel, 1979; but see Liu et al., 1993), this should enhance monitoring performance. But this is clearly not an allocation strategy that can be pursued generally for all automated tasks and at all times, for it would lead to excessive manual workload, thus defeating one of the purposes of automation. One potential solution is to allocate the automated task to the human operator for only a brief period of time, before returning it once again to automation. The benefits of temporary allocation of a task to human control may persist for some time, even after the task is returned to automation control. This hypothesis was tested in a study by Parasuraman, Mouloua, and Molloy (1996). During multiple-task flight simulation, a previously automated engine-status monitoring task was adaptively allocated to the operator for a 10-minute period in the middle of a session, and then returned to automatic control (see Figure 1.6).

Detection of engine malfunctions was better during the 10-minute block when the task was returned to human control from automation, consistent with previous reports of superior monitoring under conditions of active human control (Parasuraman et al., 1993; Wickens and Kessel, 1979). More importantly, however, detection performance under automation control was markedly superior in the post-allocation phase than in the identical pre-allocation phase (see Figure 1.6). (In both these phases, the engine-status monitoring task was automated but the post-allocation phase immediately followed one in which the task was performed manually.) The performance benefit (of about 66 percent) persisted even after the engine-status monitoring task was returned to automation, for about 20 minutes. The benefit of adaptive task allocation was attributed to this procedure, allowing human operators to update their memory of the engine-status monitoring task. A similar view was put forward by Lewandowsky and Nikolic (1995) on the basis of a connectionist (neural network) simulation of these monitoring performance data.

In addition to improved monitoring, benefits of adaptive automation for operator mental workload have also been reported in recent studies by Hilburn (1996). This research is of particular interest because it examined the utility of adaptive automation in the specific context of air traffic control. Experienced controllers worked with an advanced simulation facility, NARSIM, coupled with the CTAS automation tool, specifically the descent advisor (DA). Controllers were required to perform the role of an executive controller in a southern sector of the Amsterdam airspace. A plan view display contained traffic with associated flight data blocks, a data link status panel, and the descent advisor timeline display from CTAS. Three levels of CTAS automated assistance could be provided: none (manual, traffic status only), conflict detection only, or conflict detection plus resolution advisory. Controller workload was assessed using physiological (eye scan entropy, heart rate variability) and subjective measures (NASA-TLX). Monitoring was assessed by recording controller reaction times to respond to occasional data link anomalies. A baseline study established that controller workload increased with traffic load but was reduced by each level of automation assistance compared with manual performance.

In a second study, Hilburn (1996) examined the effects of adaptive automation for two levels of CTAS aiding: manual control or resolution advisory. In two static automation conditions, automation level remained constant throughout the simulation, irrespective of shifts in traffic load. In the adaptive condition,

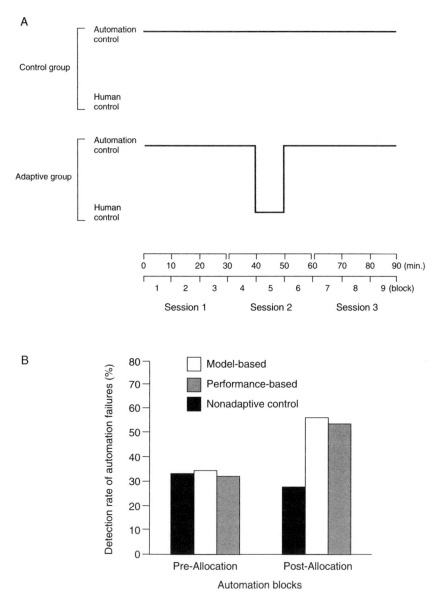

FIGURE 1.6 (A) Time line for adaptive task allocation. (B) Effects on monitoring performance. Source: Parasuraman, Mouloua, and Molloy (1996, Vol. 38, No. 4). Copyright 1996 by the Human Factors and Ergonomics Society. All rights reserved. Reprinted by permission.

shifts between manual control and resolution advisory coincided with traffic pattern shifts, giving the appearance that the adaptation was triggered by the traffic increase or decrease. Compared with the static automation conditions, the adaptive condition was associated with workload benefits, particularly under high traffic load. There was also a trend for monitoring to be better in the adaptive condition, compared with the two static conditions, consistent with the previously described study by Parasuraman, Mouloua, and Molloy (1996).

Despite these performance benefits, adaptive systems may not be free of some costs. For example, if the adaptive logic on which the system is based is oversensitive to the eliciting criteria, then the system may oscillate between automated and manual control of a task at frequent intervals. There is evidence that performance costs can occur if the cycle time between automated and manual control of a task is very short, particularly if the operator has no control over function changes (Hilburn, Parasuraman, and Mouloua, 1995; Scallen et al., 1995).

The question of operator control leads to the issue raised by Billings and Woods (1994) on adaptive versus adaptable automation. Very little empirical work has been done on this issue. Hilburn et al. (1993) had individuals perform a multitask flight simulation with the ability to turn automation on or off whenever they chose (adaptable automation). The times that automation was invoked or turned off were recorded and presented as the output of an intelligent adaptive system to another group of individuals in a yoked-control design modified from one used by Liu et al. (1993). Overall performance was superior for the adaptable automation group compared with the adaptive automation group, consistent with the findings of Billings and Woods (1994), although automation benefited both groups.

In these and other studies on adaptive automation, function changes involved allocation of entire tasks to automation or to human control. As mentioned earlier, another possibility is to partition tasks—that is, to allocate subtasks. Partitioning may lead to performance costs if tasks are partitioned in a nonmodular way (Gluckman et al., 1993). Vortac and Manning (1994) also found performance costs of partitioning in an air traffic control context. They suggested that automation benefits will accrue only if entire behavioral modules are allocated to automation. Finally, adaptive systems may not necessarily be immune from operator errors arising from misunderstanding or lack of awareness of the activities of the automation at a particular time (Sarter and Woods, 1995b). Given that adaptive systems will probably be granted higher levels of autonomy than current automation, automation-related surprises may occur, particularly if the system is slow to communicate intent to the human. Bubb-Lewis and Scerbo (1997) have considered ways in which human-computer communication can be enhanced in adaptive systems, but problems in coordination and communication remain potential concerns with such systems. It remains to be seen whether these potential costs of adaptive automation will outweigh the performance benefits that have been reported to date.

DESIGN AND MANAGEMENT INFLUENCES

Another aspect of human performance in automated systems involves the impact of other human agents in automated systems, not just those who have direct responsibility for operation of the system, whether as individuals or in teams. In an earlier part of this chapter we mentioned the influence of these other individuals—e.g., those involved in design, test and certification, and maintenance—with respect to system failures. In this section we consider their influence with respect to the human operator response to system failure.

Parasuraman and Riley (1997) discussed the system performance consequences of human usage of automation both when automation works as designed as well as when failures, unexpected automation behavior, or other anomalies occur. An important feature of their analysis is that they consider the impact of human interaction with automation for *all* humans involved with the automation: that is, not only human operators but also human designers of automation and managers and supervisors who implement and enforce policies and procedures concerning human operator use of automation.

Parasuraman and Riley (1997) showed how automation can act as a surrogate for the designer or the manager. As a result, when automation has an adverse impact on system performance, this can occur not only because of the performance of the human operator, but also because of specific decisions made by the designers of automation and by managers.

In some instances, such decisions can legitimately be called designer or management errors. Two examples taken from Parasuraman and Riley (1997) serve as illustrations. In 1993 an Airbus 320 crashed in Warsaw, Poland, when the pilot was unable to activate thrust reversers and brakes after landing because of a failure in the weight-on-wheels sensor on the landing gear (Main Commission Aircraft Accident Investigation, 1994). This system was specifically designed to prevent pilots from inadvertently deploying the spoilers to defeat lift or operate the thrust reversers while still in the air. The protections were presumably put in place due to a lack of trust in the pilot to not do something unreasonable and potentially catastrophic. Lack of trust in the pilot is the complement of trust in the (human) designer of the weight-on-wheels automated system to anticipate all possible conditions. But if the weight-on-wheels sensor fails, as it did in Warsaw, the pilot is prevented from deploying braking devices precisely when they are needed. This represents an error of the designer.

The second example from Parasuraman and Riley (1997) concerns management practices or corporate policies regarding automation. In some cases these may prevent human operators from using automation effectively, particularly under emergency conditions. The weight-on-wheels sensor case represents an example of the human operator's not being able to use automation because of prior decisions made by the designer of automation. Alternatively, even though automation may be designed to be engaged flexibly, management may not authorize its use or its disengagement in certain conditions. This appears to have been the case in a recent accident involving a subway train near Washington, D.C. The train collided with a standing train in a heavy snowstorm when the automatic speed control system failed to bring the train to a stop because of snow on the tracks. Just prior to this accident, the previous policy of allowing train operators intermittent use of manual speed control was rescinded suddenly and without explanation. The accident investigation board determined that the management policy and the decision of the central train controller (who had to enforce policy) to refuse the train operator's request to run the train manually because of the poor weather was a major factor in the accident (National Transportation Safety Board, 1997b). Thus, automation can also act as a surrogate for the manager, just as it can for the system designer, and management policy errors regarding automation can also adversely impact human performance in automated systems.

TEAM PERFORMANCE AND COORDINATION

Chapter 7 of the Phase I report discussed team aspects of air traffic control and employed a broad definition of team that includes not only controllers and their supervisors who are in face-to-face contact, but also pilots who interact indirectly. The Phase I report also highlighted the importance of shared knowledge of evolving situations for system performance. As the air traffic system becomes more automated, information sharing and team coordination issues will continue to be critical and, under some circumstances, assume greater importance.

Those needing to share information in air traffic management include not only controllers and pilots, but also traffic managers and dispatchers (Smith et al., 1996). Automation can facilitate information sharing (for example, by data link or a large CTAS display visible to all operators at a facility). However, automation can also impede shared awareness and the development of common mental models for several reasons. One is that interactions with automated devices through keyboard entries may be far less visible (or audible) to adjacent operators than interaction via more traditional media (such as voice communication or stick manipulations; see Segal, 1995). A second is that some automated systems may not provide comparable information to all participants in the system. The introduction of TCAS resolution advisories has occasionally resulted in a lack of controller awareness of an aircraft's intended maneuver (Jones, 1996; Mellone and Frank, 1993). A third is that automated systems may allow reconfiguration of system characteristics by remote operators in a way that is initially transparent to other affected operators (Sarter and Woods, 1997).

An incorrect mental model of a developing situation and the status of automation can prevent effective action by a single operator. Similarly, if team members hold different mental models about how an automated device operates and what it is doing, differing perceptions of the situation can thwart effective communication. To date there has been relatively little research in the area of shared situation awareness and mental models in the collaborative use of automation (Idaszak, 1989; Segal, 1995). Sarter (1997) argues that information requirements in the cockpit will be increased if both aircraft and controllers are to have accurate, shared mental models. This has implications for the workload of flight crews, who are responsible for all aspects of a flight's management. The keyboard mode of communication associated with data link may prove to be inefficient for team communication and conflict resolution associated with decision making under time constraints that may be imposed as aircraft near the final approach fix or in other time-critical situations (Sarter, 1997).

The ultimate goal of shared information and situation awareness is to allow users to make optimal decisions in the operating environment. If the expressed goals of a less constrained, more flexible air traffic management system are to be achieved, there will be more collaborative, shared decision making in the future than in the present system (Smith, Billings, Woods et al., 1997). Some research is currently in progress on the dynamics of distributed decision making in air traffic control (Hutton, 1997; Orasanu et al., in press). To achieve effective *team* decision making between widely separated individuals with different workloads and information displays, more research into the processes and media requirements (i.e., data link versus radio for negotiation) will be needed. Such research can benefit from knowledge of the area of collaborative technology (discussed in Chapter 2). This research should provide guidelines for training to optimize distributed decision making and the resolution of decision conflicts. Training in decision making should take into account the characteristics of expert decision making in naturalistic settings (Hutton, 1997).

The problem of collaborative decision making between air traffic control and aircraft is exacerbated because the pilot members of decision-making teams come from diverse, multicultural backgrounds. Hence, controllers will not be able to assume a common decision-making orientation. Nor will many users of the air traffic system have had formal training in collaborative decision making. This will pose a serious challenge for training and will force consideration of the range of air traffic control users (i.e., from many cultures with different approaches to decision making and communication) who may be required to collaborate with air traffic control to resolve incipient flight path conflicts.

Team issues will also become critical in situations in which the automated system's capabilities degrade. In the event of reduced capability, tasks normally accomplished by a single controller may require additional human support—a reversion to present-day team duty assignments. The Phase I report identified team communications factors in current air traffic control sector management. Jones (1996) further specified team issues associated with both operational incidents and exemplary controller performance, issues amenable to training interventions.

In a more automated air traffic control system, there is a strong possibility that team skills associated with coordination among controllers may degrade if the system functions with high reliability. Both formal training and regular practice in the use of team skills within the facility will be needed to maintain a safety buffer.

In summary, the same team skills (and formal training to gain, maintain, and reinforce them) that are needed in the current air traffic control system will be required under more automated systems. It is should be noted that Eurocontrol, the parent agency for air traffic control in the European Community, is implementing a program of team training called *team resource management* that makes use of the experience gained from *crew resource management* programs for flight crews (Barbarino, 1997; Masson and Paries, 1997). In addition, the concept of shared decision making between aircraft and air traffic control will require further training in distributed decision making and conflict resolution.

2

Emerging Technological Resources

Advances in hardware and software offer promising opportunities for automating a greater range of information-processing, decision-making, and control functions than has been possible in the past. Along with these advances comes the question of the degree to which emerging hardware and software systems can be trusted to perform functions in a reliable and valid manner. In this chapter we review and assess three technologies that relate to the functions of information acquisition, information distribution, the generation of alternative decision options, and option selection. These technologies are visualization, intelligent decision aiding and intent inferencing, and computer-supported cooperative work.

VISUALIZATION

Visualization, the process of using a visual mental model, is perhaps the most important cognitive function the controller performs. Visual mental models are what we usually think of when we speak of mental models—we "see" them in our "mind's eye" (although musicians surely have auditory mental models, professional tasters surely have olfactory and gustatory mental models, etc.). Computerized automation can enhance visualization in many ways, which is the point of revisiting the topic of visualization here.

Computer graphic displays help visualization by combining variables into a single integrated display. For example, the old mechanical attitude (8-ball) display combined roll, pitch, and yaw, enabling the pilot to visualize the aircraft attitude much more easily than if such information had to be gleaned from three separate indicators. The computer graphic display that shows three aircraft symbols (past, present, and predicted future) in roll, pitch, and yaw relative to glide slope, command heading, and altitude integrates even more information. The plan view or map display that shows waypoints, heading, other aircraft, predicted trajectories, and weather is another advanced visualization aid.

The digital representation of altitude on the radar display has remained a feature of the air traffic control workstation that is less than optimal. Although controllers adequately handle digital flight-level data, the fact remains that it is difficult to visualize vertical trends or the magnitude of altitude differences from such a representation. Designers have realized the possible advantages to visualization by representing the vertical dimension in analog format. There are in fact two ways in which this might be accomplished (Wickens, 1997). One is through addition of a vertical "profile" display, and the other is through a three-dimensional or "perspective" display.

To date, most experimental research has compared conventional plan view displays with perspective displays. Such comparisons have generally not been favorable for the latter (Wickens, Miller, and Tham, 1996; May et al., 1996). Although a perspective view does indeed represent the vertical dimension, it also compresses the three-dimensional airspace onto a two-dimensional viewing surface, leaving a certain amount of perceptual ambiguity regarding the precise lateral and vertical distance separating a pair of aircraft (McGreevy and Ellis, 1986; Merwin et al., 1997). This ambiguity can disrupt the controller's judgments of predictive separation.

Three solutions may be available. First, as noted, a profile display could be coupled with the plan view display to represent, without ambiguity, the vertical separations. This approach has proven quite successful for representing traffic separations and terrain awareness in cockpit displays (Merwin et al., 1997; Wickens, Liang, et al., 1996). Second, some designers have proposed using holographic or stereo techniques to create displays, in which the ambiguity is lessened (Wickens et al., 1989). Third, it is possible to provide a controller with interactive tools, whereby the three-dimensional viewpoint of the display can be altered, making the position of aircraft less ambiguous through the perceptual cue of motion parallax (Sollenberger and Milgram, 1993; Wickens et al., 1994); this can also be provided by holographic displays.

A more radical form of interaction is created by allowing the controller to change the viewpoint position and "immerse" himself within the airspace, thereby approximating the technology of virtual reality (Durlach and Mavor, 1995; Wickens and Baker, 1995). Certain limitations of this technology for air traffic control, however, appear evident. First, by immersing oneself within the traffic volume, aircraft to the side and behind are "out of sight," a factor that is of considerable concern if the safe separation of all traffic is to be maintained. Second, such immersion can be disorienting to one who is not in active control of the viewpoint and hence would tend to be disruptive to efforts to coordinate a view among multiple observers. As a consequence, the prospects of this technology for real-time air traffic control operations appear remote. However, the feasibility of both immersive and non-immersive three-dimensional displays in a training capacity appears more promising.

INTELLIGENT DECISION AIDING

The principal uses of intelligent computer-based decision-making systems include diagnosis, planning, decision aiding, intent inferencing, and training. They can be developed from a variety of sources, including highly structured written documents, such as military doctrine; knowledge elicitation methods used to create expert emulations; and algorithms that provide structures and strategies for learning by example or through neural networking. Although these systems may vary in underlying logic or structure, most include both domain knowledge and procedures for operating on that knowledge.

In this section we briefly review the technology of expert systems, intent inferencing systems, learning software, and blackboard systems. The current technology for expert, intent inferencing, and blackboard systems requires a programmer to make changes. Learning systems, in contrast, are designed to grow and add new knowledge through iterative operation.

In the air traffic control environment, this technology continues to hold promise for equipment troubleshooting, simulation-based training, air traffic flow planning, decision aiding, and intent inferencing for the controller and the pilot. However, caution is needed. Although computer-based systems offer advantages of speed and capacity, the increased efficiency and power predicted by the combination of these systems with human decision makers have not been realized (Mosier and Skita, 1996). Major issues concern validity and reliability and the ease and effectiveness with which human operators (controllers, pilots, and maintainers) can make use of them.

One concern is that novices who use expert systems to aid them in their decision making do not perform as well as experts. Novices and experts have different approaches or schema for structuring and solving problems (Chi et al., 1981). Also, computer systems are limited in technical knowledge and are not as versatile as the human expert (Will, 1991). The most favorable results for the combination of novice and automated aid occur when the task is routine and covered by standard procedures.

A second concern is that incorrect models of human decision making and automated decision aids may result in systems that are less effective than the human alone. Mosier and Skita (1996) suggest that these incorrect models may create decision-making environments that promote decision biases rather than enhancing human capabilities. As an example of this, Adelman et al. (1993), in a study of real-time expert system interfaces for use by air defense officers in identifying aircraft as friendly or hostile, found that aids to focus the operator's attention on most critical events led to inferior performance for important but less critical cases also requiring the operator's attention. Hockey (1986) has observed similar findings with regard to a tactical aid for managing air traffic in a combat environment.

Perhaps the most promising work, directly relevant to air traffic control goals, is in intent inferencing, an approach developed to alleviate the need for an operator to directly input his or her intentions into the system (Geddes, 1985). Intent inferencing provides an intelligent interface to the operating system by informing the system about the plan the operator is intending to implement. This technology has the potential to present controllers with better predictor information, thus overcoming an important limitation in the current air traffic control system. Most of the work in this area has been done in the context of military aircraft (Geddes, 1985; Banks and Lizza, 1991; Andes, 1996); however, a preliminary study of shared intentions for free flight has recently been completed for the National Aeronautics and Space Administration (NASA) (Geddes et al., 1996). Free flight is discussed in detail in Chapter 9.

Blackboard systems provide the architecture for the integration of several knowledge sources (expert systems, case-based systems, neural network systems) to interactively solve a problem or develop a plan. These systems also have potential, particularly for long-range strategic planning applications. However, their effectiveness may be limited by the features of the component software program representing the various knowledge sources (Corkill, 1991).

What follows is a brief overview of the technologies used in developing intelligent decision-aiding systems and a discussion of their applications.

Expert System Technology

Expert systems are computer programs designed to solve complex problems by emulating human expertise. Work on the first expert system began in the mid-1960s and resulted in a computer-based system that could function as effectively as a human expert in determining molecular structures from chemical data.

The basic structure of most expert systems includes a knowledge base and an inference procedure that operates on the knowledge base. The knowledge base contains the facts or declarative knowledge in a particular subject area and the rules of judgment developed by experts who use these facts. In most systems, this knowledge is represented in the form of production rules. Production rules are sets of condition-action pairs presented in the form of *if-then* statements. Once these pairs are formed, weights are assigned to show the relative strength of the relationship as seen by the expert.

In addition to the knowledge base, an expert system has an inference procedure. The two principal forms of reasoning used are goal-directed backward chaining and forward chaining. Backward chaining involves working from a goal to the conditions required to reach that goal. Forward chaining infers the goals from the conditions. A critical feature of all expert systems is that they can make explicit the reasoning used to reach a specific conclusion or recommendation. This is useful in validating the system and in assisting the user in assessing the value of the advice.

In the early days of expert systems development, the focus was on artificial intelligence and research in cognitive psychology that explored the nature of expert knowledge and the data structures and reasoning strategies necessary to create a software representation of the knowledge. Once it was demonstrated that usable expert systems could be developed, the focus moved from research to application. One major stumbling block in the development process is the acquisition of the appropriate knowledge from the expert and the validation of that knowledge. These processes are both labor-intensive and time-consuming and also require highly trained individuals to do the work. Another barrier is that expert systems work well only in well-known problem domains that can be described by procedural rules.

Although there have been many applications of expert systems, including training, planning, diagnosing, and scheduling, most have not been developed for real-time uses. Early work focused on such problems as providing physicians with diagnostic aids, advising geologists working with rock formations, planning experiments in DNA synthesis, and assisting in electronic troubleshooting. More recently, the majority of applications have sprung up in areas such as training, counseling (for example, Chwelos and Oatley, 1994; Wilson and Zalewski, 1994; Hile et al., 1995), management planning (for example, Liang and Teo, 1994) and test development and interpretation (Frick, 1992). Production rule systems have also been used to emulate command decision making in military simulations.

Regarding training, Chu et al. (1995) have proposed requirements for an intelligent tutoring system that specifies the instructional content and procedures to teach novice operators to manage a complex dynamic system. This approach may also be useful in developing simulations for training air traffic controllers. One well-researched intelligent tutor is the system developed by John Anderson and his colleagues at Carnegie Mellon University in which the adaptive control of thought (ACT) theory of learning and problem solving was used to build the software. They have found that the early stages of learning are dominated by declarative or factual knowledge, whereas the later stages focus on procedural knowledge (Anderson et al., 1993). An important result of this research is that the developers shifted from their earlier model of a tutor that emulates an expert to a tutor as a learning environment in which helpful information can be provided and useful problems can be selected. This work may provide important guidance to the design of computer-based training systems for air traffic controllers.

Systems That Learn

During the past 20 years substantial progress has been made in the development and testing of category learning models such as exemplar or case-based models. In these models, past and current states serve as memory cues for retrieving scenarios that are similar to the current situation, and the actions that produced favorable outcomes in the past are retrieved for use as possible future actions. In essence, the decision problem corresponds to pattern recognition based on similarity to previously stored examples. This type of learning model has been extremely successful in a wide range of rigorous experimental tests, including more complex learning problems such as controlling dynamic systems (Dienes and Fahey, 1995).

According to Pew and Mavor (1997), an appealing feature of this approach is that it bypasses the knowledge acquisition and knowledge representation bottleneck associated with expert systems by recording past behavior of real humans to form the memory base of exemplars that are retrieved. Neural network models can accomplish the same objective; however, exemplar models may be more compatible and thus more combinable with rule-based systems. Hybrid systems that result from such combinations have yet to be evaluated but contain some promise for being more useful that either pure rule-based or pure exemplar-based systems alone.

Bayles and Das (1993) examined the feasibility of using an exemplar-based approach to solving traffic flow management problems. In this study, prior cases of weather and traffic problems with their attendant solutions were documented, stored, and made available for retrieval as new situations arose. This approach, as contrasted with the rule-based approach, seemed more appropriate because of the variability in conditions from one situation to another. The approach works by selecting cases from the past that are similar to the current situation and providing them to traffic flow managers as aids to developing solutions. New solutions are generated from prior cases and these new solutions are added to the data base. Traffic flow managers found the exercise particularly useful because the system provided them with feedback linking solutions to both positive and negative outcomes.

Blackboard Systems

Blackboard technology (Nii and Aiello, 1986) is essentially an electronic emulation of a group of experts or specialists using a blackboard as the workplace for cooperatively developing a solution to a problem. It offers a problem-solving architecture that is particularly useful when the following conditions are present:

- The problem is decomposable into a number of subproblems.
- Many diverse, specialized knowledge sources are needed to address a problem.
- An integrative framework is needed to manage heterogeneous problem-solving representations.
- The development of an application involves numerous developers.
- Uncertain or limited data make it difficult to develop an absolute solution.
- Multilevel reasoning or dynamic control of problem-solving activities is needed for the application.

Blackboard systems have three major components: a collection of knowledge sources, a control module that schedules the contributions of the knowledge sources, and a blackboard or a database that saves the current state of the problem generated by the knowledge sources. The knowledge sources generate cooperative solutions on a blackboard using a variety of reasoning approaches such as expert systems, numerical analysis, exemplar systems, and neural networks. Each knowledge source represents a different area of expertise or a different perspective on the problem and can be developed independently (using different languages) from the other knowledge sources; however, each knowledge source must use an interaction language that is common to the blackboard. Also, if a knowledge source contains relevant expertise it can be used in more than one blackboard system. The heart of the system is the control module that provides for the integration of the various knowledge sources and controls the flow of the activity in the application, much the way a moderator would control a group of human experts working collaboratively on a problem (Corkill, 1991).

Blackboard control architecture has several benefits including modularity and the flexibility to adapt to a wide range of complex heuristics and rules that may change in the course of problem solving. Another strength is that the architecture places all the strategies and rules governing system behavior under system control. The primary drawback is the heavy computational and storage requirements (Hayes-Roth, 1985).

In air traffic control, blackboard systems may be useful for addressing flow control and weather prediction problems. For example, in one research project, Craig (1989) used a blackboard system named Cassandra to monitor aircraft separation in a controlled airspace. This system contained separate experts for vertical, lateral, and horizontal separation.

Although this technology may offer relevant assistance to the performance of a number of air traffic control tasks, it needs further development. As noted earlier, it combines a number of other technologies (e.g., knowledge-based systems and case-based systems) that have their own set of limitations (discussed in previous sections).

Intent Inferencing

The fundamental principle underlying intent inferencing is to keep the operator in control, even though the system is able to carry out a series of tasks automatically. Thus, when using this technology, the tasks that the system executes are based on inferences made about the goal the operator is trying to achieve and actions that relate to implementing that goal. The operator does not directly tell the system what to do but rather continues to perform activities. The intelligent system analyzes these activities and makes inferences about the goal of the operator and the best plan to execute to reach that goal. Based on this inference, the system carries out the desired process automatically.

One intent inferencing model, described by Jones et al. (1990), was developed as part of the operator function model expert system. This model, the actions interpreter, dynamically builds a model of operator goals for the current system state and then works to interpret the user's actions in terms of these goals. Each goal is decomposed into a hierarchy of plans, tasks, and operator actions required to fulfill the goal. This representation evolves over time as new information is recorded. The operator function model developed by Mitchell (1987) provides the basis for the action interpreter's knowledge about how events trigger likely operator goals. The actions interpreter has been evaluated in the Georgia Tech Multisatellite Operations Control Center simulation, an interactive simulation that supports simulated satellites and the computer and communications technology used for data capture.

Another framework used to represent intent inferencing is the plan and goal graph (Geddes, 1989; Rouse et al., 1990; Shallin et al., 1993). The plan and goal graph is a task analytic decomposition of the goals and plans for all operators interacting with the system. The top-level nodes in the graph are goals. A goal represents a specific criterion on the state of the system that can be tested by observation. The next level of nodes are plans. Plans involve activities, time frames, the use of resources, and side effects. Plans are decomposed into subgoal, subplans, and actions. Several plans may share common actions and compete for resources. Thus, a key element of the program involves resolving conflicts. The formalism of the relationship between plans and goals guides the decomposition process. The idea is to develop the goal and plan structure for the set of missions the system is expected to perform.

As noted earlier, much of the work in this area has concentrated on military aircraft, specifically the pilot associate program (Banks and Lizza, 1991) and the rotorcraft pilot associate (Andes, 1996). Currently, Geddes and his colleagues are working with NASA under the advanced air transportation technology program to demonstrate intent inferencing as an emerging technology that can be used to detect goal and plan conflicts among active participants in free flight scenarios (free flight is discussed in detail in Chapter 9). This research moves from interpreting the intent of one operator to interpreting the intent of several operators.

The heart of the project is the "shared model of intent" (using the OPAL software system) and its use in early conflict detection and resolution. In the shared model of intent, the goals and plans of all ground- and air-based participants are represented in a plan and goal graph. In addition, the system contains a knowledge base that specifies information about all objects in the system, including the conditions and time frames under which state changes may be expected to occur.

The shared model of intent has been tested in 10 free flight scenarios focusing on the transition from en route to terminal airspace with particular emphasis on the coordination between large commercial aircraft and general aviation aircraft. A simulation facility was established at Embry-Riddle Aeronautical University to run the test scenarios. As part of this facility, two manned air traffic control consoles were set up, one for the en route sector and the other for the terminal sector. The terminal airspace was a representation of the Orlando International Airport. Each scenario included 32 aircraft (2 manned and 30 digital). By the end of the evaluation scenarios, the shared model of intent was accurately accounting for over 90 percent of manned pilot actions, approximately 80 percent of digital aircraft actions, and 100 percent of the actions at the two manned air traffic control stations.

The results of early testing appear to be positive. However, further evaluation is needed with a larger number of participants and different levels of airspace complexity. According to Geddes et al. (1996:3):

> The potential scope of the shared model of intent includes conflicts in flow control between ground coordination activities as well as aircraft. It will be possible, for example, to detect that the coordination plan to increase take-off rates at Dallas Fort Worth as a plan to reduce taxiway wait time will have a more serious conflict with the plan to reduce the arrival rate at Atlanta due to high levels of thunderstorm activity in the approach area. . . . By detecting conflicts at a higher level, not only is conflict detection typically earlier, but it can also result in a more strategic resolution that re-directs resources more efficiently.

COMPUTER-SUPPORTED COOPERATIVE WORK

Distributed networking capabilities plus advances in telecommunications, multiuser applications, shared virtual environment technologies, and the like have created opportunities for users in the same or different locations engaged in interdependent activities to work together in a common computer-based environment. These capabilities have given rise to a relatively new interdisciplinary field of study known as computer-supported cooperative work (CSCW). Its goal is to use groupware technologies to facilitate communication, collaboration, and coordination in accord with the users' organizational and social contexts. Research in this area takes into account situations, roles, social interactions, and task interdependencies among participants as a guide for CSCW system design, development, implementation, and evaluation. It is easy to see how this work is relevant to the computer mediation of cooperative problem solving and scheduling among air traffic controllers, pilots, and dispatchers.

Distinctive Features

Cooperative work in this perspective is interpreted broadly to refer to work that is completed through the harmonization of acts carried out by multiple individuals (Malone and Crowston, 1990). The key issue is the use of computer support to manage effectively the interdependent activities of diverse actors so that the task goals affected by these interdependencies can be achieved. Although CSCW shares some concerns with the traditional human factors field, this orientation creates several distinctive foci.

First, CSCW tools attempt to support multiple interdependent tasks rather than individual tasks that can be completed by people acting independently. Interdependencies may stem, for example, from the fact that tasks must be completed in a specified order, that the same resource(s) is needed by multiple activities, that actions must be synchronized, and so on.

Second, existing interdependencies may be tacit or implicit, rather than explicit or articulated in task descriptions; often they are taken for granted by workers but not necessarily captured in the task analyses or needs assessments that provide input to traditional systems design. Surfacing such interdependencies has been a consistent contribution from this research.

Third, this view of cooperative work recognizes that task interdependencies may often be managed through common "artifacts" or representations of the work (see Suchman, 1995). Ethnographic studies of the use of flight strips by controllers, for example, suggest that the strips do far more than deliver information to an active controller; they also serve as transparent representations of interdependent tasks-in-progress to the incoming controller and others (Harper and Hughes, 1991).

It should be noted that studies of the use of paper versus electronic flight strips conducted by Manning (1995) have shown that electronic flight strips have the benefit of reducing workload; these issues are discussed in more detail in Chapter 4. Similar findings about visible representations of work have come from studies of the role of job tickets in equipment repair facilities (Sachs, 1995) and of the way that representations function in shipboard navigation (Hutchins, 1990). Research that focuses exclusively on independent work is likely to overlook how media function as representations and artifacts that support tacit interdependencies among tasks (see also Kyng and others in the September 1995 special issue of *Communications of the ACM* on representations of work).

Fourth, operators may be engaged in cooperative work in autonomous or semiautonomous roles, and such roles may be enacted by either individuals or computer programs (or both). Thus technology designs for CSCW do not assume a binary choice (to automate or not to automate) but instead consider an array of options for allocating functions within cooperative work activity to humans and machines (Mankin et al., 1996).

Finally, the key interdependencies to be managed may involve conflict (as in negotiations or debates) or competition (as in bidding or market-based systems) rather than conscious goal-oriented cooperation or teamwork in the usual sense (Ciborra, 1993). As with collaboration, competition may occur as an explicit or as a tacit form of task interdependence. CSCW technologies can be deployed to support either sort of interdependent activity.

Components of Applications

Different implementations may involve the use of such component technologies as electronic text or audio messaging, shared spatial views of activities and operators, formal representations of work processes, and the like to support multiple individuals engaged in interdependent work. Many kinds of cooperative action, for example, require members of the interacting group to communicate in some form.

Communication

Watts and his colleagues (Watts et al., 1996), for example, describe the use of voice loops as a method for space shuttle mission controllers to coordinate their activities. The study found that controllers monitor four voice loops: the conference loop, the support loop, the air/ground loop, and the flight director loop. The conference loop is constantly monitored to receive messages from other consoles; however, actions are taken only when a problem occurs. The support loop is used for front room controllers to communicate with the support staff in another location. The air/ground loop is used by astronauts and the flight controller; all other participants only monitor the loop to maintain awareness of the evolving situation. Finally, the flight director loop contains communication between the flight controller and the front room controllers.

Study results show that controllers are able to monitor all four loops and extract meaningful patterns of information. Typically a controller is active only on one loop. But passive awareness or preattentive reference to the other loops enables controllers to maintain shared awareness, to integrate new information about the mission, and to anticipate changes and dynamically shift their activities in response; in general it helps them to synchronize their work (see Dourish and Bellotti, 1992; Woods, 1995). Controllers can segregate loops by listening to them at different volumes, monitoring loops that are less relevant to their tasks and goals at lower volumes than loops that are providing more significant information.

A primary factor in the success of voice loops in supporting coordination appears to be the use of implicit protocols to govern which loops are monitored as well as the reliance on highly coded language and immediate response on demand to directed messages in the active loop. Passive monitoring also facilitates directed communication by helping coworkers negotiate interruptions; controllers are able to listen to colleagues' loops to determine their current workloads before contacting them. Other kinds of situations that demand coordination will require rigorous protocols that are made fully explicit. One area in which the work in voice loops may be relevant to air traffic control is in the communication and coordination required among tower controllers, airport managers, gate managers, pilots, and airline dispatchers in the surface movement advisor system.

Shared Spaces

In other applications, CSCW technologies may rely on spatial approaches to support interdependent tasks. Such approaches are particularly useful for cooperative work by representing persistence and ongoing activity in a common spatial setting, by enabling peripheral awareness of what others are doing beyond a user's focal activity, by permitting navigation and chance encounters in a shared environment, and by facilitating system usability through natural spatial metaphors. More generally, spatial approaches to CSCW can be regarded as focusing support on the contexts rather than the processes of work (Suchman, 1995; Winograd, 1994).

A number of spatial techniques, including media spaces, spatial video conferencing, collaborative virtual environments, and telepresence are reviewed in an article by Benford et al. (1996). Media spaces, for example, employ integrated audio/video communications as a means for supporting social browsing and the development of long-term working relationships between physically separated individuals. Services include views into other participants' offices and open connections with selected individuals. The main drawback to this approach has been a limited field of view and the inability to navigate freely through the shared space (Gaver, 1992). Spatial video conferencing is used to support more formal interactions (e.g., meetings). Some advanced systems include shared document editors. Limitations of this technology stem from the fact that participants find it difficult to visually determine where other members of the group are directing their attention at any given time.

Collaborative virtual environments support shared work through networked virtual reality systems. In principle, such technologies provide computer-generated worlds in which participants are graphically represented to each other and each participant controls his or her own viewpoint. The shared space provides a common frame of reference for all participants. Collaborative virtual environments have been tested for use in such applications as education, training, and scientific visualization (Durlach and Mavor, 1995). These applications often integrate representations of users and their information in a common display space (unlike multimedia systems, which typically display communication and data in separate windows). However, collaborative virtual environments are a less mature technology than either media spaces or spatial video conferencing. Finally, telepresence differs from collaborative virtual environments in that participants are given the experience of a real remote physical space rather than a space that is computer generated. Telepresence applications currently focus on the control of remote robots in hazardous or inaccessible environments (including telesurgery).

One potential application of shared media spaces and collaborative virtual environments is to facilitate strategic planning activities among central flow control staff and staff at facilities across the country. Another possible application is to allow controllers to remain at their own facilities and be trained interactively in real time with controllers located at other facilities.

Integration and Advanced Groupware

Although different types of applications are discussed separately above, it should be noted that advanced groupware systems may well integrate aspects of each type. A complex groupware application designed to support a flight crew in their interactions with one another and with the airline both in the air and on the ground, for example, is described in Benson et al. (1990). The system enables synchronous communication, both video- and audio-based, among training/technical managers, crew managers, and chief pilots—who are normally all located in different facilities. It also supports a highly structured asynchronous messaging system through which pilots can lodge bids for flights and for training periods. But because the airline has the right to allocate some flights directly and to draft pilots if a flight is still not covered a few days before departure, a built-in workflow system (which models the bidding process and flexibly reallocates tasks to resources) manages many aspects of the bidding logistics.

The authors argue that distributed but coordinated work requires groupware systems that can communicate and execute concurrently. However, they conclude that what is most important to the performance of interdependent tasks is cohesion among participants; systems to support such activity must therefore be designed with a view to increasing trust, motivation, flexibility, and the like. Improved information is not the only essential ingredient for successful human collaboration.

Issues and Implications

A primary concern of the work in CSCW is the development of methodologies to describe roles, relationships, and shared work procedures for coordination, cooperation, and communication.

A number of investigators (Hughes et al., 1994; Twidale et al., 1994; Harper and Hughes, 1991; Bikson and Eveland, 1990, 1996; Bikson and Law, 1993; Bikson, 1996; Eveland et al., 1995; Dubrovsky et al., 1991; Finholt et al., 1990) have employed a variety of social research methods (ethnography, field experiments, replicated case designs, unobtrusive measures, and realistic laboratory studies) in efforts to develop the required social knowledge and incorporate it into design and implementation processes. Less progress has been made toward developing methods for evaluation.

To date, there has been little systematic effort to apply CSCW to time-critical operations in air traffic control. However, there are several promising areas in which this approach might usefully be considered in the future. Among these are the strategic activities of air traffic management that involve coordination and communication with facilities across the country regarding local traffic and weather concerns. Such coordination of physically remote individuals is an ideal target for CSCW technology. Other examples are the interactions between pilots and controllers who are working with shared map displays (e.g., shared plan view displays, shared airport movement area safety system maps—see Chapter 5); and the interactions between local maintenance personnel and specialists at centralized maintenance control stations (see Chapter 7). Some researchers hypothesize that interdependencies increase as the number of affected task participants increases and the time-scale for task relevant actions decrease (see, for example, Benson et al., 1990). If so, the projected growth of air traffic suggests that future needs for computer support of effective interdependency management in this domain will be pressing; consequently, the potential value of CSCW technologies for air traffic control merits serious investigation.

PART II

Current and Envisioned Automation of Air Traffic Control Tasks

In this part we review automation features and associated human factors issues for a number of existing and proposed programs and products that apply automation to air traffic control tasks. In Chapter 3 we review fundamental surveillance (radar, global positioning system, and weather) and communication (bandwidth, voice switching and control system, and data link) systems. In Chapter 4 we review systems that process and present flight information to pilots (flight management system) and to air traffic controllers (ground-based flight data processing). In Chapter 5 we review systems that support immediate conflict avoidance: the traffic alert and collision avoidance system (TCAS), the converging runway display aid (CRDA), the precision runway monitor (PRM), and airport surface collision avoidance systems. In Chapter 6 we review strategic long-term planning: the center-TRACON automation system (CTAS), the conflict probe and interactive planning, four-dimensional contracts, and the surface movement advisor (SMA). In Chapter 7 we review training and maintenance systems.

The goal of our analysis for each system or component is to examine potential issues in human factors and automation, to identify strengths and weaknesses in the system, and to suggest future research directions. With regard to research, we believe that the need for data collection and comparison is indicated in a number of areas in which changes are projected and the implications for the human operator are uncertain. The framework used for analyzing human factors issues includes the categories of workload, training and selection, organizational factors, and cognitive task analysis, in which we perform our own breakdown of the cognitive components of the task. The framework used for identifying critical automation issues includes the categories of mode errors, trust, skill degradation, mental models, and communication and organization. Researchers and developers interested in the evaluation of current and future automated systems should find these frameworks useful.

This introduction includes a set of tables that map automation programs and products to controller tasks performed in each type of facility. A glossary defining the acronyms noted in the tables and elsewhere in the report appears in Appendix A. Our purpose in presenting the tables is to offer a broad framework for the more detailed discussion of specific instances of automation and to present a general overview of trends.

Tables II.1 through II.4 summarize current, developmental, and contemplated applications of automation to air traffic control tasks for the en route, TRACON, tower, and oceanic environments, respectively. The tables include traffic management and flight service tasks for each environment, as appropriate.

In the Phase I report we acknowledged and discussed in some detail the importance of the flight service station facilities and the Air Traffic Control System Command Center facility. Our current treatment of these facilities is limited here to referencing the automated features of these facilities that support traffic management functions for the en route, TRACON, tower, and oceanic environments. In addition, we note the distinction between air traffic control and airway facilities specialists; however, the tables include and the text discusses in detail the automated features of airway facilities systems that support air traffic control tasks.

The tasks identified in Tables II.1 through II.4 are grouped into the following cognitive functions and presented in descending order of cognitive complexity:

1. Planning strategies and resolving conflicts,
2. Predicting long-term events,
3. Comparing criteria and predicting short-term events,
4. Transmitting information,
5. Remembering, and
6. Identifying relevant items of information.

For each environment and for each controller task, we identify automated features of the air traffic control system that are: (1) currently implemented, having been developed, tested, and fielded (although not necessarily implemented in all facilities for a given environment); (2) in development (although future upgrades or product improvements with additional automated features may remain tentative); and (3) under future consideration (development may be planned or concepts may be under consideration). Since the third category reflects concepts rather than detailed designs, the mapping of those items to functions that they may automate is especially tentative; our mapping is based on a broad interpretation of the automation concepts for items in that category. For example,

Table II.3 identifies, for the tower environment, extensive future capabilities for the surface movement advisor (SMA); some of the capabilities (especially higher-level capabilities) are based on conceptual developments rather than on firm program plans.

Systems in development or under future consideration often include modernization of previously automated functions (i.e., improved computing speed, accuracy, capacity, memory) and may or may not add automated features beyond those already provided by the systems that they replace. The tables include such systems only when they add automated features, and only the added automation features (not those that are simply being replicated) are identified in the tables. For example, the display system replacement (DSR) will modernize the display channels and displays of the en route system. It will replicate current processing of flight and radar data and will preserve current automation features. Therefore, Table II.1 identifies only the additional conflict probe feature added by the DSR.

Some air traffic control tasks are highly automated; others are performed primarily by the air traffic controller, who receives assistance from automation. For example, the tasks of sensing, computing, and displaying the position of aircraft are highly automated; they are performed by the elements of the radar processing system. However, the task of resolving traffic conflicts is performed largely by the controller, who may receive automated assistance from such systems as the CTAS or the user request evaluation tool (URET). In the tables, features that supply a high degree of automation for a given task are highlighted; features that provide automated assistance to controllers, who perform the task, are not. The dichotomy applied here between highly automated features and automation assistance features represents a forced choice judgment. We do not attempt here to apply the more complex treatment of levels and dimensions of automation, discussed in detail in Chapter 1.

The primary sources for the automation programs identified in the tables and discussed in this section are the Federal Aviation Administration's *National Airspace System Architecture* description (1996a) and its *Aviation System Capital Investment Plan* (1996b). The primary source for the identification of controller tasks is the controller task listing developed and reported under the FAA's separation and control hiring assessment program.

BRIEF DESCRIPTION OF AUTOMATION FEATURES

Key automation features and functionality are discussed in greater detail elsewhere in this report. Here we first briefly describe areas of automation not addressed in detail in other sections: flight services and oceanic control. In addition, we outline the modernization efforts that are prerequisite for planned product improvements for en route centers, TRACONs, and towers.

Flight Services

Many flight service functions are currently automated. Preflight briefings and instrument flight rules/visual flight rules flight plan filing services are available on a walk-in basis or via telephone. These services are also available via personal computer through the direct user access terminal system (DUATS). Preflight information is also available through dial-in lines for the automated weather observing system (AWOS) and the automated surface observing system (ASOS), whose data are also broadcast automatically.

The FAA is considering virtually complete automation of flight services, with the goal of enabling pilots to self-brief and to file flight plans without contacting flight service specialists. A contemplated operational and supportability implementation system (OASIS) would address these goals.

Oceanic Automation

The current oceanic air traffic control system does not rely on radar coverage, and so direct surveillance is not used over most of the ocean. Navigation is performed primarily with on-board inertial navigation systems, and pilots report their positions to controllers via high frequency voice radio. The current oceanic display and planning system (ODAPS), deployed in Oakland and New York, provides a display of aircraft positions, based on extrapolation of periodic voice position reports from pilots and on filed flight plans. In addition, the dynamic ocean tracking system (DOTS) assists the controller to develop routes that take advantage of favorable wind and temperature conditions, and also projects aircraft movement to identify airspace competition and availability. The telecommunications processor (TP) has replaced the flight data input/output computer system (FDIO) for oceanic controllers; the processor includes a message scrolling capability.

The FAA plans future development of data link capabilities and improved navigation and surveillance data, which are required to support desired automation features for the oceanic environment. Data link capabilities would include the oceanic data link (ODL) under development, as well as future controller-to-pilot data link (CPDL). The global positioning system and automatic dependent surveillance are also considered enabling technologies for automation in this environment. An improved air traffic control interfacility data communications (AIDC) is also posited. The umbrella programs for oceanic automation are the advanced oceanic automation system (AOAS) and the oceanic automation program (OAP). These long-term programs would build on the data provided by new surveillance, navigation, and communication systems to achieve levels of automation commensurate with those of the domestic en route environment. The oceanic environment is also the locus of one of the early precursors to free flight, embodied in the procedures of oceanic in-trail climb (discussed in Chapter 9).

Data link, the global positioning system, and automatic dependent surveillance developments are discussed in greater detail in Chapter 3.

Modernization Efforts

The en route computer display channel processor, the display channel controller processor, and plan view displays are being modernized through the display system replacement (DSR). This modernization program will retain all the features of the existing system, will support an additional conflict probe capability, and is planned to accommodate future enhancements that may include automated features discussed elsewhere in this report.

The standard terminal automation replacement system (STARS) is a modernization program that will replace ARTS processors and displays. STARS will replicate ARTS functions and will therefore include the automated features of ARTS. STARS is planned as an expandable system that will accommodate future automation enhancements for the TRACON.

The FAA is planning a tower integration program whose main goals are the consolidation of the disparate displays and controls in the current tower and the addition of automation enhancements.

Each of these modernization efforts includes the provision of new workstations for controllers.

Voice Switching and Control System

The voice switching and control system is a form of air traffic control automation that employs digital logic, controlled by a touch screen interface above the controller's display, to change and reconfigure radio frequencies and communication links, in order to directly route (or reroute) communications to desired parties (Perry, 1997). It is a highly flexible and adaptable system, enabling controllers and supervisors to easily reconfigure communications within a sector, or supervisors to do so within an entire facility. The system has been well received by controllers because it replaces time consuming and inflexible operations and because of its greater reliability; however, a survey of air traffic controllers revealed that its implementation has produced certain problems (Sarter and Woods, 1997). For example, 28 of the 58 controllers responding to the survey indicated instances in which they had been "surprised" by a reconfiguration of the system that had been carried out by a remote operator; at the time they were not aware of the reconfiguration, but only discovered it later, when they tried to perform operations that failed in the new reconfigured mode. The potential for such mode errors (see Chapter 1) is perhaps an inevitable downside of the flexible aspects of some automation functions. Their presence may have serious consequences, and their possible emergence in other systems should be anticipated, with attention given to design features that make mode changes clearly observable to all participants.

KEY TRENDS

1. A considerable amount of automation has already been applied to air traffic control tasks for the en route, TRACON, and tower environments, and future automation is likely to be significant for all environments.

2. Current automation is applied to support controller tasks across all levels of cognitive complexity. However, the application of highly automated features, which often virtually replace controller actions, has to date been largely reserved for tasks of lower cognitive complexity. When automation is currently applied to tasks of higher cognitive complexity, the automation provides assistance to controllers, who perform and are responsible for the tasks.

3. Given that tasks of lower cognitive complexity have to date received "fuller" automation, the trend toward a more highly automated system appears more revolutionary—and faces its greatest challenge—at higher levels of cognitive complexity (long-term prediction, planning, and conflict resolution).

TABLE II.1 Automated Features: En Route Environment (highly automated features are in bold)

Cognitive Function/Task	Currently Implemented	In Development	Future Concepts
PLAN/RESOLVE			
Plan/resolve traffic management constraints	ETMS	CTAS, CP	**CR**
Plan clearances	ETMS	CTAS, CP	**CR**
Resolve tactical conflicts	TCAS (for pilots), ERM	CTAS, ESP/ASP	**CR**
Resolve strategic conflicts	ETMS, ERM	CTAS, CP, ESP/ASP	**CR**
Resolve MSAW condition			**CR**
Plan special-use airspace activities		CTAS, CP, SAMS/MAMS	**CR**
Resolve special-use airspace violations		CTAS, CP, SAMS/MAMS	**CR**
Resolve consequences of deviation		CTAS, CP	**CR**
Plan departure and arrival flows	ERM, ETMS	CTAS, CP, ESP/ASP	**CR**
Plan response to weather	ETMS	CTAS, CP	**WARP, ITWS, CR**
Plan emergency response	ETMS, MCC, NMCC	CTAS, CP	**CR, OCC, NOCC**
Plan search for lost or overdue aircraft			
Respond to system failures	ETMS, MCC, NMCC	CTAS, CP	**OCC, NOCC**, CR
Plan resectorization		CP	CR
PREDICT LONGER TERM			
Predict violation of separation standards		**DSR, CTAS, CP**	
Predict aircraft trajectory	ETMS	**DSR, CTAS, CP**	
Predict aircraft heading and speed	ETMS	**DSR, CTAS, CP**	
Predict aircraft position	ETMS	**DSR, CTAS, CP**	

continued on next page

TABLE II.1   (*continued*)

Cognitive Function/Task	Currently Implemented	In Development	Future Concepts
Predict violation of conformance criteria		CTAS, CP	
Predict violation of flow restrictions	ETMS	CTAS, CP	
Predict MSAW violation		CP	
Predict deviation		CTAS, CP	
Predict special-use airspace violations		SAMS/MAMS, CP	
Predict traffic sequences for arrival/ departure flows	ETMS	CTAS, CP	
Predict weather	Various services		WARP
Predict capacity and use	ETMS, ERM	CTAS	
Predict clearance slots	ETMS, ERM	CTAS	
COMPARE, PREDICT VERY SHORT TERM			
Determine violation of separation standards	RDP PRI/SEC RADAR, TCAS (for pilots)	DSR, CTAS, CP	GPS/ADS
Determine violation of conformance criteria	PRI/SEC RADAR, RDP	CTAS, CP	
Determine violation of flow restrictions	ETMS	CTAS, CP	
Determine MSAW violation	RDP		GPS/ADS
Determine violation of special-use airspace	PRI/SEC RADAR, RDP	SAMS/MAMS	GPS/ADS
Determine deviation	PRI/SEC RADAR, RDP	CTAS, CP	GPS/ADS
Determine equipment and system problems	MCC, NMCC		OCC, NOCC
Compare use vs. capacity	ETMS	CTAS	
Compare reported vs. actual position of aircraft	PRI/SEC RADAR, RDP		GPS/ADS
Predict weather	MWP, CWSU, TDWR	WARP, ITWS	

TABLE II.1 (*continued*)

Cognitive Function/Task	Currently Implemented	In Development	Future Concepts
Compare information from multiple sensors	ETMS, NMCC, **RDP, MCC**	**WARP, ITWS**	**GPS/ADS, OCC, NOCC**
TRANSMIT INFORMATION			
Receive clearance requests and generate clearances	FDP, ETMS	CTAS	**Data Link**
Receive/send traffic management restrictions	ETMS	CTAS, CP	**Data Link**
Receive flight plan information	**FDP, DUATS**	CP	**Data Link, OASIS**
Input/send flight plan information	FDP		**Data Link**
Instruct pilots: heading, speed, altitude			**Data Link**
Instruct pilots: flight paths			**Data Link**
Receive/send conflict information to pilots and/or controllers	TCAS (to pilots), RDP (to controllers)	CTAS, CP	**Data Link**
Receive/send MSAW alert	RDP		**Data Link**
Inform pilots of unsafe condition advisories			**Data Link**
Inform pilots of deviations			**Data Link**
Inform pilots of airspace restrictions		SAMS/MAMS	**Data Link**
Receive/send information about aircraft emergency			**Data Link**
Receive/send information about system degradations	MCC, NMCC		**Data Link, OCC, NOCC**
Update flight plan information	FDP, DUATS		**Data Link, OASIS**
Receive/send handoff	**FDP, RDP**		
Receive/send weather information	ACARS, MWP, CWSU	WARP, ITWS	**Data Link, OASIS**

continued on next page

TABLE II.1 *(continued)*

Cognitive Function/Task	Currently Implemented	In Development	Future Concepts
REMEMBER			
Remember history of aircraft position	**RDP**		**GPS/ADS**
Remember flight plans and updates	**DUATS, FDP, ETMS**		**OASIS**
Record conflict situations	**RDP**		
Remember noncontrolled objects	**RDP**		
Remember assigned aircraft	**FDP, RDP**		
Remember weather information	**MWP, CWSU**	**WARP**	**OASIS**
Remember clearances	**FDP,** ETMS		
Remember aircraft sequences	**FDP,** ETMS		
Remember special-use airspace restrictions	ETMS	**SAMS/MAMS**	
Remember traffic management constraints	ETMS		
Remember sectorization	**VSCS, RDP, FDP**		
Remember aircraft capabilities/ characteristics	FDP, ETMS		
IDENTIFY			
Identify navigation fixes	**FDP**		
Identify weather features	**RADAR, ACARS, NEXRAD**	**WARP**	
Identify borders of special-use airspace	**FDP**	**SAMS/MAMS**	
Identify aircraft air speed, ground speed	**PRI/SEC RADAR, RDP**		**GPS/ADS**
Identify aircraft type/designation	**SEC RADAR, FDP, RDP**		**ADS**
Identify aircraft position (altitude, plan position)	**PRI/SEC RADAR, RDP**		**GPS/ADS**
Identify noncontrolled objects	**PRI RADAR, RDP**		

NOTE: See Appendix A for a glossary of acronyms.

TABLE II.2 Automated Features: TRACON Environment (highly automated features are in bold)

Cognitive Function/Task	Currently Implemented	In Development	Future Concepts
PLAN/RESOLVE			
Plan/resolve traffic management constraints	ETMS	CTAS, CP	**CR**
Plan clearances	ETMS	CTAS, CP	**CR**
Resolve tactical conflicts	TCAS (for pilots)	CTAS	**CR**
Resolve strategic conflicts	ETMS	CTAS, CP	**CR**
Resolve MSAW condition			**CR**
Plan special-use airspace activities		CTAS, CP, SAMS/MAMS	**CR**
Resolve special-use airspace violations		CTAS, CP, SAMS/MAMS	**CR**
Resolve consequences of deviation		CTAS, CP	**CR**
Plan departure and arrival flows	ETMS	CTAS, CP	**CR**
Plan response to weather	ETMS	CTAS, CP	**ITWS, CR**
Plan emergency response	ETMS, MCC, NMCC	CTAS, CP	**CR, OCC, NOCC**
Plan search for lost or overdue aircraft			
Respond to system failures	ETMS, MCC, NMCC	CTAS, CP	**OCC, NOCC,** CR
Plan resectorization			CR
PREDICT LONGER TERM			
Predict violation of separation standards		**CTAS, CP**	
Predict aircraft trajectory	ETMS	**CTAS, CP**	
Predict aircraft heading and speed	ETMS	**CTAS, CP**	
Predict aircraft position	ETMS	**CTAS, CP**	
Predict violation of conformance criteria		CTAS, CP	
Predict violation of flow restrictions	ETMS	**CTAS, CP**	

continued on next page

TABLE II.2 (*continued*)

Cognitive Function/Task	Currently Implemented	In Development	Future Concepts
Predict MSAW violation			
Predict deviation		CTAS, CP	
Predict special-use airspace violations		**SAMS/MAMS, CP**	
Predict traffic sequences for arrival/departure flows	ETMS	**CTAS, CP**	
Predict weather	Various services		**ITWS**
Predict capacity and use	ETMS	**CTAS**	
Predict clearance slots	ETMS	**CTAS**	

COMPARE, PREDICT VERY SHORT TERM

Determine violation of separation standards	**ARTS, FMA/ PRM, CRDA** PRI/SEC RADAR, TCAS (for pilots)	CTAS, CP	GPS/ADS
Determine violation of conformance criteria	PRI/SEC RADAR, ARTS	CTAS, CP	
Determine violation of flow restrictions	ETMS	CTAS, CP	
Determine MSAW violation	**ARTS**		**GPS/ADS**
Determine violation of special-use airspace	PRI/SEC RADAR, ARTS	**SAMS/MAMS**	GPS/ADS
Determine deviation	**FMA, PRM** PRI/SEC RADAR, ARTS	**CTAS, CP**	GPS/ADS
Determine equipment and system problems	**MCC,** NMCC		**OCC, NOCC**
Compare use vs. capacity	ETMS	**CTAS**	
Compare reported vs. actual position of aircraft	PRI/SEC RADAR, RDP		GPS/ADS
Predict weather	TDWR	**ITWS**	
Compare information from multiple sensors	ETMS, NMCC, **ARTS, MCC**	**STARS**	**GPS/ADS, ITWS, OCC, NOCC**

TABLE II.2 (*continued*)

Cognitive Function/Task	Currently Implemented	In Development	Future Concepts
TRANSMIT INFORMATION			
Receive clearance requests and generate clearances	FDIO, ETMS	CTAS	**Data Link**
Receive/send traffic management restrictions	ETMS	CTAS, CP	**Data Link**
Receive flight plan information	**FDIO, ARTS, DUATS**	CP	**Data Link**
Input/send flight plan information	FDIO, ARTS		**Data Link**
Instruct pilots: heading, speed, altitude			**Data Link**
Instruct pilots: flight paths			**Data Link**
Receive/send conflict information to pilots and/or controllers	TCAS (to pilots), ARTS (to controllers)	CTAS, CP	**Data Link**
Receive/send MSAW alert	ARTS		**Data Link**
Inform pilots of unsafe condition advisories			**Data Link**
Inform pilots of deviations			**Data Link**
Inform pilots of airspace restrictions		SAMS/MAMS	**Data Link**
Receive/send information about aircraft emergency			**Data Link**
Receive/send information about system degradations	MCC, NMCC		**Data Link, OCC, NOCC**
Update flight plan information	**DUATS** FDIO		**Data Link, OASIS**
Receive/send handoff	**ARTS**		
Receive/send weather information	TDWR, ACARS	**ITWS, TWIP**	**Data Link, OASIS**

continued on next page

TABLE II.2 (*continued*)

Cognitive Function/Task	Currently Implemented	In Development	Future Concepts
REMEMBER			
Remember history of aircraft position	**ARTS**		**GPS/ADS**
Remember flight plans and updates	**DUATS, FDIO, ARTS, ETMS**		**OASIS**
Record conflict situations	**ARTS**		
Remember noncontrolled objects	**ARTS**		
Remember assigned aircraft	**ARTS**		
Remember weather information	**TDWR**	**ITWS**	**OASIS**
Remember clearances	**ARTS,** ETMS		
Remember aircraft sequences	**ARTS,** ETMS		
Remember special-use airspace restrictions	ETMS	**SAMS/MAMS**	
Remember traffic management constraints	ETMS		
Remember sectorization	**ARTS**	**TVSR**	
Remember aircraft capabilities/ characteristics	ARTS, ETMS		
IDENTIFY			
Identify navigation fixes	**ARTS**		
Identify weather features	**RADAR, ACARS, TDWR**	**ITWS**	
Identify borders of special-use airspace	**ARTS**	**SAMS/MAMS**	
Identify aircraft air speed, ground speed	**PRI/SEC RADAR, ARTS**		**GPS/ADS**
Identify aircraft type/designation	**SEC RADAR, FDP, ARTS**		**ADS**
Identify aircraft position (altitude, plan position)	**PRI/SEC RADAR, ARTS**		**GPS/ADS**
Identify noncontrolled objects	**PRI RADAR, ARTS**		

NOTE: See Appendix A for a glossary of acronyms.

TABLE II.3 Automated Features: Tower Environment (highly auutomated features are in bold)

Cognitive Function/Task	Currently Implemented	In Development	Future Concepts
PLAN/RESOLVE			
Plan/resolve traffic management constraints	ETMS		**SMA**
Plan clearances	ETMS		**SMA**
Resolve tactical conflicts	TCAS (for pilots)	AMASS	**SMA**
Resolve strategic conflicts	ETMS		**SMA**
Resolve MSAW condition			
Plan special-use airspace activities			
Resolve special-use airspace violations			
Resolve consequences of deviation			
Plan departure and arrival flows	ETMS		**SMA**
Plan response to weather	ETMS		**SMA, WSP**
Plan emergency response	ETMS, MCC, NMCC		**SMA, OCC NOCC**
Plan search for lost or overdue aircraft			
Respond to system failures	ETMS, MCC, NMCC		**SMA, OCC NOCC**
PREDICT LONGER TERM			
Predict violation of separation standards	**TCAS (for pilots)**	**AMASS**	**SMA**
Predict aircraft trajectory			
Predict aircraft heading and speed			
Predict aircraft position		**AMASS**	**SMA**
Predict violation of conformance criteria			
Predict violation of flow restrictions	ETMS		**SMA**
Predict MSAW violation			

continued on next page

TABLE II.3 *(continued)*

Cognitive Function/Task	Currently Implemented	In Development	Future Concepts
Predict deviation			
Predict special-use airspace violations			
Predict traffic sequences for arrival/ departure flows	ETMS		**SMA**
Predict weather	Various services		**WSP**
Predict capacity and use	ETMS		**SMA**
Predict clearance slots	ETMS		**SMA**
COMPARE, PREDICT VERY SHORT TERM			
Determine violation of separation standards	PRI RADAR, DBRITE, ASDE	**AMASS**	**SMA** GPS/ADS
Determine violation of conformance criteria	PRI RADAR, RDP		GPS/ADS
Determine violation of flow restrictions	ETMS		**SMA**
Determine MSAW violation	DBRITE		GPS/ADS
Determine violation of special-use airspace	PRI RADAR, DBRITE	**SAMS/MAMS**	GPS/ADS
Determine deviation	PRI RADAR, DBRITE		GPS/ADS
Determine equipment and system problems	**MCC**, NMCC		**OCC, NOCC**
Compare use vs. capacity	ETMS		**SMA**
Compare reported vs. actual position of aircraft	PRI RADAR, ASDE, DBRITE	**AMASS**	**SMA** GPS/ADS
Predict weather	ASOS, TDWR	**WSP**	
Compare information from multiple sensors	ETMS,NMCC, **MCC**	**WSP**	GPS, **ADS, OCC, NOCC**
TRANSMIT INFORMATION			
Receive clearance requests and generate clearances	FDIO, ACARS		**Data Link, SMA**

TABLE II.3 *(continued)*

Cognitive Function/Task	Currently Implemented	In Development	Future Concepts
Receive/send traffic management restrictions			**Data Link, SMA**
Receive flight plan information	FDIO, DUATS		**Data Link, SMA, OASIS**
Input/send flight plan information	FDIO		**Data Link, SMA**
Instruct pilots: heading, speed, altitude			**Data Link**
Instruct pilots: flight paths			**Data Link**
Receive/send conflict information to pilots and/or controllers	TCAS (to pilots), RDP (to controllers)	AMASS	**Data Link**
Receive/send MSAW alert	DBRITE		**Data Link**
Inform pilots of unsafe condition advisories	ACARS		**Data Link**
Inform pilots of deviations			**Data Link**
Inform pilots of airspace restrictions	ACARS	SAMS/MAMS	**Data Link**
Receive/send information about aircraft emergency			**Data Link**
Receive/send information about system degradations	MCC, NMCC		**Data Link, OCC, NOC**
Update flight plan information	FDIO, DUATS		**Data Link, OASIS**
Receive/send handoff	ARTS		
Receive/send weather information	AWOS, ASOS, LLWAS, TDWR	WSP, TWIP	**Data Link, OASIS**
REMEMBER			
Remember history of aircraft position	**ASDE, DBRITE**		**GPS/ADS, SMA**
Remember flight plans and updates	**DUATS, FDIO** ETMS		**OASIS, SMA**

continued on next page

TABLE II.3 (*continued*)

Cognitive Function/Task	Currently Implemented	In Development	Future Concepts
Record conflict situations			**SMA**
Remember noncontrolled objects	**ASDE, DBRITE**		
Remember assigned aircraft	**FDIO**		
Remember weather information	**ASOS, LLWAS, TDWR**	**WSP**	**OASIS**
Remember clearances	ETMS, FDIO		**SMA**
Remember aircraft sequences	**FDIO**, ETMS		**SMA**
Remember special-use airspace restrictions	**DBRITE** ETMS	**SAMS/MAMS**	
Remember traffic management constraints	ETMS		**SMA**
Remember aircraft capabilities/ characteristics	FDIO, ETMS		**SMA**
IDENTIFY			
Identify navigation fixes	**DBRITE**		
Identify weather features	**TDWR, ASOS, LLWAS**	**WSP**	
Identify borders of special-use airspace	**DBRITE**	**SAMS/MAMS**	
Identify aircraft air speed, ground speed	**PRI RADAR, DBRITE**		**GPS/ADS, SMA**
Identify aircraft type/designation	**DBRITE, FDIO**		**ADS, SMA**
Identify aircraft position (altitude, plan position)	**ASDE, DBRITE, PRI RADAR**		**GPS/ADS, SMA**
Identify noncontrolled objects	**ASDE, DBRITE, PRI RADAR**		**GPS/ADS, SMA**
Identify ground hazards	**ASDE, PRI RADAR**		**SMA**

NOTE: See Appendix A for a glossary of acronyms.

TABLE II.4 Automated Features: Oceanic Environment (highly automated features are in bold)

Cognitive Function/Task	Currently Implemented	In Development	Future Concepts
PLAN/RESOLVE			
Plan/resolve traffic management constraints			**AOAS**
Plan clearances			**AOAS**
Resolve tactical conflicts	**TCAS (for pilots)**		**AOAS**
Resolve strategic conflicts			**AOAS**
Resolve MSAW condition			
Plan special-use airspace activities			
Resolve special-use airspace violations			
Resolve consequences of deviation			**AOAS**
Plan departure and arrival flows			**AOAS**
Plan response to weather			**AOAS**
Plan emergency response	MCC, NMCC		**AOAS, OCC, NOCC**
Plan search for lost or overdue aircraft			
Respond to system failures	MCC, NMCC		**AOAS, OCC, NOCC**
Plan resectorization			
PREDICT LONGER TERM			
Predict violation of separation standards	DOTS		**AOAS, OAP**
Predict aircraft trajectory	DOTS		**AOAS, OAP**
Predict aircraft heading and speed	DOTS		**AOAS, OAP**
Predict aircraft position	DOTS		**AOAS, OAP**
Predict violation of conformance criteria	DOTS		**AOAS, OAP**
Predict violation of flow restrictions	DOTS		**AOAS, OAP**
Predict MSAW violation			**GPS/ADS**

continued on next page

TABLE II.4 (*continued*)

Cognitive Function/Task	Currently Implemented	In Development	Future Concepts
Predict deviation			**AOAS, OAP**
Predict special-use airspace violations			
Predict traffic sequences for arrival/ departure flows			**AOAS**
Predict weather			
Predict capacity and use	DOTS		**AOAS**
Predict clearance slots	DOTS		**AOAS**
COMPARE, PREDICT VERY SHORT TERM			
Determine violation of separation standards	TCAS (for pilots), DOTS	**ADS**	**GPS, OAP**
Determine violation of conformance criteria		**ADS**	**GPS, OAP**
Determine violation of flow restrictions	DOTS	**ADS**	**GPS, OAP**
Determine MSAW violation		**ADS**	**GPS**
Determine violation of special-use airspace		**ADS**	**GPS**
Determine deviation		**ADS**	**GPS, OAP**
Determine equipment and system problems	MCC, NMCC		**OCC, NOCC**
Compare use vs. capacity			**AIDC**
Compare reported vs. actual position of aircraft	DOTS, ODAPS	**ADS**	**AIDC, GPS, OAP**
Predict weather			
Compare information from multiple sensors		**ADS**	**AIDC, GPS, OCC, NOCC**
TRANSMIT INFORMATION			
Receive clearance requests and generate clearances			
Receive/send traffic management restrictions			**AIDC, CPDL**

TABLE II.4 (*continued*)

Cognitive Function/Task	Currently Implemented	In Development	Future Concepts
Receive flight plan information	TP	**ODL**	**AIDC, CPDL**
Input/send flight plan information	TP	**ODL**	**AIDC, CPDL**
Instruct pilots: heading, speed, altitude			**CPDL**
Instruct pilots: flight paths			**CPDL**
Receive/send conflict information to pilots and/or controllers	TCAS (to pilots)		**AIDC, CPDL**
Receive/send MSAW alert			**CPDL**
Inform pilots of unsafe condition advisories			**CPDL**
Inform pilots of deviations			**CPDL**
Inform pilots of airspace restrictions			**CPDL**
Receive/send information about aircraft emergency			**CPDL**
Receive/send information about system degradations	MCC, NMCC		OCC, NOCC
Update flight plan information	TP	**ODL**	**AIDC, CPDL**
Receive/send handoff			**AIDC, CPDL**
Receive/send weather information			**AIDC, CPDL**
REMEMBER			
Remember history of aircraft position	**ODAPS**	**ADS**	**GPS, OAP**
Remember flight plans and updates	**ODAPS, TP**		**AIDC, OAP**
Record conflict situations			**AIDC, OAP**
Remember noncontrolled objects			
Remember assigned aircraft	**ODAPS**		**AIDC, OAP**

continued on next page

TABLE II.4 (*continued*)

Cognitive Function/Task	Currently Implemented	In Development	Future Concepts
Remember weather information			
Remember clearances	**DOTS**		**AIDC, OAP**
Remember aircraft sequences	**DOTS**		**AIDC, OAP**
Remember special-use airspace restrictions			
Remember traffic management constraints			**AIDC**
Remember sectorization	**ODAPS**		**AIDC**
Remember aircraft capabilities/ characteristics			**AIDC**
IDENTIFY			
Identify navigation fixes	**ODAPS**		
Identify weather features			
Identify borders of special-use airspace			
Identify aircraft air speed, ground speed	**ODAPS**	**ODL, ADS**	**GPS, OAP**
Identify aircraft type/designation	**TP, ODAPS**	**ODL, ADS**	**OAP**
Identify aircraft position (altitude, plan position)	**ODAPS**	**ODL, ADS**	**GPS, OAP**
Identify noncontrolled objects			

NOTE: See Appendix A for a glossary of acronyms.

3

Surveillance and Communication

Surveillance and communication technologies are prerequisite for performing air traffic control functions, and they constitute critical components of the national airspace system infrastructure into which automation has been increasingly introduced. In this chapter, we review technologies that are applied to the surveillance of aircraft, ground vehicles, and weather and to the communication of information. In particular we examine the characteristics of three technologies that enable the acquisition of information (radar, the global positioning system, and weather data processing) and two key features of communication technology (bandwidth and data link).

SURVEILLANCE TECHNOLOGIES

Two critical types of information that must be acquired, processed, and displayed to controllers are aircraft situation data (e.g., position, identification, heading, speed, and altitude) and weather data. Aircraft situation data are acquired primarily through radar systems, although global positioning system/automatic dependent surveillance applications are under consideration by the Federal Aviation Administration (FAA). Weather data are acquired and presented through a variety of systems.

We treat the radar processing system and the global positioning system in detail. The radar processing system is currently the fundamental enabling technology for aircraft surveillance. The global positioning system represents new aircraft surveillance technology that is likely to be a critical component of the national airspace system in the future. The global positioning system may also permit changes to separation standards, thereby playing a significant role with respect to safety and efficiency.

Radar Processing Systems

Key Elements and Functionality

For en route, TRACON, and tower operations, radar is the primary source of surveillance data used to calculate and predict the position, speed, and course of aircraft. Radar surveillance is not provided for oceanic air traffic control. Within the national airspace system, radar is considered a *service* delivered to controllers by a radar *system* consisting of the radar equipment itself, radar processing hardware and software, the display devices used to present the resulting data, and the interfaces among the system elements. The key elements of the radar systems for en route, TRACON, and tower air traffic control are summarized below.

There are two fundamental types of radar supporting air traffic control. Primary radar relies on reflection technology that provides data sufficient to calculate the range and bearing, but not the altitude, of a detected object. All en route centers and TRACONs are fed by primary radar. En route centers use the long-range air route surveillance radar (ARSR), which scans a wide area (generally a 250-mile radius). TRACONs use a shorter-range airport surveillance radar (ASR), which scans a narrower area (generally a 60-mile radius). In addition, busy towers are supported by a specialized primary radar, called airport surface detection equipment (ASDE), that detects ground objects. Radar is also a key sensor for detection of weather features.

Secondary radar, or beacon radar, usually collocated with primary radar, transmits an interrogation pulse; when the interrogation is received by an aircraft equipped with the appropriate transponder, the transponder replies with codes that indicate the aircraft's altitude and identification; the replies are received by the secondary radar. Secondary radars support both en route centers and TRACONs. Each en route facility is serviced by multiple radar sites, whereas most TRACONs are serviced by a single radar sensor.

At the en route center, primary and secondary radar data are processed by the HOST computer's radar data processor. The radar data processor software assesses the quality of radar data and blends radar inputs from multiple sites to provide controllers with the best available targets. The HOST radar data processor, together with computer display channel or display channel complex computers—depending on the facility—process the radar data to identify targets, calculate their positions, track their movements, correlate altitude and identification data with targets, transform the data to display coordinates, and display the resulting information (including target pixels, data blocks, and warnings of conflicts and unsafe altitudes) along with maps and other data seen on the controllers' plan view displays. The enhanced direct access radar channel is a backup processing suite that performs radar processing and supplies the controllers' displays if the HOST processor fails. Controllers can manually select enhanced direct access radar channel data for display if they suspect the integrity of the HOST radar data processing.

At the TRACONs, data processing is performed by the ARTS system. The ARTS system displays relatively unprocessed radar returns to controllers and superimposes on their display alphanumeric information indicating the identity of each target, its altitude, ground speed, type, miscellaneous flight plan data, and warnings of conflicts and unsafe altitudes. TRACONs are not serviced by an enhanced direct access radar channel backup; instead, TRACONs can be supplied, if necessary, by radar data from a connected en route HOST. Under such circumstances, the TRACON relies on the less accurate air route surveillance radar, and controllers must adjust their separations accordingly. Radar data from the ARTS is also supplied to some high-volume towers through a digital BRITE display that is similar to that used by the TRACON controllers.

Both the HOST (with display channel complex or computer display channel) and the ARTS perform additional processing to compensate for radar limitations. This additional processing is discussed below.

Redundancies

Redundancies are designed into the radar processing systems at each level. Each en route facility is serviced by multiple radars that provide overlapping coverage, and each radar transmits its data to the facilities over redundant interface lines. This applies as well to those TRACONs that are serviced by more than one radar site. The en route HOST processor is backed up by the enhanced direct access radar channel processor, and the TRACON ARTS is backed up by the en route HOST. Within the en route center, each computer display channel or display channel complex is backed up by redundant processors. The TRACON ARTS system also includes redundant display processors. At both the en route centers and the TRACONs, the displays themselves are redundant with other displays. In addition, the paper flight progress strips provide backup information in the event that the radar processing system fails.

Limitations

The radar processing systems are subject to two types of limitation: limited reliability (addressed through redundancy, preventive maintenance, and modernization) and limited accuracy (addressed through processing and new technology).

Reliability The radars themselves rely on mechanical components that are subject to failure. This limitation is addressed by redundant radars with overlapping coverage, by frequent preventive maintenance, and by an aggressive modernization program within the FAA for radars that are approaching the end of their service lives.

A more serious concern has been the unreliability of the en route display channel complex and the computer display channel hardware, which represent 1960s- and 1970s-vintage computer technology that is difficult to maintain, and which operate on obsolete software languages that have been altered over the years by software patches in response to site-specific requirements. Although these processors include and are backed up by redundant components, in some cases the radar processing systems have been operating on the backup components alone, because of the difficulty of maintaining the components. However, significant improvements in reliability are anticipated in the future. The HOST processor has been recently modernized, and the display system replacement (DSR) program will modernize, in the near future, the display channel complex and computer display channel processors, as well as the controllers' displays and workstations.

Although the ARTS system has also experienced unreliability associated with aging computer hardware and software, its anticipated lack of capacity has motivated its modernization. Concerned by the prospect that its limited capacity (e.g., memory and processing speed) will not be able to withstand projected increases in air traffic and will not be able to support functional enhancements aimed at increasing the throughput of the air traffic control system, the FAA has initiated the development of the standard terminal automation replacement system (STARS), which will modernize ARTS hardware and software.

Accuracy Presuming improved reliability associated with the modernization of en route and TRACON radars and radar processing systems, the question of accuracy limitations remains. Radar inaccuracies derive from two basic sources, clutter and misregistration. These inaccuracies are addressed primarily through processing.

Clutter refers to objects that are undesirable to display but are nevertheless sensed by the radar. Depending on the perspective of the controller's task, clutter may include terrain, buildings, antennae, ground vehicles, and precipitation. Algorithms in the radar data processor can filter and adjust gains to reduce clutter, and airborne processors can suppress transmissions that confuse the radar on the ground. In addition, radar may be physically adjusted to reduce ground clutter. Processing and physical adjustments that reduce clutter, however, can carry associated risk of reducing desirable information, particularly the depiction of VFR aircraft that are not equipped with mode C transponders.

Radar systems are also subject to some inherent inaccuracies. Transponder turnaround error alone can be as large as 0.04 miles (200 ft; 61 meters). Due to azimuth variances, position errors grow linearly larger with distance from the radar site. Although terminal area radars are fairly accurate, en route surveillance and tracking radars have accuracies of 300-500 meters (Galati and Losquadro, 1986). The range of these systems is limited to 350-400 km due to the horizon. Also, at long ranges, the position error becomes comparable to the movement of the aircraft between scans. This makes aircraft trajectory difficult to determine (Gertz, 1983). Although satellite-based radar systems can provide global coverage, their accuracies are still comparable to long-range ground radars due to their distances from the targets. The high accuracy and global coverage of the global positioning system could overcome these problems, especially in the en route portion of cross-country and oceanic flights.

Radars are also subject to miscalibration or misregistration. To maintain and adjust registration, radar are periodically tested and mechanically adjusted if necessary. In addition, it is standard practice for airway facilities radar specialists to enter numerical corrections into specially designed processing routines, to achieve registration through software.

Although processing filters and corrections can significantly compensate for clutter and misregistration, the radar data processing systems are ultimately limited by the accuracies achievable by the radar technology—and these limited accuracies affect the separation standards imposed by air traffic controllers. On that account, the FAA is considering surveillance technologies whose accuracies are better than that of radar, and that could, with effective data processing, permit reduction of separation standards. An augmented global positioning system, discussed below, is a candidate as a future surveillance system.

Summary

The reliability of radar processing systems is maintained by redundancies designed into the systems at each level. These redundancies include: multiple radars that provide overlapping coverage at all en route facilities and some TRACONs, redundant interface lines, backup radar processing, and redundant display devices. In addition to their other functions, the paper flight progress strips provide backup information in the event that the radar processing system fails.

Despite redundant system design, elements of the radar processing system have reached or are reaching the end of their service lives. The FAA response has been vigorous modernization programs that are replacing major components of the national airspace system radar systems; improved reliability is therefore anticipated.

Accuracy limitations of the radars are addressed, with generally good effect, by processing filters and corrections. The FAA is considering other surveillance technologies that may provide still greater inherent accuracies.

Global Positioning System

Potential Applications

GPS and other satellite navigation systems are rapidly becoming vital technologies in hundreds of disparate applications. Aviation has been on the forefront of adopting GPS, taking advantage of its inherent accuracy and worldwide availability. There are obvious applications in air traffic control that could benefit from the use of satellite navigation. However, many complex issues must be considered before GPS can be adopted as an air traffic control standard.

GPS was developed by the Department of Defense to provide a simple but accurate worldwide navigation system. Conceived in 1973, GPS became fully operational in 1994 when the last of its 24 satellites was launched (Parkinson, 1996).

The concept of using satellites to find position comes from the basic idea that distance equals speed times time. Each GPS satellite broadcasts a radio signal that contains a highly accurate time marker. The receiver generates the same code as the satellite and compares the codes to determine how long it takes for each satellite signal to arrive. Since radio waves travel at the speed of light, the distance to the satellite can be computed. This places the receiver's location on a sphere about the satellite with radius equal to the calculated distance. If the distances from four satellites are computed and the precise locations of those satellites at any moment are known, the receiver's three-dimensional position can be computed as the point at which the four spheres of position intersect. GPS satellites are placed in high orbits that are very predictable. They also carry atomic clocks that are extremely accurate and broadcast position corrections with the timing signal.

One of the most attractive features of GPS is its simplicity. It provides the most basic information, position, with a high degree of accuracy that is nearly uniform across the globe. The system can also be used to compute attitude (from multiple receivers) and the higher-order quantities of velocity and acceleration with high accuracy as well. Because it provides such fundamental information, it can be used in all phases and aspects of flight, from takeoff to landing, as well as during taxi. The most obvious use is in aircraft automation. Stanford University has demonstrated the automatic control of a model aircraft from takeoff to landing, using only the differential GPS (DGPS, discussed below) and a pilot on the ground (Montgomery et al., 1995). A GPS taxi guidance system superimposed on a digital map can increase pilot situation awareness and airport safety. GPS also provides an accurate time signal that can be used in communications and other timing applications.

Automatic landing systems and instrument flight rules (IFR) guidance are of particular interest. GPS can replace current instrument and microwave landing systems with the added benefit of accuracy that does not degrade with distance from the runway. Also, GPS approaches can be curved, allowing safer parallel runway landings and denser packing of aircraft in a terminal area. It can effectively reduce the required spacing between planes landing on parallel runways without affecting false and late collision alarm rates. Reducing parallel runway separation or staggered landings leads to increased arrival capacity at airports and reduced delays. This can decrease the need to build new airports or expand existing ones (Gazit, 1996).

There are many other applications of GPS to the flight environment. Utilizing periodic aircraft state broadcasts, the system can provide a ground surveillance system that is more accurate and expansive than the current network of radars. This could reduce the number of radar sites that need to be maintained or possibly eliminate them completely. The higher resolution of GPS allows for long-range conflict resolution and could possibly allow smaller aircraft separation standards. This in turn leads to greater airspace capacity. Enhanced oceanic traffic management is also possible with the use of GPS.

Besides enhancing the ground control aspect of air traffic control, GPS can also shift traffic management into the hands of the pilots, if this is desirable. Knowing the exact three-dimensional position of his or her plane as well as other aircraft in the vicinity can increase the situation awareness of the pilot. Since GPS can provide the velocity and three-dimensional position information of all aircraft, collision avoidance systems can be greatly enhanced. If these systems are shifted onto aircraft, pilots may be able to react faster because the information link from the ground to the aircraft is eliminated. (However, the workload costs of this added monitoring requirement could offset benefits in response time benefits.) Furthermore, GPS can provide low-cost collision avoidance systems, equaling the current TCAS (traffic alert and collision avoidance system), for all types of aircraft, including general aviation. The three-dimensional and velocity aspects of GPS navigation can be used to augment current displays or develop entirely new ones, including advanced situational awareness displays (Gazit, 1996). GPS combined with a terrain database could provide a more effective ground proximity warning and a recommended escape route to the pilot.

All of these applications could shift air traffic control responsibility from the ground to the cockpit, an issue we discuss extensively in Chapter 9. They could lead to a more efficient flight environment by increasing the airspace capacity. Air traffic would benefit from flexible routings, reduced flight times, optimum altitudes, and increased fuel savings. These benefits support free flight concepts.

Accuracy

The biggest advantage GPS offers is its high degree of accuracy, which is fairly uniform worldwide. Its two-dimensional position information is provided with respect to a common grid reference, but can be adapted to any spheroid model. However, a number of errors degrade the ideal system accuracy, including selective availability (Hurn, 1989) imposed by the Department of Defense. The standard positioning service, broadcast on the L1 frequency (1575.42 mHz), is available to all GPS users. The Department of Defense also maintains a second frequency, L2 (1227.6 mHz), which is encrypted and can only be used by Department of Defense users. The encryption is known as anti-spoofing. This precise positioning service is more accurate than the standard positioning service, but it is not available to civilians. However, the U.S. Department of Transportation announced that it will choose a second civilian frequency for GPS. The nominal accuracy of the standard positioning service without selective availability is 20-30 meters; selective availability degrades this to 100 meters. When this restriction is removed and the second civil frequency is implemented, an accuracy of 5-6 meters could be obtained (*Aviation Week and Space Technology*, 1997).

The differential global positioning system (DGPS) accommodates the selective availability of GPS. It uses a nearby ground reference station whose position is precisely known. It acts as a static reference point and can calculate the errors in the satellite signals. These errors can then be broadcast to a GPS receiver so its position can be corrected. Differential stations can also act as system signal broadcasters. This provides the receiver with ranging signals from above and below, making the three-dimensional calculations more accurate. The use of DGPS greatly reduces the effects of selective availability. The DGPS produces accuracies of 1-10 meters, even with selective availability, and a special form of the DGPS known as carrier phase differential can yield 5-20 cm accuracies (Navtech Seminars, 1995). Carrier phase differential measures the difference in the phase of the receiver and satellite oscillators. This phase difference can be used to resolve GPS measurements to a much finer level.

DGPSs with meter accuracies can cover a wide range. Corrections can even be broadcast over AM and FM radio stations. This technique has already been demonstrated and used operationally in Norway (*Aviation Week and Space Technology*, 1994). The United States is currently developing a wide-area and local-area augmentation system, networks of differential stations to provide corrections around and between airports.

Stanford University has developed lightweight differential beacons that help achieve centimeter-level accuracies during landings by resolving carrier wave cycle ambiguities (Cohen et al., 1994). The Stanford integrity beacon landing system demonstrated the potential of the DGPS for use in the most demanding phases of flight.

Other satellite systems, such as the Russian Glonass system, could be used concurrently with GPS to possibly increase accuracies. Glonass is not limited by selective availability, has L1 and L2 frequencies that can be accessed by civilians, and is more accurate than GPS at higher latitudes because of the Russian satellite orbits.

Availability, Reliability, and Integrity

Accuracy is not the primary concern in adopting GPS as the principal means of navigation and surveillance. Questions of availability, reliability, and integrity need to be addressed.

In order for GPS receivers to navigate in three dimensions, one must lock onto a minimum of four satellites or signal sources. The current system constellation configuration ensures that at least six satellites are in view at any time from any point on the globe (Parkinson, 1996). However, geography and aircraft attitude may obscure satellites. If a satellite is damaged or fails, a hole appears in the constellation, which can move into and out of receiver view and persists until a replacement satellite can be launched. Solar activity, debris collisions, and deliberate attacks are all possibilities that could result in the loss of satellites. A nuclear detonation in space could possibly render several satellites inoperative and create massive gaps in coverage. These problems could be alleviated by using multiple antennas, launching more GPS satellites, or augmenting GPS with other satellite navigation systems like Glonass and the European INMARSAT 3, which could relay differential corrections. Also, the use of integrity beacons that broadcast system-like signals could help solve coverage problems.

Another consideration is the fact that GPS satellites are constantly moving across the sky. Therefore, receivers often have to change satellite sets to keep four satellites in view. Sudden steps in system error can occur during these transitions because of the resolution degradation with only three satellites and the highly dynamic nature of aircraft. However, a proper tracking filter can greatly reduce this problem (Gazit, 1996). Other integrity errors can occur from GPS signals being reflected, fooling the receiver into thinking the path to the satellite is longer. This is a large concern around airports, where there are many structures to reflect signals. Most buildings are extremely good reflectors of system signals. Advanced integrity monitoring, phase smoothing, and filtering can detect and minimize multipath effects (Marsh, 1994).

Interference and jamming are also major integrity concerns. "Wormholes," areas of high GPS signal interference, have been discovered in several areas of the United States and other countries. Some of these wormholes cover hundreds of square miles (*Aviation Week and Space Technology*, 1995a). Several causes of system interference are suspected, including VHF/UHF TV signals, hand-held and standard very high frequency transmissions from aircraft, mobile satellite system transmitters, and even VHF omnidirectional range stations. There is also concern about the Glonass system, whose L1 frequency is very close to that of GPS (*Aviation Week and Space Technology*, 1995a) and may cause interference for some receivers.

Besides unintentional interference, the threat of jamming and spoofing of GPS signals also exists. Because these signals are very weak, they are relatively easy to jam. The spread spectrum design of the system complicates the matter for jammers but does not eliminate the threat (*Aviation Week and Space Technology*, 1995c). In a series of tests in the United Kingdom, a 1-watt jammer completely stopped all GPS receivers in a 20-mile radius (Gerold, 1994). Defense Research Agency tests found similar results; a 1-watt jammer was able to interfere out to 16 nautical miles (*Aviation Week and Space Technology*, 1995c). The U.S. Coast Guard has shown that jammers can be constructed for as little as $50 and made small enough to be carried in a briefcase; they would also be virtually untraceable (Gerold, 1994).

Spoofing, or imitating a GPS transmitter, may be as much of a threat as jamming. Spoofing is more difficult to detect than jamming and could lead unsuspecting pilots into dangerous situations. It has been argued that wide- and local-area differential service can prevent spoofing, but it is also easier to spoof differential signals than the constantly changing satellite signals. Possible solutions to interference, jamming, and spoofing include developing better filtering techniques, encrypting differential signals, and developing better integrity monitoring systems (*Aviation Week and Space Technology*, 1995c).

Integrity monitors are key factors in improving the reliability of GPS. Ground-based integrity monitoring systems have been developed extensively, but they cannot detect faults in the aircraft. Aircraft autonomous integrity monitoring combines GPS signals with inertial navigation system signals using a Kalman filter (Marsh, 1994), but at significant cost. GPS can also be coupled with Doppler and synthetic aperture radar, and multimode receivers can use TACAN and instrument and microwave landing systems as backups.

Additional Considerations in Adopting GPS

Another major benefit GPS provides is cost savings. Receiver and differential transmitter costs are already low and falling rapidly. A Magellan receiver cost $3,000 in 1989, $1,800 in 1992, and $199 in 1995 (*Aviation Week and Space Technology*, 1995b). Receivers are much cheaper than the $100,000 ring laser gyro systems used for inertial navigation (Gazit, 1996). The Stanford integrity beacons are small and lightweight, and their price is on the order of low-powered runway lights (Cohen et al., 1994). Also, the production of receivers has increased dramatically, with over 60,000 sets being manufactured per month (Parkinson, 1996).

Many other considerations are involved in adopting GPS as a navigation and control system. GPS is currently controlled by the Department of Defense, which will not guarantee that the system will never be denied or degraded (Gerold, 1994). Implementing the system puts the navigation and control capabilities of other nations in the hands of the Department of Defense. What would happen if the United States were to adopt GPS, but other nations did not? All international flights would have to be equipped to handle GPS as well as radio navigation, and a mismatch in procedures would exist. Furthermore, if a foreign country did implement GPS navigation and control and an accident occurred due to the failure of the system, would the United States be liable?

One answer would be to guarantee uninterrupted GPS service and to share control with other nations. Countries could contribute to the costs of satellites and differential stations and to the development of application technologies. However, any kind of payment or contribution implies a say in the management of the system. Also, hostile nations would have access to the same accuracies as the United States. Except for the precise positioning service, this would eliminate any kind of force multiplier advantage the United States gains by employing GPS-based technologies (Gerold, 1994).

Special consideration must be taken in addressing the issue of using GPS in air traffic control and air traffic management applications. Utilizing the system necessitates the design concept of automatic dependent surveillance (ADS). In such a system, instead of actively looking for aircraft with radar, each aircraft reports its position and other information (such as velocity, identification, and intentions) to a ground station or other aircraft via a satellite or radio link. This is an entirely new philosophy for the FAA, which now requires that the national airspace system supply independent surveillance for air traffic control functions (Bartkiewicz and Berkowitz, 1993).

GPS offers clear benefits over radar, particularly in terms of greater universal accuracy, but the automatic dependent surveillance concept using GPS has some problems as well. Radar systems have update rates between 5 and 12 seconds. Theoretically, the automatic dependent surveillance messages could be broadcast at much faster rates, but air traffic control systems in busy control areas could quickly become overwhelmed and unable to sort a large flow of state messages. Some kind of timing system must be used to ensure automatic dependent surveillance messages can be properly received and processed. Also, in terminal areas, the FAA requires that aircraft data be less than 2.2 seconds old. Of this time, 1.4 seconds have already been budgeted for delays that would fall outside the automatic dependent surveillance link. The propagation time in using a geostationary communication link alone would account for 240 ms of the remaining 0.8 seconds in an automatic dependent surveillance system (Bartkiewicz and Berkowitz, 1993). Minimizing hardware and protocol time delays is a major concern.

It would be desirable if the changes to current air traffic control software necessary to incorporate automatic dependent surveillance were minimized. This leads to the idea of automatic dependent surveillance state messages emulating radar returns (Bartkiewicz and Berkowitz, 1993). Although this would smooth the integration of such a system, it does not take full advantage of its capabilities.

Though it would be possible for a GPS-based automatic dependent surveillance system to replace the current radar-based system, there are many reasons why this might not be desirable. First, if there is an error in the azimuth of a radar system, this error will be the same for all the aircraft that radar is tracking.

Consequently, although the reported position of the aircraft will be wrong, their positions relative to each other will be fairly accurate. This allows the controller to maintain separation safely. In an ADS system, if an aircraft is reporting an incorrect position to the system, its reported position relative to other aircraft will also be in error. This could lead to a situation in which a controller believes the aircraft is properly separated, when in fact it is not. Therefore, when used together, the two types of system must complement each other.

If a radar is jammed or fails, only a small area of airspace is affected. If a system link satellite is jammed or fails, a much larger region would be without surveillance capability (Bartkiewicz and Berkowitz, 1993). Also, there is a problem with equipping aircraft with GPS-based automatic dependent surveillance broadcasters and receivers. Not only would this be a large expense, but also aircraft without or with nonfunctioning equipment would not be detectable in a pure automatic dependent surveillance system.

Because these two types of systems are so different in principle, they naturally complement each other. Integrating the automatic dependent surveillance system with the current system may increase air traffic control operational cost and complexity, but it potentially could also increase the integrity, reliability, and overall safety of the entire system. The cost of actually implementing an automatic dependent surveillance system would potentially be less if it were to complement instead of replace independent surveillance. A detailed study of fault tolerances is needed in order to compare the overall reliability of an automatic dependent surveillance system to current independent surveillance. Also, the reliability of a combined system should be examined.

If some kind of automatic dependent surveillance system is implemented, decisions need to be made about mandates on system equipment. This is also true in the case of accepting GPS-based navigation as a standard. Will certain airspace require aircraft to be GPS or automatic dependent surveillance equipped? What about the multitude of general aviation aircraft that exist now with no navigation equipment?

Weather

The key challenges in the arena of weather data are to provide additional useful weather information, integrate information from multiple sensors, predict weather more effectively, and disseminate information more efficiently. The aviation weather distribution system includes subsystems that collect, process, display, and disseminate weather data that can affect the safety and efficiency of the national airspace system. The FAA considers the highest-priority weather functions to be those that detect phenomena posing a potential hazard to aviation and disseminate this information to controllers, traffic managers, flight service specialists, and pilots (Federal Aviation Administration, 1996a). The current weather distribution system for air traffic control relies on a variety of information sources that include: pilot reports; sensors whose data are provided by the FAA, the National Weather Service, and commercial vendors; aircraft sensors whose data are reported through the aircraft communication addressing and reporting system (ACARS); surface sensors, including wind shear sensors, operated by the FAA in the vicinity of airports; and primary radar, which is used to detect phenomena such as wind shear and thunderstorms. Surface weather observations are also generated by the automated weather observing system (AWOS) and the automated surface observing system (ASOS).

Weather data are processed and presented to controllers, traffic management specialists, and flight service specialists through a variety of systems. Controllers and flight service specialists, in turn, communicate with pilots to exchange weather information. The current system of weather information distribution for air traffic control is fragmented and does not adequately tailor information for controllers, specialists, and pilots. Therefore, the FAA is developing or planning automated features that would integrate weather data and distribute it to controllers, specialists, and pilots. Future systems would also include improved predictive capabilities and would support responses to weather conditions (Federal Aviation Administration, 1996a). Figure 3.1 summarizes current and contemplated systems for processing, displaying, and communicating weather data pertinent to air traffic control. The figure summarizes, for key data processing systems, the sources of data, the types of data processed, media by which controllers and specialists receive the data, and mechanisms by which the data are transmitted to pilots. These elements are discussed below from the perspectives of controllers and specialists within the terminal (tower and TRACON) and en route (including oceanic) environments, and then from the perspective of the pilots.

Terminal Weather Data

Controllers and traffic managers in the terminal environment, which includes tower and TRACON facilities, receive weather reports from pilots (through pilot reports), from the National Weather Service, and from commercial vendors. They also receive automated support through three systems: the automated weather observing system and automated surface observing system (AWOS/ASOS), the low-level wind shear alert system (LLWAS), and the terminal Doppler weather radar (TDWR).

The AWOS/ASOS collects data from ground sensors and provides surface weather observations to tower controllers and TRACON specialists via an automated surface observing system display. The low-level wind shear alert system processes real-time data from pole-mounted sensors in the airport vicinity to determine wind shear and microburst conditions. The alert system presents these data, along with applicable alerts, to both tower and TRACON controllers via

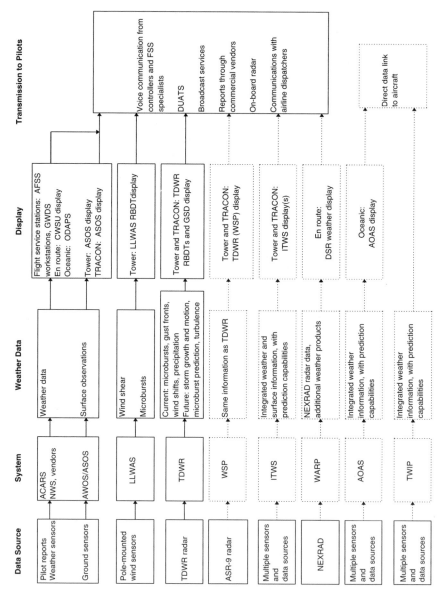

FIGURE 3.1 Processing, display, and communication of weather data. Dashed lines indicate future developments.

ribbon display terminals, which present information that is read by controllers to pilots.

The terminal Doppler weather radar is a radar-based system that detects microbursts, gust fronts, wind shifts, and precipitation intensities in the airport vicinity. The weather radar, through the ribbon display terminals, presents advisories to tower and TRACON controllers. The advisories inform controllers of wind shear and microburst events affecting runways and nearby airspace. The terminal Doppler weather radar does not detect wind shear outside the arrival and departure ends of the runways, wind shear that is not a microburst or a gust front, gusty cross-wind conditions, or turbulence. However, planned improvements include more accurate display of storm motion and gust fronts, as well as display of storm growth and decay, microburst prediction, and turbulence.

The terminal Doppler weather radar also provides to tower and TRACON graphic situation displays that present, in color, six levels of weather, gust fronts, and predicted storm movement(s). These data are used by the controllers, traffic management specialists, and supervisory personnel to plan for runway changes and arrival/departure routing changes in order to reduce aircraft delays and to increase airport capacity.

Future enhancements include the weather system processor (WSP) and the integrated terminal weather system (ITWS; Klingle-Wilson, 1995). The weather system processor will provide the same displays as the TDWR; however, its weather processing will be based on the ASR-9 primary radar, which is a less costly sensor than the TDWR radar. The ITWS is a longer-term improvement that will integrate data and products from various FAA and National Weather Service (NWS) sensors, aircraft, and NWS weather information systems. The ITWS will provide safety and planning displays that characterize the current terminal weather situation as well as forecast weather conditions 30 minutes into the future.

En Route Weather Data

Controllers and traffic managers in the en route, including oceanic, environment also receive weather reports from pilots (through pilot reports), from the National Weather Service, and from commercial vendors. En route controllers and specialists are supported by central weather service unit (CWSU) displays and by oceanic display and planning system (ODAPS) displays that present National Weather Service data. The display system replacement (DSR) system that modernizes the workstations for en route controllers will include a color graphic weather display. The weather display will present radar data based on the NEXRAD radar and processed by the weather and radar processing system (WARP), which may provide additional weather products. The advanced oceanic automation system (AOAS) will integrate weather data from multiple sources for display to oceanic controllers and specialists.

Weather Data for Pilots

Pilots currently receive weather data through voice communication with flight service specialists, automated flight service stations, controllers, other pilots, and airline dispatchers; broadcast services and reports from commercial vendors; direct user access terminal systems (DUATs) that transmit reports through personal computers; and on-board radar displays. Currently, some weather data that pilots receive from other pilots and from airline dispatchers is often better than that which can be provided through the air traffic control weather data systems. Therefore, through pilot reports, pilots are a critical source of weather information for controllers. As the weather information presented to controllers improves, future plans will include direct data link of the integrated weather data also provided to controllers through the AOAS (for transoceanic flights), and cockpit display of integrated weather information with prediction capabilities, data linked from the terminal weather information for pilots (TWIP) system. The pilots would then also be provided with graphic display and alerts for microbursts, wind shear, significant precipitation, convective activity within 30 nautical miles surrounding the terminal area, and more accurate weather predictions that could affect airport operations.

COMMUNICATION TECHNOLOGIES

The acquisition of surveillance information is necessary but not sufficient for effective air traffic management, which also depends critically on the accurate and timely exchange of information between ground and air and, increasingly, between aircraft.

Communication Bandwidth

Communication exchange was initially supported by radiotelephone and primary radar returns, necessary to locate the plane in lateral airspace. Development of secondary radar (mode C and subsequently mode S) allowed the digital packaging of information between ground and air, so that air traffic control could positively confirm an aircraft's identity, altitude, and a small amount of additional information. Secondary radar is supported by an active transponder within each aircraft. Because each message is directed to an individual respondent, it is a serial system, in which the communication links are increasingly delayed as there are more respondents (i.e., as air traffic density increases).

In addition to sending traffic information, mode S radar has supported two other functions. It has been incorporated into TCAS (discussed in Chapter 5), allowing a pair of aircraft to know their rate of closure with respect to each other, and it is being used to support a data link between ground and air (see below). The latter functionality is designed to support a far richer (but therefore slower) exchange of information, regarding such issues as clearances, instructions, and weather.

As noted, the limitation of mode S radar and data link for air-ground communications is in the availability of its data to users, which degrades (due to packet collision on a limited bandwidth) as the airspace becomes more crowded. However, considerable advances beyond this level are enabled by a satellite-based broadcast communication system that can broadcast digital data, in parallel, to a broad range of airborne and ground-based users. Because of this parallel broadcast quality, airborne surveillance, referred to as automatic dependence surveillance-broadcast mode (ADS-B), is not as constrained in its availability by the number of users (i.e., aircraft). Furthermore, the information quantity per message is considerably greater than that of mode S radar. Thus, at a frequency of 1 Hz (defined by the 1 second interval of each information packet), an ADS-B message contains each aircraft's position, trend, and, if desired, intent (e.g., flight plans in a flight management system). Because it enables an increase in both frequency and amount of information, ADS-B supports two potential expansions of the national airspace.

First, as we noted earlier in this chapter, ADS-B can potentially serve air traffic control with precise position information, thereby eventually replacing the slower, less accurate, and more expensive secondary surveillance radar. This will depend, of course, on all participating aircraft being ADS-B-equipped, a requirement that is potentially less expensive than a mode S transponder and 1090 mHz receiver. At the MITRE Corporation, work is under way to develop a system, called the universal access transceiver, which is a multipurpose broadcast communication system that enables traffic and weather information to be sent to each aircraft and ADS-B data to be provided to air traffic control (Strain et al., 1996).

Second, the higher update rate and accuracy provided by ADS-B may enable more complex flight path negotiations between aircraft than does the present TCAS system. ADS-B is the likely enabling technology to support free flight.

Data Link

Data link is a set of technologies designed to relay communications between ground and air, using digital information rather than conventional radiotelephone communication channels (Kerns, 1991, 1994). As such it depends on relatively high-bandwidth mode S radar systems at both ground and air. The proposed types of information that can be exchanged include items such as standard clearances and instructions, pilot requests, weather information, airport terminal information services (ATIS) broadcasts, and so forth. Because data link is assumed to be a two-way channel, its description distinguishes between *down-linked* (air to ground) and *up-linked* (ground to air) messages. Correspondingly, the human factors issues are somewhat different in the two environments. In the cockpit, data link interfaces are alternatively proposed to reside in a separate console, embedded within the control and display unit of the flight management computer, or embedded in the multifunction display, an option chosen in the Boeing 777 (Bresley, 1995). On the ground, the displays are positioned as close as possible to, or as windows or overlap on, the plan view or radar display. In both cases, keyboard entry and graphic displays have been the standard approach, although alternative media are being considered.

A primary impetus for data link has been traffic delays that are themselves the result of communications bottlenecks. When a controller must share a single radio channel with up to 20 or 25 aircraft, there are times when the competition for this channel can lead to substantial delays, as well as frustration by pilots. One analysis suggested that the airlines lost over $300,000,000 annually as a result of communications-induced delays (Federal Aviation Administration, 1995a; Swierenga, 1994). An equally strong rationale for the development of data link is concern over the vulnerability of standard radiotelephone communications to errors in speech perception and working memory (Morrow et al., 1993; Cardosi, 1993). Nagel (1989) concluded that over half of aircraft incidents are a result of breakdowns in communication. Furthermore, work by Billings and Cheaney (1981) identified 80 percent of information transfer problems as occurring on radio channels, and cognitive task analysis reveals the extent to which human perception and working memory are vulnerable to confusion, expectancy, and forgetting (see the panel's Phase I report). (It should be noted that confusion and expectancy errors occur within the visual display modality as well as the auditory.) These factors provide strong justification for seeking computer automation to directly transfer information, ensuring that it is "permanently" (i.e., until erased) visible (and therefore perceptible) on a display in the form in which it was sent.

As a consequence of these concerns, the FAA in 1988 initiated a data link research and study program, aggregating research that had been done prior to that time, initiating new research, and developing a program of airborne simulation and testing (Federal Aviation Administration, 1990b). Kerns (1991, 1994) provides an excellent description of the integration of the human factors work that had been done on data link up to this time. At present, aircraft such as the Boeing 777 are manufactured with the potential to host data link (Bresley, 1995), although the system is not yet implemented in operational flight. ACARS is a digital data link system currently in use, but it interfaces between aircraft and airline companies concerning company business, unlike the proposed data link system that interfaces with air traffic controllers and addresses issues of flight control.

Human Factors Implementation

A substantial effort has been undertaken by both the FAA and the National Aeronautics and Space Administration, as well as the Programme for Harmonised

Air Traffic Management Research in Eurocontrol (PHARE) in Europe, to ensure that data link is implemented in a successful fashion. Several of the earlier efforts in laboratory studies and part-task simulations are well summarized by Kerns (1991, 1994). Recent studies by the FAA (Federal Aviation Administration 1995a, 1996c) have evaluated the ground system in full mission simulations, and corresponding efforts have evaluated the air side (Federal Aviation Administration, 1996c; Lozito et al., 1993; Gent and Van, 1995). In all cases, overall measures of performance efficiency have been collected and conjoined with more specific assessments of operator workload, opinion, pilot response time, etc. In all cases, the evaluation of data link has been generally favorable, although users have expressed qualifications about its appropriateness in some circumstances. In-the-loop simulations have revealed that a combined voice-data link system enables equal levels of flight efficiency with a reduced number of voice communications and a reduced number of total communications (voice and data link), the latter reduction resulting in part because there are fewer requirements to repeat voice messages (Talotta et al., 1992a, 1992b).

The operational data have pointed to specific guidelines for design. Many of these guidelines were compiled in a set of human factors recommendations for data link (SAE Aerospace Recommended Practice, 1994). Furthermore, those studies that have directly compared a data-link-equipped aircraft with a radiotelephone-only aircraft have revealed improvements in various levels of air traffic management efficiency (e.g., increased traffic flow, reduced delays; Federal Aviation Administration 1995a, 1996c).

However, it should be noted that the most detailed analysis of efficiency gains have compared efficiency in a data link simulation environment with the operational efficiency measures of the same traffic scenario taken previously with live traffic in the facility environment. That is, the latter baseline scenario was used to estimate the efficiency of the radiotelephone performance. Hence, in comparing data link conditions with radiotelephone-only conditions, there were differences not only in the interface, but also in traffic (simulated versus live), the identity of the controllers, and operating conditions (on-the-job controllers versus those participating in an experiment). Furthermore, the baseline data did not include corresponding measures such as workload, which could be compared with the data link condition measures.

Nevertheless, it is apparent that the FAA is paying a good deal of attention to human factors issues in data link implementation, as discussed below.

Human Factors Issues

Cognitive Task Analysis As noted, the baseline system is one that relies totally on voice perception and speech. Given the difficulty a pilot may have in responding immediately to all requests, this system also then imposes on working memory, as the pilot must rehearse instructions until they are implemented in flight control (or written down), and the controller may need to rehearse requests until they are granted or denied. Furthermore, pilot working memory load will be exacerbated when controller instructions are long or complex (Cardosi, 1993; Morrow et al., 1993). As we noted in the Phase I report, both pilots and controllers often tend to hear what they expect to hear, and lengthy sequences of instructions may be partially forgotten before they can be implemented. Even though procedural safeguards are built into the current system by requiring readback of all communications, this will not prevent a controller from hearing what he or she expects to hear, namely that the pilot will read back the message as delivered (Monan, 1986). If the pilot does not, the error may go undetected.

In contrast then, the data link capability guarantees that the message sent by one party will be physically available *exactly as sent*, on a display screen viewed by the other. It then can be read accurately at any time and is not vulnerable to the same sources of forgetting as is the auditory message (although other forms of error may emerge). An analysis undertaken by Shingledecker and Talotta (1993) suggests that such a system can reduce if not eliminate about 45 percent of the existing communications errors that are made between ground and air. Some have questioned whether a message appearing on an electronic display commands the same sense of immediacy as does an oral communication. Hence, most proposed data link implementations are incorporated along with a distinct auditory alert that announces the arrival of a new text message (Gent and Van, 1995).

Although the *perception* of information by the receiver may be facilitated by a data link system, it is not apparent that the *composition* and *initiation* of a message by the sender will be equally improved. Indeed, keyboard interactions are notoriously cumbersome and error prone if they are long, in contrast to the naturalness of voice control, an issue we address in the following section. Furthermore, the interface can become cumbersome in retrieving previously received messages, if care is not taken in design.

An important issue relates to the time requirements of data link versus radio-telephone communications. On the ground side, Wickens, Miller, and Tham (1996) have observed that the delays in responding to pilot requests are approximately 3 seconds longer when controllers perceive requests presented by visual as compared to voice (radiotelephone) display. On the air side, there appear to be few substantial differences in pilot response to data link versus radiotelephone instructions (Kerns, 1994). However, Gent and Van (1995) have found that pilots respond significantly faster when data link messages are redundantly conveyed by synthetic voice (than by visual display only). Finally, analysis of the total transmission time, which is the time between the initiation of a message by air traffic control and receipt of acknowledgment that the message has been received, suggests that this may be nearly twice as long for a visual-manual data link system (around 20 seconds) as for a radiotelephone system (around 10 seconds) (Kerns, 1994; Waller and Lohr, 1989; Talotta et al., 1990). Measures of total transmission time taken in more recent simulation (Federal Aviation Administration 1995a, 1996c) suggest that the measures of data link total transmission time may be somewhat less than the values of the earlier studies, being closer to around 15 seconds on average. The total transmission time delays tend to be longer with nonroutine communications and in the final control sector before landing (Lozito et al., 1993). The total transmission time delay issue is quite important, not only because longer delays will reduce data link efficiency, but also because they will lead controllers to abandon the use of data link in preference for more rapid radiotelephone communications (Talotta et al., 1992a, 1992b).

Given the differences in response time and total transmission time between the two modes, a consensus is emerging that any effective data link system should provide redundant means of transmitting information along either channel and, furthermore, that data link messages should be primarily associated with routine communications (e.g., standard clearances, airport terminal information services), whereas radiotelephone channels should be used for the more unusual instructions and requests (Kerns, 1991, 1994; Gent and Van, 1995). This distribution has two advantages: (1) the nonroutine requests will be delivered over the more attention-capturing auditory channel and (2) more unfamiliar communications can be initiated over the more natural voice channel, hence minimizing the number of keystrokes. Thus, in summary, it appears that on both the ground side and the air side, data link provides more accurate, but slightly slower communications.

Workload   The workload issues associated with data link represent some of the greatest human factors concerns, both in the flight deck (Kerns, 1994; Groce and Boucek, 1987; Corwin, 1991) and on the ground (Programme for Harmonised Air Traffic Management Research in Eurocontrol PD1, 1996; Nirhjaus, 1993). In each environment, three issues are raised:

1. What is the workload imposed by the task of initiating and receiving communications with the data link?
2. What are the implications of the demand for the visual-manual channels necessitated by conventional data link on ongoing flight or air traffic control tasks, most of which themselves are visual-manual?
3. How does data link affect strategic workload management?

With regard to the workload of the data link task itself, there is considerable consensus that the composition and initiation of lengthy keystroke messages by either ground or air personnel involve considerably higher workload than spoken messages. This appears to be a particularly strong source of complaint for pilots (Gent and Van, 1995). One solution has been to try to predefine "macros" such that a more complex message can be sent with a single keystroke. In some cases, this may involve constructing a predefined list, prior to a flight, on which the messages can pertain to the particular geometry of the flight plan. On the air side, Hahn and Hansman (1992) have found that graphic depiction of data link routing information received from the controller and embedded in the electronic map display imposes lower workload than either text or spoken representation of the same spatial information.

Another solution, evaluated on the ground side (Programme for Harmonised Air Traffic Management Research in Eurocontrol PD1, 1996) has been to try to maximize the intuitiveness of the command interface, via a mouse windowing menu-type of environment, in which predefined options can be easily selected and then up-linked. Such approaches were documented to reduce various measures of controller workload.

With regard to the second workload issue, interference with ongoing tasks, a major concern has been the "head-down time" imposed as pilots read data link information (Gent and Van, 1995; Groce and Boucek, 1987) and, to a lesser extent, the time that the controller must divert gaze away from the plan view display (Programme for Harmonised Air Traffic Management Research in Eurocontrol PD1, 1996). It turns out that this competition for visual resources is not trivial. Even in dual-seat cockpits, when the pilot not flying is responsible for handling the procedures associated with data link, the pilot flying may avert his gaze to cross-check data link information (Gent and Van, 1995). These findings have led to proposals that a primary data link printed message be supplemented with a synthesized voice transmission of the same material, hence offering all the well-known benefits of redundancy gain (Wickens, Miller, and Tham, 1996; Wickens, 1992; Kerns, 1994). Such a procedure was found to reduce the amount of head-down time spent by the pilot flying (Gent and Van, 1995).

On the ground side, design efforts have been implemented to try to present down-linked messages visually, but as close as possible to the plan view or radar display, either as windows on the margin of the display (Programme for Harmonised Air Traffic Management Research in Eurocontrol PD1, 1996; Kerns, 1994; see Figure 3.2) or directly incorporated into the flight data blocks or the spatial depiction of flight trajectories (Wickens Miller, and Tham, 1996).

Finally, because data link does allow a relatively enduring representation of text (or graphic) information, it should allow pilots more flexibility, for example, in completing high-priority, interruption-vulnerable tasks (i.e., checklist procedures). Supporting this conclusion, Lozito et al. (1993) found that pilots were more likely to carry out other tasks, between receipt and response to communications, over data link than over radiotelephone channels.

Communication Communication is at the core of data link, and we have already discussed several issues related to this process. Another issue pertaining to the message delivery itself concerns the sorts of communication errors that might be committed by keystrokes in a data link system and the sorts of error-trapping

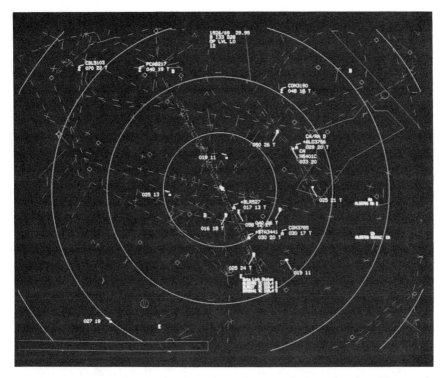

FIGURE 3.2 Sample of data link information at the controller's workstation. The sample shows experimental display of resolution advisory data downlinked from the traffic alert and collision avoidance system (TCAS). Source: Photo courtesy of the MITRE Corporation.

mechanisms that may prevent these errors from turning into system errors. Currently the data link system is designed so that the pilot, upon reading a message, can respond with a "Wilco" (will comply) message, which implicitly suggests that the message has not only been understood but also can be carried out. However, there is no guarantee that the same problems of top-down processing (seeing what one expects to see) may not be present here as they have been observed with auditory communications (Kerns, 1994). That is, a pilot might "Wilco" a message without fully considering its implications. This issue has not been examined. Furthermore, as yet, no specific examination of keystroke errors in data link usage has been carried out to compare, for example, their frequency relative to the frequency of communication errors with an radiotelephone system (Cardosi, 1993).

It is also possible that data link systems may inhibit the tendency for pilots to follow up messages with requests for clarification, as they often do with radiotelephone systems. Furthermore, data link will not permit the passage of nonlinguistic information, like the sound of urgency in a pilot's or controller's voice.

Communications with data link has at least two broader implications. First, considerable concern has been expressed that personalizing the communications channels between each pilot and the controller will deprive other pilots of important party-line information that may help them update or maintain their situation awareness of the status of the surrounding airspace (Midkiff and Hansman, 1992; Gent and Van, 1997; Federal Aviation Administration, 1996c). For example, one pilot can certainly benefit from hearing that a pilot ahead has encountered turbulence, or that several ahead are forced into holding patterns. The desirability of obtaining such party-line information by pilots is well documented (Midkiff and Hansman, 1992), and at least one case has been documented in which the advanced knowledge of an aircraft's presence, gained from party-line information, was partially responsible for preventing a midair collision (Danaher, 1980). Although no negative impacts have been observed as a consequence of party-line deprivation in data link simulations, a fairly strong recommendation can be made that a data link system should retain the capability of sharing certain forms of critical information regarding issues such as weather, particularly in the terminal area. This is consistent with the idea that nonroutine information could be allocated to radiotelephone channels. Hazardous weather conditions would certainly fall into the nonroutine category.

The second way in which data link affects communication and teamwork issues is in the sharing of duties between players, both on the flight deck and on the ground. On the flight deck, fairly clear lines of responsibility can be allocated between the pilot flying and the pilot not flying, with the latter maintaining full responsibility for managing the flight trajectory. However, as noted, the pilot flying cannot be expected to ignore data link channels entirely. Furthermore, unless data link messages are redundantly presented via voice synthesis, the pilot flying will be less aware of potentially important up-linked information that would have been shared under a radiotelephone system.

On the ground, the FAA simulations have revealed the positive benefits of data link, in terms of load sharing and the flexibility of distribution of responsibilities, when traffic load becomes quite high (Federal Aviation Administration 1996c; Talotta et al., 1992a, 1992b). Unlike the dedicated radiotelephone communicator on the R-side of a workstation with the conventional system, a data link system can allow various operators to assume temporary responsibility for certain aspects of communications (or communications with certain aircraft). In simulations, this flexibility has been found to provide an unexpected benefit to control efficiency. However, it should be noted that the flexibility of loosely defined responsibilities can have its down side, unless careful training of the team in resource management is implemented, so that shifts in responsibilities are clearly and unambiguously annunciated, a recommendation articulated by the investigators in the FAA simulation (Federal Aviation Administration, 1996c). Parallel findings have been observed in the flight deck and are incorporated into crew resource management training programs (see the panel's Phase I report, Chapter 7).

Organization   The possible direct link between data link and the flight management system (FMS) allows for the possibility that information could be directly passed from airline dispatchers to the aircraft, hence potentially bypassing the controller (and even the pilot).

Automation Issues

Data link is itself a form of computer-based automation. But within the data link system, various higher levels of automation have been proposed. Various forms of computer-based automation can assist in message composition, hence reducing workload (Kerns, 1994; Programme for Harmonised Air Traffic Management Research in Eurocontrol PD1, 1996). An even more critical concept is *message gating*. This involves a system in which an up-linked message can be directly passed into the flight management system with one or two keystrokes, without requiring the pilot to read the message and enter it manually (Gent and Van, 1995; Federal Aviation Administration, 1996c; Waller, 1992; Knox and Scanlon, 1991).

This gating process can be carried out at three critical levels of automation. At the lowest level, the pilot may read the display, acknowledge with a Wilco keystroke, and then proceed to load the information manually into the flight management system. At a higher level of automation, activation of the Wilco key will automatically load the information into the flight management system. At a still higher level, such information will automatically be loaded into the system as it is up-linked and will proceed to affect the aircraft trajectory unless the pilot intervenes.

There is relatively substantial agreement among pilots that such a gating system is of benefit, both in reducing workload (and head-down time; Gent and Van, 1995) and in reducing the possibilities of keystroke errors that might result if the data were entered manually (Waller, 1992; Knox and Scanlon, 1992; Gent and Van, 1995).

However, two concerns with such a system should be noted. First, it is possible that it might lead to complacency and relatively automatic acceptance (and entry into the flight management system) of the message, with less careful evaluation than would be done with manual entry. The lessons learned regarding complacency in response to reliable automated actions are well documented. In this regard, Hahn and Hansman (1992) found that graphic presentation of up-linked routing messages (on the horizontal situation indicator) provided a better means for the pilot to identify inappropriate instructions than did text messages.

Although Gent and Van (1995) did not find that pilots reported a loss of situation awareness with such a gating option, it is important to realize that self-report of awareness will not necessarily be the same as actual awareness. The second concern is the possibility that designers may create a system in which the message is automatically loaded into the flight management system prior to a pilot's decision and the pilot would simply have the authority to activate it. It appears that this further removal of the pilot from the control loop would be a clear invitation to complacency.

Given possibilities envisioned by the different levels of gating, it is feasible that a system could be designed that allows alternative gating modes. Such a system will invite confusion: a pilot, for example, may assume that a message was automatically loaded into the flight management system (high automation, low gating), when in fact it was not.

In conclusion, the introduction of data link has profound implications for workload, for communications, and indeed for the overall structure of the national airspace system, characterized by the relationship between pilots, controllers, dispatchers, and automation. With modest goals, it is possible to envision a system that is designed primarily to provide a visual record of material transmitted by conventional voice channels. At the other extreme, it is possible to envision a scenario in which both human elements, on the ground and in the air, are substantially removed from the control loop, while control is exercised between computers on the ground and in the air. Although planners do not currently intend such a scenario, the possibility nevertheless exists that levels of automatic control and gating could be implemented that approximate this kind of interaction.

4

Flight Information

This chapter provides an analysis of the flight information system in the air and on the ground. We begin with a description of the flight management system, its functions, its history, the human factors issues associated with its development and use, and lessons learned that may be useful in introducing other automated systems. The second part of the chapter presents a discussion of flight information processing through HOST and ARTS and the state of human factors research on flight progress strips, lists, and data blocks.

FLIGHT MANAGEMENT SYSTEM

Functionality

The flight management system (FMS) of a modern jetliner should not be thought of as a mere component or even a computer, but rather as the heart and soul of the plane. The flight management system, along with sensors, system interfaces, and a flight management computer (FMC), produces a full-flight control and information system. This system provides the aircraft with navigational guidance, thrust control, instrumentation (including the horizontal situation indicator map and other modes), vertical guidance, and flight path optimization.

The flight management system contains two flight management computers that operate independently and compare results with each other. Each supports one or more multipurpose control display units, which contain an alphanumeric keyboard and a limited cathode ray tube for text-only display.

The following are the major functions of a flight management system (Honeywell, 1989):

1. Flight planning.
2. Navigational computation of a plane's position.
3. Guidance commands for the autopilot and flight director, in conjunction with integrated thrust management and autothrottle control, to fly optimal vertical profiles while also flying the lateral path.
4. Navigation display data to generate a horizontal situation indicator map display and features.
5. Navigation radio tuning.
6. Storage of database for navigation, aerodynamic, and engine data.
7. Interface to inertial reference system (IRS).
8. Performance optimization.
9. Thrust calculation.
10. Autothrottle control.
11. Polar navigation/operation capability.
12. Simulator capability to allow for simulator training and flight operations.

The relevance of the flight management system to air traffic control is threefold. First, as we reviewed in the Phase I report, many of the human factors lessons learned in automation of the flight management system are directly relevant to air traffic control automation. Second, the flight management system provides the aircraft with opportunities to fly extremely efficient user-preferred routes, a source of frustration to the airlines that must often remain on air traffic control-preferred airways. Third, given that the aircraft flight plans are encoded digitally, when linked digitally to the ground by data link, there is the capability to send information downward to air traffic control regarding intent and upward regarding flight control, as well as to share information between aircraft. This enhanced data sharing has profound implications for the future automation of the national airspace system.

History

In the late 1970s, microprocessor technology had developed to the point at which not only were the electronic devices becoming more and more sophisticated, but also the individual devices could be linked to form a flight management system, rather than a collection of independent, albeit sophisticated, boxes (Billings, 1996b). The individual devices architecture was exemplified by the wide-body aircraft of the period: B-747, L-1011, and DC-10. In these planes, inertial and radio (e.g., Loran and Omega) navigation not only located the plane on the earth's surface, but could also provide guidance commands to the autopilot system, allowing point-to-point steering. Such systems were called generically "area navigation." The aircraft of the next decade took this a great step forward: the flight management systems that appeared on the B-767 in 1982 provided the functions listed above, tying together for the first time navigation (vertical and horizontal), thrust control, data storage, optimization, and in the extreme, autoland. Billings (1996b:40) referred to this as a "fundamental shift in aircraft automation." For a more complete history of aircraft automation, see Billings (1996b:Part 1).

The autoland system in the modern jet airliner is a combination of a number of systems. These include autopilot, autothrottles, the flight management system, and instrument landing system. The airport and its instrument landing system must have special equipment that is rigorously certified by the Federal Aviation Administration (FAA) in order to permit aircraft to land under low visibility. During the cruise phase of the flight, the autopilot is very precise in maintaining altitude and track. During an autoland, both track and height above the ground are even more precisely maintained. In the aircraft, the autoland system is normally selected by the pilot approximately 5 miles from the landing.

Human Factors Implementation

It is difficult to speak of the implementation of the flight management system as a single system, because one would have to include the entire flight regime (and some ground regime) of the aircraft. Numerous authors have written on the human factors implications of cockpit automation (see, for example, Wiener and Curry, 1980, for an early warning on the possibility of negative as well as positive consequences). In the mid-1980s these authors concentrated on field studies on various models (Curry, 1985; Wiener, 1985, 1989), and later in that decade Sarter and Woods began their highly prolific collaboration in applying cognitive engineering to the automated flight deck (e.g., Sarter and Woods, 1994, 1995a, 1995b).

All these authors wrote of both positive and adverse consequences. The adverse consequences include mode confusion, excessive head-down time, an invitation to large errors ("blunders"), automation-induced complacency, possibly diminished situation awareness, lack of an operational doctrine to govern usage, unpredictable workload, and others. Furthermore, the air traffic control systems of today are not cordial to the advanced aircraft. Wiener (1988) stated, "years from now we will look back and call this the era of clumsy automation," clumsy in the sense of hard to operate, error inducing, and at times workload inducing.

Human Factors Issues

Because of the central position of the flight management system in the advanced cockpit aircraft, it is not possible to review all human factors issues. We will take note of three basic and important issues: workload, head-down time, and cockpit communication. Readers who wish more comprehensive coverage are directed to papers and reports by Billings (1996a, 1996b), Sarter and Woods (1995b), and Wiener (1988, 1993).

Workload

Workload is at the center of automation. Especially without an effective workload measurement tool, there does not exist at this time much insight into the fundamental question: Does automation affect total workload? Or more properly put, under what conditions does automation increase or decrease workload, or have little or no effect?

What little evidence we have is based on attitude questionnaires and subject workload measures (e.g., National Aeronautics and Space Administration TLX). Wiener et al. (1991) compared subjective workload estimates of DC-9 and MD-88 pilots who had just flown the same line-oriented flight teams scenario. The MD-88 (glass cockpit version of a DC-9) pilots rated their workload higher than did the DC-9 pilots, by a slight but statistically significant amount.

Wiener (1989) also expressed the belief that the effect of automation was to increase workload when it was already high, and decrease it when it was low. Most of the researchers in the area seem to agree (Rudisil, 1996), and research using simpler single-axis autopilots supports the assertion that automation increases cognitive workload while decreasing motor workload (Wickens and Kessel, 1980). Since it is motor workload that is observable, the designers may have gained a false impression that led to their claims of workload reduction. An observer can easily see manual activities in the cockpit but can view only by inference the cognitive processes and demands of a job. Billings (1996b:131) generalizes this result: "workload removed from one element of the system will often be reflected in additional workload elsewhere."

Most people agree that a high degree of automation keeps the pilots' attention inside the cockpit (head-down), to the detriment of extra-cockpit scanning for traffic. It is not at all unusual to see both pilots "inside the cockpit" working on the control display unit. Check airmen, who observe and assess the activities of flight crews, are attuned to this, and make it part of their check ride. Langer (1990) put it most colorfully: "I have discovered that the flight management system control display units, in addition to being means of controlling the system, also act as cockpit vacuum cleaners . . . that is, they suck eyeballs and fingertips into them. I've given check rides on these airplanes and have seen four eyeballs and ten fingertips caught in two flight management system control display units at the same time. This is bad enough at cruise altitude, but it can be lethal in the terminal area."

Crew Coordination and Resource Management Issues

Relatively little has been written on the subject of crew coordination in aircraft in which electronic displays are used to present information—"the glass cockpit" (Wiener, 1993; Wiener et al., 1991). Helmreich and his colleagues have been studying attitudes about national culture and automation for several years (Sherman et al., 1997). Data have been collected on preferences for automation, and attitudes regarding automation use have been collected from pilots of glass-cockpit aircraft in 11 nations on 5 continents. The degree of variability in attitudes and preferences was surprisingly large. Preference for automated over standard aircraft across nations ranged between 34 and 98 percent. More critical were attitudes in the area of skill degradation, head-down time, and perceived company policy regarding automation use. For example, agreement with the item, "I am concerned that the use of automation will cause me to lose flying skills" ranged from 19 to 73 percent across the 11 countries. The item "When workload increases, it is better to avoid reprogamming the FMC" elicited a range of agreement between 36 and 66 percent. Similarly, the item, "My company expects me to always use automation" showed a range between 49 and 100 percent. On most items, responses of pilots from the United States fell in the middle of the distribution. The data suggest that automation is viewed very differently by respondents from different cultures. McClumpha and James (1994) have noted considerable differences in response to automation of the same aircraft among pilots from different airlines. Similar variability may be found in reactions to flight in a more automated air traffic system.

It seems clear that there are communication perils induced by the flight management computer aircraft, but it is equally clear that these can be overcome by crew resource management training and checking, as well as making effective communication part of the culture of the flight management system cockpit. Just how this should be done is not clear. Airbus Industrie has taken an aggressive approach by packaging crew resource management training, which they call AIM—airman integrated management—with the initial airplane training that they provide for customers of their new aircraft. This is a highly unusual step: customarily crew resource management training is provided by the end user airline, not the manufacturer.

The communications problem has as its origin the fact that, due to the design of the automated cockpit, it is often difficult for one pilot to see what the other is doing. The cockpit may be described as two side-by-side workstations (Segal, 1995). The placement of the control display units creates a problem. Many airlines have a procedure that requires the pilot who did not enter the data (e.g., route changes) into the control display unit to review and approve what has been input before it can be executed.[1] In practice this is seldom done, due to the

---

[1]When new data are put into the control and display unit, the system is unaffected until the Execute button is pressed. Prior to execution, a new route, for example, is shown in white, making it

difficulty of leaning across the central pedestal to see the other pilot's display. The problem may be exacerbated if there are large disparities in knowledge of the many sophisticated and complex modes of the flight management system between the two crew members in the cockpit.

Automation Issues

Error Management and Control

Error management is essential in flying FMS aircraft, as cockpit automation can be friend or foe. The previous issues are part of error control. Procedures are also an essential part: the FMS forces the issue of proper cockpit procedures to control error (Degani and Wiener, 1994). Assignment of duties ("who does what") is particularly critical in two-pilot FMS aircraft.

Complacency and Boredom

Most pilots agree that the modern FMS aircraft have very high reliability. They also frequently warn that this may lead to crews relaxing their vigilance and missing aberrations when they occur. The human factors issue is how to maintain vigilance in a somewhat boring, high-reliability environment. Evidence of the fallibility of the FMS (and its underlying database) was provided by the recent crash near Cali, Colombia (Strauch, 1997).

Training and Proficiency Maintenance

There is little written on the subject of training and proficiency maintenance for the modern cockpit. These are actually separate issues: how to conduct transition training to the glass cockpit, especially for the first-time glass pilot; the other issue is maintenance of skill through recurrent training, part-task simulator devices, and the role of line check airmen in maintaining cognitive proficiency In both instances, revealing studies by Sarter and Woods (1994, 1995a, 1995b) suggest the poor understanding that pilots have of the total mode structure of the FMS. Irving et al. (1994) and Casner (1995) have both suggested highly interactive training and simulation techniques whereby this training might be improved. A third, and somewhat obscure issue, is "reverse transition," training pilots who go from the flight management computer back to traditional cockpits as part of their career path (e.g., a high-seniority first officer on glass returns to the traditional cockpit of a less automated airplane in order to upgrade to captain).

---

easy to detect errors. This is one of the great safety features of the FMS—the ability to check out a plan before execution. When executed, the course line would change from white to magenta, the magenta line representing the course that the plane will fly.

Job Satisfaction

The question of job satisfaction in a highly automated environment was first raised by Wiener and Curry (1980). Since then, both authors have stated that in their field studies they found no trace of automation-induced apathy or job dissatisfaction (Curry, 1985; Wiener, 1985, 1989). If anything, pilots seem to be proud to be flying a modern aircraft and highly satisfied with the job. However, it should be noted that satisfaction with the automation provided by the FMS can vary greatly, depending on the attitude fostered by airline management (McClumpha and James, 1994).

Danger of Catastrophic Failure

Catastrophic failure is a threat to crew and passengers in any aircraft. There was some concern in the early days of FMS aircraft of total electrical failure, due to the fact that the aircraft is so electrically dependent. So far the only accident we are aware of that might be termed catastrophic failure was the Lauda Air B-767 that crashed in Thailand in 1991. The accident was due to an uncommanded deployment of a thrust reverser, not related to the flight management system or any other automatic feature.

Incompatibility with Current Air Traffic Control Systems

There is little argument that the current air traffic control systems are inadequate to control and optimize the flight paths of the modern aircraft. In short, the outdated air traffic control systems of today do not allow the crews of FMS aircraft to fully exploit its remarkable capabilities. This is one of the major complaints of the flight management system by aircraft pilots. The situation was explored in detail in a field study by Wiener (1989). Although the data collection of that study is now about 10 years old, the situation has changed little and will probably not change until the air traffic control systems are improved. When this occurs, and assuming that data link will enable direct digital communication between air traffic control and FMS, it will be important to ensure that there is harmony between the logic of the maneuvers in both ground and air-based systems.

Conclusion

The modern flight management system, beginning with the Boeing 767 in the early 1980s, brought a new era to flight guidance and control. It gave the pilot sophisticated, highly reliable tools to manage flight path control and power plant control with great precision. But with these ingenious tools came problems at the human-computer interface, resulting in some degree of distrust on the part of the pilots and, in the extreme, some spectacular incidents and accidents (Hughes and Dornheim, 1995). The great potential for precise, safe, and economical flight has been marred by these events. It is essential that the same mistakes not be made in the implementation of the next generation of air traffic management systems.

One of the problems that must be confronted is the incompatibility between the new flight management system aircraft and the geographic and spatial constraints of the current air traffic control system, which is not compatible with the flight management system-equipped aircraft. The full potential of the flight management system cannot be exploited in today's air traffic control environment. Put simply, the planes are far more sophisticated than the ground-based systems, resulting in suboptimal use of the vehicle. This problem may be resolved when advanced air traffic management systems come on line in the next decade. This may solve the problem of "impedance mismatch" between the vehicle and the ground-based systems, allowing more nearly optimal use of the flight management system and conservation not only of fuel, but also of that one, irreplaceable asset—airspace.

FLIGHT INFORMATION PROCESSING AND PRESENTATION

In this section we discuss key elements of the flight information processing system, as well as the human factors aspects of the presentation of flight information to controllers.

Flight Information Processing

Before complete flight information can be presented to controllers, flight plan and radar information must be acquired by the system, processed, and associated with each other. Figure 4.1 illustrates the key elements of the flight information processing and display system that supports the en route and terminal facilities. Primary elements of the system are the HOST computer, which provides processed flight plan information to terminal facilities and both radar and flight plan information to en route facilities, and the ARTS system, which processes radar data and associates them with HOST-provided flight plan information for terminal facilities.

HOST Processing

The HOST computer is divided into two systems, the flight data processor (FDP) and the radar data processor (RDP). The flight data processor provides flight planning analysis and automatically distributes flight progress strips to air route traffic control center (ARTCC) sectors and to towers and TRACONs through flight strip printers. The flight data processor takes flight plan input from the air traffic controllers and from aircraft users; determines the time it will take

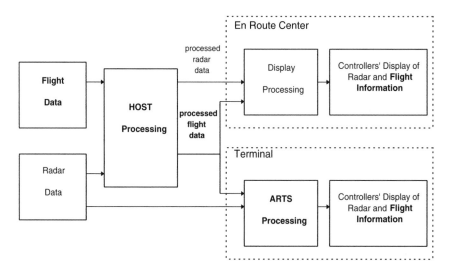

FIGURE 4.1 Key radar and flight information processing elements.

to go from the departure point to the destination; identifies the fixes the flight plan will utilize; assigns a preferential route if necessary; and then posts flight progress strips to the appropriate tower/TRACON and the ARTCCs that will control the aircraft. The strips are printed on a flight data input/output (FDIO) device located at the various ARTCC sectors and at the towers and TRACONs. The time at which the strips are printed at the various sectors and facilities is a parameter that is set to ensure that they are printed in sufficient time for the controllers to plan for their traffic.

The HOST radar data processor processes radar information from a variety of radars and supports presentation of a digital display of alphanumeric information, such as aircraft identity, altitude (mode C), climbing or descending information, ground speed, and assigned altitude. The flight plan information from the flight data processor is associated with the radar data so that the controller can project the aircraft's flight path on the radar display. The radar data processor allows the controller to make automated handoffs from one sector to another or to another ARTCC or TRACON. If the radar data processor fails, a backup system called the direct access radar channel provides the controller with alphanumeric information of aircraft on the radar display but is not associated with the flight data processor. When the flight data processor fails, there is no backup system. When this occurs, it usually has more impact on the air traffic control system than if radar fails.

Prior to automation, flight progress and flight plan analysis were done by the controller. When a flight plan was filed, a controller would develop the route and determine the time to various fixes and to the destination based on the knowledge of the aircraft's performance and the upper winds. Estimates were passed from one facility to another indicating when the receiving facility or sector could expect to have control of the flight.

The first air traffic function to see some automation was flight planning and progress strips. In the early 1960s, some of the large ARTCCs began to take advantage of rudimentary electronic computers to process flight plan information and print flight progress strips for manual distribution within the ARTCC sectors. These systems led to the development of the IBM 9020A mainframe computer. However, there was no standard computer program; each ARTCC with a 9020A developed "local programs." The first national program, developed to meet 80 to 85 percent of the requirements of each facility, became operational in 1972. Its extension to the remaining ARTCCs allowed flight progress information to be automatically passed to all air traffic control facilities throughout the United States. The radar data processor was added to the 9020s in the mid-1970s. The 9020s were replaced in the late 1980s with the HOST system, which handles more capacity with greater speed.

Automated Radar Terminal System

In the service of terminal (TRACON and tower) controllers, the automated radar terminal system (ARTS) performs radar data processing independent of the HOST computer, but relies on the HOST for flight data processing functions. ARTS performs additional processing involving a combination of radar data processor and flight data processor information. ARTS is a ground-based system that provides the air traffic controller with alphanumeric information superimposed on a raw radar target return. The information presented to the air traffic controller is aircraft identity (call sign), mode C altitude (if the aircraft is so equipped), ground speed of the aircraft, type of aircraft, whether or not the aircraft is considered a heavy jet (this is required for separation purposes), and miscellaneous information such as destination airport or first fix on the route of flight. The ARTS supports display of this information in the form of a data block that is constantly associated with the actual radar target through a software tracking program.

The ARTS system was introduced to assist the controller with memory tasks. Providing information on the display rather than only on flight progress strips, the ARTS was intended to allow the controller more time to look directly at the display and to have real-time information available, such as aircraft identity, aircraft type, altitude, and ground speed.

The first ARTS systems, called ARTS I and ARTS IA, were deployed in the New York and Atlanta facilities in the early and mid-1960s. They were essentially prototypes that led to the ARTS III, which was introduced to major TRACONs beginning in late 1969. ARTS II, which has less functionality (e.g., no tracking capabilities), was introduced to lower-activity TRACONs in the 1970s.

Presentation of Flight Information

As noted above, one of the first air traffic control functions to see some level of automation was flight planning and flight progress strips. Over the years, flight progress strips have become what Hopkin (1991a) has called the "emblem of air traffic control," and it is not surprising that there has been a marked reluctance to replace them with an electronic version as part of the automation process. It is recognized that, in the current air traffic control systems, one of the major contributors to controller workload is the requirement for manual processing and distribution of flight data within and between units.

Electronic "flight strips" of some description are necessary to support the automation of this activity. The concept of an electronic flight strip in automated systems, however, understates the objective of modernizing the processing and display of flight data. The issue that needs to be addressed in the research and development process is less one of perpetuating the current roles and functionality of paper strips than of how to achieve an effective electronic embodiment of flight data. Hopkin (1989, 1991b, 1995) has described many of the design issues that need to be addressed in a systematic integration of control information and has articulated the current challenge for interface design:

> A tabular information display of flight progress strips, whether electronic or manual, is difficult to integrate cognitively with a plan view of the air traffic. The consequent problem of cross-referral between radar and strip information is aggravated if traffic is heavy: there are more data to search through whenever there is less time to spare for searching. Windows of tabular information within the display do not wholly resolve this problem. A continuing challenge is the integration of these different kinds of information into a single practical format (1995:26).

Integration of information from the radar, progress strips, and communications has enabled the controller to build up a picture or mental model of the traffic situation (Harper and Hughes, 1991; Whitfield and Jackson, 1983). The replacement of paper flight strips with a more automated electronic mode could, unless carefully designed, affect the construction of the mental model and its cognitive strength, variables that directly impact situation awareness (Endsley and Rodgers, 1994; Isaac, 1997; Harper and Hughes, 1991). Another concern in replacing paper strips with an electronic representation is that strips have provided a kind of "witnessability" that enabled another controller to determine what was being done and what needed to be done. Air traffic control can be viewed as a collaborative activity in which strips are an embodiment of the working division of labor. In their description of an ethnographic analysis of air traffic control, Hughes,

Randall, and Shapiro (1993) refer to strips as work sites, publicly accessible to all members of the sector suite.

Thus, the gradual modernization of air traffic control and the continuing concern for the reduction of operational errors have converged on the issues surrounding workstation and interface design, and particularly on the implications for controller performance of moving to a stripless environment. The following paragraphs provide an overview of research related to these questions that has been undertaken by the FAA Technical Center, the FAA Civil Aeromedical Institute (i.e., the Vortac studies), and other air traffic control organizations.

Research Studies

Issues in Transitioning to Electronic Displays An early evaluation by the FAA Technical Center of a touch-entry electronic tabular display for an en route environment (Rosenberg and Zurinskas, 1983) produced a favorable assessment of the concept by en route specialists. However, the results of the study showed that alternative data entry and update approaches should be developed to reduce errors, increase speed, and improve accuracy.

Although empirical data to verify the purported role of flight strips are scarce, it can be reasoned that the process of physically manipulating the paper strips facilitates the controller's awareness of the physical relationships between aircraft (Hopkin, 1991a; Stein and Garland, 1993; Zingale et al., 1992; Vortac et al., 1993). Sorting the paper flight strips or cocking them on the strip board further facilitates the controller's understanding and memory for the flight data. Similarly, the automated presentation and updating of information could result in an emphasis on monitoring rather than on processing information in memory. This in turn could affect the creation and revision of the controller's mental picture and situation awareness.

A set of four studies, conducted by the FAA Civil Aeromedical Institute and the University of Oklahoma to investigate these and other possible effects on the controllers' cognitive processing of converting from paper to electronic representations of flight progress data, have been summarized by Manning (1995). One of the research interests was to evaluate the hypothesis that utilizing an electronic flight strip display would improve controller performance and cognitive processing because the computer would reduce workload by assuming much of the associated manual activity of updating and maintaining flight progress information.

The results of the studies generally supported the reduced-workload hypothesis. Their aggregate observations suggest that an interactive integrated display or interface that provides more direct access to both flight and radar data could enhance controllers' performance without a reduction in situation awareness. None of the studies, however, was intended to evaluate directly this automation option.

Integrated Interfaces with Automation Operational evaluations of integrated displays have been undertaken to support the development of the Canadian Automated Air Traffic System (CAATS) (Stager, 1991, 1996). Experimentation on the design requirements for a stripless system was performed in France by the Eurocontrol Experimental Centre (EEC) (David, 1991) and the Centre D'études de la navigation aérienne (CENA) (Dujardin, 1990, 1993). In 1986, the EEC formed the Operational Display and Input Development (ODID) Group that subsequently performed a series of operational simulations. ODID is a subgroup of the Eurocontrol Member States' Expert Group for the Coordination of the Studies, Tests, and Applied Research (STAR) Programme on Color Displays and Stripless Systems. One of its responsibilities is to "design and establish an operationally acceptable and efficient control environment using electronic displays to replace strips" (Prosser et al., 1991:1).

The first ODID simulation (Prosser and David, 1988) studied the use of colored electronic data displays as a means of replacing traditional flight progress strips. The second ODID simulation (Prosser and David, 1989) studied the use of the colored electronic displays and raster-scan colored situation displays. The results indicated a need for more closely integrated displays.

In the third study, ODID III (Prosser et al., 1991), an electronic version of the then-current strip format was compared with a set of analog displays for the planning controller. In addition, the performance of two controllers working side-by-side was compared with their performance when separated and communicating only through their displays and communications link. Initially, the electronic strip display held too much permanently displayed data without a visible depiction of which tasks were outstanding; the planning controller, without a dynamic radar display, had to refer constantly to the display of the executive controller. In a second organizational format, a dynamic radar display was included for the planning controller, and there was a minimum display of tabular data.

Speed of input is critical to the success of future automation in air traffic control. ODID IV (Day and Strut, 1993; Graham et al., 1994) used a graphical point-and-click interface. ODID IV was a stripless environment that took advantage of advanced planning aids used by the controller to assist the tactical radar (executive) controller in separating and optimizing air traffic flow. The ODID IV simulation is now a testbed for advanced air traffic control concepts and design principles, which are developed under the ODID program and then applied to other air traffic control systems.

The PHIDIAS project (Dujardin, 1990, 1993) at CENA has worked in liaison with the ODID program to develop the controller interface, primarily for an en route sector, based on a stripless environment. The working positions are an integral component in the upgrading of the air traffic control system in France and will involve a phased introduction of a new radar system, an air-ground data link capability, and intelligent control aids. Research programs are currently in place to make comparative evaluations between ODID and the traditional PVD workstation. Such comparisons appear to offer promising benefits for ODID (Skiles et al., 1997).

The Transition from Paper Strips The transition away from the use of conventional flight strips has provided particular challenges in design that have been largely common to all systems undergoing a modernization process.

The design requirements that affect operational acceptability include the need to:

1. Compensate for the redundancies provided by paper flight strips without being constrained by the direct replication of a paper-based model;
2. Recognize how the characteristics of flight progress paper strips (and procedures associated with them) support the cognitive processes of the controller and are integral to task organization;
3. Develop effective (i.e., rapid and simple) means of data entry;
4. Fully integrate flight data within an electronic work environment; and
5. Provide for a gradual operational transition period.

Human Factors Issues in En Route and Terminal Flight Data Processing

Workload When the HOST and ARTS flight information processing systems were first introduced, the keyboard entries were somewhat lengthy. Functions had to be identified by a keystroke followed by entering the appropriate data for that function (flight data, handoff information, etc.) Although the information was displayed on the radar display, the controller had to look away from the display to make the entries. The more keystrokes required, the longer his or her attention was diverted from the radar display. Data entry by point-and-click procedures were rare. With the introduction of programming enhancements called implied functions, the en route and terminal flight information processing systems were able to identify relevant functions on the basis of the context of displayed information. These implied functions eliminated the need to repetitively select function keys and then to enter data and command actions through the keyboard. They also provided for greater use of the point-and-click method for data entry.

Training Training for the initial implementation of ARTS III was extremely efficient and effective. Teams of air traffic control specialists were trained on the system at either the developer's site or the Aeronautical Center in Oklahoma City. These specialists were then deployed to their home facilities prior to implementation, where they taught a cadre of on-site instructors how to use the system. This cadre of facility instructors then taught the remaining facility personnel.

When the system was ready for operational use, it was introduced gradually to allow controllers to adjust to the system and gain trust. Small, quick-reference cards were available to the controllers as cues for keyboard entries.

Communication and Coordination Pilot-controller communications were reduced by the introduction of the en route and terminal flight information processing systems. Constant updates on altitude and speed were no longer needed, since they were displayed on the radar screen. Automated acquisition of aircraft as they entered the radar range of the controller reduced the need for asking pilots to verify where they were in relation to a fix or geographic reference point. The human role in interfacility coordination was significantly reduced by the introduction of automated handoffs, a feature of the ARTS software and the ARTCC radar data processor. There was no longer a need for verbal coordination between air traffic control facilities when making or receiving handoffs. This was, however, evolutionary. In the early stages of the use of ARTS and the radar data processor, verbal coordination was required to verify the data that were transferred electronically. As the system became trusted, the requirement to verify data was eliminated.

System Reliability Display errors with the initial en route and terminal flight information processing systems were very rare, and trust in the systems was quickly earned. Two major safety enhancements, the minimum safe altitude warning, the ground version of the airborne ground proximity warning system, and the conflict alert, were installed. Both enhancements generated a large number of false alerts in the ARTS system—a result of the programming. The algorithms used in the program are based on predictions of where the target will be in a given number of seconds and minutes rather than the actual proximity. In the case of the minimum safe altitude warning, aircraft that are in a planned steep rate of descent or are being vectored in an area of terrain will usually generate an alarm even though there is no danger. Aircraft that are operating under visual flight rules but are being tracked in the ARTS for traffic advisories and are flying below the minimal vectoring altitude will also generate an alarm. The conflict alert creates the same problem. Aircraft being tracked in the ARTS are usually within an airport area of minimum airspace, and as they are vectored to final approach courses, they are predicted to come within close proximity to other traffic. Although the separation is under control in this situation, the computer program does not know this and generates an alarm. Although both of these enhancements can be selectively inhibited, they usually are not (minimum safe altitude warning is inhibited for aircraft that are on visual flight rules transponder codes), because controllers value the correct alarms. More sophisticated versions of the same predictive function, the conflict probe tool, are discussed in Chapter 6.

Team Environment   Although controllers still work in teams, and their supervisors are called team supervisors, the en route and terminal flight information processing systems permit controllers to work more independently than they did before the introduction of these systems.   With automatic handoffs and radar target acquisition and data being presented on the radar display, there is less need for controllers to seek help from a coordinator or handoff person, and, since requests for assistance have been reduced, there is an associated tendency on the part of coordinators and handoff persons to pay less attention to what the radar controller is doing.

5

Immediate Conflict Avoidance

In this chapter we present an analysis of human factors issues and considerations in four current and proposed automation efforts associated with performing immediate conflict avoidance tasks: the traffic alert and collision avoidance system, the converging runway display aid, the precision runway monitor, and tools for airport surface conflict avoidance. Some of these efforts involve systems that are large and already implemented, such as the traffic alert and collision avoidance system. Others are small and at the early stages of pilot testing; examples include the precision runway monitor and the converging runway display aid. All of the systems included in the following discussion represent serious efforts to automate functions that have changed or will change the role of the human operator.

For each item of automation, our analysis covers the functions to be performed; the historical context for development; the involvement of human factors in the implementation process; generic human factors issues including cognitive task analysis, workload, training and selection, and communication; and the human factors issues specific to automation that were discussed generically in Chapter 1. In describing these subsystems, one important message that we wish to convey is that each subsystem can independently aid the controller in performing the core functions of air traffic control; however, implementation will progress faster and more smoothly if each subsystem is compatible with its neighbors and its predecessors.

TRAFFIC ALERT AND COLLISION AVOIDANCE SYSTEM

Functionality

The traffic alert and collision avoidance system (TCAS) is an airborne system designed to: (1) *advise* pilots visually on a horizontal situation display if there is traffic in the nearby vicinity (a range extending beyond that defining an operational error for controllers); (2) *alert* them both visually and aurally if a possible collision is imminent (assuming both aircraft remain on the same course); and ultimately, if necessary, (3) *issue* a redundant (visual and auditory) *resolution advisory*, instructing the pilot on a vertical maneuver to avoid the possible collision. In the current TCAS II (Federal Aviation Administration, 1990b), the advisory is issued by depicting a vertical speed to seek (on the vertical speed indicator of the pilot's instrument panel) and another to avoid and by presenting an aural advisory such as "climb climb climb" or "reduce descent reduce descent" (*Avionics*, 1990; Federal Aviation Administration, 1990b). Figure 5.1 presents a sample TCAS display. TCAS II version 7, which is planned for release in 1998, will improve the conflict resolution algorithms and provide some added display functionality (Klass, 1997).

TCAS is essentially an automated system that is a redundant monitoring backup for the air traffic controller in instrument meteorological conditions, and for both the controller and pilot in visual meteorological conditions; it is also a control advisor for the pilot in the crisis situation when a potential collision is imminent.

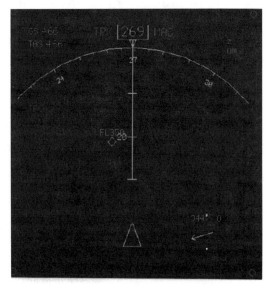

FIGURE 5.1 Sample traffic alert and collision avoidance (TCAS) display, showing a target 19 miles ahead. Source: Photo courtesy of the MITRE Corporation.

History

The seeds for TCAS were planted both in concern over the rare midair collisions that have occurred (Wiener, 1989) and in the earlier efforts by the National Aeronautics and Space Administration to develop the cockpit display of traffic information (Abbott et al., 1980; Kreifeldt, 1980; Hart and Loomis, 1980). In the early 1980s, there was some concern over the visual workload imposed on pilots by giving them a full picture of all local traffic, as well as possible concerns about inadvertent shifts in authority away from air traffic control to the flight deck. The more restricted TCAS concept was developed following an FAA commitment to the system in 1981 and has been gradually phased into commercial air traffic. A great impetus (and a congressional mandate) were provided by the midair crashes over San Diego (in 1987) and Cerritos, California (in 1986; Wiener, 1989). By 1993, all the U.S. commercial carriers were equipped with TCAS.

Human Factors Implementation

The process of implementation of TCAS has benefited from some of the lessons learned by the earlier introduction of the ground proximity warning system, which suffered extensively from a high false alarm rate and as a result led pilots to develop a corresponding mistrust (Hanson, 1992). As a consequence, National Aeronautics and Space Administration's Ames Research Center undertook a systematic human factors research program prior to the introduction of TCAS (Chappell, 1990). This program entailed the collection of a considerable amount of laboratory and simulation data and the use of these data in fabricating many of the display parameters. Correspondingly, the implementation of the system on commercial aircraft has followed a gradual and closely monitored course, allowing early experience to guide redesign and refinement. A formal TCAS transition program established by the FAA has provided a vehicle for integrating lessons learned and disseminating them to the national airspace system community via a newsletter. The MITRE Corporation has been continually involved in refining the collision prediction and alerting algorithms on the basis of field problems and to address the still nontrivial false alarm problem (Klass, 1997). Human factors issues related to pilot compliance (or noncompliance) with resolution advisories are being closely monitored (Adam, 1995).

An important Aviation Safety Reporting System report (Mellone and Frank, 1993) provided an early warning of some of the unanticipated system-wide human factors consequences of TCAS. Following a set of National Transportation Safety Board safety recommendations (National Transportation Safety Board, 1993), these have led to FAA intervention in issuing regulations on the use of TCAS in the cockpit. Three of these consequences have direct implications for air traffic control and are discussed further below: (1) pilots following a resolution advisory were changing altitude by nearly twice the amount recommended by the user manual (600 versus 300 feet, with some deviations exceeding 1,000 feet) and hence intruding on a higher or lower flight level; (2) pilots were not always informing controllers that they were undertaking a resolution maneuver, even after the fact; and (3) pilots were sometimes using the traffic status display to maintain separation from nearby aircraft, hence implicitly shifting separation control from ground to air. More recent, still emerging lessons are continually being applied, as the TCAS transition program remains in effect and the aviation safety reporting system continues to cull through its database to keep track of recurring problems. Although clearly imperfect, it does appear that this implementation program of TCAS has adhered to many of the important procedures to ensure that human factors are considered. Some of the more specific human factors issues, also discussed in the Phase I report, are considered below.

Human Factors Issues

Cognitive Task Analysis

It is clear that TCAS accomplishes two functions designed to assist human performance in areas in which the latter is vulnerable: monitoring for low probability events and predicting the interactions between complex speed-varying trajectories. Furthermore, its role as a situation awareness support, by providing the pilot with a graphic description of the state of nearby traffic, is a beneficial one. It can also be argued that the effectiveness of a resolution advisory, offered as guidance for action in a stressful, time-critical period, is one that supports human performance, because of the tendency for self-initiated actions to suffer a speed/accuracy trade-off under stress (Hockey, 1986; Wickens, 1996). At the same time, it is evident from task analysis and controller reports (Mellone and Frank, 1993) regarding the current implementation of the system that the sometimes unanticipated corrective actions initiated by aircraft in response to a resolution advisory can drastically disrupt the controller's situation awareness. This disruption is amplified because the direction of the advisory (i.e., a vertical maneuver) is one that is not spatially evident in the display but must be perceived from the digital data tags.

Workload

TCAS has workload implications both on the ground and in the air. For the controller, the enhanced workload of dealing with an unanticipated and often complex event is evident and has been the subject of explicit complaints (Mellone and Frank, 1993). For the pilot, the workload effects may come in two forms. First, responding to a resolution advisory is obviously a high-workload event, but one that is justified and acceptable if the advisory is "legitimate." If it is a false alarm, this unnecessary distraction from other aspects of flying will have undesirable consequences. For example, recent reports have noted the frequency of hard and fast landings, resulting from false advisories issued during airport approaches. Second, a more insidious workload effect was anticipated by the earlier research on the cockpit display of traffic information. To the extent that pilots begin to navigate using the system's status display, their workload is likely to increase, both as a function of visual attention allocated to this new channel of input and as a function of added control decisions that may now be based on the system's input.

Training and Selection

Training issues were anticipated to some extent prior to TCAS implementation, and manuals were printed for both pilots and air traffic controllers. However, in some respects, reports from the field have indicated that initial training was not fully adequate (Hanson, 1992; Vickers, 1992; National Transportation Safety Board, 1993). From the controller's standpoint, many of the training manuals did not actually reach their destinations in the field (Vickers, 1992), and the initial training focused more on how the system *should* work, rather than how it *did* work in practice. For example, controllers were not alerted to the possible problems that would arise if pilots exceeded the recommended 300 foot altitude deviation, as many did (Mellone and Frank, 1993). For pilots, the simple instruction manuals were probably inadequate to prepare them for executing the actual maneuvers that might be required at infrequent and unexpected times. There is a need to train them to consistently follow the procedures that the controller would expect. At present, the fact that 30 to 50 percent of resolution alerts are *not* followed (i.e., ignored or followed incorrectly) (Steenblik, 1996; Adam, 1995) would suggest that there is great variance across pilots and occasions in the manner in which TCAS is used, suggesting a lack of adequate standardized training.

Communication and Coordination

The role of consistent training is particularly critical in systems like TCAS, with joint ground-air implications, because of the importance of shared situation awareness and a shared mental model between pilot and controller regarding how a pilot is likely to react and how the pilot actually is reacting to a conflict situation. The initial reports of Mellone and Frank indicated the magnitude of the problem. Subsequent reports of the large number of resolution advisories that are not followed (Steenblik, 1996; Ciemer et al., 1993) suggest that controllers cannot easily guess what the pilots will do in a conflict situation. (Only a minority of the cases in which pilots ignored resolution advisories resulted because the pilot was following explicit controller instructions). We may infer that this issue lies at the heart of potential human factors problems with this system.

Two solutions to this problem are implicitly suggested. First, greater and more effective training for pilots must focus on the need for consistent response to TCAS, so that the response will be predictable to the controller. Second, there should be a concerted effort to down-link the representation of resolution advisory responses (and possibly traffic alert information) to controllers (Hoffman et al., 1995; Flavin, 1996), to ensure that pilots and controllers have shared situation awareness of the nature of maneuver advisories. This represents an active program of research in air traffic control human factors that has been undertaken by the FAA. The program has included two pilot tests in a medium-fidelity simulation at the MITRE Corporation (Hoffman et al., 1995), which primarily employed user opinion (10 air traffic control specialists) to evaluate the value of this information, its format, and level of detail. It also includes a field test at Boston's Logan Airport.

Organization

Intended or not, TCAS has clearly produced a slight shift in authority from ground to air, resulting in ambiguity as to who is responsible for errors and possible accidents that may result. This shift is particularly evident in the use of the TCAS traffic display to navigate and maintain separation (Mellone and Frank, 1993), although this function is specifically acknowledged for oceanic in-trail climbs and, with the introduction of TCAS II version 7, for air traffic control authorized clearances for visual approach (Mundra et al., 1997). Issues involved in developing procedures for dealing with unintended consequences are also nontrivial, and the FAA is addressing this. Another organizational issue that is emerging relates to differences across and within airlines in the manner in which the system's procedures are followed. As noted above, the greater the inconsistency of procedure following, the less controllers will be able to anticipate maneuvers or remotely judge the pilot's assumed responsibility, and hence the greater the workload imposed on the controller. Furthermore, TCAS logic itself makes assumptions that the maneuvers of both aircraft involved in an engagement will proceed as advised. If this advice is unheeded by one aircraft but not the other, a bad situation could become worse.

Automation Issues

Mode Errors

Although originally anticipated as a single mode system, early lessons indicated the need for certain modes to be deactivated at certain times, in order to avoid high false alarm rates. For example, the presence of other TCAS-equipped aircraft on an adjacent runway (or in a parallel approach) during landing, where known close proximity encounters exist, requires that advisory and aural alert modes be deactivated. Yet such decisions will invite the possibility that other encounters may not be alerted. The existence of this issue is acknowledged, but its magnitude is uncertain.

Trust

As noted above and as discussed in Chapter 1, the mistrust engendered by false alerts and unnecessary resolution advisories, and also reflected in the frequent failures to comply with the resolution advisories, is the most critical issue. This issues is being addressed in part through continuous refinement of the algorithms by the MITRE Corporation. Issues of overtrust and complacency have not yet surfaced as identifiable concerns (perhaps because the nontrivial false alarm rate currently prevents complacency from occurring). However, greatly improved algorithms could increase the level of sensitivity of the system and significantly reduce the false alarm rate; such design changes should be accompanied by safeguards against complacency (automatically following the resolution advisory without a cross-check).

Skill Degradation

Skill degradation would not appear to be an issue for pilots, but for controllers the potential issue is very real; if TCAS supersedes controllers in issuing instructions to disentangle aircraft from complex traffic encounters, these skills may be lost by controllers. Similar concerns, of course, arise for controllers if ground-based automation accomplishes the task, as we discuss in the next chapter.

Mental Models

The issue of mental models can be defined at two levels. The first concerns the extent to which any operator (pilot or controller) has an accurate mental model of the algorithm by which resolution advisories are issued. In the absence of an accurate model, it is easy to envision circumstances in which an appropriate resolution advisory might not be followed.

The issue at the second level concerns the extent to which both pilots and controllers develop the *same* mental model of the algorithms operating in the system. If the mental models do not coincide, mistrust and hence misuse may result (Parasuraman and Riley, 1997). Since the controller's explicit model of separation violation is based on a purely space-based geometry (e.g., 5 miles, 1,000 feet), whereas the system's resolution advisories are based on a time-based geometry (i.e., predicted time to impact), there is an invitation for misunderstanding. A recent simulation study by Pritchett and Hansman (1997a, 1997b) attributed the failure of pilots to follow many of the resolution advisories issued on parallel approaches in a flight simulator to the pilots' judgment of separation on the basis of distance, rather than on the time algorithms used in the resolution advisories. Such confusion may be amplified, to the extent that the system evolves to incorporate *intent inferencing* (see Chapter 2), based on programmed flight management system logic within the two aircraft involved in a potential encounter.

Communication and Organization

The main issues of communication and organization were discussed earlier. However, the discussion of mental models reiterates the critical factors involved in the information and assumptions shared among the four agents involved in TCAS: the two pilots, the automated system logic, and the controller. Since the dynamics of the situation will jointly emerge from the knowledge and expectancies that each agent has about the likely behavior of the others, as well as from the momentary situation awareness (or knowledge of the dynamic state) that each has of the conflict geometry, the predicted complexity of this system is great.

Conclusion

Although TCAS was originally intended to be a purely air-based system and designed to be a final backup to breakdowns in ground-based control, it is evident that it has much more profound implications for air traffic control. These implications will grow as the system is extended forward to recapture more elements of the cockpit display of traffic information, in the implementation of certain levels of free flight (e.g., the role of TCAS in approaches, the role of TCAS in oceanic in-trail climbs—Mundra et al., 1997). It is clear that considerable thought was given to human factors issues in the initial implementation and subsequent fielding of the system. However, it may be argued that more early attention could have been given to trying to discover the complex pilot-controller interactions that emerged, and that have subsequently forced revision of procedures, policy, training, and software. It is likely that more extensive reliance on system models (with valid models of human components), as well as complex human-in-the-loop simulation, could have anticipated some of these problems. It is encouraging to see movement in this direction as other future air traffic control technologies are envisioned (e.g., data link).

CONVERGING RUNWAY DISPLAY AID

Functionality

The converging runway display aid (CRDA) is a computer program that can reside on the ARTS III computer used in the terminal area for air traffic control. Its main function is to aid controllers in sequencing traffic for arrival at converging runways (Mundra, 1989; Mundra and Levin, 1990).

At terminals with converging runways, there are two final approach paths. These two paths typically are separated by an angle of up to 90 degrees. When approaching aircraft are under positive radar control, the controller uses range markers on the radar display to determine the relative sequential spacing of aircraft on the two different descent paths. The goal is to maintain separation of at least 2 nautical miles as long as the aircraft are airborne. The critical stage is the point at which the two approach paths come together; arrival at that point must be staggered.

The separation task is particularly difficult when the arriving traffic is diverse so that, for example, velocity on final approach varies from aircraft to aircraft. When inclement weather complicates the situation, loss of capacity can run to 50 percent.

The converging runway display aid shows each aircraft on both approach paths by means of a "ghost" image. That is, the position of aircraft number 1 on approach path A is also shown on approach path B as a virtual or ghost representation. Thus the in-trail separation of the aircraft on both paths can be directly observed and adjusted through standard air traffic control procedures in a continuous manner. When the converging runway display aid is desired, it may be activated. A single switch brings up the converging runway display aid on the radar display.

History

Computer-aided metering and spacing were functions considered in system design exercises in the late 1960s when computer processing of radar images was first implemented. The basic response was to provide time-distance vectors for each aircraft under positive control. Thus the processed radar display generated a line that projected the path of future movement for each aircraft for a particular time duration. Since distance scale was constant for the radar display, the controller could assess momentary separation and also infer future separations (or violations), because the vector permitted explicit predictions.

In 1988, the concept of providing ghost images as an aid in maintaining separation at the point of path intersection was first articulated and documented (Mundra, 1989). There followed an engineering development effort that was typified by the use of rapid prototyping techniques and the early engagement of representatives of the user population in the assessment of these prototypes. Continuing domestic evaluation of the resultant computer program package is under way in St. Louis, Missouri; Norfolk, Virginia; El Paso, Texas; Cincinnati, Ohio; Tulsa, Oklahoma; Philadelphia, Pennsylvania; Birmingham, Alabama; Boston, Massachusetts; and Newark, New Jersey. The system is also being evaluated at Schiphol Airport in Amsterdam, the Netherlands, at the National Aerospace Laboratory using the NARSIM air traffic control simulator. These evaluations are complicated by the site-specific procedures employed in the use of the CRDA. There are also problems related to skill maintenance because the system is used only intermittently under conditions of particularly low visibility.

Human Factors Implementation

As indicated, the original ARTS III capability for maintaining aircraft separation on converging paths was based on the controller's perceptions aided by range rings on the display. When development of the converging runway display aid was initiated by the systems engineers at the MITRE Corporation, the goal was to improve this limited capability. The developers of the aid could simply assume that the provision of any means for direct determination of the spacing would mean improvement.

The central questions during the engineering development were the demonstration of the concept and user acceptance. These questions were addressed by the provision of prototype models that could be exercised first in a simulation setting and later in the setting of operational TRACONs at terminals, such as Lambert Field in St. Louis, that have converging runways. User feedback from such exercises was used to guide each successive stage in the modification of the computer program.

Human Factors Issues

Cognitive Task Analysis

No formal task analyses were performed for the specific purpose of designing the converging runway display aid. However, an obvious cognitive problem in the basic system was the mental representation and visualization of in-trail separations for laterally separated, nonparallel radar images.

It was evident to the systems analysts that there was a reduction in arrival capacity at operational TRACONs that had converging runways when instrument flight rules were ordered. It was ascertained informally that the drop in capacity came from controller uncertainty about separation distances. In short, the controllers were generating a larger margin for error and setting spacing above the minimums stipulated by the rules.

Workload

The main workload in the predecessor system came from the need for the controllers to shift their attention back and forth between the two approach paths. The advent of the converging runway display aid was intended to eliminate the need to carry out such transfers of attention. The aid thus generates a net reduction in workload.

Training and Selection

In adopting the converging runway display aid, two learned discriminations are required. The first is simply the determination that the aid should be uploaded. The cue for this action would be the controller's sense that the spacing interval was creeping upward. Sensitivity for such a determination is trainable but could be acquired by ordinary practice in the normal course of air traffic control operations.

The second learning situation involves making judgments to adjust the spacing between aircraft with different descent speeds once the converging runway display aid is operating. It would also unfold in actual operations (or in a task simulator). A possibly crucial factor is the achievement of confidence in the system on the part of the controller so that such judgments are acted on with no hesitation.

Communication and Coordination

It is conceivable that a team of two controllers could be assigned to approach control during heavy traffic periods and that each controller would be responsible for one of the converging approach paths. The base case in this situation is dual operations without the converging runway display aid. The question is: Does the introduction of the aid change the communication and coordination needs and procedures?

With the display aid installed, each controller would see the aircraft under the other's control as a ghost target. This circumstance should actually reduce the need for communication and explicit coordination.

Organization

There is no indication that organizational dynamics change with the introduction of the converging runway display aid. However, it should be noted that field testing has been limited to a select subset of terminals; therefore, strong generalizations about organizational dynamics cannot be made.

Automation Issues

Mode Errors

The main opportunity for mode errors is in the decision to upload the system. However, the consequences of being either premature or late are not severe. Specifically, premature uploading has no apparent negative consequences. Late uploading would lead to the prolongation of some partial decline in acceptance rates—but no discernible degradation of the safety factor.

Trust

The latitude available to the controller in the decision to upload the program suggests that, if there is a lack of trust, use of the system can be delayed or avoided. The program of prototype exposure and the elicitation of feedback from the controllers suggests that the developers were sensitive to the problem of trust and undertook to provide a means to ensure that trust and confidence in the system would be established prior to its installation. Trust may, of course, be modified on the basis of controllers' operational experience with the converging runway display aid.

Skill Degradation

Since the converging runway display aid will be running only a relatively small proportion of the time, there is little likelihood that the skills required for the less automated conditions will decline.

Mental Models

The initial impetus for the converging runway display aid came from a recognition of human limitation in conceptualizing rapid changes in three-dimensional space. Another way of looking at the converging runway display aid is that it instantiates one of the mental models used by some controllers. Even if this assumption applies to only some controllers and not to others, the system provides an analogic representation of the traffic environment that reduces the need for the controller to formulate such a mental model or to employ some other cognitive means for ensuring proper separation.

Conclusion

The converging runway display aid is a modest, incremental step toward advanced air traffic control automation of information presentation and integration. It appears to work well as a sequencing tool in those relatively few situations for which it was designed—namely, low visibility conditions at a relatively high-traffic-density terminal with converging runways.

By extrapolation, the converging runway display aid technology may also be applicable to all terminal operations for arrival spacing. In the single runway situation, there is a final path that can begin as far as 10 miles or more from the runway threshold. All arrivals converge to this path. Preliminary studies of the use of "slot markers"—that are equivalent to virtual images or ghosts—have been conducted at the MITRE Corporation (Mundra, 1989; Mundra and Levin, 1990).

Other approaches to computer-aiding of approach spacing are under development, for example, the final approach spacing tool at NASA Ames (Lee and Davis, 1995; see Chapter 6) and the final monitor aid (FMA) at Lincoln Laboratories (Lind, 1993), discussed later in this chapter. There is no obvious reason that the concepts underlying the converging runway display aid, the final approach spacing tool, and the final monitor aid could not be integrated. In any case, the human factors issues and concerns raised with respect to the converging runway display aid would be the same if a virtual image generation capability were introduced in all situations in which convergence may be a problem.

PRECISION RUNWAY MONITOR AND FINAL MONITOR AID

Functionality

Like the converging runway display aid described in the previous section, the objective of the combined precision runway monitor/final monitor aid system is to increase the capacity for the acceptance of flight arrivals at terminals (Federal Aviation Administration, 1991c). However, this system is designed to function at terminals that have two or more parallel runways rather than converging runways. The system permits two aircraft to occupy their respective parallel approach paths under low-visibility conditions in a side-by-side rather than in a staggered arrangement. The system is particularly suited to high-density-traffic situations at major hubs, where demand for arrival slots has reached the upper limit of the terminal capabilities. Such saturation or near saturation contains the prospect of a double disturbance in air traffic flow. Whenever poor visibility or bad weather enters the picture, local traffic is delayed in the air. Moreover, the delay effect tends to radiate outward from the affected terminal—leading to delays on the ground for flights destined for the affected terminal or even flights that are scheduled to pass through the regional airspace.

The essential ingredients of the precision runway monitor/final monitor aid system are a high speed/high precision radar, a computer program that processes the radar signals, and a display subsystem that portrays the runways and their parallel approach paths. The high speed/high precision radar is needed to reduce the uncertainty about the position of radar targets. With reduced uncertainty, it becomes permissible to reduce the separation minimums to the distance between the parallel runways. The computer program actually does more than process the radar signals. It also generates the context in the form of color-coded images of the runways, the approach paths, and the area between the two runways that is designated as the no-transgression zone. It attaches predictive vector lines to each radar image and triggers a shift in color coding of the aircraft icon from green to yellow when one of the aircraft veers off its proper flight path. If the aircraft enters the no-transgression zone, the program initiates a second color change for the aircraft icon, from yellow to red, and initiates an auditory alarm.

History

When it became apparent in the late 1970s that building additional runways was not a complete or a cost-effective solution to the airport delay problem, steps were taken to minimize the problems associated with weather and visibility at major hubs that already had multiple runways. The initial approach to the problem began in 1975 and extended in 1981 through a study conducted by the MITRE Corporation (Haines and Swedish, 1981). The strategy focused on the development and installation of more precise radars. Development was undertaken at two contractor sites: Massachusetts Institute of Technology's Lincoln Laboratory and MSI Services, Inc./Bendix. Prototype models of the mode S sensor (Lincoln Laboratory) and the e-scan sensor (MSI/Bendix) were installed in 1989 at the Memphis International and Raleigh-Durham International airports, respectively.

The first tests in the field were focused on the actual precision of the radar. However, it was soon apparent that there might be some nonelectronic problems. Specifically, there were questions about pilots' ability and willingness to perform a missed approach maneuver at the last minute of the approach. That is, if one of the aircraft on the final approach to one of the parallel runways was to blunder across the lateral separation and infringe on the path of an adjacent aircraft, would there be time—even with the greater location precision and more rapid update cycle—to implement a conflict avoidance maneuver? In particular, the prospect was raised that the aircraft perpetrating the blunder might not be responsive to controller instructions and so resolution of the crisis would depend on the responsiveness of the pilot flying the nonintrusive aircraft. As a consequence of this concern, simulation studies were initiated to make sure that pilots could and would respond in a timely manner to an incursion that could take place at very low altitudes.

The results of the early simulation tests were somewhat equivocal—particularly for those cases in which the runways were relatively close. Consequently, attention was shifted to the possibility that the air traffic controller might be able to act sooner on potential conflicts if given an improved display. In 1990, work was initiated to introduce a new, high-resolution display to complement the new, high-precision and rapid-update characteristics of the radar. The result was the display design characterized as the final monitor aid.

Human Factors Implementation

Two studies that included human factors evaluations were carried out at the Memphis installation site by MITRE Corporation staff scientists in 1990-1991 and reported in 1993 (Lind, 1993). In these studies, experienced controllers and experienced pilots served as test subjects. The operational precision runway monitor/final monitor aid equipment was used in conjunction with high-performance cockpit simulators.

The performance data indicated a modest advantage for the rapid update feature of the radar. Other data taken from the test installation at Memphis were mainly in the form of subjective responses during debriefing sessions for controllers and pilots. Controllers generally judged the system to be acceptable. Concurrently, evaluation studies were also being carried out by FAA staff at the Technical Center near Atlantic City, New Jersey (Ozmore and Morrow, 1996). Between 1988 and 1995, 18 experiments were conducted in the simulation laboratory. Most of these studies were focused on the effectiveness of high-precision radar and the physical configuration of runways and ground-based navigational aids. Only one study was exclusively dedicated to human factors (see Ozmore and Morrow, 1996). In this study, for example, there was a "surprise" aspect on the part of pilots when instructed to execute an avoidance maneuver while on the final approach. The unexpectedness of the request led to some major delays in the actual execution of the act. A second informal observation was the relatively high frequency of false positive reactions, whereby avoidance maneuvers were called for when no incursion of the safety zone had actually taken place. The main engineering response to this effect was to emphasize the need to have a position update rate at least as rapid as once every 2.4 seconds.

The overall consequence of this series of experiments was the approval of the FMA to be used on parallel approaches for triple runways a mile or more apart and for dual runways as close together as 3,000 feet, if e-scan radar is installed.

Human Factors Issues

Cognitive Task Analysis

The cognitive aspects of the task confronting the air traffic controller when using the precision runway monitor/final monitor aid system are not particularly challenging. For example, the status of every aircraft within the final approach area is color-coded: aircraft on proper course are designated by green, those that deviate from their prescribed course are yellow, and those that have entered the no-transgression zone are red. Furthermore, an aircraft that loses its transponder is coded red regardless of its flight path. In addition, the runway is imaged as a bright, white rectangle and the extension of the center line beyond the runway threshold is shown as a dotted white line. Range markers for the distance between the multiple runways take the form of blue lines and the no-transgression zone itself is solid red. Finally, there are future course projections for each aircraft. In short, the major indicators of the actual situation are color-coded to minimize the requirement for spatial judgments by the controller. Since the aircraft are already on their final leg, the controller's task becomes one of vigilant monitoring, with the need to rapidly intervene if the no-transgression zone is violated or is about to be.

Workload

Tasks that require infrequent responses can lead to inattention. When such a loss of vigilance takes place, it is attributed to a condition of underload (Hancock and Warm, 1989; Wiener and Nagel, 1988). However, there are safeguards, such as the auditory alarm built into this system and the procedures recommended for its use. The procedural feature is the provision for relatively short duty tours. Controllers are detailed to the precision runway monitor/final monitor aid for two hours at a time without rest breaks. However, system operators can lose vigilance after only 15 minutes of passive monitoring (Parasuraman, 1986), so this safeguard may not be effective.

Training and Selection

A full-performance-level controller should be able to use the system flawlessly within minutes. However, it should be noted that, in the evaluation studies, the controllers were given a full eight hours of practice before being employed as test subjects.

A developmental controller may require more practice under supervision. However, being assigned to the precision runway monitor/final monitor aid may be an ideal way to introduce a developmental controller to live traffic.

Communication and Coordination

The effective functioning of the system is extremely time dependent. That is, the controller must react very promptly to an incursion blunder because of the low altitude and descent inertia of the aircraft. Indeed, airlines often have rules that prohibit the initiation of a missed approach maneuver below a specified altitude. This can be as high as 1,000 feet—well above the location of some of the incursions. At best, this means that the controller has less than 10 seconds to request a missed approach if an incursion is detected near the outer marker. As the landing proceeds, the time shrinks. Likewise, some leeway must be held for the pilot to implement the turn. Pilots may hesitate for any number of reasons—such as an aversion to violating company rules and a desire to avoid upsetting passengers with violent maneuvers near the ground. Another source of delay in pilot's compliance with controller instructions revealed in the simulation studies was the low expectation on the part of the pilots for receiving a landing abort message so late in the approach sequence. Under the instrument flight rules conditions prescribed for the activation of the final monitor aid, pilots will not see intruders that are the ultimate cause of the imposed missed approach. There is no opportunity for the pilots to start to tune their sensorium for the receipt of an emergency message. These observations are congruent with long-standing research on the relationship of expectancy to response time (Fitts and Posner, 1967).

A related issue is the failure of the pilots to react to the term "immediately" when it was used as a preface to an instruction. Although this term is used to convey urgency, it is used so infrequently that pilots may forget what it means to their own safety. In the simulation experiments, delays of over 10 seconds were recorded even when the controller was evincing concern by tone of voice as well as use of the supposedly alerting phrase (Ozmore and Morrow, 1996).

This may represent an opportunity for one form of automation to be used to compensate for the design limits of another automated system. Specifically, it may be ideal for a special application of data link technology. It is particularly apt since the controller *is* given an alert message by an mechanical annunciator. To activate an aural alarm in the cockpit of the aircraft that must make the avoidance maneuver should be a relatively simple step. Such options are discussed in more detail in the data link section in Chapter 3.

Organization

A possible organizational issue is that controllers with seniority may prefer to avoid assignment to operate the system—even for short duty cycles. The reason given by the senior controllers in the demonstration for this preference was boredom. For all its attractive attributes, such as the color-coded display, senior controllers apparently perceived that their talents would be wasted in operating this particular system.

Automation Issues

Mode Errors

The system, as presently configured, is either off or on. There is no intermediate state, and there is no justification for providing any. If the system fails while in action, the response of the controller would be to immediately revert to the manual mode—invoking separation standards that were otherwise obviated by the precision monitor aid capabilities.

Trust

In the prototype operations, standard ARTS computers were used to mediate between the high-speed radar and the display. It is not clear whether the controllers were aware of this particular configuration, but there was no indication in the open response sessions that the controllers were either particularly trusting or nontrusting of the system. It seems likely that, except for the issue of the false alarm rate of the final monitor aid, they would express levels of trust quite similar to the responses to the whole of the current TRACON ARTS system.

With respect to the actual properties of the system, there are few data on the possibility of a system false alarm (e.g., advice to maneuver when it was not required). It can be inferred from other studies that false alarms quickly and strongly undermine trust on the part of operators of automated systems (Parasuraman et al., 1997). The logic of operation is, however, very straightforward and is based on actual separation distance rather than closing rates. This approach is easily grasped by operators and can be tuned to select shorter or longer separations if issues of trust arise during operational experience.

Skill Degradation

The mode of operation with the final monitor aid does not appear to be substantially different from the controller's functions while monitoring a conventional instrument landing system approach. In fact, the controller should be seeing more targets with the final monitor aid—up to the limits of the flow rates under visual flight rules conditions. It is even conceivable that controllers will want to leave the final monitor aid display active under visual flight rules conditions for use as a supplementary tool. The radar with its faster update cycle, combined with the colorful display, could serve as a backup tool for ensuring proper spacing.

Mental Models

The conventionally two-dimensional display provides support for the maintenance of situation awareness by providing a color-coded, physical model of the controller's task environment. The results of the user survey suggest close congruence between the display configuration and the typical controller's mental model.

Organization

If the precision runway monitor/final monitor aid system is brought into play only in severe instrument flight rules conditions, the controller who is assigned as system operator has three entities with whom coordination is essential. The first is the pilot of an aircraft who commits a blunder on final approach and intrudes into the buffer zone between parallel runways. It seems likely that such a blunder will be symptomatic of other serious problems, so the controller might be well advised to minimize the time spent in coordinating efforts with this pilot. A second point of coordination is the pilot of the aircraft immediately adjacent to and affected by the blunder event. The effort made in reaching this person is crucial to the outcome of the episode. The third collaborator should be the arrival controller, who has responsibility for safe separation starting at the boundary of the terminal area up to the point of turn onto final approach. Ideally, a procedural arrangement would take place between the two controllers, so that aircraft would be metered onto the final approach in balanced numbers between the left and the right runways. Also important is the metering into the precision runway monitor/final monitor aid system such that sequence intervals are maintainable during the final approach.

To a somewhat lesser extent, coordination will also be needed with the tower controllers, who are responsible for separation and expeditious flow from runway to arrival gates. In effect, the precision runway monitor/final monitor aid system preempts some of the functions of the tower controller. Some review of the clearability of taxiways under instrument flight rules conditions should be done when the flow of landing airplanes is upgraded by the use of the precision runway monitor/final monitor aid. That is, the question arises as to whether surface control might not be overwhelmed in adverse weather conditions if the arrival rate is sustained at the higher level made possible by the precision runway monitor/final monitor aid.

Airborne Parallel Approach Monitoring

The organizational issues associated with the precision runway monitor are closely linked to an alternative plan for monitoring closely spaced parallel approaches via displays in the cockpit. This system, called airborne information for lateral spacing, has been under development at the National Aeronautics and Space Administration for the past few years and has a similar philosophy to that of the precision runway monitor. On the primary traffic display, the pilot will view his own approach and that of the parallel traffic. In the event of a deviation, or the prediction of penetration of the no-transgression zone, a graded series of alerts are presented in coordinated fashion between the two participating aircraft (the "intruder" and the "evader"). These involve first alerting the intruder, then alerting the evader, then commanding the intruder to maneuver (climb and turn right or left), and, as a last resort, commanding the evader to maneuver. The implicit assumption here is that the intruder bears initial responsibility for the conflict and hence shall be the first to execute a missed approach, an assumption opposite to the one incorporated in the ground-based precision runway monitor/ final monitor aid. Traffic alerts are presented redundantly on the horizontal situation indicator (traffic display) and the primary flight display, while maneuver advisories are presented via voice synthesis.

Unlike the radar-based precision runway monitor/final monitor aid, the airborne information for lateral spacing system is based on global positioning system sensing of aircraft position, and ADS-B communications between aircraft. The system thus has many analogies with TCAS, and the role of the controller would be assumed to be secondary (i.e., advised concurrently or following the maneuver, but not assumed to be an active participant in commanding the maneuver).

Simulation tests of the airborne information for lateral spacing system at NASA Ames revealed relatively rapid response times (on the order of 1 second) by the pilot to the resolution advisories. However it should be noted that, in this simulation, there were occasional long responses of 10 seconds or more and furthermore that the simulations were conducted under best-case high-expectancy conditions, in which evading pilots knew that deviations by the intruding pilot would sometimes occur.

Further work at the Massachusetts Institute of Technology (Pritchett and Hansman, 1997a, 1997b) has examined various traffic display enhancements and established that the redundant presentation of traffic information across the horizontal situation indicator and primary flight display is valuable, and that predictor (or trend) information is also useful. One important issue revealed by the simulation tests at the Massachusetts Institute of Technology pertains to the relatively high rate of *noncompliance* with resolution advisories, a finding echoing those observed in TCAS alerts. The authors attribute this in part to the fact that the time-to-conflict algorithms used by the system are different from the easy-to-visualize space-based algorithms (the no-transgression zone) that pilots generally use to monitor spatial separation (and that underlie the precision runway monitor/ final monitor aid).

At the present time, it does not appear that airborne information for lateral spacing and the precision runway monitor have been closely compared with each other or evaluated in head-to-head tests. On one hand, the airborne information for lateral spacing clearly has the advantage of a shorter loop time, because it eliminates the time delays associated with controller detection and voice communications. On the other hand, it may well be that the shortcomings of the precision runway monitor with the longer loop time are more than offset by the greater compliance rate that pilots have in following advisories given by a human controller, than those given by an automated algorithm with a synthetic voice. As noted, the two systems also rely on very different technologies (high-precision radar for the precision runway monitor, and global positioning system and ADS-B for the airborne information for lateral spacing), as well as different algorithms (space-based versus time-based). These differences in technology dependence have important organizational implications should a redundant system involving both ground- and air-based alerts be considered. If the technologies are different, and they provide conflicting advice (as they may on occasion), which should be followed? Indeed, it could be argued that the possible confusion or blurring of responsibility resulting from the implementation of both systems could be counterproductive, leading to certain ambiguous scenarios in which the pilot of one or the other aircraft is uncertain of whether to maneuver.

Conclusion

The precision runway monitor/final monitor aid system has good user acceptance, although with some reservations expressed by highly experienced controllers about the passive-monitoring role of the system operator. Even with runway separation distances reduced to 3,000 feet between dual runways (as approved in November 1995), the incident frequency is likely to be too small to allow the controller to sustain a reasonable level of alertness. More investigation of the duty cycle should be done with this concern in mind. For example, a duty cycle of 1 hour or less might be optimum.

The main areas of ambiguity about human factors considerations are communications and organization. Specific studies are needed to establish the utility and feasibility of the use of audible warning signals to alert pilots to the urgency of the missed approach message. A delay of 10 or more seconds in activating the pull-out maneuver is too long a period when the aircraft has only a few hundred feet of altitude.

Another issue that deserves some further study is the prospect that the flow of arrivals with the precision runway monitor/final monitor aid in operation may saturate the capabilities of the surface controllers, who will also be suffering from restricted visibility, for which the equivalent automated capabilities for surface operations may not be as mature (see the following section).

Finally, it will be extremely important for researchers and system designers to consider the trade-offs between the ground-based (precision runway monitor) and the cockpit-based (airborne information for lateral spacing) systems and the human factors implications of their possible joint use.

AUTOMATION FOR CONFLICT AVOIDANCE ON THE GROUND

Increased automation has been viewed by the FAA as a means of improving airport area safety on the ground. Approximately 200 runway incursions occur each year in the United States (Castaldo et al., 1996). The National Transportation Safety Board (NTSB) has considered the prevention of runway incursions and of ground collisions of aircraft a high-priority safety issue (National Transportation Safety Board, 1995a, 1995b). In response to ground accidents at Atlanta (1990), Detroit (1990), Los Angeles (1991), and St. Louis (1994), the National Transportation Safety Board issued a series of recommendations for the prevention of ground collisions of aircraft. These recommendations included the reiteration of a 1991 recommendation that the FAA "expedite efforts to fund the development and implementation of an operational system analogous to the airborne conflict alert system to alert controllers to pending runway incursions" on the ground (National Transportation Safety Board, 1995b).

To address safety concerns in a manner that may also yield efficiency gains, the FAA is undertaking a broad set of activities that, taken together, are intended to provide controllers and pilots with automated warnings of potential and actual runway incursions and ground traffic conflicts, with automated means of communication, with positive identification of surface targets, and with the capability to maintain situation awareness in low-visibility conditions. These initiatives range from current implementation through near-term enhancement to long-term development programs.

The primary goal of the automation systems for the tower described below is to enhance the safety of airport operations. These systems provide to controllers and, in some cases, to pilots information that augments the current direct visual observations and verbal communications. In addition, these systems are based on surveillance technology that provides information under conditions of poor visibility (National Aeronautics and Space Administration, 1995). As with technologies that improve the availability and accuracy of in-flight position, trajectory, and identification information, these systems may also permit improved efficiency by reducing delays otherwise dictated by less reliable information. Figure 5.2 presents the interrelationships among surveillance, processing, and tower and cockpit display systems.

Airport surface detection equipment (ASDE-3) includes an advanced digital radar that penetrates rain, snow, and fog and provides to controllers a display of superimposed radar images of airplanes and vehicles over a map of the airport surface. It permits controllers in the tower to view a continuous, real-time display of all movements on runways and taxiways in the terminal area. Airport surface detection equipment does not, however, provide identification of targets, so controllers cannot readily identify specific aircraft by looking at the radar display. The controller therefore has to rely on visual contact and voice communication to positively identify aircraft. In addition, the airport surface detection equipment has limitations that include blockage of certain terminal areas and some false returns. The equipment is currently installed in some airports and is targeted for wider implementation.

The airport movement area safety system (AMASS) augments the airport surface detection equipment with an automated alerting system. The airport

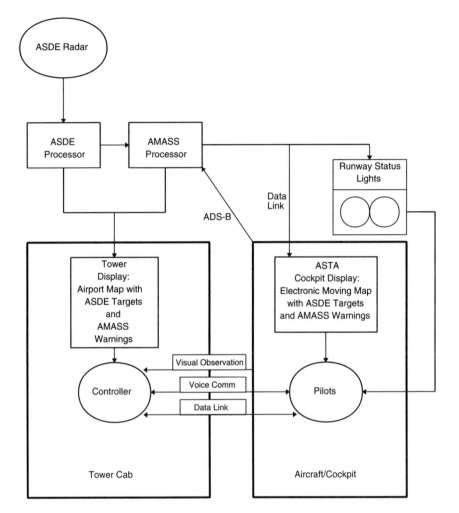

FIGURE 5.2 Elements of systems for monitoring airport area ground traffic.

movement area safety system uses the surface detection equipment data to track ground operations, compare movements of aircraft and ground vehicles, and automatically provide to controllers visual and audio alerts of potential conflicts and of deviation from airport procedures. The airport movement area safety system also provides "runway in use" alerts to controllers when it determines that targets are moving at high speed along a runway. The FAA is accelerating the implementation of airport movement area safety system displays in busy tower environments. Like the airport surface detection equipment, the airport movement area safety system does not provide controllers with identification of targets.

The aircraft target identification system (ATIDS), under study, would use triangulation and automatic dependent surveillance—rather than airport surface detection equipment radar—to pinpoint the location of aircraft on the ground. The airport target identification system would also use the secondary surveillance radar signal (mode A/C/S) to identify aircraft and to provide to controllers call sign information in association with ASDE-3 and AMASS-like target displays (Castaldo et al., 1996; Smith et al., 1996). An aircraft target identification system prototype has been undergoing tests at the Atlanta airport.

Automated aids under consideration include the capability to present displays to pilots that indicate both the situation information provided to controllers and controller instructions. The runway status lights (RWSL) system is a radar-based safety system intended to improve on-airfield situation awareness by providing pilots a visual advisory of runway status. The system consists of a series of "stop/go" lights on the airport surface that indicate to pilots whether it is safe or unsafe to enter or cross a runway or to begin or hold takeoff. The runway status lights system, whose prototype has been undergoing field tests, controls the lights according to target position, status, and logic information derived from the airport movement area safety system. The runway status lights are intended as an independent backup to controllers' assessments and instructions; procedures dictate that, when pilots identify a discrepancy between the lights and controller instructions, pilots must resolve the discrepancy with controllers before proceeding (Architecture Technology Corporation, 1996; Federal Aviation Administration, 1996d).

The airport surface traffic automation (ASTA) system would extend the mode S surface surveillance system to provide a two-way data link between the tower and the cockpit. The system may introduce into the cockpit an electronic moving map display that provides to pilots the target position, identification, and movement information presented to controllers, as well as the airport movement area safety system and controller instructions and alerts (Architecture Technology Corporation, 1996; Jones and Young, 1996; National Aeronautics and Space Administration, 1995). The airport surface traffic automation system is currently undergoing in-field prototype testing.

Enhancements to cockpit displays, integrated with the airport surface traffic automation system, may also permit improvements in the efficiency of taxiway navigation. The taxi navigation and situation awareness (T-NASA) system, under development for NASA's terminal area productivity (TAP) low-visibility landing and surface operations (LVLAS) program, is intended to support the goals of increased nonvisual ground capacity, runway occupancy time for instrument flight rules equivalent to that for clear weather, and maintenance of safety (National Aeronautics and Space Administration, 1997a). The T-NASA system includes three features intended to provide situation awareness to pilots during taxi: (1) an electronic moving map display that provides a layout of the airport, own ship position, positions of other traffic, graphical route guidance, and heading and clearance indicators; (2) a head-up display that projects symbology, correlated with a virtual out-the-window scene, displaying scene enhancements (e.g., center line markers) and scene augmentations (e.g., virtual turn signs and taxiway edge cones) as well as commanded taxiway indicators and other data; and (3) a three-dimensional audio ground collision and warning system that provides auditory warnings that include indication of the direction of approaching aircraft (Foyle et al., 1996; McCann et al., 1996, 1997; Bryant, 1993; National Aeronautics and Space Administration, 1997b, 1997c). The T-NASA system is under development; its conceptual designs are being evaluated by simulation studies and field tests at Atlanta's Hartsfield Airport.

Human Factors Implementation

There has been an encouraging general trend in the arena of airport surface automation toward earlier user and human factors involvement, coupled with a "build a little, test a little" development philosophy that includes earlier evaluations using mixed methodologies (discussed in Chapter 8). The development of the AMASS system, at its inception, was delayed by failure to structure the inputs of users, representing the air traffic requirements office and controllers, and failure to apply human factors analyses in the earliest requirements definition phases, resulting in "requirements creep" that prevented the timeliest implementation of this valuable system (National Transportation Safety Board, 1995a). Now, however, the refinement of the AMASS is supported by a MITRE Corporation laboratory, where AMASS logic and displays are prototyped and concepts are demonstrated and tested (MITRE, 1997a). The runway status lights system also underwent prototype evaluations with user involvement before its ongoing operational assessment at Boston's Logan Airport (Architecture Technology Corporation, 1996).

The ASTA and TAP T-NASA programs have both involved controllers, pilots, and human factors professionals during analyses and concept development. Their involvement is also evident in ongoing and planned evaluations that are supported by modeling (e.g., NASA Ames' Air-MIDAS model, Pisanich and Corker, 1997), by simulation (Pisanich et al., 1994; Foyle et al., 1996; McCann et al., 1996, 1997; Bryant, 1993), and by flight demonstrations (Mejdrich, 1995).

Human Factors Issues

Trust

Both the introduction of runway status lights and the addition of new surveillance technologies introduce related considerations of reliability, redundancy, and trust that can have serious implications for the usability and effectiveness of the system. The runway status lights are planned as a backup safety net—a check against controller error. Similarly, should the lights be in error, the controller is expected to serve as a cross-check. Pilots will be expected to compare the instructions presented by the lights (e.g., taxi hold) against those communicated by the controller. The assumption is that when the instructions from the lights disagree with those from the controller, one of the two sources of instruction represents an error that has been caught by the other. The converse assumption is that when both sources of instruction are in agreement, a double-check is in evidence. These assumptions would tend to increase pilots' trust in the overall system, even if trust in one of the instruction sources (lights or controller) decreases.

However, these assumptions are questionable. A double-check by redundant sources requires that the observation by each source is independent. In the present case, however, the runway lights are driven by the sensors and logic of the airport surface detection equipment/airport movement area safety system displays, which includes information presented to the controller. If the controller's instructions are also based on the airport surface detection equipment/airport movement area safety system displays, then the controller and the runway lights do not serve as independent double-checks. Rather, both the controller and the pilot are, in this case, trusting the same system.

Even when independent observations occur, dual redundancy cannot always be presumed to yield a trustworthy result. For example, airport area automation plans include the introduction of ADS-B surveillance and communication technology, which may provide observations of aircraft position in addition to those provided by surface radar. If the observations from ADS-B conflict with those of the surface radar, the result is a "two-sensor problem." Which observation is to be trusted? The general solution is to provide a third sensor (e.g., controller direct observation or confirmation with the pilot).

At issue in each case is the distinction between trust in the system and trust in its components. Although individual components may vary in their trustworthiness (which may change over time), a thorough understanding of the capabilities of each component as well as how the components work together (e.g., whether they serve as independent sources of information and when the system relies more on one than on the others) is required to permit pilots and controllers to develop an appropriate level of trust in the system. This argues against any temptation to "dumb down" training of automation systems and argues for training that provides a useful and appropriately detailed mental model of how the system works.

Mental Models, Situation Awareness, and Loss of Skill

As noted in Chapter 1, one of the greatest causes of mistrust or misapplied trust is the inability of operators to develop mental models appropriate to the system and task at hand in order to maintain situation awareness. Both controllers and pilots will be expected to develop mental models and maintain situation awareness pertinent to the prevention of ground accidents and runway incursions (i.e., awareness of the current and near-term positions and movements of aircraft and vehicles, as well as immediate controller intentions and instructions).

Lasswell and Wickens (1995) distinguished between local and global awareness in connection with taxi operations. Local guidance refers to the control task of maneuvering the aircraft along a route; global awareness refers to the task of maintaining position awareness relative to the gate and other airport features. To provide both forms of situation awareness, Lasswell and Wickens recommended displays that provide both an egocentric (pilot eyepoint) forward view, supplying local guidance, and a plan view supplying global awareness information. The designers of the T-NASA system have adopted this recommendation (Foyle et al., 1996; McCann et al., 1997), providing a head-up display that enhances local visual guidance cues, and a head-down display that augments global awareness cues (although the separate head-up/head-down display configuration represents a distinct design decision).

As noted in Chapter 1, it is often the case that operators are less aware of the changes of state made by other agents than of changes they make themselves. Particularly when system automation (e.g., improved surveillance accuracy coupled with sophisticated airport movement area safety system logic) permits more complex activities (e.g., the movement of greater numbers of aircraft), the risk of operator complacency—or of simply being unable to keep up with automated actions—and associated loss of situation awareness is introduced. The loss of situation awareness may be accompanied by degradation of skills, if the operator has not maintained proficiency in tasks that are normally performed by the automation. The combination of loss of situation awareness and skill degradation can result in the operator's inability to respond adequately to the failure of the automation. This general theme is central to this report, and it is reemphasized here because airport area automation may become extensive in the future (e.g., enhancements to the airport area movement safety system encouraging more low-visibility operations; runway lights duplicating controller functions; and automated schedulers recommending high-efficiency actions). On that account, each new automation feature should be evaluated for its impact on situation awareness, controllers should be trained to maintain proficiency in automated tasks whenever they are expected to be able to perform those tasks in response to automation failures, and the capability of controllers to manage the complexities permitted by automation should be evaluated.

Teams

Airport area automation holds the potential for changing the roles of controllers and pilots. The introduction of runway status lights and of cockpit electronic moving maps (providing to flight crews information similar to that provided to controllers through the airport surface detection equipment/airport movement area safety system display) increases shared responsibility for ground control between controllers and pilots. The implications of shared responsibility and authority, and the importance of clear and effective associated procedures, is discussed in detail in the earlier sections of this chapter and in Chapter 9 in the discussion of free flight.

Effects of Combining Systems

Chapter 8 discusses in detail the importance of considering the human factors implications of both phased and simultaneous implementation of two or more automated functions. The combination of automation features can potentially introduce effects that are not predicted from studies or tests of each feature independently. Airport surface automation includes contemplated introduction of additions or changes to surveillance technology, addition of features to airport surface detection equipment and airport movement area safety system displays, and simultaneous presentation to pilots of runway status lights and controller instructions (through visual as well as voice communication). The general guidance presented in Chapter 8 applies here: each change introduced should be studied within the operational context, taking into account all other changes introduced, and the evolution of changes should be centrally monitored and coordinated by a human factors research and development oversight organization.

Conclusion

To address both safety and efficiency concerns, the FAA is undertaking a set of activities that, taken together, is intended to provide controllers and pilots with automated warnings of potential and actual runway incursions and ground traffic conflicts, with automated means of communication, and with the capability to maintain situation awareness in low-visibility conditions. These initiatives range from current implementation through near-term enhancement to long-term development programs.

The combination of automation features can potentially introduce effects that are not predicted from studies or tests of each feature independently. This may be particularly true to the extent that pilot and controller are receiving redundant sources of information. Also at issue is the distinction between trust in the system and trust in its components. Individual components may vary in their trustworthiness (which may change over time). A thorough understanding of the capabilities of each component as well as how the components work together is required to permit pilots and controllers to develop an appropriate level of trust in the system. In addition, since these new systems are specifically intended as safety enhancements and may also be used to increase usage of airport surface capacity, it is particularly important that controllers and pilots are able to respond effectively to system failures, including those that regress the system to lower levels of automation.

6

Strategic Long-Range Planning

Ⅰn this chapter, we provide an analysis of the human factors issues associated with four automation efforts designed to facilitate strategic air traffic control: the center TRACON automation system, the automated conflict probe, the development of four-dimensional contracts, and the surface movement advisor. As we did in the previous chapter, we analyze each piece of automation in terms of the functions performed, the context for development, and the human factors issues.

CENTER TRACON AUTOMATION SYSTEM

Functionality

The primary objective of the center TRACON automation system (CTAS) is to assist the air traffic controller in optimizing the traffic flow in the terminal area (Erzberger et al., 1993). Delays are reduced and flight paths are flown in a more economical fashion so that potential fuel savings are estimated to range from 45 to 135 kg per landing (Scott, 1994). These benefits are accomplished by providing assistance in planning and control in both routine and unexpected circumstances (e.g., changes in runway configuration). CTAS is also capable of providing advice to controllers regarding particular airline preferences. CTAS is comprised of three separate tools or elements, each supporting different classes of air traffic control personnel, located in different facilities, and coordinating different phases of the approach (Figure 6.1):

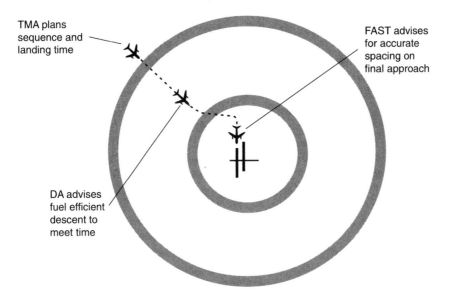

TMA plans
sequence and
landing time

FAST advises
for accurate
spacing on
final approach

DA advises
fuel efficient
descent to
meet time

FIGURE 6.1 Elements of the center TRACON automation system (CTAS). Source: National Aeronautics and Space Administration.

1. The *traffic management advisor* (TMA) supports the TRACON and en route traffic management controllers, primarily in developing an optimal *plan*, to assign each aircraft a *scheduled time of arrival* at a downstream point, like a final approach fix or runway threshold, and a *sequence of arrival*, relative to other aircraft approaching the terminal area. The traffic management advisor begins to compute these for inbound aircraft at a point about 200 miles or 45 minutes from the final approach. The plan is designed to optimize the overall flow of the set of aircraft, as well as the fuel consumption of each individual aircraft. At the same time, it accounts for various constraints on runway availability and aircraft maneuverability. The plan is also accompanied by an assessment of flight path changes to be implemented in order to accomplish the plan. A set of three displays assists the traffic management coordinator in evaluating the plan (Figure 6.2, see color plate). These include a time line of scheduled and estimated times of arrivals for the aircraft, a listing of alternative runway configurations, and a load graph, which indicates the anticipated traffic load across designated points in the airspace in 15-minute increments. The displays can be presented in large-screen formats for group viewing (Figure 6.3, see color plate). The actual implementation of the plan generated by the traffic management coordinator with the assistance of the traffic management advisor is carried out by the other two elements of CTAS, the descent advisor, and the final approach spacing tool.

2. The *descent advisor* (DA) provides controllers at the final sector of the en

route center with advice on proper speed, altitude, and (occasionally) heading control necessary to accomplish the plan generated by the traffic management advisor. The critical algorithm underlying the descent advisor is a four-dimensional predictor that is individually tailored for each aircraft, based on that aircraft's type and preferred maneuver, along with local atmospheric data. This predictor generates a set of possible trajectories for the aircraft to implement the traffic management advisor plan. The descent advisor then provides the controller with a set of advisories regarding speed, top of descent point, and descent speed. In cases in which these parameters are not sufficient to accomplish the plan, *path stretching* advisories are offered that advise lateral maneuvers. The descent advisor also contains a conflict probe that will monitor for possible conflicts up to 20 minutes ahead. If such conflicts are detected, it will offer resolution advisories, based initially on speed and altitude changes. If none of these is feasible, lateral maneuvers will be offered as a solution.

Figure 6.4 (see color plate) illustrates the descent advisor display. Controllers read the advice of the descent advisor on the fourth line of the data tag for each aircraft. In addition, markers on the plan view displays indicate the location at which flight path trajectory changes should be issued. Time lines, similar to those provided by the traffic management advisor, are also available at the side of the display.

3. The *final approach spacing tool* (FAST) is the corresponding advisory tool designed to support the TRACON controller in implementing the traffic management advisor plan, by issuing speed and heading advisories and runway assignments necessary to maintain optimal spacing between aircraft of different classes (Davis et al., 1994; Lee and Davis, 1995). An important secondary function of the final approach spacing tool is its ability to rapidly adjust to—and reschedule on the basis of—unexpected events like a missed approach or a sudden unexpected runway closure. Like the descent advisor, the controller receives advice in the fourth line of the data tag, and also has access to time lines (Figure 6.5, see color plate). The final approach spacing tool exists in two versions: the passive FAST provides only aircraft sequence and runway assignments, and the active FAST includes speed and heading advisories.

A system with similar functions, known as COMPAS (computer-oriented metering planning and advisory system), was developed by the German Aerospace Research Establishment and has been operational in Frankfurt since 1991 (Völckers, 1991). The system attempts to assist the controller in the planning and control of approach traffic. Based on flight plans and radar data, the system calculates the arrival time of each aircraft, taking into consideration such parameters as aircraft performance, traffic proximity, and wake vortex separation minima. On the basis of these calculated arrival times, the system establishes a landing sequence, as well as a nominal gate arrival time for each aircraft. The difference between the calculated time and the nominal time is then transformed into a medium-term plan by which traffic flow can be smoothed, starting outside the terminal area. The goal of this plan is to reduce aggregate delay across the entire traffic stream.

The interface for the COMPAS presents the controller with a sequencing time line, with arrivals ordered from latest to earliest, top to bottom. The time associated with each aircraft represents the estimated arrival time, over either the metering fix (in the case of the en route controller) or the approach gate (for the approach controller). Aircraft weight class and approach direction are represented in the display. The control advisories themselves are presented as one of four possible characters beside the aircraft label: X to expedite up to two minutes, O for no action, R for delay up to four minutes, and H to hold for more than four minutes.

Operational experience with COMPAS has demonstrated reductions in planning and coordination workload, as well as reductions in the time spent on coordination and smoothing of the traffic flow in the terminal area.

Notice that COMPAS provides general resolution advisories (e.g., "hold for more than four minutes"); the descent advisor of CTAS provides another level of assistance—namely, the specific action by which a conflict should be resolved (e.g., "descend to flight level 70").

History

The main impetus toward the development of CTAS has been the loss of capacity in airport arrival and landings. Limitations in prediction of trajectories and weather have led to spaces on the final approaches that are not occupied by an aircraft, thus creating delays or not meeting the actual capabilities of an airport's true capacity. In the 1980s, the National Aeronautics and Space Administration (NASA) and the Federal Aviation Administration Technical Center began an in-house research and development project to develop the software tools for achieving this optimization (Erzberger and Tobias, 1986), working closely with controllers and human factors professionals to create a fielded system. During the mid-1990s, this system has received several field tests at Dallas-Fort Worth International Airport and at the Denver airport and center. It is also being installed at Schiphol Airport in Amsterdam, the Netherlands.

Human Factors Implementation

Human factors has played a relatively important role in the maturation of CTAS, from concept, to laboratory prototype, to simulation, to field test (Erzberger and Tobias, 1986; Tobias et al., 1989; Harwood et al., in press). From 1992 to 1997, approximately 30,000 person hours of human factors expertise have been devoted to CTAS development and fielding. In part, the successful implementation of the human factors input was a result of the fact that the development took place at NASA laboratories, with ready access to human factors professionals and active participation of controllers in developing the specifications. The development was not under constraints related to contract delivery time or required specifications. Human factors implementation was also facilitated in part by the frequent input of controllers to the design concepts of functions at all phases and frequent human-in-the-loop evaluations at varying levels of simulation fidelity. The controller's input was filtered by human factors professionals (Lee and Davis, 1995; Harwood et al., in press).

Another important factor is that these evaluations (and system changes based thereon) have continued as the system is being field tested at the Dallas and Denver facilities (Harwood et al., in press). In particular, developers realized the need for extensive input from a team of controllers at the facility, in order to tailor the system to facility-specific characteristics. The introduction process was quite time-consuming, taking place over several years. This proved necessary (and advantageous), both in order to secure inputs from controllers at all levels, and also in order for human factors professionals and engineers on the design team to thoroughly familiarize themselves with the culture and operating procedures at the Denver and Dallas-Fort Worth facilities; this, in turn, was necessary in order for the trust of the operational controllers to be gained and for the CTAS advisories to be employed successfully.

It is also important to note that the system was designed to have a minimal effect on the existing automated systems (HOST and the automated radar terminal system, ARTS) and on existing procedures. Finally, it should be stressed that CTAS is presented to controllers with the philosophy that it is an advisory aid, designed to improve their capabilities, rather than as an automation replacement. That is, nothing in CTAS qualitatively alters the way in which controllers implement their control over the aircraft.

Human Factors Issues

Cognitive Task Analysis

A cognitive task analysis reveals that CTAS supports the controller's task in three critical respects, addressing the vulnerabilities identified in the panel's Phase I report. First, its four-dimensional predictive capabilities compensate for difficulties that the unaided controller will have in predicting and visualizing the long-term (i.e., five minutes) implications of multiple, complex, speed-varying trajectories subjected to various constraints, such as fuel consumption, winds, and runway configuration. With the current system, these limits of the unaided human constrain the flexibility of considering a variety of traffic plans. Second, its interactive planning and scheduling capabilities allow multiple solutions to be evaluated off-line, with the graphics feedback available in the time lines, to facilitate the choice of plans. Here also the system supports the workload-intensive aspects of planning (Johannsen and Rouse, 1983; Tulga and Sheridan, 1980), particularly prevalent when multiple plans need to be compared. Finally, CTAS, particularly the final approach spacing tool, supports the controller's ability to deal with the high workload imposed by unexpected and complex events, characterized for example by a missed approach or an unanticipated runway closure. The first and second of these tasks primarily affect the efficiency of system performance, whereas the latter appears to have direct and beneficial safety implications.

Workload

A stated objective of CTAS is that it will not increase controller workload; indeed, field tests of the system reveal that this criterion has been met (Harwood et al., in press). As noted above, CTAS has the potential to reduce workload during the "spikes" imposed by unexpected scheduling and spacing requirements due to a missed approach or closed runway. However, it is also the case that workload may be shifted somewhat with the introduction of CTAS. Relying on an added channel of display information, rather than the controller's own mental judgment, may impose an increase in visual workload. In fact, any new set of procedures (such as those associated with CTAS) would be likely to impose some transient workload increase.

Finally, although not yet reported, a tool such as CTAS does have the potential of advising maneuvers that create an airspace considerably more complex than that viewed under unaided conditions (Wyndemere, 1996). In such a case, controller monitoring and perceptual workload may be increased by the controller's effort to maintain a full level of situation awareness of the more complex airspace, an issue that we revisit later in this chapter and in Chapter 10.

Training

The general approach to CTAS is to first provide simulation, then provide a shadowing of the real traffic off-line in the system. In the shadowing mode, CTAS elements provide the advice, and the controller can compare clearances that he or she might provide on the basis of that advice with clearances more typical of an unadvised controller and evaluate the differences (Lee and Davis, 1995). The controller can then determine the rationale behind the automated advisory. This builds confidence that the computer can provide advice to maintain separation. One might anticipate the need for some training of pilots regarding the CTAS system, not because procedures are altered, but because the nature of the clearances and instructions may be changed, relative to the more standardized, space-based approaches (i.e., using the standard terminal arrival system) in a non-CTAS facility.

Communication and Coordination

Because of the philosophy by which the traffic management advisor plans are implemented via the descent advisor and the final approach spacing tool advisories, CTAS imposes a relatively heavy communication load between operators and facilities. This is supported via digital data transfer rather than voice communications. Furthermore, the philosophy of repeated displays across different environments (e.g., the time line seen in Figure 6.2) supports greater communications and coordination between operators, in that these can better support a shared situation awareness of the implications of different schedules. The extent to which ground-air communications are altered by CTAS remains unclear. At least one field study of the final approach spacing tool (Harwood et al., 1997), carried out at the Dallas Airport over a 6-month period indicated that the system imposed no increase in overall communications, although the nature of the communications was altered somewhat, involving more messages pertaining to runway assignments and sequencing.

Automation Issues

CTAS is sufficiently recent in its introduction that there has not been time to identify specific human factors automation issues on the basis of operational experience (e.g., operational errors or aviation safety reporting system incidents). However, analysis of system capabilities suggests at least some of these that may surface.

Mode Errors

CTAS does contain some multimode operations. For example, with the descent advisor, controllers can choose a route intercept or a waypoint capture mode for individual aircraft, as well as one of three possible speed control modes for all aircraft (Erzberger and Nedell, 1989). However, the system appears to be designed so that different modes are prominently displayed, and active decisions must be carried out to change modes, so that mode errors would appear to be very unlikely.

Mistrust

There would appear to be a real possibility that the advice offered by CTAS could be initially mistrusted by controllers if it differed substantially from the way in which control is typically accomplished. It would seem that such trust must be carefully built through careful training with both simulated and live traffic. Indeed, Harwood et al. (in press) noted the increase in controller confidence after they had used the system (and relied on the final approach spacing tool advice) with live traffic. This provided the opportunity to see the real improvement in traffic flow (13 percent) that was achieved.

FIGURE 6.2 Center TRACON automation system (CTAS) traffic management advisor (TMA) display. Source: National Aeronautics and Space Administration.

FIGURE 6.3 Center TRACON automation system (CTAS) traffic management advisor (TMA) large screen displays. Source: National Aeronautics and Space Administration.

FIGURE 6.4 Center TRACON automation system (CTAS) descent advisor (DA) display. Source: National Aeronautics and Space Administration.

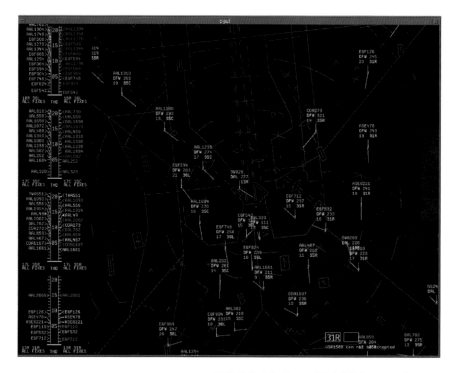

FIGURE 6.5 Center TRACON automation system (CTAS) final approach spacing tool (FAST) display. Source: National Aeronautics and Space Administration.

FIGURE 6.6 Center TRACON automation
system (CTAS) conflict probe display. Source:
National Aeronautics and Space Administration.

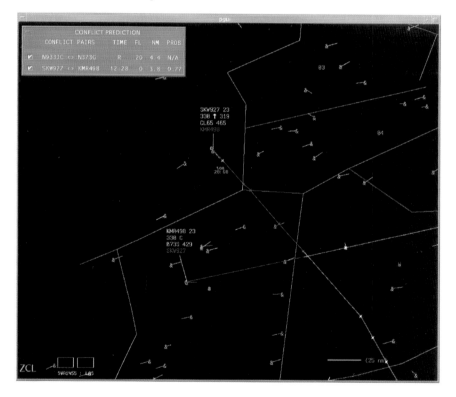

FIGURE 6.8 User request evaluation tool (URET) at controller's workstation. Source: Photo courtesy of the MITRE Corporation.

FIGURE 6.9 User request evaluation tool
(URET) display. Source: Photo courtesy of
the MITRE Corporation.

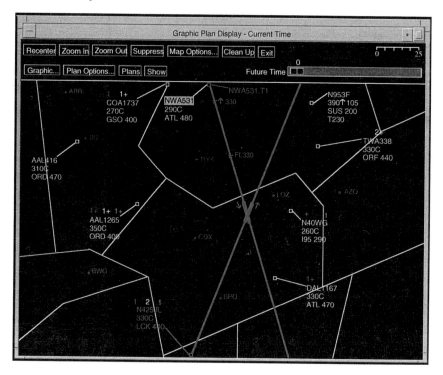

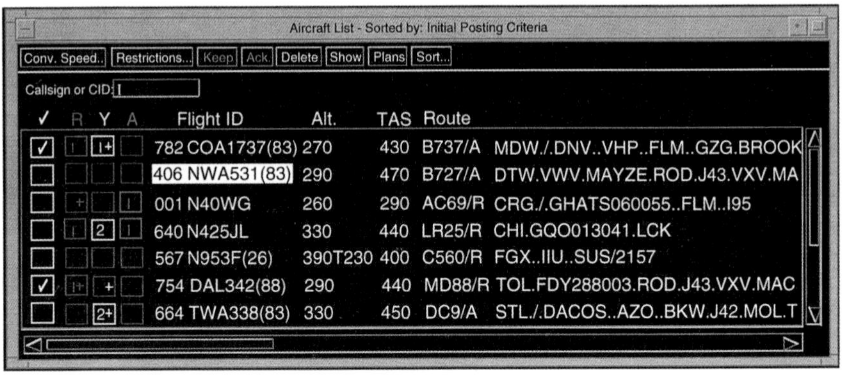

FIGURE 6.10 User request evaluation tool (URET) list display. Source: Photo courtesy of the MITRE Corporation.

Overtrust and Complacency

Currently, the philosophy of system implementation safeguards against undue complacency. This is because controllers must still give the actual clearances orally, as they would in a nonaided situation. Hence, they remain more likely to actively think about those clearances, for example, than they would in a system in which clearances could be relayed via data link with a simple keystroke (i.e., automation of response execution in Chapter 1). Complacency is not generally recognized as a concern until an incident of automation failure occurs, in which the human's failure to intervene or resume control appropriately is attributed to such complacency. No such incidents have been observed with CTAS. The advice-giving algorithms were thoroughly tested, and in operational trials have yet to fail; alternatively, if inappropriate advice was ever provided, controllers were sufficiently noncomplacent that they chose to ignore it. In short, the system has been in use for an insufficient time for trust to reach the possible excessive level at which it could be described as complacency.

Past experience with other systems indicates that systems can fail, in ways that cannot be foreseen in advance (e.g., the software does not anticipate a particular unusual circumstance). Furthermore, despite the design philosophy that appears to keep the controller a relatively active participant in the control loop, it is also the case that the primary objective of CTAS is to increase the efficiency (and therefore saturation) of the terminal airspace. Such a circumstance would make recovery more difficult, should problems emerge for which CTAS would be unable to offer reliable advice.

Skill Degradation

As with complacency, so with skill degradation: CTAS has not been used long enough to determine whether this is an issue. Yet it is easy to imagine circumstances in which controllers increasingly begin to rely on CTAS advice, relaying this as instructions to pilots, losing the skills at selecting maneuvers on their own. This may be more problematic still, to the extent that the maneuvers recommended by CTAS are qualitatively different from those that would previously have been issued by unaided controllers. At this time, a clear tabulation of maneuver differences with and without CTAS has not been carried out.

Organization

The organizational implications of CTAS remain uncertain. A strength of the system is that it is designed to be advisory only; by not directly affecting required procedures, the negative impact on organizational functioning should be minimized. However, it is possible that subtle shifts in authority from the R-side controller to the D-side (who is more likely to have direct access to CTAS advisories) could have unpredictable consequences. We explore these consequences further in the discussion of conflict probes in the following section.

Conclusion

CTAS appears to be a well-conceived automation concept, addressing a valid concern of the less automated system and designed with an appropriate philosophy that is based on automated advice-giving, rather than automation-based control. As such it is characterized by a relatively low point on the level of automation action scale, discussed in Chapter 1, which accordingly diminishes (but does not eliminate) the extent of concern for complacency. Finally, CTAS has been developed and introduced gradually, in a manner sensitive to human factors issues, and to the importance of filtered controller input into the functioning of the system. Careful human factors monitoring of the system's field use should be continued.

CONFLICT PROBE AND INTERACTIVE PLANNING

The core of the controller's job is to maintain a continuous flow of air traffic while also preserving adequate separation. There are three interrelated automation functionalities that can potentially assist in these goals: conflict probes, interactive planning tools, and conflict resolution advisors. The conflict probe is essentially a preview of the current flight trajectory of a given aircraft, to assess whether it will create a loss of separation with another aircraft at some time in the future. Current probes exist in the ARTS and HOST computer systems, yielding alerts if conflicts are predicted (discussed in Chapter 4). Similar conflict probe logic also characterizes the TCAS system (discussed in Chapter 5). These current air traffic control probes are not sophisticated, in the sense that their predictive logic is based on an extrapolation of the current ground velocity (or, in the case of TCAS, the rate of closure). They may also be described as tactical, in that they forecast only a short duration (i.e., a few minutes or less) into the future.

In contrast, however, far more intelligent probes, such as those embedded in CTAS, can include models of different aircraft capabilities, head winds, and even flight plans, to more accurately estimate the future four-dimensional trajectory of the aircraft. Smart probes, such as those incorporated into CTAS and COMPAS are far more strategic in nature, allowing much longer look-aheads. Figure 6.6 illustrates a CTAS conflict probe display (see color plate). It should be noted, however, that, although systems such as COMPAS and CTAS are highly sophisticated conflict resolution systems, they leave the final authority for implementing that resolution squarely with the human. Some other development efforts over the years (e.g., the U.S. AERA system, the European ARC2000 developed by Eurocontrol) have not always embraced the same approach and have investigated the potential for fully automated conflict resolution. The ARC2000 program, for example, sought to develop a fully automated strategic resolution system. Although the development of efficient conflict resolution algorithms proved somewhat difficult, the ARC2000 is directly credited with the development of later PHARE tools (such as the PHARE HIPS, described below).

Any conflict probe is by definition based on a prediction of future behavior of the aircraft involved. Such prediction or intent inferencing must of necessity be imperfect, and it will be more so, the farther into the future that behavior is predicted. Hence, a conflict probe should be able to differentiate most likely scenarios from worst-case scenarios, the former being defined by the best guess on future behavior, and the latter being defined by the margins of uncertainty if the two aircraft maneuver toward a conflict. This uncertainty can either be portrayed graphically and continuously over time (Figure 6.7), or discretely, at a given time horizon (often selected as 20 minutes).

Once a conflict is probed and identified, it must then be negotiated. Automation has the capability of providing two further services to assist with this negotiation. Computers can recommend a course of action to resolve the conflict (automated *conflict resolution*), or they can provide interactive graphical tools as a decision aid, to assist controllers in developing a solution themselves to resolve the conflict.

Using the framework presented at the beginning of Chapter 1, we note that conflict resolution is a higher level of automation than tool-based decision aiding. Ironically, however, air traffic control has proceeded more directly to implementing conflict resolution than to providing interactive tools for decision aiding. For example, we note that CTAS and COMPAS both employ automation to formulate recommended solutions for the controller to either accept (and implement through traditional procedures) or reject, and both are in active service at certain airports (Frankfurt, Denver, Dallas-Fort Worth). A less mature level of development characterizes interactive decision aids, two of which we describe in some detail below: the user request evaluation tool developed for use in the United States and the highly interactive problem solver (HIPS) developed by Eurocontrol.

User Request Evaluation Tool

Functionality

The user request evaluation tool (URET), developed by the MITRE Corporation for assistance to the en route controller, provides a conflict probe based on a 20-minute look-ahead capability (Brudnicki et al., 1996). The probe is a "smart" one, accounting for different flight plans, aircraft models (i.e., flight capabilities), and anticipated head winds, in determining the best estimate of each aircraft's

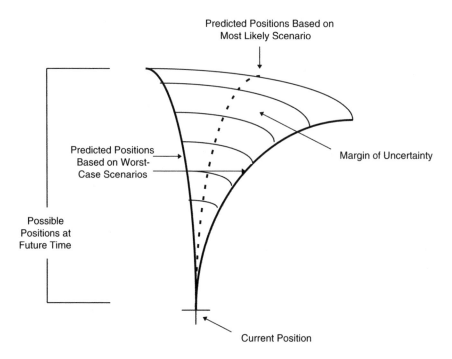

FIGURE 6.7 Margin of uncertainty in conflict probe prediction.

position 20 minutes into the future. (It does not, however, take into account any future flight plans based on scheduled mode changes in a flight management system).

The results of the probe are displayed to the D-side controller in two modes: a graphic mode portrays the flight path on a large-scale electronic map (Figure 6.8, see color plate). Projected flight paths are color-coded: a red code indicates a likely future conflict, and an amber code indicates a possible conflict (Figure 6.9, see color plate). The latter represents a wider bound of uncertainty of future behavior. A tabular mode, visible concurrently, characterizes each aircraft by a line of text portraying flight information; it will also color-code any pair of aircraft involved in a predicted conflict (Figure 6.10, see color plate).

The key interactive feature of the user request evaluation tool is the *planning mode*, which allows the D-side controller to play what-if scenarios by graphically examining the implications of alternative instructions that could be given to one or both aircraft. Thus, for example, a controller might see that a current predicted conflict can be eliminated by increasing the air speed of one of the aircraft by 30 knots. The recommended change can then be suggested to the R-side controller, who may then choose to implement the instructions. Clear and salient indications are provided on the display to show that it is in the planning mode (i.e., that changed flight paths have not actually been provided to the aircraft in question).

Human Factors Implementation

As developed at the MITRE Corporation, the user request evaluation tool received a substantial amount of input from controllers in specifying both functionality and the interface, and such input was guided by human factors professionals. Equally important, current field tests, now under way at the Indianapolis Center, are being closely monitored by human factors personnel to evaluate both strengths and deficiencies of the system in operational use (Brudnicki et al., 1996; Brudnicki and McFarland, 1997).

The field evaluation at Indianapolis was preceded by providing four teams of three controllers with 16 hours of training on the system. A series of tests were then carried out, with R-side and D-side controllers advised by the third controller on the team working with the user request evaluation tool. The study revealed that the tool was positively evaluated by the controllers, and all felt that it could be easily used by the D-side controller. Use of the tool resulted in fewer maneuvers instructed to the aircraft with no loss of separation and greater efficiency. This difference resulted because the longer (and more accurate) look-ahead capability of the user request evaluation tool would often reveal that current trajectories were conflict free, whereas the unaided controller, behaving conservatively, might judge that the same trajectories could generate a conflict and hence instruct a maneuver. In this regard, the user request evaluation tool nicely supported and augmented the predictive capabilities of the human controller (see the Phase I report).

A second, less expected observed benefit was that the user request evaluation tool enabled controllers to more efficiently assess pilot requests for preferred routes and deviations, since a quick interaction with the planning aid could determine if such a request was conflict free.

Programme for Harmonised Air Traffic Management Research in Eurocontrol Demonstration Tool Set

In Europe, PHARE (Programme for Harmonised Air Traffic Management Research in Eurocontrol) is developing a research set of integrated tools, designed to assist the controller in determining and ensuring conflict-free and efficient trajectories. The system is based on a concept of closed-loop four-dimensional trajectory negotiation and control, whereby sophisticated air and ground systems can negotiate a suitable trajectory, and an airborne flight management system can issue appropriate clearances to track the agreed trajectory (Maignan, 1994). Principal developments of PHARE include an experimental flight management system, advanced data link capability, and a set of advanced controller tools. A phased development of the PHARE demonstration tool set is taking place, with the three consecutive phases focusing on en route, terminal, and multisector operations, respectively. Among the core set of PHARE automation tools (as embodied in the en route interface) is the highly interactive problem solver (HIPS), which is increasingly referred to as the PHARE Advanced Tools (PATS) Problem Solver.

Functionality

The highly interactive problem solver is a sophisticated interface tool that permits the controller to view, edit, negotiate, and approve trajectories (National Air Traffic Services, 1996). The other PHARE advanced tools are not directly visible to the controller; instead, he or she interacts with these other tools through the HIPS interface. HIPS takes the form of both profile and plan view display windows, in which time-related conflict regions are graphically represented as "blobs" that the controller must separate. A controller can use HIPS to assess a trajectory, generate an alternative clearance, or modify an existing clearance (via altitude, heading, or speed modifications).

The developmental PHARE en route interface, including the HIPS, is shown in Figure 6.11. When the flight path monitoring algorithm predicts a loss of separation between two (or more) aircraft, the HIPS display presents the time-weighted (four-dimensional) conflict zones as red regions (potential conflict regions are color-coded yellow). A loss of separation occurs whenever an aircraft's predicted trajectory passes through any region of potential conflict, known as no-go zones or, more commonly, blobs. Using HIPS, the controller is then able to implement prospective solutions using one of three possible maneuver spaces (altitude, speed, or heading). Resolving the conflict thus involves mouse-dragging aircraft in one of the maneuver windows, so as to physically separate red blobs, which in turn (once the solution is accepted) triggers the issuance of an appropriate clearance. Since controllers are free to implement solutions in any maneuver space, the HIPS concept permits alternative control strategies. Furthermore, it provides salient and immediate feedback on the utility of various strategies. For example, a controller can compare the efficiency of a heading-versus speed-based solution, before actually implementing either.

Human Factors Implementation

Human factors considerations appear to have been paramount at all stages of the HIPS development (Jorna, 1997). Although elements of the system were inspired by the earlier ARC2000 European prototype system, unlike its predecessor HIPS does not implement automatic conflict resolution. Instead, HIPS is explicitly based on a human-centered approach and, like the user request evaluation tool described above, tries to keep the controller in the loop by restructuring

FIGURE 6.11 PHARE HIPS display. Source: Eurocontrol (1997). The copyright vests in the European Organisation for the Safety of Air Navigation (EUROCONTROL); the CENA (Centre d'études de la navigation aérienne); the STNA (Service technique de la navigation aérienne); the NLR (Nationaal Lucht- en Ruimtevaartlaboratorium); the RLD (Rijksluchtvaartdienst); the LVB (Luchtverkeersbeveiliging); the DLR (Deutsche Forschungsanstalt für Luft- und Raumfahrt); the DFS (Deutsche Flugsicherung GmbH); the UK CAA (Civil Aviation Authority); the NATS (National Air Traffic Services), and the DRA (Defence Research Agency).

the data in a way that facilitates strategic air traffic management decisions. Under HIPS, such decisions remain very much the domain of the air traffic controller.

Empirical trials of the initial PHARE en route system were carried out during late 1995 in the United Kingdom, using 32 active controllers from eight different European air traffic control organizations (National Air Traffic Services, 1996). The trials were aimed at evaluating the effects of both the PHARE advanced tool set and the presence of advanced (4-D-capable, data link-equipped) aircraft, in terms of controller workload, traffic throughput, and situation awareness.

Subjective workload data suggest that the PHARE advanced tools may beneficially redistribute workload between the tactical and the planning controller (under baseline conditions, reported workload had been higher for the tactical than for the planning controller), albeit at the cost of higher total team workload. Survey data revealed that, overall, controllers were very positive about the display aspects of the PHARE system. Although controllers gave the advanced tools mixed reviews in general, they were extremely enthusiastic about HIPS. In terms of flight efficiency, the full PHARE scenario (advanced tools combined with advanced aircraft capability) yielded better flight-level-request performance (that is, aircraft spent a significantly greater percentage of time at or near their requested flight level) than either the baseline or the advanced tools condition. The data did not, however, reveal hypothesized situation awareness benefits.

Automation Issues

Like other advanced or proposed automation concepts, conflict probes and interactive problem-solving tools are sufficiently recent that major problems have not yet had a chance to surface. Nevertheless, extrapolating from other systems, we can identify certain potential sources of problems.

New Error Forms: Mode Errors

These systems appear to have been designed to be relatively simple, with few modes to invite confusion. For the user request evaluation tool, a concern is whether the portrayal of flight paths in the planning mode could become confused with its portrayal in the active traffic mode. To guard against this, both it and the highly interactive problem solver employ salient color-coding (e.g., of adjacent sectors under HIPS). In addition to color-coding, HIPS also guards against team mode confusion through different displays for the planning and the tactical controllers. The planning controller can work in either look-ahead or real-time mode (and therefore has no radiotelephony communication capability), whereas the tactical controller's display operates only in real time.

Workload and Situation Awareness

By providing visual representations of future flight paths, tools such as the user request evaluation tool and the highly interactive problem solver should serve to increase situation awareness and reduce the workload of planning, which conventionally must be done on a cognitive basis by interpreting and mentally visualizing digital information (i.e., from flight strips). In this sense, as long as the planning tool remains within the domain of the D-side controller, workload may be reduced. Should, however, the R-side controller begin to shift attention to the user request evaluation tool to or the highly interactive problem solver display, one can envision negative workload implications, to the extent that visual resources are removed from the plan view display. Also, it is possible that R-side situation awareness could degrade if the controller adopts a strategy of automatically accepting recommendations based on the tool, without carefully thinking through the implications of those suggestions. Finally, an indirect negative effect on workload could result if the planning tools are used extensively to divert aircraft from FAA-preferred routes to user-preferred routes in order to expedite flying. The resulting increase of complexity in the traffic pattern will negatively affect both perceptual workload and situation awareness, as documented by recent studies (Wyndemere, 1996). We revisit this issue in Chapter 10.

Mistrust

Adequate trust in the systems can and should be developed by careful training, as has been undertaken in the field tests at Indianapolis and advised on the basis of work with HIPS. The algorithms and assumptions of conflict probe devices should be consistent with the controller's means of prediction and the controller's mental model. Excessive false alarm rates for conflict alerts, a source of user mistrust, have been addressed in the user request evaluation tool by the philosophy of providing two levels of alert (amber and red), which implicitly characterize the automation's uncertainty of future traffic behavior. This bilevel or "likelihood alarm" philosophy has been shown to be a useful remediation to problems of mistrust resulting from false alarms (Sorkin et al., 1988).

Overtrust and Complacency

The impacts of complacency and overtrust remain to be determined. This is because such states are not of operational concern until automation fails, and as yet there have been no documented instances of tool failure. (It is important to note here that, in the development of the tools, there was no apparent effort to develop a fault tree analysis of the possible causes and consequences of such low-probability events). A key feature of both the user request evaluation tool and the highly interactive problem solver is to keep the controller actively involved in the problem-solving and decision formulations. Hence, there is no likelihood of overtrusting automated solutions (which may be in error), since automation is not involved in recommending the solutions. (This, of course, is in contrast to the conflict resolution tools, discussed in the context of CTAS.) One important issue related to trust concerns the extent to which the intelligence within an interactive planning tool may not be cognizant of other hazard information (e.g., weather) that a controller normally considers.

Skill Degradation

As with overtrust and complacency, discussed in the previous section, skill degradation does not appear to present an issue. Controllers will continue to practice their skills in constructing conflict-free trajectories, but they will be better supported with graphical tools to implement those skills. Indeed, an argument can be made that such a tool will improve skill development by providing real-time feedback. For instance, en route controllers tend to achieve separation through either vertical (flight level) or direction (heading) control. In part this tendency derives from the small speed envelope of cruising jets and the resulting limited utility of speed control in en route airspace. Because the effects of speed manipulations become apparent only gradually, they can be difficult for the controller to visualize. As a result, the feedback provided by graphical look-ahead tools may enable the controller to develop better speed control skills.

Communication and Coordination

Both the user request evaluation tool and the highly interactive problem solver are designed to support more long-range strategic planning. As such, they have the potential to shift more control from the R-side to the D-side. Indeed, one can envision a scenario in which the R-side controller has little to do but implement long-range suggestions made by the tool-supported D-side controller, thereby guaranteeing conflict-free flights, with little need for active controlling. Hence, while the controller *team* may not suffer a loss of skills, there may well be a transference of skills from one controller to another within the team.

A second coordination issue emanating from the strategic, long-term nature of these interactive tools may be an increased need for coordination between sectors, since it seems more likely that aircraft will be maneuvered either on the basis of implications of an aircraft in a different sector, or in a manner that will affect that aircraft when it enters a different sector. A controller in one sector may then need to be increasingly vigilant of the behavior of controllers in adjacent sectors who are using the user request evaluation tool.

Failure Recovery

The prime issues for failure recovery are twofold, both emanating from potential problems identified above. First, it is possible to envision a scenario in which the deployment of interactive tools has enabled more complex (and possibly more densely packed) traffic flow. Second, this scenario situation has also left the R-side controller with reduced situation awareness of the current airspace (because trajectory changes were not imposed by his own decisions). A sudden failure of the user request evaluation tool or conflict probe system could thereby leave the R-side controller more vulnerable in issuing the rapid tactical commands necessary to avoid conflict situations.

User Acceptance

As with many sophisticated forms of automation, if systems like these are not carefully designed and introduced with adequate concern for controller training, the potential exists for limited user acceptance to threaten job satisfaction, which may in turn be reflected in perceived job insecurity. The more capable such automated systems are, the more likely such fears become. Furthermore, history suggests that such fears are not always unwarranted; in 1982, the FAA's modernization plans were presented to the U.S. Congress with the promise that they would reduce future staffing requirements (Stix, 1994). Some also fear that advanced air traffic control automation, if not well designed, may erode the job satisfaction a controller derives from resolving a challenging situation (Harwood, 1993).

Conclusion

Interactive planning tools appear to offer many of the benefits of automated information collection and integration (providing more easily visualizable predictive information to support human problem solving), without inviting some of the most obvious costs associated with automation of response (complacency and skill degradation). Nevertheless, predicted effects, discussed above, remain uncertain and should be the focus of continued evaluation.

FOUR-DIMENSIONAL CONTRACTS

Air traffic management seeks to solve a four-dimensional space-time problem. Aircraft flight paths in three dimensions of space (latitude, longitude, altitude) must be coordinated over time so as to be conflict free. Currently, controllers and flow managers solve this four-dimensional problem by forming a mental picture of aircraft trajectories in the future. The picture of the future traffic pattern is updated periodically as new data about aircraft positions and weather are obtained. Moreover, current procedures dictate that controllers have control over the aircraft's flight path, so that they can anticipate potential conflicts and plan for the future. The controller also has available display tools for short-term projection of flight paths. Thus, the controller's cognitive skills in planning and the spatiotemporal projection of flight paths, combined with display aids, form the basis for the current system of air traffic management.

Although experienced controllers have developed considerable cognitive skill in trajectory prediction, additional tools may be necessary to facilitate this skill under high workload and as traffic density increases. Such tools have also been proposed because current air traffic management is thought to be less than optimal. There is a disparity between the accurate, fuel-efficient trajectory that an aircraft fitted with a flight management system (FMS) can fly and the more limited, constrained flight path that air traffic management can offer. As a result, the benefits offered by the FMS cannot be realized.

One solution to this problem is to down-link FMS-derived information on the current and future aircraft trajectory to ground air traffic management systems. Automated tools could then be developed to help the controller in using this information to negotiate with the pilot a flight trajectory more compatible with the FMS-derived path and to detect and resolve conflicts over longer periods of time. In particular, automated tools have been proposed to improve capacity through more accurate navigation in four dimensions. Recent work in Europe has been aimed at developing such four-dimensional tools.

Functionality

The Programme for Harmonised Air Traffic Management Research in Eurocontrol (PHARE) has specified a medium-term future air traffic management scenario that comprises (among other things) a suite of tools for pilots and controllers aimed at facilitating trajectory prediction and conflict detection. The medium-term scenario envisions a process of negotiation between airborne and ground-based systems, whereby an agreed flight path can be flown with minimal ground intervention. The resultant trajectory for a given aircraft could then be represented as a four-dimensional "tube" through space (Eurocontrol, 1996). Each aircraft would be assigned a tube, resulting in a number of tubes representing all the traffic in a given airspace (Figure 6.12).

The four-dimensional tube can be represented as a three-dimensional "bubble" that moves through space such that its position and size are specified functions of time (see Figure 6.13). The precise cross-sectional dimensions of such a tube would vary dynamically with such factors as traffic density and weather disturbances. The tube may grow or shrink asymmetrically along any of the three possible dimensions of space, but it will always remain aligned with respect to the anticipated route. An aircraft would be required to remain within

4-dimensional tubes in space

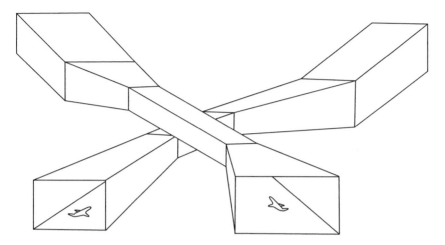

FIGURE 6.12 Four-dimensional (4-D) contract concept. Source: Eurocontrol (1996). The copyright vests in the European Organisation for the Safety of Air Navigation (EU-ROCONTROL); the CENA (Centre d'études de la navigation aérienne); the STNA (Service technique de la navigation aérienne); the NLR (Nationaal Lucht- en Ruimtevaartlaboratorium); the RLD (Rijksluchtvaartdienst); the LVB (Luchtverkeersbeveiliging); the DLR (Deutsche Forschungsanstalt für Luft- und Raumfahrt); the DFS (Deutsche Flugsicherung GmbH); the UK CAA (Civil Aviation Authority); the NATS (National Air Traffic Services), and the DRA (Defence Research Agency).

the tube at all times. In fact, the tube is the basis for a negotiated "contract" between the pilot and the controller; hence the term *4-D contract*.

Negotiation of the contract will necessarily involve heavy use of data link to support air-ground communication. In an experimental flight management system concept being evaluated by Eurocontrol, aircraft intentions (a four-dimensional trajectory derived by the system) would be down-linked to air traffic management, who would then up-link their requirements in terms of route or time constraints. A prediction system would then calculate the detailed four-dimensional trajectory in a manner that meets the system's specifications within the air traffic management constraints. This would then be down-linked to air traffic management, who will then have to approve the trajectory tube. In principle, the entire trajectory tube, from origin to destination, would be specified and agreed on as the basis for the contract. To reduce data link overhead, default tube parameters could be used for different flight segments, so that only limited tube reference information would need to be up-linked (Eurocontrol, 1996).

In the 4-D contract scenario, the pilot will be free to modify the flight path within the tube (Flohr, 1997). For example, the pilot may deviate laterally at will

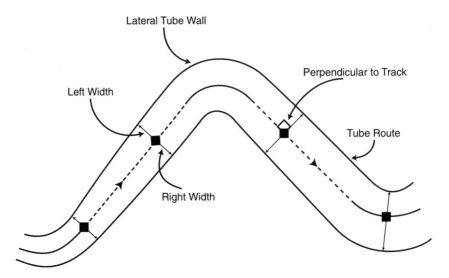

FIGURE 6.13 Lateral route and tube for four-dimensional (4-D) contract. Source: Eurocontrol (1996). The copyright vests in the European Organisation for the Safety of Air Navigation (EUROCONTROL); the CENA (Centre d'études de la navigation aérienne); the STNA (Service technique de la navigation aérienne); the NLR (Nationaal Lucht- en Ruimtevaartlaboratorium); the RLD (Rijksluchtvaartdienst); the LVB (Luchtverkeersbeveiliging); the DLR (Deutsche Forschungsanstalt für Luft- und Raumfahrt); the DFS (Deutsche Flugsicherung GmbH); the UK CAA (Civil Aviation Authority); the NATS (National Air Traffic Services), and the DRA (Defence Research Agency).

so long as the left and right tube boundaries are not breached (see Figure 6.13). In this respect, the 4-D contract concept is similar to the U.S. air traffic management concept of free flight, albeit in a more limited form: the degree of pilot freedom lies somewhere between current practices and "advanced" free flight, in which aircraft have much greater flexibility in setting and changing flight paths (RTCA, 1995b).

Human Factors Issues

The 4-D contract concept is relatively new, and validations of the concept and human factors studies (simulations and field trials) are still ongoing. Two demonstration projects have been completed to date: PHARE Demonstration 1 and 2, PD/1 and PD/2. PD/1 examined, among other issues, acceptance by controllers of a sector-based 4-D contract system for en route air traffic management. As mentioned earlier, initial analyses suggest that such a system can reduce subjective tactical workload without any cost in user acceptance (Schroter, 1996; National Air Traffic Services Limited, 1996).

An important technical and procedural issue in the 4-D contract concept is whether the contract applies locally (e.g., to a sector) or globally (to multiple sectors). The original concept envisages a negotiated contract from origin to destination, gate to gate. This is clearly what the pilot and the airlines would prefer, because it would be consistent with the capabilities that the FMS provides and would facilitate pilot flight planning. Controllers, however, may prefer to negotiate contracts sector by sector, because this would give them greater flexibility in management of the traffic pattern, particularly in response to unexpected events, weather disturbances, etc.

Of course, whether or not 4-D contracts are negotiated within or across sectors, the controller will still be responsible for the separation of aircraft. Also, controllers will be able to cancel a contract in response to unanticipated conditions at any time. When this is done, the aircraft will be under tactical control from the ground, as in current practice. Once the condition has passed, however, a new contract can be negotiated. A significant human factors concern is whether such negotiations can be undertaken efficiently and safely in a time-critical environment. Procedures for unambiguous and uninterruptable trajectory or clearance negotiation must be worked out. Thus, 4-D contracts will change aspects of the controller's job, but will not fundamentally alter responsibility for separation. The question is, will the changes affect the ability of controllers to maintain separation?

Only limited data are available to answer this question. On one hand, limited, routine clearances that are communicated to the pilot under the current system may be eliminated, so that controllers may be able to devote greater time to longer-range conflict prediction and planning. On the other hand, the current system is one in which the controller knows that the aircraft will follow a precise, specified path. This will be replaced by a system in which there will be some uncertainty about the aircraft's future position. The larger the 4-D tube, the greater the uncertainty. It is difficult to predict how controllers will react to such a system. One possibility is that they will attempt to reduce the uncertainty by querying pilots more frequently, which would tend to increase communications workload. Endsley (1996b) reported such an effect in an experimental evaluation of a free-flight scenario. However, it is also possible that controllers will adapt to the system and attempt to calibrate their level of uncertainty in advance by negotiating narrower tubes for anticipated problem areas within a sector and larger tubes elsewhere.

The development of the 4-D contract concept has been accompanied by attention to human factors enhancements, particularly in the controller's tools and operating procedures. One product of the PHARE effort will be a set of integrated controller tools, known as the PHARE advanced tools, that incorporates the following capabilities:

- The *trajectory predictor* predicts the onward path of aircraft in four dimensions.
- The *conflict probe* predicts conflicts based on the output of the trajectory predictor.
- The *flight path monitor* detects deviations from planned flight trajectories.
- The *negotiation manager* processes communication (air-ground and ground-ground) to facilitate flight path negotiation.
- The *problem solver* proposes solutions to resolve conflicts (as predicted by the conflict probe) or other problems.
- The *arrival manager* provides scheduling/sequencing information for arrival traffic within the terminal maneuvering area.
- The *departure manager* provides departure advisories to optimize flow into the en route sector.
- The *cooperative tools* manage controller workload by monitoring, predicting, and adapting to future task demands.
- The *tactical load smoother* creates interface enhancements aimed at improving high-level, multisector flow planning.

Another important human factors issue concerns how controllers will interact with displays of the 4-D contracts. Given the graphical and spatial qualities of the four-dimensional concept, it would seem appropriate to make controller interaction with the display also graphical and spatial rather than alphanumeric. This is consistent with a direct-manipulation approach to human-computer interaction (Norman, 1993; Robertson et al., 1993). The PHARE advanced tools incorporate the highly interactive problem solver (discussed in the previous section) that permits the controller to resolve traffic conflicts by interacting directly with graphical depictions of tubes in the sky for a given traffic sample. Dynamic data from underlying databases (with respect, for example, to weather and aircraft performance) are transformed and integrated into the displayed flight navigation tubes. Initial trials with active controllers have suggested that this approach can provide substantial benefits in conflict resolution time (and hence traffic throughput), as well as high levels of user acceptance (National Air Traffic Services Limited, 1996).

Failure Recovery

When the system has saturated the airspace and a partial failure occurs, the use of 4-D contracting tools, like CTAS and interactive conflict resolution tools, may lead to problems in achieving effective and timely recovery.

AUTOMATED SUPPORT FOR AIRPORT OPERATIONS:
THE SURFACE MOVEMENT ADVISOR PROGRAM

Functionality

Increased automation has been viewed by the FAA as a means of improving the efficiency of airport operations while maintaining safe taxiway navigation, takeoffs, and landings, especially during low-visibility operations. Delays in air traffic translate to extensive costs for airlines and passengers. In response to projected increases in air traffic, the U.S. aviation industry and the FAA are investing billions of dollars to increase airport capacity. However, capacity increases must be supported with improvements in the ability of the national airspace system to take advantage of capacity. Airport operations are a significant candidate for improvement (Jones and Young, 1996). To address efficiency concerns, the FAA, in collaboration with NASA, is undertaking large-scale development activities to provide controllers, pilots, airfield managers, and airline operations personnel with cues that enhance situation awareness and with automated support of surface traffic planning.

The surface movement advisor project, a joint activity of the FAA and NASA, is being developed to improve the efficiency with which airport facilities operate. The advisor, which is in the concept development and demonstration phase and is undergoing prototype testing at the Atlanta airport, would integrate information from and share information among FAA controllers and air traffic control supervisors, FAA traffic management coordinators (as well as the ATCSCC central flow control facility), ramp operators, airport managers, airline operators, and pilots.

The surface movement advisor architectural concept, illustrated in Figure 6.14, is based on a server that collects the following data: information from the FAA tower (e.g., runway configurations), surveillance data (e.g., radar data), weather, real-time aircraft status updates, gate information, airline schedules, and flight plans. The advisor includes automated analysis, prediction, and planning tools (i.e., performance histograms, prediction algorithms, airport operations procedure aids, and statistical analyzers) and distributes, as appropriate, collected data as well as analyses, predictions, and plans to FAA, airport, and airline personnel. This information will assist cooperating personnel to optimize gate resource utilization; balance taxi departure loads; improve gate scheduling and rescheduling; facilitate airport operations analysis; improve crew scheduling; and reduce voice radio traffic (National Aeronautics and Space Administration, 1996).

Potential long-term upgrades to the surface movement advisor include performance improvements based on actual customer use and feedback; integration of air traffic management technologies such as CTAS; implementation of data warehousing and data mining of on-line airport traffic data (e.g., analysis of cause

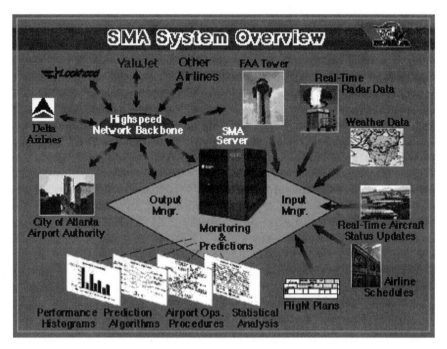

FIGURE 6.14 Surface movement advisor (SMA) system overview. Source: Federal
Aviation Administration.

and effect relationships between data sources such as weather, operations, and
schedules); implementation of wireless mobile computing technologies to promote wider surface movement advisor data access; and integration of the advisor
with surface traffic development and test facilities (National Aeronautics and
Space Administration, 1996).

Human Factors Implementation

The surface movement advisor is being developed according to the "build a
little, test a little" development philosophy that includes early involvement of
users and human factors professionals and ongoing evaluations using mixed methodologies (see Chapter 9 for a discussion of the advantages of these activities).
Its subsystems and features are developed with the support of a surface development and test facility sponsored jointly by NASA and the FAA. The facility
supports prototyping and simulation studies that involve test designs developed
by human factors professionals and the participation of air traffic controllers,
flight data and clearance delivery personnel, traffic management coordinators,
tower cab coordinators, supervisors, ramp controllers, "pseudo-pilots," and air-

port operators. It provides a real-time, interactive, simulated operational airport environment, and its studies support validation of designs as well as development of site-specific adaptations for the surface movement advisor (National Aeronautics and Space Administration, 1997d). The facility is therefore both a research and a development tool. In particular, it holds great promise as a testbed for evaluating the interactive effects of introducing multiple automation features into the extant system over time.

Human Factors Issues

Trust

As this report notes repeatedly with respect to conflict avoidance in ground operations, one of the greatest causes of mistrust or misapplied trust results when controllers or pilots fail to develop mental models appropriate to the system and task at hand. An appropriate mental model may be considered prerequisite for situation awareness. Both controllers and pilots, as well as airport managers and airline operations personnel, will be expected to develop mental models and situation awareness pertinent to the efficiency of airport operations (e.g., awareness of schedules, gate availabilities, and clearances).

Mental Models, Situation Awareness, and Loss of Skill

The risks of operator inability to develop and apply a mental model of the system's activity, operator inability to monitor fast-paced machine actions, and associated loss of situation awareness are introduced when system automation (e.g., improved surveillance accuracy coupled with sophisticated airport movement area safety system logic, as well as automated planners and schedulers that advise high-efficiency operations relying upon the automated surveillance and processing technology) permits more complex activities (e.g., the movement of greater numbers of aircraft, including under low visibility conditions). The loss of situation awareness may be accompanied by degradation of skills, if the operator has not maintained proficiency in tasks that are normally performed by the automation. For the surface movement advisor, such tasks may include monitoring the positions and movements of aircraft on the ground (if the surface movement advisor introduces substantial automation to this task), scheduling clearances, coordinating flight plans, and assessing capacity and use of airport resources. The combination of loss of situation awareness and skill degradation can result in the operator's inability to respond adequately to the failure of the automation. In the case of the surface movement advisor, these risks are introduced at multiple points in the team structure that includes controllers, pilots, airport managers, and airline operations personnel. On that account, each new automation feature should be evaluated for its impact on situation awareness, all team members should be trained to maintain proficiency in automated tasks whenever they are expected to be able to perform those tasks in response to automation failures, and the capability of team members to manage the complexities permitted by automation should be evaluated.

Teams

Airport area automation holds the potential for changing the roles of controllers vis-à-vis pilots, airport personnel, and airline personnel. The data distribution and analysis capabilities of the surface movement advisor introduce the potential for realigning responsibility and authority for performing and managing airport operations among controllers, airport managers, traffic managers, and airline dispatchers and analysts. Realignment may include new responsibilities, new authority structures, new communication and cooperative work links, and new measures of effectiveness (e.g., increasing emphasis on efficiency).

The impact of the surface movement advisor on individual roles should be considered during advisor analysis, design, and test activities. The teamwork associated with it should also be considered. One promising avenue that can contribute to the design of an effective surface movement advisor is the study of computer-supported cooperative work (discussed in Chapter 3). Such a study should include attention to workload implications of the work requirements and distribution, as well as of the automation of tasks and functions.

Effects of Combining Systems

As noted in Chapter 5 (with respect to automated ground control systems) and Chapter 8 (with respect to general principles of system development), it is critically important to consider the human factors implications of both phased and simultaneous implementation of two or more automated functions. The combination of automation features can potentially introduce effects that are not predicted from studies or tests of each feature independently. Airport surface automation includes contemplated introduction of many additions or changes to airport operations support tools and, possibly, associated procedures. For example, tools currently available only to some personnel selectively provide such information as airline schedules, flight plans, gate information, various weather parameters, and runway configuration; the surface movement advisor may combine these tools, or future versions of them, and redistribute the information to additional personnel. In addition to the issue of developing a consistent human-computer interface across the integrated tools, their combination may introduce possibilities for redefining tasks. The redefinition of tasks and potentially more timely and accurate information may introduce possibilities for new procedures. The general guidance presented in Chapter 8 applies here: each change introduced should be studied within the operational context, taking into account all other changes introduced. Such changes may include, for example, the center TRACON automation system final approach spacing tool and the surface conflict avoidance technologies discussed in the previous chapter. The evolution of changes should be centrally monitored and coordinated by a human factors research and development oversight organization.

7

Support Functions

The operation of the air traffic control system is supported by training and maintenance. In both cases, technology plays an important role in how the services are designed and delivered. In this chapter we review trends in technology and the human factors questions surrounding the implementation of new approaches.

TRAINING

Technology Advances

Advances in computing and networking technology have expanded the options for training design and delivery. In addition to classroom and traditional simulation facilities (which are dynamic interactive mockups), training is now possible through personal computer-based simulations and by exercises that are embedded in operational equipment. Moreover, the future holds promise for the use of virtual environment technology in both standalone and networked applications.

As noted in the panel's Phase I report, the Federal Aviation Administration is currently examining methods for providing simulations on personal computers. These computers will provide a high-fidelity emulation of the radar and keyboard as they appear in the live environment. Some specific advantages offered over traditional training simulators are that they can be started, stopped, and rewound at any point in the simulation; they can use voice recognition technology to simulate pseudo-pilots, thus saving on personnel to play these roles; they have software that can generate user-friendly scenarios in minutes; and the costs of purchase and operation are lower.

Another approach to training that is being actively pursued by the military services is to build training capabilities into operational systems. This approach, known as embedded training, can be used either by interrupting or overlying normal operations, allowing operators to enter the training mode using their own equipment. Embedded training can be used to acquire initial skills or for skill maintenance. According to Strasel et al. (1988), a fully functional embedded training system should:

- Require operators and maintainers to perform normal tasks in response to simulated inputs,
- Present realistic scenarios including degraded modes of operation,
- Provide an interactive capability whereby the system would assess the action of the operator and respond realistically, and
- Record performance and provide feedback after the session.

In the face of increasing automation of the decision-making functions of the air traffic control system, embedded training appears to be an extremely useful approach to helping controllers maintain their skills in manual separation of aircraft—a skill that will be called on when an automated system degrades or otherwise forces the controller to function at a lower level of automation. Such training can be scheduled for periods when regular operations are slow.

A number of concerns associated with embedded training should be mentioned. One is that it may cause additional wear on the operational equipment and, as a result, increase the potential for down time and the need for maintenance support. Another is the concern that embedded training must not interfere with operational capabilities or with safety. Yet another is the question of whether the operational system can support embedded training given the requirements for the reliability, availability, maintenance, and staffing associated with training delivery. Good developmental studies can resolve these issues.

Work is also being conducted on using virtual reality in training. In 1996, Science Applications International Corporation conducted a review of virtual reality technology and assessed its readiness for use in training for the FAA. A virtual environment system consists of a human operator, a human-machine interface, and a computer. The computer and the displays and controls in the interface are designed to immerse the operator in a computer-generated three-dimensional environment. In a fully immersive system, the user would experience the virtual world though sight, sound, and touch (Durlach and Mavor, 1995). At the current level of development, there is not sufficient knowledge and computing power to create high-fidelity virtual environment that is interactive with the user in real time. Systems such as SIMNET, which provide real-time interactive training over a computer network, use tank simulators (which provide realistic force feedback) and low-fidelity images.

As the virtual environment technology continues to develop, it will open new opportunities for knowledge acquisition and skill training. Hughes Aircraft (1995) has introduced the virtual tower and the virtual controller. The virtual tower is a desktop trainer with a 180-degree field of view of the airport. It includes a radar situation display and training for the following positions: local tower controller station, ground controller station, flight data position, supervisor station, and pseudo-pilot station air/ground. This system runs on a pentium or 486-66 with 32-bit multitasking processors.

The virtual controller (Hughes Aircraft, 1995) is based on an extension of video game logic. It is a turnkey system that includes voice communications across all training positions as well as radar data, maps, video overlays, fixes, navigational aids, air routes, airspace sectorization, and weather data. The displays are high-resolution color or monochrome. Scenarios can be built rapidly and, once initiated, exercises can be frozen, reversed, and replayed in every detail. This system can be used as a single terminal facility or as a network.

Human Factors Issues

The major concern in designing a training experience is how well the knowledge and skill acquired in the training environment transfers to job performance in the operational environment. This has led to a continuing and not yet well answered question regarding the degree of required fidelity or realism. Transfer of training research suggests that single theories of transfer will not hold for both cognitive and motor tasks (Schmidt and Young, 1987). Hays and Singer (1989) suggest starting with an analysis to determine the major emphasis of the task to be trained—if the task is cognitively oriented, it is likely that the training system should emphasize functional fidelity, which refers to the accuracy of representation of the system's procedures. If there are strong psychomotor elements, then physical fidelity should be emphasized. Physical fidelity refers to the accuracy of representation of the physical design and layout of the system. Virtual environment training may be particularly suited to increasing the probability of transfer because of its flexibility and feedback capabilities (Durlach and Mavor, 1995). A more complete discussion of training transfer and the surrounding methodological difficulties can be found in Druckman and Bjork (1994).

MAINTENANCE

Functionality

The equipment, systems, and facilities that support air traffic control and that must be monitored, controlled, and maintained by airway facilities specialists include: equipment internal to facilities (e.g., flight and radar data processors, displays, and workstation devices); equipment that interfaces with the facilities (e.g., radars and communications equipment); and airport local equipment (e.g., runway lighting, local navigation aids, and instrumentation). Automation has been increasingly applied, at varying levels, to the following maintenance tasks: monitoring of equipment status, configuration, and performance; control (including adjustment and configuration); diagnosis of hardware and software problems for equipment and some subsystems; restoration of equipment and some subsystems experiencing outages; validation that equipment is ready for use in air traffic control; logging of maintenance events and related data; and supporting aircraft accident and other incident investigations.

Automation and computer assistance are applied at different levels in different systems. Automation has been widely applied to maintenance activities through built-in equipment-level diagnostic tests and off-line diagnostic tools. A logging system that prompts the manual entry of maintenance and incident data supports both maintenance and incident/accident investigations. In general, automation and computer assistance are provided to support such functions as information retrieval, alarm reporting, remote control, and data recording. Only rarely is automation used to perform such higher-level cognitive functions as trend analysis, failure anticipation, system-level diagnostics and problem determination, and final certification judgments.

History

Historically, the application of automation to relatively lower-level cognitive tasks has been supported by FAA policy. Federal Aviation Administration Order 6000.30B (1991d) and Order 6000.39 (1991a) establish a long-term policy for national airspace system maintenance by recommending that automation be applied to repetitive maintenance tasks and that the airway facilities specialist be left "free to accomplish higher level, decision-oriented work" (p. 5).

However, changes in this policy have been spurred by recent programs aimed at modernizing the air traffic control system and introducing automation on a large scale. These modernization programs include the advanced automation system (AAS) and its progeny: the replacement of the en route HOST computer; the display system replacement (DSR), which modernizes en route processors and workstations; the standard terminal automation replacement system (STARS), which modernizes the automated radar terminal system processors and workstations; and the tower control computer complex, which modernizes tower processors and workstations. Each of these systems includes new distributed architectures, networks, and built-in automated features that diagnose system faults and perform on-line reconfigurations to maintain system availability.

Formal certification of national airspace system equipment, systems, and services is an especially critical procedural and legal responsibility of system maintainers. This certification responsibility involves the validation by airway facilities specialists that the equipment, systems, and services are performing within specified tolerances—as well as the legal attestation of certification with accompanying accountability. Equipment, systems, and the services they provide (e.g., radar data) can be accepted for use by air traffic controllers only if they have undergone a process of verification followed by formal, written certification. Certification is performed when the equipment or systems are first accepted for use, when they are restored to use after interruption or maintenance, and periodically as scheduled.

The increased reliability of computer-based systems and the automation support for diagnostics that are often embedded in such systems offer the following possibilities for certification: extension of the acceptable certification intervals; increasing reliance on the results of built-in diagnostics that can support certification while the equipment remains in operation; more performance of remote certification, replacing the need to examine the equipment directly; and more automated maintenance logging and equipment performance recording.

These trends and the application of automation to the certification process must be considered in the light of the current formal procedures for performing certification, defined in FAA Order 6000.15B (1991b) and FAA Order 6000.39 (1991a), which emphasize that the choice of methods used for certification—including the use of available automation assistance—must be left to the professional judgment of the certifying technician. A major challenge in the maintenance context is therefore whether and how to apply automation to such higher-level cognitive tasks as estimating trends and predicting, diagnosing interactions between systems, responding to outages that involve interacting system components, and planning maintenance tasks. Such automation would support the turn in maintenance philosophy away from an emphasis on corrective and regularly scheduled preventive maintenance toward an emphasis on performance-based maintenance that takes advantage of automated trend analyses to identify the most efficient scheduling for maintenance to prevent failures.

Under the assumption that sufficient automation support will be available, maintenance philosophy is also turning away from concentration on on-site diagnosis and repair of elements of equipment (using local maintenance control centers) toward more centralized and consolidated operational control centers that remotely monitor and control equipment and systems across facilities, accompanied by automated localization of problems to line-replaceable units that are replaced and sent to contractors for repair. The focus on "systems within one's jurisdiction" is being replaced by a focus on sharing of information, resources, and responsibilities across jurisdictions (Federal Aviation Administration, 1995b, 1995c).

Human Factors Implementation

The maintenance control center (MCC) is the central workstation suite from which maintenance specialists monitor and control the air traffic control system for a given facility or set of sites. The maintenance control center at an en route center, for example, typically consists of an extensive set of separate indicator panels, control panels, keyboards, video displays, and printers that, taken together, provide the capability to monitor and control: radars and radar processing; the HOST components and peripheral devices; computers that process the radar and flight data for presentation at the controllers' workstations; the controllers' plan view displays; communications equipment; and facility environment systems.

Because modernization has been accomplished through many different programs in the FAA involving many different vendors of equipment and systems, and because the national airspace system is the focus of rapidly advancing technologies, maintenance specialists face a variety of new technologies, provided by different vendors, with varying levels of automation and different human-machine interface designs. In contrast, the procedures and human-machine interface for air traffic controllers have undergone more controlled growth and change. The specialists who monitor and control the supporting equipment are typically provided with new monitoring and control devices that are tacked onto the array of such devices for other equipment in a loosely arranged maintenance control center that lacks integration (Theisen et al., 1987).

The FAA has specified standardized protocols and data acquisition and processing requirements to guide the integration of new national airspace system components and systems in a manner that continues to support the centralized monitoring and control workstations (Federal Aviation Administration, 1994a). However, these and other recommendations (Federal Aviation Administration, 1991a) address only the lower-level automation tasks mentioned above. They do not address the allocation of higher-level tasks between human and machine, the integration of automation functions across disparate systems, or the integration of the associated human-machine interface.

There appears to be a significant need for the specification of a maintenance control center human-computer interface into which all new designs must fit well, and a corresponding need for an overall maintenance control center automation strategy against which proposed automation designs can be evaluated. These same needs apply to the design of tools that support other airway facilities activities, such as off-line diagnosis of equipment, maintenance logging, and maintenance of software.

The ongoing development of the national airspace system infrastructure management system is an opportunity to address this need. It consolidates the existing 79 maintenance control centers into four centralized operations control centers and modernizes the current national maintenance coordination center into a national operations coordination center. It will be automatically fed data from the centralized operations control centers and may include automation enhancements that support prediction, response, and planning tasks. The success of this consolidation and integration effort hinges on the degree to which new systems pass relevant data to the centralized operations control centers, the manner in which automation is applied at the centralized operations control centers and the national operations coordination center to support the cognitive tasks of the maintainers, and the successful application of human factors research and design efforts to the development of effective centralized operations control centers and national operations coordination center workstations. It is therefore encouraging that the FAA Technical Center human factors organization is undertaking research and providing design support for the effort.

Human Factors Issues

The impact of automation when new components or systems are introduced is often experienced more directly by maintainers than by air traffic controllers. The new components or systems occasionally include increased automation of air traffic control functions; often they represent modernization of aging equipment without significant change to the human-machine interface for the air traffic controllers. In either case, the new systems increasingly include automation of such maintenance functions as diagnostics, fault localization, status and performance monitoring, logging, and reconfiguration using backup components when the primary components fail. Although these automation enhancements are likely to prove transparent to the air traffic controllers, they can impose on maintenance specialists the requirements to learn new and often complex functional and human-machine characteristics of the modernized equipment.

Cognitive Task Analysis

The FAA has developed detailed job task analyses for maintenance tasks and has applied these analyses to the development of training plans and programs (Federal Aviation Administration, 1993a). The job task analyses have been accompanied by identification of knowledge, skills, and abilities prerequisite for effective task performance, as well as 14 cognitive and sensory attributes of 4 types of task (entry, receipt, analysis, and communication). The cognitive and sensory attributes identified for the national airspace system operations manager are listed in Table 7.1.

Table 7.2 provides examples that illustrate the meanings of the cognitive/sensory attributes listed in Table 7.1. These attributes map well to the hierarchy of cognitive functions applied to the summary of automation applications in this report (see the introduction to Part II), as shown in Table 7.3 (which also includes

TABLE 7.1 Task Set and Cognitive/Sensory Attributes of the National Airspace System Operations Manager

Task Set	Cognitive/Sensory Attributes	Number of Tasks
Entry	Coding	134
Receipt	Movement detection	3
	Spatial scanning	34
	Filtering	43
	Image/pattern recognition	42
	Decoding	157
Analysis	Visualization	7
	Short-term memory	35
	Long-term memory	10
	Deductive reasoning	107
	Inductive reasoning	16
	Probabilistic reasoning	43
	Prioritization	23
Communication	Verbal filtering	132

TABLE 7.2 Examples of Cognitive/Sensory Attributes

Attributes	Examples
Coding	Enter information into the maintenance log
Movement detection	Listen for alarm printouts
Spatial scanning	Observe status panels for status data
Filtering	Identify significant status data on status panel
Pattern recognition	Form mental picture of facility status
Decoding	Read a facility configuration display screen
Visualization	Determine operations impacts from weather picture
Short-term memory	Remember status information to record in log
Long-term memory	Remember procedures
Deductive reasoning	Determine that facility data are questionable
Inductive reasoning	Estimate impact from historical trend data
Probabilistic reasoning	Evaluate the nature of a degradation
Prioritization	Establish order for restoring equipment
Verbal filtering	Identify relevant verbal information

TABLE 7.3 Cognitive/Sensory Attributes Arranged by Cognitive Function
Hierarchy

Cognitive Functions (Higher To Lower)	Cognitive/Sensory Attributes	Number of Tasks
Plan/resolve	Prioritizing	23
Predict longer term	Inductive reasoning	16
Compare, predict shorter term	Deductive reasoning, pattern recognition, probabilistic reasoning, visualization	199
Transmit information	Coding, decoding, verbal filtering	423
Remember	Short-term memory, long-term memory	45
Identify	Filtering, movement detection, spatial scanning	80

summation of the tasks to which the cognitive/sensory attributes were found to
apply). The information in Table 7.3 suggests that:

1. Since lower-level cognitive tasks (identifying and remembering) may be
presumed to underlie higher-level cognitive tasks, the relatively small number of
maintainer tasks for which lower-level cognitive/sensory attributes are currently
required supports the general conclusion that automation has been widely applied
to these lower-level tasks.

2. The relatively large number of tasks for which moderate-complexity
(transmit information, compare, predict shorter term) cognitive/sensory attributes
are required suggests an opportunity for automation of these moderate-complexity tasks.

3. Although the number of tasks for which higher-level (plan, resolve, predict longer-term) cognitive attributes are required is relatively small, these tasks
may be taken as a critical culmination of the results of lower-level cognitive tasks
and represent a significant challenge for future automation.

In addition, Blanchard and Vardaman (1994) have developed an outage assessment inventory to study factors relating to equipment and system outages,
such as system and equipment design factors; human behavioral processes; personnel factors; logistics factors; and physical environment factors. Expanding
Blanchard and Vardaman's work to address cognitive tasks and attributes in
greater detail might represent a useful framework for investigating, within the

context of a standard maintenance task sequence, variables that may interact with automation to mediate the effectiveness of automation applied to maintenance.

Workload

FAA maintenance specialists experience sudden transition from low-workload troughs to high-workload peaks. Scheduling of preventive maintenance and certification tasks is currently a commonly applied method to average workload. Maintainers also schedule tasks that affect air traffic control operations in coordination with air traffic controllers, taking into consideration the controllers' workload. The most significant high-workload challenge for maintenance personnel occurs when multiple critical elements fail, creating or threatening service outage. Under these situations, maintenance personnel face the complex task of rapidly diagnosing the cause from the pattern of failures, while simultaneously assessing the progress of the diagnosis, logistics support factors, and the utility of applying alternative solutions to maintain or restore service.

Training and Selection

Selection of maintenance technicians has been neither centralized nor standardized. Each region hires new technicians by evaluating the experience and education reported in candidates' SF-171 applications against knowledge and skill criteria for the specializations that the regional office requires. These specializations have traditionally included: navigation, communication, radar, and computers. Guidance for the knowledge and skill criteria applicable to each specialization is available in formal qualifications standards and position descriptions. There is no prehire selection test for maintenance personnel. Hirees typically have electronics backgrounds, usually developed in military service and/or through technical education.

Until 1994, the focus of electronics specialists was on specific subsystems or items of equipment to which they were assigned. In recognition of the need to develop generalists who focus on system-level functions and the delivery of services across interacting systems, the FAA created the GS-2101 job classification, which emphasizes systems engineering skills. The knowledge, skills, and task emphases of the GS-2101 specialist include: ability to work with automation tools for diagnostics and maintenance, ability to perform centralized monitoring and control, ability to perform system- and service-level certification, breadth of knowledge across systems rather than depth of knowledge of specific items of equipment, knowledge of how information flows between systems, ability to work with information management systems, maintaining end-product services for national airspace system users, performance of independent actions, and ability to work well in interaction with others (Federal Aviation Administration, 1995d).

The GS-2101 job classification, which now covers the majority of electronics technicians, is likely to require change in the population from which hirees are selected. There is no known FAA documentation of the strategy for identifying this population or for determining the precise relationship between selection criteria, performance during training, and on-the-job performance.

Demographic data for the FAA's maintenance workforce suggest that, within 10 years, there will be a simultaneous retirement of significant percentages of experienced technicians and the equipment on which they have developed their experience (Federal Aviation Administration, 1993b). Whereas this suggests that the introduction of the GS-2101 job classification is quite timely—fostering the hiring and training of new types of people for new types of equipment—it also adds to the urgency of validating the GS-2101 hiring and training devices and procedures.

The training process has two goals: (1) certification of the technician's abilities with respect to given systems and equipment, so that he or she may be authorized to certify the systems and equipment for use in air traffic control and (2) career progression of the technician, so that, by demonstrating proficiency, he or she can progress to journeyman status. In principle, these goals are met by providing theory through course material and application through subsequent on-the-job training.

There is currently no training track that specifically addresses the position descriptions of the GS-2101; these trainees currently receive tailored instruction selected from among the pool of instructional sources that were developed to train the specialists in radar, navigation, communications, and computer systems.

Communication and Coordination

Restoration to service of failed equipment, systems, or entire facilities requires close cooperation between maintainers and air traffic controllers, both on site and across sector, regional, and national levels, because outages at one facility can affect systems and services at other facilities, and because the responses to outages may require support and approval from the other locations. In addition, each maintenance coordination center reports all equipment and system outages and restoration activities to the national maintenance coordination center, whose staff monitor situations and coordinate resolutions with the national, centralized air traffic control system command center.

In all cases involving interruption and restoration of items affecting air traffic control, maintainers function in a supportive capacity. Controllers must decide the priorities by which maintainers apply their resources. However, in so doing, controllers must consider recommendations from maintainers that take into account the likelihood of restoring the affected item(s) within desired time frames, the levels of functioning available with degraded equipment, and potential temporary work-around strategies. The outage of automated systems or functions is a problem that must be jointly solved. Such cooperative problem solving is currently addressed by experience and procedures rather than by automated supports, at both the local and national levels.

The responsibility for restoration also highlights the need for teamwork within the maintenance organization. Maintainers currently rely on one another's expertise to solve problems. A frequent requirement during restoration is to call back needed off-duty specialists, when those on duty do not possess specialized knowledge to address a given problem. A move toward more breadth of responsibility, as reflected by the GS-2101 job description, may affect the dynamics of such teamwork.

The FAA has recently begun to study maintenance teamwork at its Civil Aeromedical Institute in the following areas: knowledge and skills that predict successful membership in and leadership of self-managed teams; tools to assess the progress of work teams; organizational culture factors that inhibit or facilitate acceptance of new technology by the maintenance workforce; and methods for introducing new technology (e.g., quality circles, town hall meetings, goal setting, and teaming).

Organization

Traditionally, the national airspace system operations manager has been supported by specialists in computer systems, radar, communications, and navigation aids equipment, and these specialists have been supported by hardware and software technicians. National airspace system operations managers have been traditionally selected from among the ranks of specialists whose expertise crosses the computer systems and radar areas. In the past, they have represented systems-level expertise. The reclassification of virtually all specialists as GS-2101 "automation systems specialists" brings into question this traditional understanding of organizational ties and roads to promotion and introduces the possibility of considering new organizational arrangements for maintainers.

The primary staffing unit for maintenance technical activities in support of en route and terminal operations is the airway facilities sector, which is staffed as a "self-contained and self-sufficient" work unit. The FAA is in the process of consolidating the 79 existing sectors into 33 system management offices. The planned consolidation of these offices into four operations control centers will introduce a new, as yet unknown, organizational structure.

Automation Issues

Error

Human error, particularly by maintenance staff who control the automation equipment, can cause or contribute to outages. One option frequently considered by maintenance specialists when complex systems demonstrate performance dec-rements is to do nothing, since experience has shown that frequently performance decrements are transient, and complex systems sometimes salvage themselves. One general rule followed by experienced maintenance specialists is: analyze before you act. This suggests that important features of automation for mainte-nance are the extent to which the design of the device contributes to system self-stabilization, the extent to which it supports system analysis, and the extent to which it discourages (e.g., foolproofs) human error and recovers from them.

Trust

Certification provides an example of how questions of trust with respect to automation of maintenance tasks are considered within the FAA. A significant practical consideration is: How does the automation of certification affect legal liability? If automation is relied on for certification and it errs, is it appropriate (legally) to blame the machine or to blame the certifier whose judgment accepted the machine's error?

It is important to emphasize that the certification process represents formal-ization and operationalization of trust. When a maintenance specialist certifies a system, that specialist formally and legally expresses the FAA's conclusion that the system is trustworthy. When the specialist ceases to trust a system, the specialist formally decertifies the system. Therefore, when a certified system fails, the issue of trust extends through multiple orders: the air traffic controllers may question not only their trust in the system and its equipment, but also their trust in the individual(s) who certified the system. This introduces mistrust in the qualifications of the certifier (and therefore in the process by which the certifier was "certified to certify") and in the process of equipment/system certification, which ultimately and formally (by FAA Order 6000.15B) relies on the "profes-sional judgment of the certifier." One response to these concerns has been the suggestion that the certification process should be as automated as possible—in which case the question arises: Who will certify *that* certifier?

A significant question regarding the application of automation to mainte-nance is: Will the maintenance specialists be able to effectively restore equip-ment and systems to service when (1) the equipment or systems that have failed contain automation on which air traffic controllers rely heavily to perform their duties and when (2) maintainers themselves rely on automation to perform the restoration, but the maintenance automation has failed or is difficult to work with? Improper design or application of automation to both air traffic control and maintenance can produce a compounding of difficulties that complicates ex-tremely any problems relating to failure of the automation supporting air traffic tasks, as discussed elsewhere in this report.

Skill Degradation

The rationale for the GS-2101 job classification relies partly on the expectations that new systems are likely to automate current component- and subsystem-level monitoring, diagnostic, and reconfiguration functions and that the systems will be modularized to permit failed components to be removed, replaced with equivalent modules (pull-and-replace maintenance), and returned to the manufacturer for repair. The concern is that these assumptions may lead to the conclusion that the new class of employees can focus on system- and service-level activities, relying on automation to monitor and control lower-level functions— and that training for these lower-level functions can therefore be eliminated. Such "dumbing down" of training would be suspect in the light of questions about what will happen when the automation fails, and how the GS-2101 will maintain proficiency in the automated tasks.

Mental Models

There are no known descriptions of the maintainer's mental model of the national airspace system. However, to the extent that maintainers and controllers must communicate on the diagnosis and repair of automated function, as we discuss below, it would appear to be important that they both maintain simulation mental models of the equipment.

Communication and Organization

Currently, air traffic controllers and maintainers share supervisory control tasks. Controllers monitor and control air traffic patterns and activities. In the process of doing so, they also monitor the apparent quality of the data appearing on their workstations and the performance of their display and control devices. For example, controllers will question the quality of radar-provided data and have limited control over the selection of radar parameters for display. However, it is the responsibility of maintainers to monitor and control all equipment that ultimately supports the controllers, to inform the controllers of the status and performance of equipment and systems on which their tasks depend (including the controllers' workstations), to reconfigure and maintain degraded or failed equipment in a manner that minimizes interference with air traffic control tasks, and to respond to requests for service from controllers. Air traffic supervisory control tasks must therefore be viewed as cooperative efforts of both controllers and maintainers. In addition, controllers and maintainers share the responsibility for installing and evaluating new, increasingly automated equipment as well as software and hardware upgrades to existing equipment.

Maintainers have always shared with controllers the responsibility for and the philosophy of maintaining the safe and efficient flow of air traffic; it is open to question whether the maintainer roles within the team will actually increase with increased automation, or whether increased automation will require that the controller roles expand into supervisory control functions currently performed by maintainers.

The results of the FAA's recent employee attitude survey (Federal Aviation Administration, 1995e) indicate that maintenance employees report low to moderate satisfaction with the impact of new technologies on their jobs. Attitudes were assessed about whether new technology is appropriate and sufficient, whether timely information on the new technology is provided by management, and whether the organization is generally quick to adopt new work methods. Such attitudes form part of the organizational culture within which user involvement transpires during the acquisition of new systems and users accept or reject new technology.

Conclusion

The FAA is reconceptualizing its approach to maintenance. This reconceptualization is reflected in several trends:

1. Centralization of monitoring and control functions and capabilities (into work centers, centralized operations control centers, and an overriding national maintenance coordination center). This presumes a significant amount of additional automation to support system-level diagnostics, certification, and restoration after outages.

2. Increased automation of higher-level cognitive tasks, permitted and required by the centralization mentioned above, and accompanying large-scale modernization of the technology supporting both air traffic control and maintenance activities. In the past, the focus has been on automating lower-level cognitive functions.

3. Changing roles within the maintenance organization (e.g., the shift away from specialization toward broader systems engineering required by the new GS-2101 job classification); changing roles between maintenance and air traffic personnel, which will result from the movement of maintenance specialists to centralized facilities (e.g., differing lines of communication, possibly different responsibilities).

4. Changing maintenance philosophy toward more preventive and predictive maintenance.

5. Changing culture, emphasizing management and delivery of services to customers (e.g., system reliability and availability maintained for air traffic control) and to internal business managers (e.g., meeting goals for efficient use of resources).

This new culture of performance-based management is expected to be fostered by the introduction of supporting automation that includes: shared distributed databases, expert systems, distributed systems, data and telecommunications networks, decision support systems, mobile computing, computer-based planning tools, and simulation and modeling tools (Federal Aviation Administration, 1995c). Adkisson et al. (1994) identified applications of artificial intelligence (e.g., expert systems, artificial neural networks, expert neural systems, fuzzy logic, natural language processing, intelligent databases, distributed artificial intelligence, and machine learning) to such maintenance activities as alarm processing, monitoring, information retrieval, administrative functions, problem resolution, certification, preventive maintenance, and training. There is, however, scant discussion of human factors research in descriptions of these shifts in direction for maintenance.

PART III

Integration

In Parts I and II we have considered various components of air traffic control automated technology and related human factors issues. In this third part, we take a broader perspective regarding how these research approaches and technologies could and should be integrated into the national airspace system.

We addressed several issues in the Phase I report regarding the introduction of new technologies to the workplace and how the FAA structure can facilitate them. Chapter 8 focuses the discussion much more directly on new and emerging automated technology.

Chapter 9 takes a broad look at two alternative views of where the national airspace system is heading: free flight and high-level automation. We discuss the relative costs and benefits of both, primarily from the perspective of the air traffic controller.

Chapter 10 contains the panel's full set of conclusions and recommendations.

8

Integration of Research and Development

As a result of the panel's studies of various existing and proposed systems in air traffic control, human factors lessons learned from other systems (e.g., the flight deck), and our understanding of good human factors practices in other fields, we have identified several key issues that are critical to the successful development and integration of new technology. We describe these issues below and note, where relevant, both positive and negative ways in which certain aspects of air traffic control automation represent them.

One common theme underlying all issues is the need for close harmony between research and development. That is, research is necessary for good product development, and many issues encountered during development directly contribute to the research base or at least feed back to define important research questions. As a consequence, these two concepts are closely linked in this chapter.

Human factors activities should be integrated comprehensively across the development cycle. Too often, program managers perceive human factors as a marginal design function constrained to the details of the human-computer interface (e.g., color-coding, character height, workstation anthropometry). This perception ignores the importance of human factors throughout the analysis, functional specification, detail design, test and evaluation, and implementation phases of development (Booher, 1990).

As noted in the Phase I report and as recommended by the Federal Aviation Administration's Subcommittee on Human Factors of the agency's Research, Engineering, and Development Council (Federal Aviation Administration, 1996e), integration of effort would be enhanced if human factors research were treated as a unified program. To do so will require the establishment of a single locus within the FAA organization that has, at minimum, an oversight function for all such research and development. Ideally, such a unit would also have the authority to establish research goals and standards of rigor in the conduct of the program of studies. This arrangement would not reallocate roles and responsibilities now assigned to the FAA's Civil Aeromedical Institute and the FAA Technical Center, but it would impose central management of the human factors support for the integrated product teams. General recommendations for integrating human factors research and development activities into a comprehensive, iterative program are echoed in the earlier reports of three technical meetings, sponsored in part by the FAA (Wise, Hopkin, and Smith, 1991; Wise, Hopkin, and Stager, 1993; Wise, Hopkin, and Garland, 1994).

Our emphasis here is on the integration of research and development activities into a systematic and comprehensive human factors *program*. Such a program involves the coordinated actions of many contributors (including managers, systems engineers, a variety of users, and human factors specialists) at the FAA, cooperating government agencies, and subcontractors. These activities occur across all phases of acquisition and implementation (including analysis, definition of requirements, design, test and evaluation, and training and selection of personnel) and involve a mix of research and evaluation methodologies (including analysis, modeling, simulation, prototyping, laboratory studies, and field studies). This comprehensive approach must be applied to individual subsystems and to the wider national airspace system into which the subsystems must be integrated. We note here that the maintenance of such a comprehensive program requires the commitment and support of FAA management, as well as of those constituents with whom the agency interacts (e.g., legislators, regulators, commercial users of the national airspace system, and representatives of employee unions). This commitment must be demonstrated by continuous allocation of resources (e.g., budget, staffing, facilities, and educational materials) sufficient to accomplish both the breadth and depth of research and development activities we discuss below. In systems with direct safety implications, such as those that the FAA is developing, the resource commitment to human factors during development and testing should be at least as large as that associated with hardware and software reliability.

APPROPRIATE APPLICATIONS OF
RESEARCH METHODOLOGIES

In the Phase I report, we identified a wide range of research methodologies that could contribute to understanding the information needs and task requirements of controllers, as well as to the appropriate design of equipment and interfaces to serve those needs. These methodologies include literature searches, incident analysis, modeling, laboratory studies, simulation studies, and field tests.

Each is briefly discussed below as it relates to human factors work on the current and proposed systems presented in Part II of this report.

Literature Searches

There is an extensive body of literature that describes fundamental principles, methodology, data, and lessons learned relevant to the general activity of human factors development and testing. However, despite valuable sets of technical reports produced through such organizations as the FAA's Civil Aeromedical Institute and the FAA Technical Center, the body of literature has been largely derived from domains other than air traffic control. Caution must be exercised before lessons, data, and recommendations derived from other domains are applied to air traffic control; in many cases such information is best used to formulate and refine hypotheses that must be tested in the air traffic control setting. This represents the fundamental principle of replication, important in scientific settings, whereby the external validity of findings is demonstrated across different domains.

Within the domain of air traffic control, the human factors literature evinces uneven coverage. For example, although Kerns (1994) seems to have done an exemplary job of amassing and organizing literature specifically relevant to the development of data link, there is a paucity of relevant literature for such developments as the user request evaluation tool (URET), the precision runway monitor (PRM), and the converging runway display aid (CRDA). The operational impacts of these latter developments may be smaller than those of data link, yet efforts to document the human factors issues, findings, and decisions during their development and evaluation would contribute useful data and lessons learned to the human factors database.

Incident Analysis

Incident analysis is a useful methodology that has been used heavily and productively, for example, in the refinement of the traffic alerting and collision avoidance system (TCAS) (Mellone and Frank, 1993). Incident analysis can serve as an important trigger for developing a particular automation functionality by revealing the existence of a problem. For example, reported problems in the cleared for visual approach situation have triggered exploratory investigations of means to extend TCAS to support visual clearances (Mundra et al., 1997). A limitation of the incident analysis methodology, however, is that the post hoc analysis process identifies a problem only (which automation may address); incident analysis can be used as a tool for evaluating the proposed solution only if it is applied early in implementation. Another limitation is that post hoc analysis using reports of incidents often relies on data that have been filtered through a conceptual system that is reflected in the classification structure of the database itself. That is, the elicitation of the data may be constrained by the structure of the database in a manner that does not garner needed human factors data or that combines data in ways that obscure meaningful parameters.

The continuing challenges for the improvement of incident analysis databases are to centralize and connect relevant data; encourage data input by users; structure data inputs and analyses to permit addressing specific questions pertinent to the automation of air traffic control functions; and develop user-friendly interfaces for analysts.

Computational Models

Progress has been made in recent years and new work is currently under way to increase the usefulness of computable models in the analysis and evaluation of complex systems. A major center for such work at a basic, generic level is located at Carnegie Mellon University, where the SOAR (state, operator, and results) model has been developed and used as the computational framework for studies in artificial intelligence as an aid to human performance. Such work is currently being carried forward in support of the development of operational systems (Tambe et al., 1995). The expansion of such models to incorporate many of the details of human behavior is currently being supported by the Defense Modeling and Simulation Office (Pew and Mavor, 1997). Advanced modeling of specific air traffic control operations is under way at the Massachusetts Institute of Technology and elsewhere in the FAA and NASA (see Odoni et al., 1997, for a review). The FAA has also used SIMMOD and other human performance models for feasibility and certification analyses of the precision runway monitor and the converging runway display aid. In addition, NASA is sponsoring work to develop modeling capabilities specifically suited to examination of the human performance component of air traffic management systems (Corker et al., 1997). Air traffic control workload models are being developed in the United Kingdom at the National Air Traffic Control Simulation facility (Evans et al., 1997).

Valid models of air traffic control error generation and situation awareness, however, remain insufficient. The uses of such models in human-centered systems research are multiple. One use is the forward testing of major changes in system composition. The large advantage is that radical innovations can be given a preliminary evaluation at low cost and zero risk. An even more attractive use is the ranking of alternative design solutions to a particular, generic operational problem. An example of a generic problem is the variation in performance profiles between aircraft landing on a common runway. Should aircraft having higher speed and rate of descent be automatically slotted in ahead of slower planes? Such a situation is inherently computable because the phenomena in question are quantitative. Many different mixtures of aircraft types could be evaluated through modeling in a short time. For example, spacing between pairs of aircraft is computable in four dimensions. Automatic adjustments in separation could be engendered by situations such as the presence of a slow aircraft in trail behind a faster aircraft (taking into account such variables as wake turbulence). In such cases, the separation will increase over time with no intervention by the controller.

It is increasingly possible to include some dimensions of human capabilities in such models. Consequently, although modeling cannot directly answer many human factors questions, it can serve as the means to carry out exploratory studies. Such studies can point to specific issues that need resolution through the use of other methods. For example, if human abilities to discriminate speed and rates of closure are included in the model, it should be possible to form highly focused hypotheses about the relationship between aircraft heterogeneity and subjective workload.

Another area of usefulness for operational models is the simultaneous testing of more than one innovation. This use gets directly at the problem of systems integration. It could be very cumbersome if not dangerous to evaluate the levels of compatibility between data link, the center TRACON automation system (CTAS), and free flight by other methods. For example, under free flight it can be assumed that arrivals to the terminal area could appear at any spot on the boundary rather than at the intersection with one of the standard air routes. In effect, this transition will take the arriving aircraft out of the free flight mode and into a nominal instrument flight rules mode. CTAS will designate a landing slot. Data link will transmit a standard greeting and local meteorological data (i.e., information from the automatic terminal information service). In short, many events will be under way at the moment of entry to the terminal area. Will there be some way to assure both pilot and controller that situation awareness is complete on both sides? Will cognitive load effects become excessive when arrival rates peak at more than one per minute? Will vectoring of the aircraft to adjust orientation to the final approach line disrupt the slot assignment provided by CTAS? If there is clear-air turbulence at the threshold to the runway, will the controller need to override the data link to ensure that the pilots take this hazard into account in choosing the ideal altitude at the point of threshold crossing?

Examples of areas in which computational modeling is being productively applied include the terminal area productivity (TAP), CTAS, and TCAS projects. Examples of areas in which modeling would be helpful, although modeling applications have not been extensively applied or planned for, are the CRDA, airport movement area safety system (AMASS), airport surface traffic automation (ASTA), and the airway facilities operations control center (OCC) projects.

Laboratory Studies

Laboratory studies, which permit rigorous control over experimental conditions, can be very valuable for investigating issues that arise early during the development of automated systems and that may not have been predicted prior to system specification or preliminary design. For example, within the domain of air traffic control, laboratory studies at the FAA's Civil Aeromedical Institute contributed important understanding pertinent to the design and use of flight strips (see Chapter 4); laboratory studies at the University of Illinois resulted in useful guidance for the design of displays to present three-dimensional information; and laboratory studies were effectively employed to address specific design questions during the improvement of TCAS (Chappel, 1990). Examples of good candidates for additional laboratory study address workload issues associated with data link and vigilance issues associated with PRM and TCAS. In addition, laboratory studies can be very valuable for examining variables that are too complex or numerous to study in more costly, full-mission simulations. Often such laboratory studies serve to identify the most critical variables for incorporation into the full-mission simulations.

There is concern that researchers conducting applied laboratory studies retain understanding of the need to transition experiments into a contextually real environment, and that they also ask operationally important questions. Still, because laboratory studies generally represent low-cost, high-power (i.e., experimental power) methodologies, their value should not be undersold.

Simulation Studies

Simulation provides a more relevant context for study. Simulation has been applied successfully to study human factors aspects of data link, of the PRM, and of European conflict probe designs. Simulation can be especially useful in support of investigating how multiple systems do or do not harmonize and of the impacts of new systems on teamwork.

Simulation has been used effectively to study the combinatorial effects of CTAS with existing tools and tasks, and the Canadian automated air traffic system (CAATS) program (see Stager, 1991) used simulation effectively to study electronic flight information presentation, considering how the relevant subtasks of flight information processing fit into the overall air traffic control task set. Simulation can also be usefully applied to the study of combining effects, for example, of CTAS and URET predictive capabilities, of PRM with CRDA for landing coordination, of multiple components of ASTA and the taxi navigational situation awareness (T-NASA) system for surface conflict avoidance, and of all the components of the surface movement advisor (SMA).

Simulation has also been, and should continue to be, productively applied to evaluate data link innovations. An example of such simulation is described in the *Airborne Data Link Program Plan* for fiscal 1995 (Rehmann, 1995), which identifies projects that use the air traffic control simulator at the FAA Technical Center in combination with the reconfigurable cockpit simulator. This simulation requires the valid representation of the whole avionics subsystem that would probably be in use in the cockpit alongside the data link equipment. The early research is aimed at determining whether there are gross incompatibilities between data link and existing instrumentation.

The team setting is a key context for introducing technologies and is amenable to study through simulation. The teamwork aspects of TCAS, including shifts of authority between controllers and pilots, have increasingly been studied through simulation, with productive results (Hoffman et al., 1995). Other candidates for simulation study of teamwork are the maintenance OCC (considering teamwork within maintenance organizations and between controllers and maintainers), and airport surface automation projects such as ASTA, T-NASA, and the SMA. The manner in which controllers perform complementary strategic and tactical tasks during the use of conflict probes such as URET merits study to determine whether specific design (or procedural) features affect the cooperative task performance.

One concern with respect to simulation studies is that statistical power is preserved by the introduction of as much experimental control as feasible and by the use of large numbers and representative types of subjects. Another concern is that, because of expense and complexity, all of the relevant real-world variables may not be included in a given simulation study. Some of these variables (e.g., those associated with low frequency, unexpected events, or error recovery) can have significant implications for operational safety and should be included. Others, however, while contributing to the operational realism of the simulation, may be superfluous to the task performance characteristics that are to be measured and hence impose unnecessary expense. Objective guidelines exist to help identify the latter classes of variables (Sheridan and Hennessy, 1984; Druckman and Bjork, 1994).

Field Studies

When an advanced prototype or preproduction model of a new subsystem is available, field investigations can be conducted. Field tests are almost always a formal stage preceding approval and certification. They provide the opportunity for operational evaluations of elements of a system to be conducted on integral equipment that is being used online in the control process. In addition, field studies are useful when the interactions of a comprehensive set of variables (including the interaction of new equipment with one another and with existing equipment) can be observed dependably only in the actual operational environment.

One of the advantages of collecting human factors information in a field setting rather than in real-time simulation is that the live operational environment provides a means of capturing the subtleties in operational practices and work habits that may not carry over into a simulation environment. The ability to capture controllers' experience with new technology, for example, is especially important for complex automation in which the implications of the interactions between system components are largely unknown prior to implementation.

Field studies, which are inherently face-valid, can serve as a comprehensive source of information. Although they are retrospective in the sense that some design decisions will have been made, the resultant information can also tell the designers whether the system retains major flaws. Examples of programs that are harvesting useful data through field studies are CRDA, CTAS, URET, runway status lights (RWSL), PRM, ASTA, and T-NASA. The HOST/ARTS field experience, resulting in implementation of the implied functions capability that reduces the requirements for manual data entry, is a representative example of the use of field study data to improve design. We wish to emphasize that the concept of field study must also include the ongoing efforts to collect operational data from new systems well after they have been installed, as well as a proceduralized willingness to consider design modifications if field lessons reveal nontrivial human factors concerns. The TCAS system with its newsletter and continued refinement of algorithms provides a positive example of this.

As with simulation studies, one concern with respect to field studies is that, depending on the design of the study, the full range of relevant operating conditions may not necessarily be assessed. Another concern is that the validity of the study can be jeopardized if a representative sample (i.e., representing the range of relevant characteristics of intended users) of properly trained operators are not observed.

System Analysis

In parallel with system development, starting with early conceptual development and continuing through installation, a system-specific analysis of the interactions between system attributes and operators' capabilities should be undertaken—even though the procedures for a given controller position may be well known. In doing so, opportunities to compensate for operator limitations and to take advantage of operator strengths, as well as specific compatibilities and incompatibilities, should be identified.

It is always important—and especially so when the design includes automation features—that human factors participation begin at the earliest phases of analysis, when decisions are usually made about which functions to automate. Human factors activities should not be confined to the implementation of specifications; they should precede and contribute to the development of the specifications. System specifications typically include both *functional requirements* (what the system shall do) and *performance requirements* (how well the system shall perform its functions). These requirements are usually quite detailed in specifications for hardware and software elements of systems. However, functional requirements for the human user are often less clearly specified, and human performance requirements are often not specified at all. A significant reason for the absence of useful human functional and performance requirements is the lack of supporting analyses that link human performance to system performance. Analyses must also be supported by a database of human performance metrics derived from research and from tests and evaluations. Stager (1993, 1994) provides a comprehensive treatment of methodological issues pertaining to the validation and certification of complex systems, including air traffic control systems. Applying research to fill existing gaps in the body of applicable performance metrics is a challenge that requires commitment and investment by program management (Stein and Wagner, 1994).

Integration of Research Methodologies

The discussion above leads to the suggestion that all methodologies have strengths and weaknesses (Chapter 10 in the Phase I report provides a detailed discussion of the strengths and weaknesses). The best approach to successfully fielding a system is to integrate lessons learned across methodologies. Kerns (1994) provides a good example of this integration across laboratory studies, simulations, and field tests for data link. The TCAS, OCC, ASTA, T-NASA, and SMA projects have applied, or plan to apply, a mix of research methodologies that includes modeling, simulation, and field tests; laboratory studies are conspicuously scarce for these programs. Other projects, such as URET, PRM, CRDA, and AMASS, are examples of an imbalance of methodologies, focusing on field tests with little or no evidence of incremental laboratory, modeling, and experimental simulation study. Such imbalance can reflect fractionation of research and development activities. For PRM, CRDA, and AMASS, in particular, the reports describing the functionality do not provide evidence that a comprehensive human factors methodology has been applied.

USER AND HUMAN FACTORS PRACTITIONER INVOLVEMENT IN SYSTEM DESIGN

The advantages of involving users include a better identification of operational needs that drive specifications, garnering useful operational perspectives as the design develops, identifying procedural and organizational implications of design features, and enhancing user acceptance in advance of fielding the system. Recognizing the importance of user involvement, the FAA has established an integrated product team approach to the development of new systems. This approach brings together representatives from systems engineering, users (including air traffic controllers and airway facilities specialists), human factors, and others for the duration of the development cycle (the team works together from earliest analysis of needs and requirements, through post-fielding evaluations). However, as Small (1994) points out, such teams must have a clear understanding of the roles of each member.

Integrated product teams constitute a useful vehicle for cooperative work, but they are not always successful in practice if user inputs are not appropriately structured and filtered by the guidance of the human factors practitioner, and if the advice of the human factors practitioner is not provided or heeded. It is helpful if the users are familiar with fundamental human factors principles and methodology, and if the human factors practitioner has received adequate training in both human factors and air traffic control operations.

User involvement should not be accepted as a substitute for engineering or human factors expertise. A significant risk associated with overreliance on user inputs is the common divergence of user preference and actual performance. Users may prefer one design option but actually perform better with a less preferred option (Andre and Wickens, 1995; see also Chapter 9 in the Phase I report). Small (1994) recommends that users be expected and encouraged to express their findings in terms of operational needs and tasks, rather than in contractual system specification language. However, Small also stipulates (e.g., on the basis of lessons learned from the AAS program) that users not be allowed to specify a system's detailed design (e.g., the human-computer interface).

Human factors practitioners must be involved in defining the functionality (including the allocation of functions to human or to automation), not just the human-computer interface. The most valuable contributions of users occur during the definition of requirements, including functional requirements and performance requirements. These requirements are typically defined in system-level specifications. User inputs are less valuable, and may be counterproductive, if not filtered by human factors professionals, for specifying the detailed design of the system, including the human-computer interface characteristics.

Human factors guidance is properly provided at all phases of development: recommending task analysis techniques, filtering and integrating user input and subjective opinion, and designing assessment tools (including appropriate use of rapid prototypes, experiments, simulations, and literature searches). The CTAS program, for example, illustrates early and continued involvement of human factors practitioners applying a variety of methods in concert with user involvement (Harwood et al., in press). The CTAS project represents exemplary cooperation between users, human factors practitioners, and engineers during the definition of system functionality. The AAS and the AMASS systems, in contrast, illustrate that user control of detailed design decisions can result in "requirements creep" that delays system development and can engender costly reengineering.

Rapid prototyping is a technique for gathering the comments and impressions of future users and others regarding the capabilities and limitations of a simulated air traffic control workstation or workspace while it can still be changed without major cost or schedule impacts. Prototyping is not a substitute for testing, but it can be a useful technique to discard fundamentally flawed options quickly, to identify crucial combinations of circumstances that require testing, and to discover main topics of agreement and of disagreement among evaluators. Prototyping has been usefully applied to such projects as CTAS, TCAS enhancements, data link, and URET, and is planned for application to such projects as SMA and the maintenance OCC. European developers make much use of effective prototyping, as did Canadian developers of electronic flight data presentation for CAATS (see Stager, 1996, for a discussion of automation in CAATS).

To be most effective, user inputs must be structured. The question "Is this design option usable or operationally suitable?" often engenders costly and time-consuming debate that cannot be resolved solely on the basis of the preference of users or of design engineers. The standard human factors task analysis (e.g., see MIL-H-46855B) is a powerful tool that can constitute a common ground for deliberation of operational suitability, as well as for the development of specifications, training requirements, and testing procedures (Small, 1994). Recent efforts have expanded traditional task analysis into the domain of cognitive task analysis, targeted specifically at air- and ground-based aviation systems (Seamster et al., 1997). The task analysis formally defines the tasks that the system and its users are expected to perform to accomplish required functions. When users contribute to the definition of operational scenarios that drive the analysis, when systems engineers contribute to the definition of data flows and machine functions, and when human factors specialists contribute to the definition of operator tasks—and when all team members formalize performance requirements (e.g., time, error) for functions and tasks—then operational suitability decisions can be cooperatively made by asking "Applying a given design option, will the tasks and functions be accomplished within the performance constraints?"

By structuring team roles and inputs, the formal task analysis assists the team in addressing two corollary questions. One is "Where do we need more information to make a decision?" When the team is unable to specify the human performance data associated with a given task, clear direction is implied for supporting research (laboratory, modeling, or prototyping). A second question is "When is the design suitable *enough*?" This question introduces the issue of cost-effectiveness of development efforts. Too often, users and designers identify design options and ask "Which option is more suitable?" This, however, is not necessarily the appropriate design question. The search for the most suitable (or the most preferred) design can lead the team to unnecessarily expensive options. In fact, the decision to automate a task or function can sometimes result in unnecessary expense. To determine operational suitability, it may not be productive to compare options against one another (e.g., comparing automating a function against performing it manually, or comparing one human-computer interface feature against another) without also comparing both options against some specification of acceptable suitability (e.g., the option must permit the performance of a given function within specified time and error constraints). If neither option meets requirements, then neither is suitable. If both options meet requirements, then the relatively "better" (or preferred) option is not necessarily more suitable, and the decision should include considerations of cost-effectiveness (Small, 1994), as well as harmonization with existing equipment and procedures.

INCREMENTAL DEVELOPMENT

In the Phase I report we advanced an incremental approach to testing and validation that reflects a general "build a little, test a little" development and test philosophy from the Phase I report (Del Balzo, 1995). U.S. developers of air traffic control systems have experienced difficulties when they have followed a philosophy that relies on building a complete system according to complex specifications that must be amended as designs develop unforeseen problems, as new technologies appear, and as more is discovered about human performance. The AAS represents a recent example of the difficulties attendant to reworking specifications for a complex air traffic control system (Del Balzo, 1995). In contrast, European developers have adopted an approach that encourages more exploratory research prior to specification (so that problems are discovered early). The CAATS program (see, for example, Stager, 1991) in Canada fell somewhere between these two approaches to system development. For CAATS it was recognized that many design specifications for the controller workstations and displays could not be stated in the absence of additional human engineering data, and that the specifications would need to be resolved through the human engineering program plan.

Automation will be associated with larger conceptual and technological leaps than have characterized past developments. Particularly for large, complex systems (e.g., AAS) this argues all the more for earlier concept exploration activity prior to the writing of system specifications, as well as for the incremental development of system specifications, rather than a traditional approach that specifies all requirements at detailed levels (see Stager, 1993, for an in-depth discussion of the interplay between validation methodologies and system development). The "build a little, test a little" philosophy also relies less on specification of a large system (which takes a long time to develop and to discover whether it is successful) than on the piecemeal development of subsystems, which are flexibly specified and implemented as they are validated (Del Balzo, 1995). In any case, operational testing, evaluation, and validation activities should begin early in the development cycle (Grossberg, 1994) and can be significantly facilitated by cost-effective prototyping and simulation (Small, 1994).

Examples of good incremental development appear to include the CTAS, data link, T-NASA, ASTA, and SMA—all of which remain under development. An example of poor incremental development is the AAS program, whose overall failure was due in part to ambitious attempts to specify in advance a very large and complicated system with many development risks (Del Balzo, 1995).

SYSTEM INSTALLATION

The introduction of automated tools into the workplace should proceed gradually, with adequate attention given to user training, to facility differences, and to user requirements. The operational experience from initial introduction should be very carefully monitored, with mechanisms in place to respond rapidly to both positive and negative lessons learned from those experiences. Adequate funding should be provided at all stages of system development and field evaluations both before and after systems acquisition.

Human Factors and Training

Operators chosen to work with new systems or subsystems should be given an understanding of the principles of system operation. They should be educated with respect to the logic and algorithms underlying the system as well as the practice of system operations. The panel has previously discussed the features of air traffic control training programs and the importance of human factors support of training in detail (see Chapters 3 and 9 in the Phase I report). It remains important that users of systems with automation be trained to perform any manual tasks that will be required in the event of the failure of automation, that they be trained in recovery procedures (which may represent totally new tasks), and that this training be reinforced periodically to maintain appropriate manual skill levels.

Training should include familiarization and part-task instruction on automated systems, but such training should progress quickly to the level of real-time exercises in the setting of interactive simulations. Embedded training should be considered as a useful approach to help controllers maintain skills with automated systems.

The goal of training is to bring each candidate to a high standard of proficiency. Therefore, valid and reliable performance measures should be defined, and proficiency should be determined in regard to the specific measures. The training activity also represents an opportunity to collect data on user performance and to elicit comments and criticisms of the new system.

The TCAS program stands as an example of inadequate initial training (see Chapter 5), whereas training for transition to the ARTS was effective (see Chapter 4). In both cases, as with CTAS, training was enhanced by vendors or by such organizations as the MITRE Corporation and NASA, which, as sponsors of the tools, contributed understanding of the facility climate.

User Acceptance

Several aspects of human factors involvement encourage user transition to and acceptance of new systems. The interaction between human factors specialists and users during early analyses, detail development, and testing forms a working relationship that inspires confidence in prospective users, as well as a structure for training and for field evaluations. This confidence can be reinforced by continued data collection that promises responsive review by program management. Trust is also reinforced by a transition strategy, generally followed by the FAA, that maintains previous equipment and procedures as backup until controllers develop confidence in the new system.

Training that provides to controllers an adequate mental model of how the system works, why it can be expected to be reliable, and how the controller can fulfill assigned responsibilities in the event of system degradation also contributes to trust—whereas "dumbed down" training that does not provide such information can detract from trust. It is important that users possess a clear understanding of their expected tasks in the event of system degradation or failure. These expectations will vary depending on system design and procedures. If the system design includes the expectation that, in the event of system failure, users will perform manually some of the same tasks performed by automation, then users must be trained (and the training must be periodically reinforced) to perform the manual tasks. However, if the system design includes the expectation that users will not be able to perform certain automated tasks manually, then this expectation must be made clear, and users must be trained to perform other recovery tasks (which may be quite distinct from performing the automated tasks manually). In addition, the general "build a little, test a little" philosophy introduces new systems in a manner that allows for an easier absorption rate by users; this may help smooth transition.

Continued human factors involvement throughout training, testing, and implementation contributed to user acceptance of ARTS and is contributing to user acceptance of CTAS and URET. In contrast, AMASS had poor user acceptance due to improper structuring of user involvement (National Transportation Safety Board, 1995b).

Ongoing Data Collection

It is a hallmark of the integrated product team process that team members serve a program throughout the life cycle of its product. This has also been a hallmark of effective human factors programs, which include activities during implementation of systems. MIL-H-46855B is one example of a well-known guide that specifies a comprehensive human factors program to be applied throughout the life cycle of military systems. Continued human factors activity after system installation has three key advantages: development and administration of effective training programs, collection of data for long-term validation of systems, and facilitation of user transition and acceptance.

Performance data and user feedback should be collected throughout the early field use of the system. All data should be applied, when appropriate, to validation (or contradiction) of prior system analyses (which include assumptions about how tasks will be performed and how well they will be performed) and, if necessary, to system upgrades. An additional area of investigation should be the interaction effects between the procedures associated with use of the new system and the organizational context (including formal structure and informal culture) into which the system is introduced.

It is very important, then, to establish a method for ongoing data collection, error and incident analysis, and sharing of lessons learned. TCAS, CTAS, and URET, for example, share lessons learned through newsletters. The ASTA and SMA projects update findings through the Internet. Technical and peer review reports are also important means of sharing findings (see the discussion of literature searches, above). It is not clear that the PRM project has established a method for performing and sharing the results of continued evaluation.

HARMONIZATION OF MULTIPLE SYSTEMS

Currently in the developmental pipeline are a series of substantial air traffic control subsystems that are prospective inclusions in the national airspace system. These systems are described in Chapters 3 through 7 of this report. More research is needed to determine if these new subsystems can perform as well as expected and whether they fit together to make an effective total system. So far, subsystems have been developed in relative isolation from one another and from the overall modernization program. For example, the STARS and DSR specifications require that developers provide an architecture that will allow future plug-in of preplanned product enhancements; however, no human factors analysis of how those enhancements will be integrated with one another or with the standard terminal automation replacement system (STARS) and display system replacement (DSR) baselines is evident. As examples of products being developed in isolation from one another, URET is being tested in a different facility from CTAS, and there does not appear to be research considering the consequences of using both tools simultaneously. There is also little coordination evident between PRM and CTAS and between ASTA and SMA. As we discussed in detail in the Phase I report, the airway facilities monitoring and control workstation is a long-standing example of the negative effects (e.g., inconsistent human-computer interface, haphazard workstation configurations) of failing to consider in advance the integration of multiple components.

The lack of evidence of a unifying human factors analysis for advanced automation products, in order to guide their integration into complementary workstation designs or procedures, is also exemplified by CTAS. Although NASA's in-house scientists and their supporting contractors are also working on projects such as cockpit automation and data link in air traffic control, the role of data link with respect to CTAS, and the potential constraints of data link on CTAS, have not received significant attention of researchers.

In general, tests that determine intersubsystem compatibility should follow the tests that demonstrate subsystem performance. When the compatibility between pairs of subsystems has been established, and possible sources of confusion resulting from conflicting sensors, databases, and algorithms have been identified, the assembly should be enlarged to include other innovations until the subsystems that must be used together have been included in an overall test. At each stage, the evaluation should include a comparison against the base case represented by the current operational system.

Typically, despite careful analysis and validation efforts, not all human errors can be predicted. The human-computer interface is not the only source of error; new systems can introduce new sources of error (e.g., mode, logic, and procedural errors). This may be especially true when a given system will be integrated within a set of existing systems, or when systems in parallel development will be implemented together, because such integration can produce unexpected and unintended consequences. Reason and Zapf (1994) note that testing components in isolation and then putting them together opens the opportunity for previously unidentified "resident pathogens" to strike. Systems designed without consideration of the implementation context risk incorporating such error-inducing features as computer-interface logic that conflicts with that of other systems, information that unnecessarily duplicates (and possibly conflicts with) that provided by other systems, information whose interpretation or use requires data from other remotely located systems, information that confuses what is offered by other systems, alarms that distract the user from those of other systems, and disruption of team work flow (Miller et al., 1996). It should be noted that even field testing can miss unanticipated errors, caused by combining new systems, if systems planned for simultaneous implementation are not field tested together.

Such cumulative or interactive effects should be taken into account throughout a system development process that anticipates the integration of system elements, as discussed in detail above. In addition, since controller training, sector staffing, operational procedures, control room conditions, and equipment maintenance affect system effectiveness, system development and testing should include attention to how these context factors affect controller tasks, workload, and performance during use of the system under development and test (Grossberg, 1994). Modeling and analytical techniques, as well as prototyping and simulation, are all important methodologies for examining possible interactions between new technologies and the equipment and procedural contexts into which they are introduced. These techniques do not, however, obviate the need for operational validation in the actual air traffic control context.

COMMERCIAL OFF-THE-SHELF AND
NONDEVELOPMENTAL ITEMS

The acquisition of commercial off-the-shelf (COTS) and nondevelopmental items (NDIs) does not warrant exemption from human factors analytical, design, or evaluation scrutiny. In the Phase I report, we suggested that human factors analysis, test, and evaluation activities should be applied, for a given application, to these items to ensure that they are compatible with the capabilities and limitations of users. In fact, there are aspects of such acquisitions that require human factors support beyond that provided for developmental acquisitions. For example, COTS items and NDIs may require modification of designs; such modifications can require design and evaluation activities that take into account the constraints imposed by the designs and procedures that come part and parcel with the items—while developmental acquisitions may proceed without these constraints. In addition, integrating the COTS items or NDIs into existing equipment, human-computer interfaces, and procedures may require additional study.

The FAA recognizes that human factors activities must be applied to COTS items and NDIs. The primary human factors policy document within the agency (Order 9550.8, Federal Aviation Administration, 1993c) emphasizes that human factors considerations must be applied to all acquisitions that involve human users. The agency's *Human Factors Acquisition Requirements and Planning* (HARP) document emphasizes the importance of human factors support of the following early phases of acquisition, which apply equally to developmental and nondevelopmental items: (1) mission analysis (e.g., conducting function analysis, identifying human performance and safety shortfalls, and developing the mission need statement); (2) investment analysis (e.g., performing trade-off studies, identifying staffing and training concerns); (3) solution implementation (e.g., conducting prototyping and simulation studies, conducting test and evaluation, and performing risk assessments); and (4) in-service management (e.g., supporting equipment installation and transition, conducting follow-on tests, monitoring staffing and training programs, and identifying requirements for modifications or redesign).

The FAA's human factors guidelines documents (*Human Factors in the Design and Evaluation of Air Traffic Control Systems* [Federal Aviation Administration, 1995f] and *Human Factors Design Guide for Acquisition of Commercial Off-the-shelf Subsystems, Non-developmental Items, and Developmental Systems* [Federal Aviation Administration, 1996f]) provide comprehensive descriptions of procedures for developing a program of human factors activities.

A special concern for COTS items and NDIs is the evaluation of system performance data and operational lessons learned. From the point of view of system validation, the acquisition process should include garnering of available system data relevant to human factors, including: specifications to which the system was built; modifications to those specifications, as well as rationale for those modifications; the human factors program plan applied to the development of the system; documentation of approaches applied to define the functionality of the system (including the allocation of functions to human or to machine) and the human-computer interface (including options considered and rationale for selecting the options implemented and for rejecting others); test procedures and results; field evaluation data; program trouble reports; and training experiences. Ideally, human factors specialists and representative users from the FAA should interview past and current users of the system proposed for acquisition, as well as human factors and engineering personnel involved in its design, if feasible.

Currently, the STARS program represents a significant COTS/NDI acquisition. Since the STARS acquisition is quite recent, the program should be closely monitored for lessons learned.

MANAGEMENT OF THE HUMAN FACTORS PROGRAM

Research

A description of the current distribution of human factors research responsibilities by the FAA appears in the panel's Phase I report. In general terms, the headquarters unit is responsible for the coordination of information at high management levels. CAMI at Oklahoma City is responsible for research and development in support of controller selection and training and for short-term applied research requested by program management offices. The human factors unit at the Technical Center in Atlantic City is responsible for supporting the evaluation of operational alternatives, including new subsystems. The Volpe Center in Cambridge, Massachusetts, is not an interior part of the Federal Aviation Administration but has some responsibility for supporting the human engineering aspect of system design.

Much of the advanced research and technical development is delegated to contractors. In this regard, the NASA research facility at the Ames Center functions as a contract research and development unit. Here, advanced systems such as CTAS are developed with human factors participation from the resident staff of human factors specialists. Some exploratory research on human factors issues (e.g., advanced data link usage procedures) is also performed in this setting. Similar responsibilities have been allocated to the MITRE Corporation in McLean, Virginia, and the Lincoln Laboratory in Bedford, Massachusetts. Other commercial organizations and university research units are engaged in relevant research under contract from time to time.

The general picture presented of the human factors research and development effort within the FAA is that of a patchwork arrangement (Federal Aviation Administration, 1996e). This circumstance is not necessarily adverse except for the evident lack of coordination between units and the absence of a common set of conceptual objectives. These negative attributes are partially balanced by positive features such as the stability of established role structures and a degree of local autonomy. For example, the relationships between researchers and operational people in the various FAA regions are generally mutually beneficial (and are reinforced by recent memoranda of understanding under which NASA researchers are supporting developments in such areas as the terminal area productivity program and the AATT/free flight initiative). Consequently, change in the present delegation of human factors research responsibilities for the sake of centralization of functions is not recommended. However, the need for serious reforms in the scope of activities should be considered. For example, the present provision for long-range feasibility studies is not adequate given the conditions of rapid evolution in computer technology. Such work should probably be done by organizations outside the Federal Aviation Administration and, indeed, outside the government. The in-house laboratories and those other facilities with close linkages to specific systems or subsystems need to continue in their current modes of operation. However, there is need for much more investment in generic studies and what might be called basic research.

Reliable mechanisms for the management of forward-looking research activities exist in settings such as the National Institutes of Health. In that setting, mission-oriented research and development activities are undertaken by the researchers employed within each institute. This arrangement corresponds to the present one within the FAA. However, each institute also sponsors extramural programs and projects by means of grants and contracts with organizations such as independent research centers and university departments. Proposals for research from such outside organizations are subject to rigorous evaluation by expert panels of peer scientists who are not employees of the institutes. Consequently, the record of scientific quality of the research sponsored by the National Institutes of Health has been exemplary. Applying this model to the management of extramural human factors research for the FAA would require special attention to the prevention of such potential problems as accepting research proposals that do not demonstrate expertise in air traffic control operations, that are not predicted to contribute knowledge useful to the development of air traffic control systems, and that do not support an integrated research and development program.

The budgetary allotment for such research by the Federal Aviation Administration would be many times smaller than that established by the National Institutes of Health. However, there is no reason why the quality of the science should be any lower.

Applications

One conclusion of the panel's Phase I report is that effectiveness of human factors activities also requires coordination and oversight by a central human factors management within the Federal Aviation Administration. In reaching that conclusion, we considered requirements for an effective human factors *program* (as opposed to fragmented human factors research and development activities) identified in the following FAA documents: (1) the Human Factors Policy (FAA Order 9550.8, Federal Aviation Administration, 1993c), (2) the report of the Human Factors Subcommittee of the Research, Engineering, and Development Council (*Report of the Committee on the Status and Organization of Human Factors Within the FAA*, Federal Aviation Administration, 1996e), and (3) the *National Plan for Civil Aviation Human Factors* (Federal Aviation Administration, 1995g). Although our conclusion applies to all human factors activities within the agency, we reemphasize here, with respect to the development and acquisition of automation systems for air traffic control, that a centralized human factors program management for the Federal Aviation Administration should:

- Coordinate communication of human factors performance data across integrated product teams and between researchers, developers, users, and testers in the United States as well as in other countries;
- Develop and monitor human factors program plans;
- Monitor and guide the activities of contractors' human factors representatives;
- Develop policies and procedures for the application of human factors to the development, testing, and implementation of automated systems;
- Evaluate the qualifications and performance of human factors specialists; and
- Guide trade-offs pertaining to cost and schedule of human factors activities.

Human factors management should play a key role in identifying the appropriate mix of research and test methods that support system development. Human factors management should interface with engineering and program management personnel at the FAA and at support contractors to ensure that human performance requirements drive specifications and that hardware and software developers are responsive to the human performance requirements. Poor alternatives are the unfortunate situations in which human factors specialists become documenters of previously written computer code for the human-computer interface, or in which training is expected to compensate for poor design.

It is also the role of human factors management to remind program managers, as necessary, that good human factors is a "pay now or pay more later" proposition. By the time a system reaches late stages of development or testing, major design commitments have been made, resources have been spent, and there is reduced motivation to discover design flaws that threaten deployment schedules. It is not unusual for system designers or program managers to request that human factors specialists devise improved training programs to compensate for discovered design problems, after system designs are frozen. Training, however, should not be considered a substitute for effective design (reliance on training will not prevent errors if the design itself is inadequate), and flawed systems often require redesign despite improved training methods. Systems in which human factors are not properly addressed may require costly redesign after inadequacies are discovered (Grossberg, 1994; Stein and Wagner, 1994).

Of course, an effective human factors program presumes the activity of knowledgeable human factors specialists. In addition, it is important that researchers, system developers, and developers of policies, procedures, and regulations share appreciation of the importance of human factors activities and understanding of fundamental human factors principles. There are several avenues by which the FAA can pursue development of human factors understanding throughout the agency, as well as the enhancement of human factors expertise:

• The human factors management function, as stated above, should include coordination of information sharing between researchers and system developers. One appropriate vehicle would be a human factors (in air traffic control or in aviation) newsletter, broadly disseminated within and beyond the agency to summarize studies, lessons learned, and issues raised by fielded systems, analogous in some respects to *ASRS CALL BACK*.

• The existing Human Factors Coordinating Committee, established by FAA Policy Order 9550.8 (Federal Aviation Administration, 1993c), represents a vehicle whereby FAA program managers can identify human factors needs and human factors specialists can provide (or link managers with sources of) information. To be effective, the committee must meet frequently.

• Widespread appreciation of fundamental human factors principles requires education of those within the agency who perform research, support system development and testing, and establish regulations and procedures. The FAA has developed at least four useful educational tools: (1) the *National Plan for Civil Aviation Human Factors* (Federal Aviation Administration, 1995g), which identifies key general human factors goals and principles for agency activities; (2) the guidebook *Human Factors in the Design and Evaluation of Air Traffic Control Systems* (Federal Aviation Administration, 1995f), which provides a comprehensive discussion of human factors principles, is written specifically to educate agency personnel, and includes a software tool for assessing systems under development; (3) the *Human Factors Design Guide for Acquisition of Commercial Off-the-shelf Subsystems, Non-developmental Items, and Developmental Systems* (Federal Aviation Administration, 1996f) , which provides reference information for the selection, analysis, design, development, and evaluation of new and modified air traffic control systems and equipment; and (4) FAA human factors web sites (e.g., for the AAR-100 organization and for the FAA Technical Center) that contain useful human factors resources and identify human factors contacts within the agency. We trust that this panel's two reports will constitute a fifth key educational tool. We note here that such educational materials are expected to convey an appreciation for fundamental human factors issues and methodologies, not expertise in human factors. We also note that there are many other documents that provide useful guidance for those interested in human factors (see Chapter 10 in the Phase I report for a detailed discussion of sources of human factors guidance and information).

• FAA acquisition programs have generally relied on development contractors and subcontractors to perform human factors activities. Qualifications of good human factors specialists, however, are not often made clear during the hiring of personnel by contractors, and the FAA has not generally reviewed the qualifications of human factors specialists hired by contractors. One function of FAA human factors management should be to do so.

• Training within the agency and hiring from without the agency remain alternative means of enhancing the human data base of human factors principles and criteria. Two additional resources are available. (1) Other government or government-funded agencies are repositories of human factors expertise and data. For example, the FAA shares a memorandum of agreement with NASA, whereby NASA human factors specialists support FAA research and development activities. (2) Academic programs throughout the country offer programs of study in human factors, at both the graduate and undergraduate levels. The FAA (e.g., through AAR-100, the Technical Center, and the Civil Aeromedical Research Institute, as well as through NASA) seeks the support of faculty from these institutions. In addition, the students at these institutions represent valuable sources of actual and potential human factors knowledge. The training they receive in human factors principles, methods, and criteria could be usefully augmented by increased opportunities for apprenticeships and internships within the FAA—whereby the agency would be increasing the very restricted pool of individuals whose expertise includes both human factors and air traffic control knowledge.

• The FAA should continue to work toward an agency infrastructure in which some human factors training is provided to personnel and program managers at all levels of the organization (and to contract teams).

• The FAA should continue to support integrated product teams with well-trained human factors specialists assigned to the team. These specialists should be responsible to human factors management within the FAA as well as to project managers.

9

Airspace System Integration: The Concept of Free Flight

The national airspace system involves four key components: (1) air traffic control personnel, (2) dispatchers and management of the airline industry, (3) pilots and their aircraft systems, and (4) ground-based automation. Perceived inefficiencies in the national airspace have spurred serious planning toward a concept in which pilots, airline dispatchers, and managers may be assuming more authority for flight path management (RTCA, 1995a, 1995b). In this chapter, we take a systems perspective in considering the roles of these four components in the concept of free flight (Figure 9.1). Our discussion includes an overview, system-level issues, and related human factors issues, revisiting issues discussed in detail in the panel's Phase I report. We then propose an alternative vision of the evolution of automation in the national airspace system in the next decade.

We begin by characterizing differences among the key components in three critical variables:

1. *Goals* may differ, in terms of the relative emphasis on safety versus efficiency (and productivity) and in terms of local optimization versus global optimization.

2. *Information* may reside differently within different components, and such information may or may not be shared between them.

3. *Authority* for different aspects of air traffic management exists in certain places. Furthermore, authority may "flow" along certain paths, and these paths may change with future changes in air traffic management procedures.

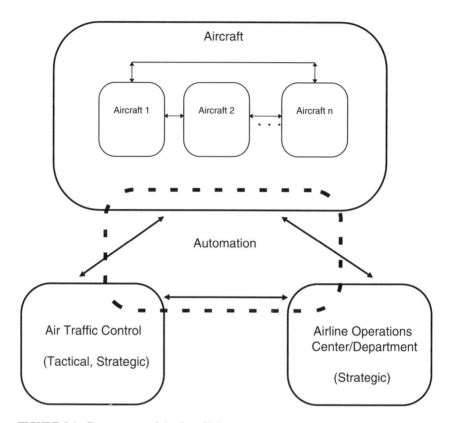

FIGURE 9.1 Components of the free flight concept. Goals, information, and authority (both perceived and actual) may differ among the four major elements.

First, air traffic controllers maintain primary responsibility for the goal of overall safety of *all* aircraft in the system, and their concerns about efficiency are distributed across *all* occupants of the airspace, including general aviation and military aviation flying in civilian airspace. Airline management, as reflected by the influence of the airline operations center, although concerned with safety, has relatively greater interest in expediency and efficiency, as well as a more local interest in the efficiency of its own fleet of aircraft. Profit is a heavy driver of the expediency goal, given the low profit margin of most airlines and the high cost of delays to company profit. The pilot's interests are still more local, concerned primarily with the safety and expediency of a single aircraft. Automation may be conceived to be relatively goal-neutral with regard to safety and efficiency, in that these goals are defined by the designers of the system. However, many aspects of automation proposed for the national airspace system are specifically intended to increase efficiency, with the explicit requirement that they be *safety-*

neutral. The fact remains that automation may sometimes be safety-compromising if it is not carefully implemented (Parasuraman and Riley, 1997).

Second, each component retains somewhat different information about the airspace. That information can vary in its geographical scope (global to local), its level of detail, and its accuracy or currency. For example, airline dispatchers and management at the airline operations department may currently possess the best information about global weather patterns (of regions containing its flying fleet). Relatively high levels of automation can provide them with accurate projections of ideal flight routes. Air traffic controllers (en route and central flow control) have slightly less precise current weather information (see Chapter 3), but the best information regarding global traffic patterns and global intents. Controllers at TRACON facilities and towers have still more restricted but detailed information, and pilots generally have the most restricted but most detailed information regarding the capabilities and intent of their own aircraft. Thus, across these components, there tends to be a trade-off between information scope and detail. An advantage of automation is that it has the ability to retain, digest, and share information that is at once global *and* detailed and thus to contribute in a beneficial way to information sharing.

Third, the Federal Aviation Administration (FAA) has set up clearly defined lines of *actual* authority (responsibility) for different aspects of flight path management. For example, controllers have authority to issue clearances and instructions to aircraft only within their sector. Controllers, not pilots, have authority to direct instrument flight rules aircraft to different flight levels and headings. However, it is not clear that *perceived* authority necessarily follows procedurally defined authority lines. For example, the possible loss of situation awareness and skill induced by high levels of flight deck automation can create a potential shift in perceived authority for trajectory management away from the pilot (Sarter and Woods, 1995b). If the automation is trusted, reliable, and introduced carefully into the workplace, this shift can be voluntary (i.e., the human can willingly give up some aspects of control to automation). However, if the automation is mistrusted, clumsy, and introduced without consideration of user inputs, the shift may be involuntary, with the user feeling that authority has been taken away. In either case, there are possible concerns: complacency in the former case, loss of job satisfaction or even possible abuse of automation in the latter.

From a controller's perspective, the loss of authority and information may have similar implications, no matter which component in the airspace (pilot or automation) is perceived to preempt that authority. Most of this report has addressed a scenario in which authority potentially flows to automation. However, the concept of free flight in which pilots, airline dispatchers, and managers, rather than automation, may be assuming more authority, has many implications for the controller similar to those of high automation levels. In Chapter 5 we note a precursor to this effect when we discuss the issue of maneuver authority in the traffic alert and collision avoidance system (TCAS).

HISTORY

Many participants in commercial aviation have become frustrated by what they view as inefficiencies in the national airspace. These inefficiencies translate into flight delays, occasionally missed connections, passenger complaints, excess fuel consumption, excess crew time, and, ultimately, loss of revenue, for companies that already have a very thin profit margin. Such inefficiencies are viewed to result, in part, from three factors: (1) standard linear airways that rarely allow the most direct flight between two points (e.g., a great circle route), (2) strict adherence to air traffic control procedures for route changes, which sometimes imposes delays, inefficiencies, or denial of requests that in fact might be entirely safe, and (3) dependence on radar for separation standards, which are therefore constrained by the resolution of radar in estimating position (see Chapter 3).

In response to these concerns, since 1994 an effort triggered by the airline industry has begun to examine the concept of *user-preferred routing* or *free flight*, a concept in which pilots are better able to select their preferred routes, unconstrained by air traffic control (RTCA, 1995a, 1995b; Planzer and Jenny, 1995). This system is designed to allow pilots to take better advantage of local information (e.g., weather) that may not be available to air traffic control and, most important, will allow pilots to rely on the global positioning system (GPS) for navigation and separation that is far more precise than the radar-based guidance available from air traffic control (see Chapter 3). The concept has been developed by a working committee on free flight sponsored by the RTCA, who propose the following definition:

> A safe and efficient flight operating capability under instrument flight rules (IFR) in which the operators have the freedom to select their path and speed in real time. Air traffic restrictions are only imposed to ensure separation, to preclude exceeding airport capacity, to prevent unauthorized flight through special use airspace, and to ensure safety of flight. Restrictions are limited in extent and duration to correct the identified problem. Any activity which removes restrictions represents a move toward free flight.

More recently, free flight has been the subject of an intense federally sponsored research program on advanced aircraft transport technologies (AATT), sponsored by the National Aeronautics and Space Administration (NASA) and coordinated by a memorandum of agreement between NASA and the FAA. The FAA has recently published a document identifying 46 critical issues for free flight (Federal Aviation Administration, 1996g), and strategists have been working to define a global plan for the national airspace that maximizes flexibility for all users (Runnels, 1996). Reports based on the AATT program can be obtained from NASA Ames Research Center.

There are three drivers for free flight. Two are economic and the third is related jointly to comfort and safety:

1. Horizontal free flight results in fuel saving by allowing the flying of shorter, more direct routes, ideally following great circle paths, avoiding headwinds or capitalizing on tailwinds.

2. Vertical free flight results in fuel saving by allowing flying at altitudes that have the most favorable winds.

3. Flying around bad weather and clear air turbulence (both horizontally and vertically) results in passenger comfort and safety.

It is important to realize that the concept of free flight is not defined by a universally accepted set of procedures. Different players have very different notions of what it should be, how free it will be, and over what domains of the airspace it will apply (e.g., en route versus TRACON, high altitude versus all altitudes, continental versus oceanic). Some of these dimensions are explored below. However, an important distinction contrasts *strategic* free flight, in which route planning is done in a manner that is unconstrained by air traffic control (i.e., free scheduling and free routing), with *tactical* free flight, in which executions of flight path changes, including maneuvers to avoid conflicts, are carried out without air traffic control guidance or instructions (i.e., free maneuvering—Runnels, 1996). A continuum of levels exists between strategic and tactical maneuvering.

It should also be noted that at least four characteristics of the current airspace take on some aspects of free flight:

1. Standard flying by visual flight rules removes air traffic control from a great deal of responsibility for route planning and separation maintenance, outside the TRACON area.

2. The FAA is in the process of expanding the national route program, in which aircraft are allowed to file flight plans for preferred or direct routes (e.g., great circle routes, or those that take greater advantage of favorable winds or minimize the effect of unfavorable winds). Initially allowed only at highest altitudes, the expanded program has been "stepping down" flight levels to a current level of 29,000 ft.

3. The resolution advisories generated by the traffic alert and collision avoidance system (TCAS), discussed in Chapter 5, allow pilots to fly emergency conflict avoidance maneuvers in a manner that is not cleared in advance by air traffic control. Problems revealed by the TCAS program may anticipate some of the issues raised by free flight (Mellone and Frank, 1993).

4. Taking advantage of the high navigational accuracy of the TCAS situation display, the FAA has authorized a procedure called oceanic in-trail climb, whereby aircraft on transoceanic flights can adjust their flight levels and spatial positions to overtake and pass a leading aircraft that may be slower, hence avoiding the very time-consuming processes of mediating communications with oceanic controllers who have no radar coverage of the aircraft involved (*Aviation Week and Space Technology*, 1994).

SYSTEM ELEMENTS AND FUNCTIONS

The numerous versions of proposed free flight architectures have in common a set of key elements.

Global Positioning System and Position Broadcasting

Any aircraft must have a very accurate estimate of own position and that of its nearest neighbors. The global positioning system (see Chapter 3) appears to provide this facility and, when coupled with automatic dependent surveillance (ADS-B, see Chapter 3), will enable rapid communications of accurate navigational information between aircraft in close (and hence potentially threatening) spatial proximity. Such information can also be broadcast to air traffic control and airline operations centers.

Traffic Display

In order to plan conflict-free trajectories and to maneuver around possible conflicts in the absence of air traffic control advisories, pilots will need an accurate cockpit display of traffic information, whose precision and format remain to be determined (Johnson et al., 1997; Merwin et al., 1997; Kerns and Small, 1995). These requirements make relevant a large body of research carried out on the cockpit display of traffic information by NASA in the 1970s and 1980s (e.g., Ellis et al., 1987; Kreifeldt, 1980; Abbott et al., 1980). Such displays are proposed to include an important distinction between a *conflict or protected zone*, the region of space that would formally define a loss of separation or operational error, and an *alert zone*. The latter is less clearly defined but would be the level of separation at which an advisory to maneuver would be offered to one or both aircraft. It may also define a time at which air traffic control might be alerted to the possibility that active control from the ground might be required, as such control would need to be exerted prior to a formal loss of separation. Since the parameter dictating the degree of urgency to maneuver is the predicted *time to contact* (rather than spatial separation), many have considered the alert zone to be time based, rather than space based, and hence not simply represented in its geometrical form (e.g., Corker et al., 1997). Current thinking also suggests the need to define different levels of urgency within the alert zone (Johnson et al., 1997).

Intent Inferencing

Any traffic display designed to alert the pilot to potential conflicts will be beneficial to the extent that it can account for reliable predictive information regarding the trajectory of both aircraft involved. Accounting for the current velocity and acceleration vector provides a good deal of accuracy in this prediction. But considerably more valid estimates of future trajectories can be gained by knowledge of intent of one or both aircraft in a conflict: Does the potential intruder intend to level off? Will it slow within the next few minutes? (Geddes et al., 1996).

Such intent inferencing (discussed in Chapter 2) can be gained from a variety of sources: current velocity vectors, filed flight plans, information resident in the flight management system, even the active queries of the pilots involved. The further into the future that reliable intent inferences can be made, the more flexibility pilots will have in selecting routes to avoid conflict situations.

Rules of the Road

The kind and precedence of maneuvers undertaken as two aircraft present a potential future conflict situation will need to be formally established. These will need to go beyond standard FAA guidelines to maintain traffic in sight, yield to the aircraft on the right, or to turn to the right to avoid conflict (FAR 34291, Section 91.113). For example, how much will the same rules apply to all aircraft, and to what extent will smaller (and hence more maneuverable) aircraft be expected to bear a greater burden of maneuvering? How should the pilot trade off the costs and benefits of lateral versus vertical versus speed change maneuvering (Krozell and Peters, 1997)? A substantial part of these rules may be left flexible to be negotiated between aircraft at the encounter, as discussed below.

Air Traffic Control

All players acknowledge the critical sustaining role of air traffic control in a free flight system. This role is seen in at least two ways:

1. Any free flight system will need to include both unconstrained (free flight) and constrained airspace. In the latter, conditions of high traffic density or the need to maintain regular flow militate against user-preferred routing. For example, it is assumed by most planners that TRACON regions will remain under positive air traffic control.

2. There is always a danger that a potential conflict situation may develop for which pilots involved are unable or unwilling to formulate a satisfactory solution. Air traffic control then must be alert to "bail out" the pilots from catastrophe in such a situation.

A large number of issues must be addressed and resolved before determining if a free flight system is feasible in an airspace whose regulators and occupants are committed to safety as a primary goal (White House Commission on Aviation Safety and Security, 1997). We discuss these issues below in two categories, those pertaining to the airspace system as a whole, and those focusing more directly on human factors.

SYSTEM-LEVEL ISSUES

Air Traffic Control Role

The role of air traffic control in a free flight regime will continue to remain a critical and controversial issue. Indeed, one of the thornier issues concerns the appropriate *level of authority* that should be maintained by air traffic control (Endsley et al., 1997). On one extreme is a system in which aircraft maneuver as they choose, allowing air traffic control to be only a passive monitor of the changing trajectories, until or unless these lead to danger, and then intervening with control. A more conservative system will require pilots to inform air traffic control of their maneuvers but proceed to carry them out unless vetoed by air traffic control; this level captures the procedural rules involved in following TCAS resolution advisories. Still more conservative is a system not unlike that in existence today, in which pilots request deviations and air traffic control approves. However, under a free flight regime, such requests would be far more frequent (as would approvals), given that pilots would have the equipment (GPS, ADS-B, cockpit display of traffic information) and training to carry them out safely.

Pilot's and the Airline Operations Center's Roles

Our discussion here has implicitly assumed that the pilot is the one calling the shots in a free flight regime. However, from the standpoint of commercial aviation, the pilot is not necessarily the best originator of unconstrained maneuver plans. Instead, the airline operations center, and its agent the aircraft dispatcher, will probably have far better global knowledge of weather patterns, winds, traffic scheduling, and regional traffic density, in order to make more nearly optimal decisions on route and trajectory changes. Hence, although the pilot may become free from air traffic control constraints, these may be replaced by constraints from the dispatcher.

System-Wide Efficiency

On paper, convincing cases can be made for the cost savings of direct routings and other free flight concepts (Lee et al., 1997). However, in practice, savings that appear in one place may be lost in others. For example, complex simulation runs have revealed that free flight can considerably lessen the cruise flight time en route between TRACONs (Lee et al., 1997). But much of the time saved may then be lost, as a large stack of rapidly arriving aircraft must now wait at the feeder gate to a TRACON (constrained airspace), in order to be handled in a less efficient, more sequential fashion by air traffic control. Also, losses of efficiency may emerge from group behavior in ways that cannot easily be predicted in advance. One such loss was revealed by an analysis of aircraft behavior in the expanded national route program by Denning et al. (1996) and Smith, Woods, McCoy et al. (1997). The analysis revealed a phenomenon whereby several aircraft, all requesting the same preferred routing, created a bunching on that preferred route that ultimately slowed their flight, and in some cases required redirection back to the earlier nonpreferred route, now with a considerable loss of time. In this case, flight time is not saved, nor is any workload reduced for the controller. It may well be difficult or impossible to predict other such system-wide effects until or unless a full operational test of the system is in place.

Safety Versus Efficiency

The pressure toward free flight is primarily efficiency driven. Lee et al. (1997) simulated flying on a set of cross-country routes and estimated a 6 percent fuel savings and, with equal fuel burn between preferred and nonpreferred routing, found an average 15-minute time savings. The FAA has rightfully maintained a conservative stance, driven by safety, in responding to pressures to move toward free flight. But given the recent commitment to reduce accident rates by a factor of five over the next decade (White House Commission on Aviation Safety and Security, 1997), it can be argued that any radical change to an already safe system will at least have the possibility of being safety-compromising. And given the complexity of the free flight concept, accurate assessment of its safety benefits may not be achievable for several years after its implementation.

In the Phase I report we pointed out the need for sophisticated modeling of both safety and efficiency parameters of new technologies and procedures. Shepherd et al. (1997) confirm this need and are developing a reduced aircraft separation risk assessment model (RASROM), with the goal of assessing the overall level of safety associated with reducing separation standards and with the introduction of new technology and procedures. Developed under the aegis of NASA's terminal area productivity program, the model incorporates both fault trees and event trees (see Chapter 2 for a discussion of the use of these techniques in failure and recovery analysis). The model takes into account events, behaviors, and parameters (e.g., response times) at levels that do not include elaborate, detailed modeling of the internal processes of complex technologies or of human factors (Shepherd et al., 1997).

Valid airspace safety models that include contributions of human operator (pilot or controller) processing are greatly needed in order to predict safety implications of free flight, and compare these implications with those supported by higher levels of ground-based automation, discussed below. For example, Corker et al. (1997) have applied MIDAS, a human-machine system model with valid estimates of human processing times for different cognitive components, to predicting decision time requirements in different conflict situations. Riley et al. (1996) are working to extend MIDAS to account for errors in interaction between pilots and automation.

Equipment

Free flight demands special technical equipment: accurate global positioning systems, automatic dependent surveillance communications, and high-resolution cockpit displays of traffic information. Using such technology, the position of fully equipped commercial aircraft can be estimated within a standard deviation of 30 m both horizontally and vertically. However, any airspace that contains at least one aircraft without such equipment is placed at risk in a free flight regime. The FAA will need to continue to protect the interests of general, corporate, and military aviation, so that movement toward free flight will not price these players out of the national airspace.

HUMAN FACTORS ISSUES

Many of the human factors issues to be addressed in free flight pertain to the infrequent situations in which two aircraft have selected routes that will bring them into conflict. The times available to deal with these conflicts may be predicted to vary from as long as 20 to 30 minutes, to as short as a minute or two.

Level of Air Traffic Control Authority

How easy will it be for air traffic control to veto inappropriate maneuvers and flight plans, or should these indeed be subject to preapproval? If a controller's conflict probe (discussed in Chapter 6) enables him to predict a conflict within 20 minutes, should the controller intervene or offer an advisory to two aircraft in free flight? One issue concerns the extent to which controllers, rather than pilots, may have better skills, and more global displays, to appreciate global traffic patterns and may therefore be better equipped than pilots to judge the long-range implications of maneuvers. At least one simulation that compared different levels of authority in a free flight simulation revealed that more separation losses occurred under conditions in which pilots had the greatest degree of authority (Endsley et al., 1997). This simulation also revealed that the higher levels of pilot authority led to a degradation of the controllers' situation awareness, an issue we consider next.

Equally important are issues associated with ambiguity in authority. Almost any envisioned free flight system assumes regions (or times) in which air traffic control has authority and those in which they do not. At issue are the transition periods between such authority assignments (e.g., transferring from unconstrained to constrained airspace or from pilot-centered strategic maneuvering to controller-centered tactical maneuvering to resolve a conflict.) Such regions invite ambiguity, and such ambiguity in turn will invite noncooperative maneuvering or unnecessary and time-consuming negotiations (discussed below).

Situation Awareness

As noted, at least one experimental simulation study revealed the loss of controller situation awareness that resulted from progressively higher levels of pilot authority in free flight (Endsley et al., 1997). The controller's awareness of the big picture may be degraded under free flight for one of three reasons. First, as noted above and repeatedly observed in basic and applied psychological research, when people do not actively direct changes but only observe them passively, they are less likely to remember them (Slameca and Graf, 1978; Hopkin, 1991a). Hence, a controller who passively witnesses a pilot changing altitude will be less likely to be aware of and remember the implications of that new altitude for another aircraft, than if the controller had actively selected the change (or even had to consider and approve it). Second, an airspace that functions under free flight rules will, almost by definition, lose the structured order that enables the controller to easily grasp the big picture (Wyndemere, 1996). Aircraft will no longer be flying linearly along predefined routes, and flight levels may no longer be evenly spaced and predictably occupied. It is quite possible that an airspace under free flight will yield unpredictable shifts in traffic density, and this in turn may require some degree of "dynamic resectorization." Given the strong dependence of the controller's mental model on the static, enduring characteristics of a sector (see the Phase I report), these dynamic and inconsistent characteristics invite greater difficulty in maintaining situation awareness. Finally, as noted above, free flight separation algorithms, like those of TCAS, are likely to be time based rather than space based. Space can be easily visualized by the controller, but time less so. It is unclear the extent to which this shift may also inhibit controller situation awareness.

Controller Workload

As previously noted, workload and situation awareness are closely and often reciprocally related, and the mediation of these two concepts by a free flight regime leads to several possible implications. First, under routine conditions, controller workload in decision making and communications may be reduced by free flight (Hilburn et al., 1997), but monitoring workload—a nontrivial source of stress—may be increased. Second, the likely decrease in traffic structure and increase in traffic complexity (Wyndemere, 1996) will impose greater cognitive workload in trying to predict traffic behavior to maintain adequate situation awareness. The increase in controller workload with the decreased structure of the free flight airspace was observed in the simulation experiment carried out by Endsley et al. (1997). Third, controller workload is likely to be substantially increased under the infrequent but safety-critical circumstances in which two or more aircraft cannot negotiate a conflict-free solution and the controller must intervene. Fourth, as has been noted, increased efficiency of free flight in the unconstrained region may produce traffic bottlenecks at the borders of the constrained regions, hence imposing high workload to deal with the resulting traffic rush, although the center TRACON automation system (CTAS) can provide a valuable aid here.

For the pilot, there is a clear assumption that shifting responsibility for traffic avoidance to the cockpit will increase flight deck workload to some extent. Indeed, the decision in the 1980s not to proceed with introduction of the cockpit display of traffic information was based in part on pilot workload concerns. How much added head-down time will be imposed, as pilots attempt to resolve conflicts with a cockpit display, remains poorly understood, as does the level of cognitive load imposed on pilots as they attempt to chose an appropriate maneuver and communicate with other traffic in doing so.

Pilot Maneuver Selection

In the tactical aspects of maneuver selection required for predicted conflict avoidance, it is unclear how pilots will allow various factors to influence their chosen maneuvers. Different maneuvers (i.e., speed, heading, altitude control), executed at varying times in advance of a potential conflict, have quite different economic consequences (Krozel and Peters, 1997). But it is not at all apparent that these correlate with safety, and it is not clear how well (or how homogeneously) pilots will achieve the appropriate balance between safety and efficiency. We have noted above that automated assistance in recommending maneuvers will benefit from accurate intent inferencing capabilities. But recent lessons learned from TCAS compliance (Pritchett and Hansman, 1997a, 1997b) suggest that automated advice in air traffic avoidance maneuvers will not always be followed, particularly if the algorithms governing that advice are not well understood by the pilots.

In a recent study, Patrick (1996) interviewed a group of 747-400 pilots and dispatchers concerning the qualitative criteria they used (e.g., safety, time efficiency, fuel efficiency) and their relative importance in establishing a flight plan. The results suggest that pilots differ from dispatchers in how criteria are weighted. For example, pilots are charged with ride comfort, which they weigh move heavily than dispatchers; pilots also use a nonlinear trade-off function between time and fuel, whereas dispatchers follow a linear trade-off function.

Negotiations

A minimum of two players are potentially involved in any conflict resolution scenario. If conflicts are predicted far in advance, then only the two pilots may be involved in negotiations to avoid. If such negotiations are not completed (or not initiated) progressively close to the predicted time of separation loss, air traffic control is more likely to get involved and possibly desire to intervene. It is also easy to imagine circumstances in which a third aircraft can be a party to the negotiations, if a maneuver by one of the first two may turn it toward the third. The organizational psychology of negotiations and group behavior is poorly understood. Any negotiations once air traffic control becomes a concerned party (because, for example, the alert zone has been penetrated) will be complicated by the fact that pilot-pilot communications may be more rapid (and based on better local information) than pilot-controller communications; there may therefore be times when the lines of authority are blurred.

The application of negotiation theory to the free flight regime will become simpler to the extent that clearly defined rules of the road are laid out (e.g., always turn right; the lower aircraft always descends, etc.). Indeed, as in TCAS, it is in theory possible to embody these rules in software, providing expert advice on resolution to two cooperating aircraft. But the lessons learned from TCAS are that these algorithms are far from perfect, even in the relatively simple case of two aircraft and one degree of resolution freedom (vertical maneuvering). It is easy to imagine the far greater limitations of automation advice when applied to free flight conflict maneuvering, given two human pilots who may concurrently possess information that is not available to the automated advice giver.

RESEARCH APPROACHES

To some extent, knowledge of how best to implement technology in free flight can be gained by applying existing research results (Kerns and Small, 1995). However, any free flight concept now under consideration will involve relatively substantial changes in procedures and equipment from today's practices. One of the greatest challenges is to try to predict the implications of changes in free flight to overall system safety. This is particularly important, given hard numbers on target safety levels imposed by the federal government (White House Commission on Aviation Safety and Security, 1997). Three parallel research approaches are essential to estimate safety implications.

First, simulation modeling must be continued and refined. Initial simulations, revealing efficiency changes under a free flight regime (Lee et al., 1997), represent a valid starting point. But, as suggested by Odoni et al. (1997), it is essential that simulation models begin to make assumptions about the human operator. NASA's recent AATT initiative appears to be taking promising initial steps in this direction. A good example of such models is provided by MIDAS, a complex model including estimates of human processing time, developed at NASA Ames (Corker et al., 1997) and being extended to account for errors (Riley et al., 1996). Major efforts should be made to continue development of these modeling efforts and their validation.

Second, it is necessary to collect sufficient amounts of human-in-the-loop simulation data, so that the infrequent but catastrophic consequences are revealed and understood—for example, two pilots involved in a nearly unresolvable conflict. Such data appear to be very difficult and time-consuming to collect (Endsley et al., 1997). Third, extensive reliance can be made on scenario walkthroughs and focus group sessions among controllers and pilots who have been provided with clear descriptions of future assumed capabilities (Smith, Woods, McCoy et al., 1997). These can reveal potential bottleneck areas. A final approach involves not research but rather a design change to greatly increase the safety margin between aircraft, even as the procedures are altered to allow more regular flow (i.e., improve efficiency).

In conclusion, we note that free flight is only one of two possible trajectories that may be taken toward increasing flight efficiency. The other—increasing air traffic automation rather than the flight deck capabilities underlying free flight—has been the focus of this report. It is not at all clear whether these represent two closely intertwined parallel paths to the future, or whether their implications for authority are so different that they represent very different paths. Nevertheless, the common concern that both impose for controller awareness, workload, skills, and authority requires a close sharing of lessons between them.

THE PANEL'S VISION FOR APPLICATIONS OF AUTOMATION

In the panel's judgment, pursuing the free flight concept to achieve high and broad levels of pilot authority has a number of risks for the national airspace, given that the stated policy of the FAA is to guarantee that any proposed changes to the national airspace system's architecture will be at least safety-neutral and should be projected to be safety-enhancing. Considering the number of uncertainties associated with free flight, it seems very difficult to project with any high degree of confidence that it will produce an *increase* in safety, unless extensive research and modeling is continued.

An alternative approach, which we believe has lower safety risks, capitalizes on the strengths of advanced technology and human-centered automation and does so in a way that maintains clear authority for separation with air traffic control on the ground. We project what such a system should look like, anchoring it in our assumptions about human-centered automation and our knowledge of human factors, and also spelling out certain expectations about the evolution of the national airspace system in the next decade. These expectations are consistent with Federal Aviation Administration forecasts (Federal Aviation Administration, 1996a). We also reiterate some important human-centered automation concerns and show how these should be applied, in order to move toward a national airspace system with increased capacity but no compromise of safety.

Expectations

In the coming decade, we expect the following developments:

1. The FAA's goal will continue to be one of *improving* safety (decreasing risk of midair collision and collisions on the ground).
2. Current air routes will become obsolete and will be replaced by many more direct routings.
3. Satellite-based navigation and ADS-B communications, coupled with current radar, and integration of sensor data will allow ground-based air traffic control to obtain increasingly precise and timely estimates of three-dimensional aircraft position, thereby enabling reduced separation and greater capacity in some regions of the airspace.
4. The global positioning system, data link, and ADS-B will be available in nearly all instrument flight rules aircraft, allowing rapid sharing of various kinds of textual and graphical information.
5. Weather information will be greatly enhanced and will be shared among all ground facilities and aircraft.
6. Flight strips will be eliminated and replaced by electronic packages of data that may be represented in different ways on the controller's display and can be readily shared among all relevant parties.
7. Automated tools for medium- and long-range conflict probes (10 to 20 minutes) will be available at all air traffic control facilities (perhaps with the exception of level 3 and below TRACONs). These will provide interactive planning tools, enabling controllers to examine what-if scenarios.
8. The center TRACON Automation System (CTAS) will be available at many air traffic control facilities.

Human-Centered Automation Concerns

Authority for Maintaining Separation

We distinguish between actual authority and perceived authority for separation, and our concern is with both kinds of authority. First, the residence of authority should be as unambiguous as possible to minimize opportunity for confusion between perceived and actual authority. Second, both actual and perceived authority should reside consistently and unambiguously on the ground. The justification is that, if authority is on the ground, it is centralized. Authority in the air in a free flight regime is of necessity distributed among multiple aircraft, dispatchers, and controllers, and its residence will vary over time. Such variation is an invitation for ambiguity, which in turn will jeopardize safety. An additional justification is that, even in advanced visions of free flight that emphasize airborne self-separation with reduced ground-based control, it is recognized (RTCA, 1995a, 1995b) that ground-based controllers will continue to be responsible for separation assurance and overall safety. Controllers should thus be given an authority that is commensurate with this ultimate responsibility.

Failure Recovery

Although automation can and does assist the controller in separating traffic, the system should be designed to allow for human control and preservation of safe flight should automation fail, or should there be a failure of one or more components of the system on which the automation depends to function properly. In order to meet this criterion, it is necessary that (1) traffic density is never so great that human controllers cannot make decisions in time to ensure separation because of the effects of density on controller workload, and (2) traffic complexity is low enough so that the controller can maintain situation awareness of traffic patterns (Wyndemere, 1996). Neither traffic density nor traffic complexity should be so high as to preclude the safe performance of failure recovery tasks. Both variables need to be addressed in recovery procedures planning that supports the controllers' ability to perform recovery tasks.

Airspace Structural Consistency

As we noted in the Phase I report, a major component of the controller's mental model of the airspace is associated with the enduring characteristics of a particular sector (i.e., special use airspace, traffic patterns, hazards, sector shape). Therefore, although air routes can and should be substantially modified from their current structure in order to improve efficiency, these modifications, once in place, should be relatively enduring. Air routes should not be altered on a flight-by-flight basis. Although more alternative direct routes may be in place, thereby allowing far greater flight path efficiency than in the current airspace, there should be a fixed database of what these direct routes are, and an expectation that pilots will adhere to them (subject to controllers' granting of pilots' requests).

Automation of Decision and Action Selection

For functions in which decisions are made under uncertainty and impose safety risks, automation of decision and action selection should not proceed beyond the level of suggesting a decision/action alternative as discussed in Chapter 1. If, on the other hand, the risk is low, automation of decision/action selection can proceed to higher levels. An example of the latter is the automated handoff, for which automation of both information acquisition and decision/

action selection has been implemented at a high level because risk and uncertainty are low.

Anticipated System Features

In order to achieve these goals in a manner consistent with our expectations for the national airspace system, we foresee a system in which the air route structures are considerably altered, enabling far more direct routing and far greater efficiency. More alternate routes between airports may be available, which can be selected given winds aloft and weather conditions. However, these options will remain relatively fixed, and all aircraft are expected to fly along one of the (more numerous) routes, in this way preserving some consistency in the airspace. Flight efficiency will be greatly improved by the availability of these alternatives, but it will not necessarily be maximized.

Controllers will have the option of granting special-case excursions from the new standard routes (e.g., because of turbulence or unexpected weather), but these should be exceptions rather than standard procedures. Interactive planning tools will enable these alternatives to be rapidly computed, while maintaining the controller active in the loop.

Pilot authority for independent maneuvering (maneuver first, inform controller after) will remain restricted to following TCAS advisories, and possibly intruder avoidance during parallel runway approaches. All such maneuvers will be made immediately visible and clearly understandable by salient cues presented to ground controllers on their displays (Hoffman et al., 1995).

Maximum effort will be made to capitalize on existing and future computer technology to facilitate information sharing between ground elements (controller facilities and airline operations centers), thereby preserving and even enhancing the high levels of redundancy that now characterize the air traffic control system.

The workstation itself will rely heavily on computer-based automation to make digital flight data available rapidly (and in flexible formats) to multiple agents. These data will be available on the plan view display as well as corresponding representations on the workstations of downstream sectors that aircraft will soon enter. This multiple shared information represents a key feature required for preserving shared situation awareness and the redundancy of the current air traffic control system.

Controllers will have available longer-term strategic graphic displays (including surrounding sectors) that provide a greater lead time to assist in interactive planning and utilization of decision aids. The plan view or situation displays, however, will always include the presentation of unambiguous status information. Depending on specific system designs and associated procedures, the tasks of the R-side and D-side controllers, as these roles have traditionally been defined, may involve a reallocation of strategic and tactical responsibilities. Electronic flight data are likely to be positioned within the workstations by the controllers themselves in a way that best enhances them to meet these responsibilities.

In conclusion, the panel does not project the above description of such a system as a proposal for what the future air traffic control system should be. We recognize the many person years of effort that the Federal Aviation Administration has given to strategic planning of the future national airspace system (Federal Aviation Administration, 1994b, 1995h, 1995i, 1995j, 1996a, 1996b). The description is not intended to represent a superior alternative proposal. Rather, it represents one alternative that capitalizes on the human-centered automation principles described in this book, is geared toward considerable efficiency improvement, maintains authority for separation in the hands of air traffic control and, by doing so, best serves the interests of safety.

10

Conclusions and Recommendations

AUTOMATION ISSUES AND EMERGING TECHNOLOGIES

Levels of Automation

The levels of automation of any system vary along three dimensions: (1) information acquisition and integration (information automation), (2) decision and action selection, and (3) action implementation. The level of information automation is determined by the presence or absence of computer functions enabling filtering, information distribution, information transformations, confidence expressions, integration checks, and flexible information offerings based on the requests of users. Systems that possess all of these features have high levels of information automation, those possessing some have intermediate levels, and those possessing none have low levels. Automation of decision and action selection refers to the extent to which the controller's decision and action choices are constrained. Systems that have no or few constraints have low levels of automation on this dimension. Those that impose many constraints on operator selection of decision and action choices have high levels of automation of decision and action selection. Action automation refers to the actual implementation of an action choice and has only two levels: manual or automated.

RECOMMENDATION 1: The panel recommends that automation efforts focus on reliable, high-level automation applications for information acquisition, integration, and presentation and for aiding controller decision making in order to support all system functions. Especially important in the

near future is the development of decision aids for conflict resolution and maintaining separation. These aids should be directed primarily toward ensuring proper spacing between aircraft in preparation for the final stages of approach to landing and toward en route flight path efficiency improvement.

RECOMMENDATION 2: The panel recommends implementation of high levels of automation of decision and action selection for system tasks involving relatively little uncertainty and risk. However, for system tasks associated with greater uncertainty and risk, automation of decision and action selection should not proceed beyond the level of suggesting a preferred decision/action alternative. Any consideration for automation above this level must be designed to prevent: loss of vigilance, loss of situation awareness, degradation of operational skills, and degradation of teamwork and communication. Such designs should also ensure the ability to overcome or counteract complacency, recover from failure, and provide a means of conflict resolution if loss of separation occurs.

RECOMMENDATION 3: The panel recommends that the choice of manual (operator initiated) or automatic action implementation be guided by the level of automation of decision and action selection. Manual (or vocal) implementation is advised at the higher levels of automation of decision and action selection, at which automation narrows the decision action alternatives to a few, and more particularly at the level of automation of decision and action selection at which a single preferred decision/action is suggested. This manual (vocal) implementation will encourage the operator to review the contents of the recommended decision.

RECOMMENDATION 4: The panel recommends that the availability of computer technology not be a reason for automation in and of itself. Clear requirements for functionality that can be achieved only by computer technology should drive design choices.

RECOMMENDATION 5: The panel recommends that the choice of what functions to automate be guided by recognizing human strengths and the need to compensate for human vulnerabilities.

Adaptable Automation

Adaptable automation can benefit system performance by providing for the regulation of operator workload, reduction of complacency, and maintenance of manual skills.

RECOMMENDATION: If high degrees of automation of decision and action selection are to be introduced, adaptable automation should be considered so as to allow users to tailor the degree of automation to current needs and workload.

Recovery

Automation may increase capacity, but it will also increase traffic density and may increase airspace complexity by inducing changes in traffic flow from standard air routes. We conclude that continued use of automation of most functions eventually risks degradation of manual skills of operators who perform those functions. As a result, operators are likely to react more slowly to emergencies if they require use of those manual skills. And to the extent that the system requires manual recovery, those skills need to be preserved through recurrent training. To the extent that alternative skills will be required in emergencies, these new skills should be practiced and trained. Although automation may be highly reliable, either the automation or a resource on which it depends can be expected to fail or degrade at some time. Failure or degraded performance may come from software bugs, poor design, or aging hardware. Recovery response time will be greatly modulated by individual differences, redundant characteristics of the team environment, the complexity of the airspace (number of response options), and the familiarity versus the novelty of procedures necessary to cope with a degraded system. All important safety consequences of these failures are related to the margin by which available time exceeds the recovery response time.

RECOMMENDATION 1: The panel recommends investing sufficient resources in studies of human response to low-probability emergencies. First, studies should be designed (1) to measure human response time (and accuracy) to improbable events, (2) to determine how to extrapolate to operational situations, using data on response times observed in experimental simulations in which it is known that a low-probability event could happen, and (3) to determine how response times are modulated by skill level. These studies should be conducted in the context of a specific system architecture and specified procedures for emergency recovery and system restoration.

Second, failure modes/fault tree analyses should be actively pursued, particularly to identify situations in which two or more coordinating agents receive information inputs that are incongruous or contradictory. These analyses should be conducted on specific designs as part of the validation and verification process.

Finally, human factors specialists should be involved in the development and testing of system recovery procedures. A research simulation facility should be available to these specialists for the study of human response to rare, unanticipated system events in the national airspace system.

RECOMMENDATION 2: The panel recommends the development of models, for given designs and procedures, to examine the implications of recovery in a high-density, unstructured airspace created by increased capabilities of ground-based automation or free flight.

RECOMMENDATION 3: The panel recommends the development of airspace safety models that can predict the likelihood of midair collisions, as a function of the frequency and parameters of near-midair collisions and losses of separation, for varying standards of traffic separation. This will enable better prediction of the safety implications of capacity-increasing automation tools.

RECOMMENDATION 4: In order to support airspace safety models, models should be developed that are sensitive to loss of situation awareness and possible degradation of skills that may result from moving operators to progressively higher levels of automation of decision and action selection. These models should be elaborated to incorporate compensatory gains that can be achieved by appropriate workload reductions and better integrated information.

RECOMMENDATION 5: The panel recommends that air traffic control subject-matter experts collaborate with specialists in the behavioral sciences to model individual and team response to emergency situations and to populate the models with data to be collected in studies of human response time to low-probability emergencies. Policy makers should be made aware that choosing median response times to model these situations can have very different implications from those based on worst-case (longest) response times; these kinds of modeling choices must be carefully made and justified.

RECOMMENDATION 6: The panel recommends that system functionality should be designed so that failure recovery will not depend on skills that are likely to degrade.

Locus of Authority

Future airspace projections dictate a need for increases in capacity without sacrificing safety. Two alternative vehicles for accomplishing these goals have been proposed: a free flight scenario and a scenario involving ground-based authority; both presume automation. Several different design concepts for free flight have been proposed, which vary in the degree of authority over control of the flight path allocated to airborne and ground systems. Those versions of free flight that assume high levels of airborne authority have the predicted capability for greatly increasing airspace flexibility and hence potentially increasing capacity as well. However, a large number of uncertainties are associated with safety. These include uncertainties as to how pilot-to-pilot negotiations will be resolved in worst-case scenarios; problems relating to controllers' maintaining awareness of the tactical situation in an airspace made more complex and dense by the implementation of free flight; the workload impact of both increasing decision load in the cockpit and increasing monitoring load on the ground; and issues regarding possible confusion in the residence of authority among air traffic controllers, pilots, and airline operations center personnel.

A ground-based alternative can incorporate the best features of projected air traffic control automation functionality related to interactive planning tools, conflict probes, and decision aids, all deployed with sensitivity to human-centered automation. It assumes greatly improved surveillance and communications bandwidth and accuracy. It also assumes greater availability of direct (user-preferred) routes than are currently available as a means to improve efficiency but maintains some consistency among those routes in order to limit airspace complexity and thereby support the controller's mental model of the airspace and facilitate failure recovery. Automated tools will enable negotiation of route changes as necessary.

RECOMMENDATION 1: A ground-based scenario consistent with formulated plans of the Federal Aviation Administration can increase efficiency without radical changes in authority structure from the current system (e.g., the expanded national route program). The panel therefore recommends the development and fielding of current and proposed automation tools for ground-based air traffic control following the guidelines specified in this report regarding the selection of levels of automation. We also recommend the vigorous pursuit of projections of how various tools will operate in concert.

RECOMMENDATION 2: Because free flight design concepts that assume a high level of airborne authority over control of aircraft flight paths have more uncertainties than design options involving ground-based authority with increased automation, the panel recommends extreme caution before existing levels of free flight are further expanded to greater levels of pilot authority for separation. Furthermore, we recommend the conduct of extensive human-in-the-loop simulation studies and validation of human performance models before decisions are made regarding the further implementation of free flight; this is needed to obtain reliable prediction of the safety implication of worst-case scenarios. We also recommend heavy reliance on scenario walk-throughs and focus group sessions with controllers, pilots, traffic managers, and airline dispatchers.

Teamwork

Interpersonal communications and decision making between controllers and aircraft to resolve potential conflicts will continue to be an important component of air traffic control; it may assume greater importance under conditions of greater freedom in flight path choice.

RECOMMENDATION 1: The panel recommends the continuation of formal training for controllers in teamwork, communications, distributed decision making, conflict resolutions, and coordinated response to unexpected events as a central aspect of controller training. Additional training for supervisors in interpersonal work skills should be a part of training and qualification.

Automation of information representation and distribution has the capability to greatly facilitate teamwork between remote operators, by supporting shared situation awareness.

RECOMMENDATION 2: The panel recommends the active pursuit of efforts to share dynamic information graphically among the various affected participants in the national airspace.

Cross-Cultural Issues

Research has demonstrated that there are large national differences in attitudes about and reliance on automation. Such differences may influence interactions between air traffic control and pilots of foreign air carriers flying in U.S. airspace.

RECOMMENDATION: The panel recommends continuing to examine differences among nations in automation use in accordance with the recommendations of the Federal Aviation Administration's human factors team report on flight deck automation. Pilots from other nations that operate in U.S. airspace should be included in user tests of air traffic control automation.

Emerging Technological Resources

Visualization and Remote Control

Computer graphic displays help visualization by combining variables into a single integrated display. The digital representation of altitude on the radar display has remained a feature of the air traffic control workstation that is less than optimal. Although controllers can adequately handle digital flight-level data, it is difficult to visualize vertical trends from such a representation. One way of representing the vertical dimension in an analog format is through a vertical profile display; the other is through a perspective display. To date, the ambiguity associated with perspective displays remains a limitation for real-time air traffic control but offers promise for training.

Intelligent Decision Aids

Development of most decision aids requires a time-consuming and labor-intensive knowledge acquisition phase. Systems that learn may eventually reduce this bottleneck. However, at the present time, learning systems are not far enough along for operational use. Intent inferencing systems appear promising, but evaluations are needed of situations with more airspace complexity.

Computer-Supported Cooperative Work

Computer-supported cooperative work uses groupware technology to facilitate coordination, communication, and collaboration in accordance with the users' organizational and social context. New questions are raised about how to take social context and social process into account effectively when designing systems. To date there has been little systematic effort to apply this technology to time-critical operations such as air traffic control; however, there are some promising areas in which this approach may be useful, including strategic activities of air traffic management and interactions among tower controllers, airport managers, gate managers, pilots, and airline dispatchers in the surface movement advisor system.

CURRENT AND ENVISIONED AUTOMATED SYSTEMS

Surveillance and Communication

Surveillance and Information Acquisition

In order to maintain reliable performance, the radar processing system includes redundant equipment and is backed up by paper flight progress strips. Ongoing efforts to modernize aging equipment are expected to lead to systems with greater reliability.

An alternative technology, the global positioning system, offers a high degree of accuracy; however, questions of its reliability, availability, and accuracy still need to be addressed. Satellites can be damaged, causing a hole in the constellation; satellites are always moving, causing receivers to change satellite sets to keep the necessary number (four) in view to establish an accurate position (this can result in sudden steps in system error); jamming and spoofing are major concerns.

The current distribution system of weather information for air traffic control is fragmented and does not adequately tailor information for controllers, traffic management specialists, and pilots. The key challenges are to provide additional useful weather information, integrate information from multiple sensors, predict weather more effectively, and disseminate information more efficiently to controllers, traffic management specialists, and pilots.

Communications: Automatic Dependent Surveillance-Broadcast Mode

Effective air traffic management depends critically on the accurate and timely exchange of information between ground and air and, increasingly, between aircraft. Considerable advances are derived from a communication system that can broadcast digital data, in parallel, to a broad range of airborne and ground-based users.

Because automatic dependent surveillance-broadcast mode (ADS-B) provides an increase in both frequency and amount of information, it supports two potential expansions of the national airspace. First, it can potentially serve air traffic control with precise position information, thereby eventually replacing the slower, less accurate, and more expensive secondary surveillance radar. Second, the higher update rate and accuracy that ADS-B provides may enable more complex flight path negotiations between aircraft than does the present TCAS system. ADS-B is a likely enabling technology to support free flight.

Communication: Data Link

The use of visual and manual channels in data link substantially alters the process of communications, compared with traditional voice channels. The introduction of data link has very profound potential implications for the overall structure of the national airspace system and for the relationship among pilots, controllers, and automation. At one extreme, it is possible to envision a scenario in which humans, both on the ground and in the air, are substantially removed from the control loop, while control is exercised between computers on the ground and in the air. Although planners do not currently intend such a scenario, the possibility nevertheless exists that levels of automatic control and gating messages could be implemented that approximate this kind of interaction. This scenario leads to the high probability of loss of pilot awareness of the message content.

RECOMMENDATION 1: The panel recommends the following approaches to ensuring redundancy in data link transmissions:

(a) Provide redundant means of transmitting information contained in data link messages along conventional voice (radiotelephone) channels. Data link messages should be used primarily for routine communications (e.g., standard clearances, airport terminal information services). Radiotelephone channels should be reserved for the more unusual instructions and requests and for high-priority messages in high-workload (e.g., terminal) areas.

(b) Employ redundant voice synthesis of uplink messages as a design option, operated in parallel with visual (text and graphics) display of the message.

RECOMMENDATION 2: The panel recommends the following approaches to defining the roles of flight crews and controllers in data link communications:

(a) Carefully analyze the possible role shifts and workload redistribution between personnel on the flight deck and between controllers at the workstation caused by data link. Training or design features should be used to address these role shifts if they are found to occur.

(b) Uplinked messages that directly pertain to aircraft control should not be automatically uploaded into the flight management system. Loading must be accomplished by an active choice by the pilot. This recommendation is consistent with our general recommendation concerning the need for careful evaluation of applying automation to high-level system tasks.

Flight Information

Flight Management System

The flight management system gives the pilot sophisticated, highly reliable tools to manage flight path control and power plant control with great precision. But with these ingenious tools have come problems at the human-computer interface, resulting in some degree of mistrust, overtrust, or mode confusion on the part of the pilots and, in the extreme, some spectacular incidents and accidents. It is essential that the same mistakes not be made in the implementation of the next generation of air traffic management systems.

One of the problems that must be confronted is the incompatibility between the new flight management system aircraft and the constraints of the current air traffic control system. The full potential of the flight management system cannot be exploited in today's air traffic control environment.

RECOMMENDATION 1: The panel recommends that the development of automation of air traffic control account for the capabilities of the flight management system and, to the extent that safety is not compromised, be harmonized with those capabilities.

RECOMMENDATION 2: The panel recommends that the lessons learned from the flight management system regarding mode errors and mode confusions be carefully applied to the design of air traffic control automation.

Flight Data

The design and implementation of electronic flight strips has been seen as a major risk to user acceptance in system automation. However, the electronic flight strip is only one means of modernizing the processing and display of flight data. The issue that needs to be addressed in the research and development process is less one of perpetuating the current roles and functionality of paper strips than of how to achieve an effective electronic embodiment of flight data. An electronic format for computerized flight information will facilitate the distribution of flight data and contribute to the reduction of controller workload.

RECOMMENDATION 1: To facilitate operational acceptability of electronic flight information to replace paper strips, the design requirements should:

- **Compensate for the redundancies provided by paper flight strips;**
- **Recognize how the characteristics of the paper strips (and procedures associated with them) support the cognitive processes of the controller;**
- **Develop a rapid and simple means of data entry; and**
- **Fully integrate flight data in an electronic work environment.**

RECOMMENDATION 2: The panel recommends that research studies undertaken to validate concepts for the integration of electronic flight data represent enough aspects of operational environments to allow for generalization of the results across operational settings.

Immediate Conflict Avoidance

Traffic Alert and Collision Avoidance System

Although the traffic alert and collision avoidance system (TCAS) was originally intended to be a purely air-based system, designed to be a final backup to breakdowns in ground-based control, it is evident that it has much more profound implications for air traffic control. These implications will grow, as the system is extended to recapture more elements of the cockpit display of traffic information, in the implementation of low levels of free flight (e.g., the role of TCAS in approaches; the role of TCAS in oceanic in-trail climbs). It appears that considerable thought was given to human factors issues in the initial implementation and subsequent fielding of the system. However, more early attention could have been given to trying to discover the complex pilot-controller interactions that have emerged, and that have subsequently forced revision of procedures, policy, training, and software. It is likely that more extensive reliance on system models (with valid models of human components), as well as complex human-in-the-loop simulation, could have anticipated some of these problems. It is encouraging to see movement in this direction as other future air traffic control technologies are envisioned.

RECOMMENDATION 1: The panel recommends more effective training for pilots in order to foster greater consistency in response to TCAS alerts.

RECOMMENDATION 2: The panel recommends that communication within the system be comprehensive in the sense that the information held by the controller with respect to neighboring traffic is accessible in the cockpit, and data on trajectory change instructions initiated by TCAS resolution advisories are electronically available and can be displayed to the controller as needed.

Converging Runway Display Aid

The converging runway display aid (CRDA) is a useful subsystem for TRACON operations at terminals where arrivals are directed to either one of two converging runways during normal operations.

RECOMMENDATION: The panel recommends that (a) the methodological experiences with the converging runway display aid, including site adaptation procedures, should be used to inform the introduction of other new, special-purpose subsystems in the evolving national airspace system and (b) the mode of slot assignment and separation maintenance used by the converging runway display aid should be considered as a possible benchmark in the design and refinement of alternative subsystems for terminal area operations.

Precision Runway Monitor

The precision runway monitor/final monitor aid system has generally good user acceptance. However, some highly experienced controllers have voiced reservations about the passive monitoring role of the system operator. Even with runway separation distances reduced to 3,000 feet between dual runways (as approved in November 1995), the frequency of transmissions may be too low to allow the controller to sustain a reasonable level of alertness.

RECOMMENDATION: The panel recommends that (a) studies be conducted to determine whether the problem of vigilance decrement can be avoided by the integration of the precision runway monitor/final monitor aid system with the approach control system and (b) the trade-offs between ground-based and cockpit-based systems for lateral separation be carefully considered. If redundant systems are implemented in the air and on the ground, all possibilities by which conflicting guidance from the two systems might be given should be analyzed (e.g., because of different sensors, different conflict prediction algorithms, different communication bandwidths).

Avoiding Collisions on the Ground

To address both safety and efficiency concerns, the Federal Aviation Administration is undertaking a set of activities that, taken together, are intended to provide controllers and pilots with automated warnings of potential and actual runway incursions and ground traffic conflicts, with automated means of communication and with the capability to maintain situation awareness in low-visibility conditions. These initiatives range from current implementation, through near-term enhancement, to long-term development programs.

The combination of automated functions can potentially introduce effects that are not predicted from studies or tests of each automated function independently. Also at issue is the distinction between trust in the system and trust in its components. Individual components may vary in their trustworthiness (e.g., ASDE radar and GPS/ADS-B), and a thorough understanding of the capabilities of each component, as well as how the components work together (e.g., AMASS display and runway status lights), is required to permit pilots and controllers to develop an appropriate level of trust in the system. In addition, since these new systems are specifically intended as safety enhancements and may also be used to support increased usage of airport surface capacity, it is particularly important that controllers and pilots are able to respond effectively to failures (e.g., degradation of sensors or sensor integration software).

RECOMMENDATION: Because a variety of ground-based and aircraft-based sensors and information processors are envisioned, the panel recommends that a careful analysis of failure modes and effects for the total system be undertaken to ensure that conflicting information is never provided to pilots and controllers regarding the status and safety of runway and taxiway paths. Controllers and pilots should receive specific training that allows their understanding of system functions and limitations.

Strategic Long-Range Planning

Center TRACON Automation System

The organizational implications of the center TRACON automation system remain uncertain. A strength of the system is that it is designed to be advisory only. Therefore, by not directly affecting required procedures, the potentially negative impact on organizational functioning should be minimized. It derives useful advice for the controller that without the system would be cognitively difficult to derive. It also facilitates sharing of information between controllers. There is a possibility that extensive reliance on CTAS could create an airspace that is denser and more complex, creating higher levels of controller perceptual workload.

RECOMMENDATION: The panel recommends the active role of human factors resources at all stages of development of the center TRACON automation system, including ongoing field tests. In addition, the informed input of users should be secured in defining and refining the functionality as well as the interface. This process should be repeated in the fielding of other systems. Adequate and extensive training should continue to be given to users regarding the assumptions underlying the system's advisories.

Conflict Probe and Interactive Planning

Although experienced controllers have developed considerable cognitive skill in predicting aircraft trajectories, additional tools for controllers may facilitate this skill. Conflict probe and interactive planning tools are designed to support more long-range strategic planning and to address human visualizations in this regard. They represent appropriate higher levels of automation of information gathering and low levels of automation of response. Both tools have the potential, depending on specific design characteristics and associated procedures, to permit reallocation of control tasks between the R-side and the D-side controllers.

For failure recovery the primary issues are twofold. It is possible to envision a scenario based on one set of design characteristics in which an interactive planning tool—the user request evaluation tool or the conflict probe system—first has enabled more complex (and possibly more densely packed) traffic flow, enabling user-preferred trajectories and, second, has left the R-side or tactical controllers with reduced situation awareness of the current airspace (because changed trajectories were not imposed by their decisions). A sudden failure within the system could leave the tactical or R-side controller more vulnerable in issuing the rapid tactical commands necessary to avoid conflict situations.

RECOMMENDATION: Simulations should be conducted to examine traffic complexity levels that are generated by the use of interactive tools to grant user-preferred trajectories. The system should be introduced in such a way that all controllers on a team can maintain full situation awareness of routing changes supported by the tool.

Four-Dimensional Contracts

Four-dimensional contracts will change aspects of the controller's job and are likely to create a less well-structured, more densely packed airspace, but they will not fundamentally alter responsibility for separation.

RECOMMENDATION: The panel recommends closely following European demonstration projects concerning the usability of four-dimensional trajectory planning and flight path negotiation tolls for lessons learned and potential application in the United States.

Surface Movement Advisor

The surface movement advisor (SMA) is intended to provide controllers, pilots, airfield managers, ramp operators, and airline operations personnel with automated support of surface traffic planning. Airport area automation holds the potential for changing the roles of controllers vis-à-vis pilots and airport and airline personnel. Realignment may include new responsibilities, new authority structures, new communication and cooperative work links, and new measures of effectiveness (e.g., increasing emphasis on efficiency). Since a prerequisite for its design is data distribution through computerized networks to cooperating team members, one promising avenue that can contribute to the design of an effective surface movement advisor is the combination of analyses and tools that pertain to emerging computer-supported cooperative work technology.

RECOMMENDATION: The panel recommends that (a) the impact of the surface movement advisor on individual roles and on teamwork be carefully analyzed during analysis, design, and test activities and (b) computer-supported cooperative work analyses of the surface movement advisor be performed. Related tools should be applied when analyses deem the applications appropriate.

Support Functions

The planned centralization of maintenance activities and the projected trend toward automating more complex cognitive functions now performed by maintainers represent a fundamental shift for maintenance design, operations, and organization. The skills of the maintainers are a significant factor in system integrity. The recently developed GS-2101 classification, increasingly applied to airway facilities specialists, outlines requirements for systems engineering skills (as opposed to component or subsystem maintenance skills) needed to support this shift. These changes are proceeding amidst a paucity of knowledge regarding: (1) maintainer task performance and error while interacting with highly automated systems, (2) the mental models of the system that guide maintainer decisions and actions, and (3) the variables of teamwork—both among maintainers and between maintainers and air traffic controllers—involved in system monitoring, control, and maintenance. In addition, the GS-2101 classification has proceeded without supporting development of validated selection, training, and performance standards for the anticipated systems engineering task requirements.

RECOMMENDATION 1: **The panel recommends that representations of maintainers' mental models be developed to complement cognitive task analyses for maintainers. These models and analyses, as well as human factors principles, should be used to develop a reasoned approach to automation and to the design of new maintainer's workstations, especially for centralized operations control centers and the national maintenance control center.**

RECOMMENDATION 2: **Selection, training, and performance standards should be developed and validated appropriate to the knowledge, skills, and abilities required to maintain highly automated systems.**

RECOMMENDATION 3: **The maintenance teamwork and the coordination between maintainers and air traffic controllers should be examined in the context of new centralized operations control centers. The increased role that controllers may assume in maintenance tasks, given digital technology of automated systems, should be considered.**

RECOMMENDATION 4: **The reliability of maintainers in automation-supported maintenance tasks should be studied, and an error-tolerant design should be applied to maintenance equipment.**

INTEGRATION

The Future National Airspace System

Authority is a critical concept in the evolution of the national airspace system, whether this evolution is toward a concept of free flight or ground-based automation.

RECOMMENDATION: The panel recommends that the momentary residence of authority with controller, an automated agent, or the pilot is unambiguously announced and displayed to all relevant agents, especially in systems in which this authority may shift dynamically.

It is important to realize that the concept of free flight remains somewhat ill defined. Different players have very different notions of what it should be, how free it should be, and over what domains of the airspace it should apply (e.g., en route versus TRACON, high altitude versus all altitudes, continental versus oceanic). One of the contentious issues to be addressed regarding free flight concerns the appropriate *level of authority* that should be maintained by air traffic controllers in a free flight regime.

An airspace that functions under free flight rules will lose the structured order that enables the controller to easily grasp the big picture. It is quite possible that an airspace under free flight will yield unpredictable shifts in traffic density, and this in turn may require some degree of "dynamic resectorization." Finally, free flight separation algorithms, like those of TCAS, are likely to be time based rather than space based. Space can be easily visualized by the controller, but time less so. It is unclear the extent to which this shift may also inhibit controller situation awareness. One of the greatest challenges is to try to predict the implications of changes in free flight procedures to overall system safety.

RECOMMENDATION 1: The panel recommends three parallel research approaches to estimate safety implications:

(a) Continue to refine simulation and modeling with an emphasis on modeling safety parameters.

(b) Collect sufficient amounts of human-in-the-loop data to populate simulation models that can be used to identify, understand, and compensate for infrequent (but catastrophic) consequences. The results should provide the basis for understanding responses to such events under conditions that approximate realistic occurrences.

(c) Rely heavily on scenario walk-throughs and focus group sessions among controllers and pilots who have been provided with clear descriptions of future assumed capabilities; these can reveal potential bottleneck areas.

RECOMMENDATION 2: The panel urges exploration of design changes that offer the possibility of greatly increasing the safety margin between aircraft, even as the procedures are altered to allow more regular flow (i.e., improve efficiency). Examples of design changes include satellite navigation, ADS-B communications, and automated tools for medium- and long-range conflict probes.

Introducing Automation

Development and Installation of Advanced Systems

The introduction of automation, whether incremental or comprehensive, involves some interference with an ongoing process that cannot be disrupted. Consequently, careful planning is required so that the transition can be made with minimum interruption.

Despite the FAA's management efforts to foster greater human factors involvement in the development and implementation of advanced air traffic control systems, the agency's success record has been mixed at best. However, a recently completed, FAA-commissioned, independent study (by the Human Factors Subcommittee of the FAA's Research, Engineering, and Development Advisory Council) examined the current FAA organizational structure, staffing, and operating practices as they relate to human factors support activities, and made recommendations for improving the effectiveness of this function. These recommendations appear to be well founded and offer the potential for better integration of human factors concerns in the development of advanced automation technologies.

RECOMMENDATION 1: The panel recommends that senior Federal Aviation Administration management should reexamine the results of the study by the Human Factors Subcommittee of the FAA's Research, Engineering, and Development Advisory Council, with a view toward implementing those recommendations that appear most likely to achieve more active, continued, and effective involvement of both users and trained human factors practitioners. All aspects of human-centered automation should be considered in fielding new automated systems.

RECOMMENDATION 2: The Federal Aviation Administration should continue to support integrated product teams with well-trained human factors specialists assigned to the teams. Both users and human factors specialists should be involved at the early stages to help define the functionality of the proposed automation system. These specialists should be responsible to report to human factors management within the Federal Aviation Administration as well as to project managers.

RECOMMENDATION 3: The Federal Aviation Administration should continue to work toward an infrastructure in which some human factors training is provided to personnel and program managers at all levels of the organization (and contract teams).

RECOMMENDATION 4: The Federal Aviation Administration should ensure that adequate funding for human factors work is provided at all stages of system development and field evaluations both before and after systems acquisition.

RECOMMENDATION 5: Starting with early conceptual development and continuing through installation, a system-specific analysis should be undertaken of the interactions between system attributes and operators' capabilities. Implicit interdependencies among controllers and between them and other human operators or automated agents should be taken into account.

RECOMMENDATION 6: Contextually valid controller-in-the-loop experiments and simulations should be conducted to validate, test, and refine system design. Human factors professionals should advise in the conduct of these experiments, with attention to good experimental design and adequate sample size. Organizations such as the Federal Aviation Administration Technical Center, the Civil Aeromedical Institute, and NASA should remain heavily involved in these developmental efforts.

RECOMMENDATION 7: The panel recommends proceeding gradually with the *introduction* of automated tools into the workplace, giving adequate attention to user training, to facility differences, and to user requirements, and carefully monitoring the *operational experience* from initial introduction, putting mechanisms in place to respond rapidly to both positive and negative lessons learned from those experiences.

RECOMMENDATION 8: The panel recommends that operators chosen to work with new systems or subsystems should be given an understanding of the principles of system operation, including the logic and algorithms underlying the system as well as the practice of system operations. Training should progress quickly to the level of real-time exercises in the setting of interactive simulations. Embedded training should be considered as a useful approach to help controllers maintain skills. Valid and reliable performance measures should be developed and proficiency should be defined with regard to the specific measures.

Long-Range Planning

The pace of events is such that some advanced subsystems, such as the converging runway display aid, are already installed at selected locations, and others, such as the center TRACON automation system, are on the verge of operational installation. Meanwhile, system-specific studies are under way on other systems such as the global positioning system and data link. Now is the time for the design and implementation of studies that deal with some of the generic problems of air traffic control and advanced technology, such as the effects on system performance of passive monitoring by controllers using the precision runway monitor. Only by building the knowledge base now will the FAA be able to make sound decisions about the future cycles of automation and to help eliminate surprises from each successive wave.

RECOMMENDATION 1: During development of each automation function, system developers should consider possible interactions with other automation functions (under development or already existing), tools, and task requirements that form (or will form) the operational context into which the specific automation feature will be introduced.

RECOMMENDATION 2: Various research methods should be integrated: models, high- and medium-fidelity simulations, and more controlled laboratory experiments at all levels of system development. Laboratory experiments that can address many useful questions of interface design must consider contextual relevance. Results of these experiments should be used to inform more realistic simulations about what variables should be investigated. The results from these experiments should be used to help estimate and validate human (pilot and controller) performance parameters for computational models.

References

Abbott, T.S., G.C. Moen, L.H. Person, Jr., G.L. Keyser, Jr., K.R. Yenni, and J.F. Garren, Jr.
  1980   Flight Investigation of Cockpit-Displayed Traffic Information Utilizing Coded Symbiology in an Advanced Operational Environment. NASA Technical Paper 1684, AVRADCOM Technical Report 80-B-4. NASA Langley Research Center, Hampton, VA.
Adam, G.L.
  1995   Human Factors Considerations for TCAS II Resolution Advisory Displays and Aural Annunciations. MTR 95W0000007. MITRE Corporation, McLean, VA.
Adams, J.
  1982   Issues in human reliability. *Human Factors* 24:1-10.
Adelman, L., M.S. Cohen, T.A. Bresnick, J.O. Chinnis, Jr., and K.B. Laskey
  1993   Real-time expert system interfaces, cognitive processes, and task performance: An empirical assessment. *Human Factors* 35(2):243-261.
Adkisson, L., K. Karna, D. Katz, A. Karna, and K. Dontas
  1994   Identification of Artificial Intelligence Applications for Maintenance, Monitoring, and Control of Airway Facilities. Federal Aviation Report Number DOT/FAA/CT-TN92/41. U.S. Department of Transportation, Washington, DC.
Ammerman, H.L., L.J. Bergen, D.K. Davies, C.M. Hostetler, E.E. Inman, and G.W. Jones
  1987   FAA Air Traffic Control Operations Concepts Volume VI: ARTCC/HOST En Route Controllers. DOT/FAA/AP/87-01. Federal Aviation Administration, Washington, DC.
Anderson, J.R., A.T. Corbett, K.R. Koedinger, and R. Pelletier
  1993   Cognitive Tutors: Lessons Learned. Unpublished paper. A copy may be obtained by contacting John R. Anderson at Carnegie Mellon University via electronic mail: ja0s@andrew.cmu.edu.
Andes, R.
  1996   Crew intent estimation in the CIM. *Rotorcraft's Pilot's Associate Inside the Vision* III(2):3.
Andre, A.D., and C.D. Wickens
  1995   When users want what's not best for them. *Ergonomics in Design* (October):10-14.

Architecture Technology Corporation
1996   ASTA and runway status lights. Internet: http://www.atcorp.com/projects/
Aviation Week and Space Technology
1994   Growing demand boosts GPS progress. *Aviation Week and Space Technology* September 19:62-63.
1995a   "Worm Holes" in GPS coverage raise interference concerns. *Aviation Week and Space Technology* June 5:32-33.
1995b   GPS technology ripens for consumer market. *Aviation Week and Space Technology* October 9:50-51.
1995c   GPS experts suggest way to avoid terrorism. *Aviation Week and Space Technology* October 9: 56-57.
1997   Filter center. *Aviation Week and Space Technology*. January 27:59.
Avionics
1990   TCAS for transports: Part III. *Avionics* (December):23-27.
Bainbridge, L.
1983   Ironies of automation. *Automatica* 19:775-779.
Banks, S.B., and C.S. Lizza
1991   Pilot's Associate: A Cooperative, Knowledge-Based System Application. DARPA Strategic Computing Initiative 0885/9000/91/0600-0018. The Institute of Electrical and Electronics Engineers, Inc., Piscataway, NJ.
Barbarino, M.
1997   Team resource management in European air traffic services. In *Proceedings of the Ninth International Symposium on Aviation Psychology*. Columbus: Ohio State University.
Bartkiewicz, G.W., and R.L. Berkowitz
1993   Preliminary requirements for satellite based automatic dependent surveillance (ADS). Pp. 209-214 in *Proceedings of the IEEE/AIAA 12th Digital Avionics Systems Conference*. Piscataway, NJ: IEEE.
Bayles, S., and B. Das
1993   Using Artificial Intelligence to Support Traffic Flow Management Problem Resolution. MTR 93W0000245. Center for Advanced Aviation System Development, MITRE Corporation, McLean, VA.
Benford, S., C. Brown, G. Reynard, and C. Greenhalgh
1996   Shared spaces: Transportation, artificiality, and spatiality. Pp. 77-86 in *Computer Supported Cooperative Work '96*. ACM 0-89791-765-0/96/11. Cambridge, MA: ACM, Inc.
Benson, I., C. Ciborra, and S. Proffitt
1990   Some social and economic consequences of groupware for flight crew. Pp. 119-129 in *CSCW 90 Proceedings*. ACM 089791-402-3/90/0010/0129. Cambridge, MA: ACM, Inc.
Bikson, T.K.
1996   Groupware at the World Bank. In *Groupware and Teamwork*, C. Ciborra, ed. Somerset, NJ: Wiley.
Bikson, T.K., and J.D. Eveland
1990   The interplay of work group structures and computer support. In *Intellectual Teamwork*, J. Gallagher, R. Kraut, and C. Egido, eds. Hillsdale, NJ: Erlbaum.
1996   Groupware implementation: Reinvention in the sociotechnical frame. In *Proceedings of the Conference on Computer Supported Cooperative Work*. New York: ACM, Inc.
Bikson, T.K., and S.A. Law
1993   Electronic mail use at the World Bank: Messages from users. *The Information Society* 9(2):89-124.
Billings, C.E.
1996a   Human-Centered Aviation Automation: Principles and Guidelines. NASA TM 110381. NASA Ames Research Center, Moffett Field, CA.

1996b   *Aviation Automation: The Search for a Human-Centered Approach.*   Mahwah, NJ: Erlbaum.

Billings, C.E., and E.S. Cheaney
1981   Information Transfer Problems in the Aviation System. NASA Tech. Paper 1875. NASA Ames Research Center, Moffett Field, CA.

Billings, C.E., and D.D. Woods
1994   Concerns about adaptive automation in aviation systems. Pp. 264-269 in *Human Perfor- mance in Automated Systems: Current Research and Trends*, M. Mouloua and R. Parasuraman, eds. Hillsdale, NJ: Erlbaum.

Blanchard, R.E., and J.J. Vardaman
1994   Human Factors in Airway Facilities Maintenance: Development of a Prototype Outage Assessment Inventory.   Document number DOT/FAA/AM-94/5.   Office of Aviation Medicine, Civil Aeromedical Institute, Federal Aviation Administration. U.S. Depart- ment of Transportation, Washington, DC.

Booher, H.R.
1990   *MANPRINT: An Approach to Systems Integration.* New York: Van Nostrand Reinhold.

Bresley, B.
1995   777 flight deck design. *Airliner* (April-June):1-9.

Brudnicki, D.J., and A.L. McFarland
1997   User Request Evaluation Tool (URET) Conflict Probe Performance and Benefits Assess- ment. MITRE Corporation, McLean, VA.

Brudnicki, D.J., A.L. McFarland, and S.M. Schultheis
1996   Conflict Probe Benefits to Controllers and Users. MP 96W0000194. MITRE Corpora- tion, McLean, VA.

Bryant, W.H.
1993   Low-Visibility Landing and Surface Operations. National Aeronautics and Space Ad- ministration, Langley Research Center, Langley, VA.

Bubb-Lewis, C., and M.W. Scerbo, M.W.
1997   Getting to know you: Human-computer communication in adaptive automation. Pp. 92- 99 in *Human-Automation Interaction: Research and Practice*, M. Mouloua and J. Koonce, eds. Mahwah, NJ: Erlbaum.

Cardosi, K.M.
1993   Time required for transmission of time critical air traffic control messages. *International Journal of Aviation Psychology* 3:303-314.

Casner, S.
1995   A personal laptop CBT for the 737-300 autoflight system. In *Proceedings of the Eighth International Symposium on Aviation Psychology*, R. Jensen and L.A. Rakovan, eds. Columbus, OH: Ohio State University.

Castaldo, R., C. Evers, and A. Smith
1996   Positive Identification of Aircraft on Surface Movement Areas—Results of FAA Trials. Report by Rannoch Corporation for the Federal Aviation Administration.

Chappell, S.L.
1990   Human factors research for TCAS. *Proceedings of the Royal Aeronautical Society Con- ference on the Traffic Alert and Collision Avoidance System (TCAS)—Its Development, Testing, Installation and Operational Use* (6-1/6-19).

Chi, M., P. Feltovich, and R. Glaser
1981   Categorization and representation of physics problems by experts and novices. *Cognitive Science* 5:121-152.

Chu, R.W., C.M. Mitchell, and P.M. Jones
1995   Using the operator function model and OFMspert as the basis for an intelligent tutoring system: Towards a tutor/aid paradigm for operators of supervisory control systems. *IEEE Transactions on Systems, Man, and Cybernetics* 25(7):1054-1075.

Chwelos, G., and K. Oatley
    1994   Appraisal, computational models, and Scherer's expert system. *Cognition and Emotion* 8(3):245-257.

Ciborra, C.
    1993   *Teams, Markets and Systems*. Cambridge, England: Cambridge University Press.

Ciemer, C.E., G.P. Gabrarani, E.H. Sheridan, S.C. Stangel, R.P. Stead, and D.H. Tillotson
    1993   The Results of the TCAS II Transition Program (TTP). ARINC Research Corporation, Annapolis, MD, April.

Cohen, C.E., D.G. Lawrence, B.S. Pervan, H. S. Cobb, A.K. Barrows, J.D. Powell, and B.W. Parkinson
    1994   Flight Test Results of Autocoupled Approaches Using GPS and Integrity Beacons. Presented at ION GPS-94, Salt Lake City, UT, September 20-23.

Corker, K., G. Pisanich, and M. Bunzo
    1997   A cognitive system model for human/automation dynamics in airspace management. In *Proceedings of the First European /U.S. Symposium on Air Traffic Management*. Saclay, France, June 16-19.

Corkill, D.D.
    1991   Blackboard Systems. Original manuscript of article appearing in *Artificial Intelligence Expert* 6(9):40-47.

Corwin, W.H.
    1991   Data link integration in commercial transport operations. In *Proceedings of the 6th International Symposium on Aviation Psychology*, R. Jensen, ed. Columbus, OH: Ohio State University.

Craig, I.D.
    1989   *The Cassandra Architecture: Distributed Control in a Blackboard System*. New York: Halsted Press.

Curry, R.E.
    1985   The Introduction of New Cockpit Technology: A Human Factors Study. NASA TM 86659. NASA Ames Research Center, Moffett Field, CA.

Danaher, J.
    1980   Human error in ATC system operations. *Human Factors* 22:535-545.

David, H.
    1991   Artificial intelligence and human factors in ATC: Current activity at Eurocontrol Experimental Centre. Pp. 173-179 in *Automation And Systems Issues in Air Traffic Control*, J.A. Wise, V.D. Hopkin, and M.L. Smith, eds. NATO ASI Series, Vol. F73. Berlin: Springer-Verlag.

Davis, T.J., K.J. Krzeczowski, and C. Bergh
    1994   The final approach spacing tool. Pp. 70-76 in *Proceedings of the 13th IFAC Symposium on Automatic Control in Aerospace-Aerospace Control '94*. Palo Alto, CA.

Day, V., and G. Strut
    1993   ODID: Operational display and input development. *The Controller* (December):21.

Degani, A., and E.L Wiener
    1994   On the Design of Flight-Deck Procedures. NASA CR 177642. NASA Ames Research Center, Moffett Field, CA.

Del Balzo, J.
    1995   Lessons learned from the introduction of automation of ATC systems in the USA. *Transmit* 3:23-25.

Della Rocco, P., C.A. Manning, and H. Wing
    1991   Selection of air traffic controllers for automated systems: Applications from today's research. Pp. 429-451 in *Automation and Systems Issues in Air Traffic Control*, J.A. Wise, V.D. Hopkin, and M.L. Smith, eds. NATO ASI Series, Vol. F73. Berlin Heidelberg: Springer-Verlag.

Denning, R., P.J. Smith, E. McCoy, J. Orasanu, C. Billings, A. Van Horn, and M. Rodvold
1996   Initial experiences with the expanded national route program. In *Proceedings of the Human Factors and Ergonomics Society 40th Annual Meeting.*

Dienes, Z., and R. Fahey
1995   Role of specific instances on controlling a dynamic system. *Journal of Experimental Psychology: Learning, Memory, and Cognition* 21:848-862.

Dornheim, M.A.
1995   Dramatic incidents highlight mode problems in cockpits. *Aviation Week and Space Technology* (January 30):57-59.

Dougherty, E.M.
1990   Human reliability analysis—Where shouldst thou turn? *Reliability Engineering and System Safety* 29:283-299.

Dourish, P., and V. Bellotti
1992   Awareness and coordination in shared workspaces. In *Proceedings of the Conference on Computer Supported Cooperative Work.* New York: ACM.

Druckman, D., and R.A. Bjork, eds.
1994   *Learning, Remembering, Believing: Enhancing Human Performance.* Committee on Techniques for the Enhancement of Human Performance, National Research Council. Washington, DC: National Academy Press.

Dubrovsky, V.J., S. Kiesler, and B.J. Sethna
1991   The equalization phenomena: Status effects in computer-mediated and face-to-face decisionmaking groups. *Human-Computer Interaction* 6:119-146.

Dujardin, P.
1990   *PHIDIAS Project: Synthesis of the Work Conducted at CENA. (Release 2).* Centre d'études de la navigation aérienne Report CENA/90-019. Paris, France: Direction de la navigation.
1993   The inclusion of future users in the design and evaluation process. Pp. 435-441 in *Verification and Validation of Complex Systems: Human Factors Issues,* J.A. Wise, V.D. Hopkin, and P. Stager, eds. NATO ASI Series, Vol. F110. Berlin: Springer-Verlag.

Durlach, N.I., and A.S. Mavor, eds.
1995   *Virtual Reality: Scientific and Technological Challenges.* Committee on Virtual Reality Research and Development, National Research Council. Washington, DC: National Academy Press.

Ei-feldt, H.
1991   Automation in ATC: How does it affect the selection of controllers? Pp. 461-465 in *Automation and Systems Issues in Air Traffic Control,* J.A. Wise, V.D. Hopkin, and M.L. Smith, eds. NATO ASI Series, Vol. F73. Berlin Heidelberg: Springer-Verlag.

Ellis, S.R., M.W. McGreevy, and R.J. Hitchcock
1987   Perspective traffic display format and airline pilot traffic avoidance. *Human Factors Society* 29(4):371-382.

Endsley, M.
1996a   Automation and situation awareness. Pp. 163-181 in *Automation and Human Performance: Theory and Applications,* R. Parasuraman and M. Mouloua, eds. Mahwah, NJ: Erlbaum.
1996b   Situation Awareness in Free Flight. Presentation at meeting of the Panel on Human Factors in Air Traffic Control Automation, National Research Council, September 1996, Boston.

Endsley, M., and E.O. Kiris
1995   The out-of-the-loop performance problem and level of control in automation. *Human Factors* 37:381-394.

Endsley, M.R., and M.D. Rodgers
  1994   Situation Awareness Information Requirements for En Route Air Traffic Control. Final
         Report. FAA Technical Report No. DOT/FAA/AM-94/27. Office of Aviation Medicine.
         Federal Aviation Administration, Washington, DC.
  1996   Attention distribution and situation awareness in air traffic control. Pp. 82-85 in *Proceed-
         ings of the 40th Annual Meeting of the Human Factors and Ergonomics Society*. Santa
         Monica, CA: Human Factors and Ergonomics Society.
Endsley, M.R., R. Mogford, K. Allendoerfer, and E. Stein
  1997   Effect of Free Flight Conditions on Controller Performance, Workload and Situation
         Awareness: A Preliminary Investigation of Changes in Locus of Control Using Existing
         Technologies. Texas Tech University, Lubbock.
Erzberger, H., and W. Nedell
  1989   Design of Automated System for Management of Arrival Traffic. NASA Technical
         Memorandum 102201. Ames Research Center, Moffett Field, CA.
Erzberger, H., and L. Tobias
  1986   A time-based concept for terminal-area traffic management. Pp. 52-1 - 52-14 in *AGARD
         Conference Proceedings 410: Efficient Conduct of Individual Flights and Air Traffic*.
         Neuilly-sur-Seine, France: Advisory Group for Aerospace Research and Development.
Erzberger, H., T.J. Davis, and S.M. Green
  1993   Design of center-TRACON automation system. Pp. 11-1 - 11-12 in *Proceedings of the
         AGARD Guidance and Control Panel 56th Symposium on Machine Intelligence in Air
         Traffic Management*. Neuilly-sur-Seine, France: Advisory Group for Aerospace Re-
         search and Development.
Eurocontrol
  1996   *PHARE: EFMS Phase 2. User Requirements Document for EFMS and EFMS/AHMI
         Interface*. Brussels: Eurocontrol.
Evans, A., I. Donohoe, A. Kilner, T. Lamoureux, T. Atkinson, H. Mackendrick, and B. Kirwan
  1997   ATC, automation, and human factors: Research challenges. In *Proceedings of the IAS-
         97 International Aviation Safety Conference*, The Netherlands, August 27-29.
Eveland, J.D., A. Blanchard, W. Brown, and J. Mattocks
  1995   The role of "help networks" in facilitating use of CSCW tools. *The Information Society*
         11(2):113-130.
Federal Aviation Administration
  1990a Introduction to TCAS II. U.S. Department of Transportation, Washington, DC.
  1990b *The National Plan for Aviation Human Factors*. Draft. Washington, DC: U.S. Depart-
         ment of Transportation.
  1991a Maintenance Control Center (MCC) Operations Concept. Order number 6000.39, August
         8. U.S. Department of Transportation, Washington, DC.
  1991b General Maintenance Handbook—Airway Facilities. Order number 6000.15B, August
         15. U.S. Department of Transportation, Washington, DC.
  1991c Precision Runway Monitor Demonstration Report. DOT/FAA/RD-91/5. Federal Avia-
         tion Administration, Washington, DC.
  1991d Policy for Maintenance of the National Airspace System (NAS) Through the Year 2000.
         Order Number 6000.30B, October 8. U.S. Department of Transportation, Washington,
         DC.
  1993a FAA Airway Facilities Job Task Analysis, Volume II: ARTCC NAS Operations Man-
         ager. Final. January 29.
  1993b Demographic Profiles of the Airway Facilities Work Force. U.S. Department of Trans-
         portation, Washington, DC.
  1993c Human Factors Policy. FAA Order 9550.8. October.

1994a   Remote Maintenance Monitoring System (RMMS), Remote Monitoring Subsystem (RMS) Requirements. Document number NAS-MD-793A. U.S. Department of Transportation, Washington, DC.

1994b   *Automation Strategic Plan.* Washington, DC: U.S. Department of Transportation.

1995a   User Benefits of Two-Way Data Link ATC Communications: Aircraft Delay and Flight Efficiency in Congested En Route Airspace. DOT/FAA/CT-95/4. Data Link Benefits Study Team Report. U.S. Department of Transportation, Washington, DC.

1995b   *Airway Facilities Strategic Plan.* Washington, DC: U.S. Department of Transportation.

1995c   *Airway Facilities Concept of Operations for the Future.* Washington, DC: U.S. Department of Transportation.

1995d   Classification Guide and Qualification Standard. GS-2101.

1995e   *Annotated Summary Briefing of the Results of the Employee Attitude Survey for 1995.* Washington, DC: U.S. Department of Transportation.

1995f   *Human Factors in the Design and Evaluation of Air Traffic Control Systems.* Report #DOT/FAA/RD-95/3. Washington, DC: U.S. Department of Transportation.

1995g   *National Plan for Civil Aviation Human Factors: An Initiative for Research and Application.* March. Washington, DC: U.S. Department of Transportation.

1995h   *Strategic Plan, Volume 2.* Washington, DC: Federal Aviation Administration.

1995i   *Plan for Engineering, Research, and Development.* Washington, DC: U.S. Department of Transportation.

1995j   *Air Traffic Service Plan 1995-2000.* Washington, DC: U.S. Department of Transportation.

1996a   *National Airspace System Architecture Version 2.0.* Office of Systems Architecture and Program Evaluation (ASD). October. Washington, DC: U.S. Department of Transportation.

1996b   *Aviation System Capital Investment Plan.* January. Washington, DC: U.S. Department of Transportation.

1996c   Data Link Benefits Study Team Report: 1996.

1996d   Runway status lights. Internet: http://www.faa.gov/and/and400/and410/rwsl1.htm

1996e   *Report to the Committee on the Status and Organization of Human Factors Within the FAA.* Final report of the Human Factors Subcommittee, August 5. Washington, DC: U.S. Department of Transportation.

1996f   *Human Factors Design Guide for Acquisition of Commercial Off-the-Shelf, Subsystems, Non-Developmental Items, and Developmental Systems.* Report #DOT/FAA/CT-96/1. Washington, DC: U.S. Department of Transportation.

1996g   Free flight action plan. Federal Aviation Administration, Washington, DC.

Finholt, T., L. Sproull, and S. Kiesler

1990   Communication and performance in ad hoc tasks groups. In *Intellectual Teamwork*, J. Gallagher, R. Kraut, and C. Egido, eds. Hillsdale, NJ: Erlbaum.

Fitts, P.M., and M.I. Posner

1967   *Human Performance.* Westport, CT: Greenwood Press.

Flavin, J.M.

1996   System-Level Requirements for the Field Evaluation of TCAS RA Downlink in the ARTS IIIA. Technical Memorandum 42PM-TCAS-0067. Lincoln Laboratory. Massachusetts Institute of Technology, Lexington, MA.

Flohr, E.

1997   Perspective primary flight displays in the 4D ATM environment. In *Proceedings of the Eighth Symposium on Aviation Psychology*, R. Jensen, ed. Department of Aviation. Columbus, OH: Ohio State University.

Foyle, D.C., A.D. Andre, R.S. McCann, E.M. Wenzel, D.R. Begault, and V. Battiste
  1996   Taxiway navigation and situation awareness (T-NASA) system: Problem, design philosophy, and description of an integrated display suite for low-visibility airport surface operations. Paper 965551 in *Proceedings of the SAE/AIAA World Aviation Congress*, Los Angeles, California, October 21-24, 1996.

Frick, T.W.
  1992   Computerized adaptive mastery tests as expert systems. *Journal of Educational Computing Research* 8(2):187-213.

Galati, G., and G. Losquadro
  1986   *Space-Based Multifunction Radar Systems: Future Tool for Civilian and Military Surveillance.* Advisory Group for Aerospace Research and Development, Neuilly-sur-Seine (France). December.

Galati, G., G. Perrotta, S. Di Girolamo, and R. Mura
  1996   Space-based SSR constellation for global air traffic control. *IEEE Transaction on Aerospace and Electronic Systems* (July):1088-1106.

Gaver, W.
  1992   The affordances of media spaces for collaboration. In *Proceedings of the Conference on Computer Supported Cooperative Work.* New York: ACM.

Gazit, R.Y.
  1996   Aircraft Surveillance and Collision Avoidance Using GPS. Unpublished dissertation, Department of Aeronautics and Astronautics, Stanford University. August.

Geddes, N.D.
  1985   Intent inferencing using scripts and plans. In *Proceedings of the First Annual Aerospace Application of Artificial Intelligence Conference*, Dayton, OH. September.
  1989   Understanding Human Operators' Intentions in Complex Systems. ASI-TR-90-01. Applied Systems Intelligence, Inc., Gainesville, GA.

Geddes, N.D., W.S. Beamon, III, J.A. Wise, J.L. Brown, W. Hamilton, B. Lee, J. Zyzniewski, P. Auman, and T. Player
  1996   Final Report, Shared Model of Intentions for Free Flight: A Level Three Study for the NASA Advanced Air Traffic Technologies Program. Contract No. NAS2-14287, National Aeronautics and Space Administration. Applied Systems Intelligence, Inc., Roswell, GA.

Gent, R.N., and H.W. Van
  1995   Human Factors Issues with Airborne Data Link. NLR Technical Publication 95666L. National Aeronautics Laboratory, Amsterdam, Netherlands.

Gerold, A.
  1994   Searching for the holy grail of avionics. *Avionics* (August):26-28.

Gertz, J.L.
  1983   Mode S Surveillance Netting. Project Report. Lincoln Laboratory, Massachusetts Institute of Technology. November 4.

Getty, D.J., J.A. Swets, R.M. Pickett, and D. Gounthier
  1995   System operator response to warnings of danger: A laboratory investigation of the effects of the predictive value of a warning on human response time. *Journal of Experimental Psychology: Applied* 1:19-33.

Gluckman, J.P., M. Carmody, J.G. Morrison, E.M. Hitchcock, and J.S. Warm
  1993   Effects of allocation and partitioning strategies of adaptive automation in task performance and perceived workload in aviation relevant tasks. Pp. 150-155 in *Proceedings of the Seventh International Symposium on Aviation Psychology*, Columbus, OH.

Graham, R.V., D. Young, I. Pichancourt, A. Marsden, and A. Irkiz
  1994   ODID IV Simulation Report. EEC Report No. 269/94, Task AS08. Eurocontrol Experimental Centre, Brétigny-sur-Orge, France.

Groce, J.L., and G.P. Boucek
    1987   Air Transport Crew Tasking in an ATC Data Link Environment. SAE Technical paper
            871764. Warrendale, PA: SAE International.
Grossberg, M.
    1994   Issues in operational test and evaluation of air traffic control systems. *Journal of Air
            Traffic Control* (October-December):4-5.
Hahn, E.C., and R.J. Hansman, Jr.
    1992   Experimental Studies on the Effect of Automation on Pilot Situational Awareness in the
            Data Link ATC Environment. SAE Technical Paper 922022. Warrendale, PA: SAE
            International.
Haines, A.L., and W.J. Swedish
    1981   Requirements for Independent and Dependent Parallel Instrument Approaches at Re-
            duced Runway Spacing. MITRE Corporation, McLean, VA.
Hall, R.E., P.K. Samanta, and A.L. Swoboda
    1981   Sensitivity of Risk Parameters to Human Errors in Reactor Safety Study for a PWR.
            Report 51322 NUREG/CR-1879 (January). Brookhaven National Laboratory.
Hancock, P.A., and J.S. Warm
    1989   A dynamic model of stress and sustained attention. *Human Factors* 31:519-537.
Hancock, P.A., and M.H. Chignell, eds.
    1989   *Intelligent Interfaces: Theory, Research, and Design.* Amsterdam: North Holland.
Hanson, Jr., E.R.T.
    1992   An airline pilot's views on TCAS. *Journal of Air Traffic Control* (January-March):15-16.
Harper, R., and J. Hughes
    1991   What a F-ing System! Send 'em All to the Same Place and Then Expect Us to Stop 'Em
            Hitting: Making Technology Work in Air Traffic Control. Technical Report EPC-91-
            125. Rank Xerox Cambridge EuroPARC, Cambridge, England.
Hart, S., and L. Loomis
    1980   Evaluation of the potential format and content of a cockpit display of traffic information.
            Human Factors 22(5):591-604.
Harwood, K.
    1993   Defining human-centered issues for verifying and validating air traffic control systems.
            In *Verification and Validation of Complex Systems: Human Factors Issues*, J.A. Wise,
            V.D. Hopkin, and P. Stager, eds. Berlin: Springer-Verlag.
Harwood, K., B. Sanford, and K. Lee
in press   Developing ATC automation in the field: It pays to get your hands dirty. *Air Traffic
            Control Quarterly.*
Hayes-Roth, B.
    1985   A blackboard architecture for control. *Artificial Intelligence* 26:251-321.
Hays, R.T., and M.J. Singer
    1989   *Simulation Fidelity in Training System Design.* New York: Springer-Verlag.
Hilburn, B.G.
    1996   The Impact of Advanced Decision Aiding Automation on Mental Workload and Human/
            Machine System Performance. PhD dissertation, Department of Psychology, Catholic
            University of America, Washington, DC.
Hilburn, B., R. Molloy, D. Wong, R. Parasuraman
    1993   Operator versus computer control of adaptive automation. Pp. 161-166 in *Proceedings of
            the Seventh International Symposium on Aviation* Psychology. Columbus, OH.
Hilburn, B., R. Parasuraman, and M. Mouloua
    1995   Effects of short- and long-cycle adaptive function allocation on performance of flight-
            related tasks. Pp. 347-353 in *Aviation Psychology: Training and Selection*, N. Johnston,
            R. Fuller, and N. McDonald, eds. Aldershot: Ashgate.

Hilburn, B.G., M.W.P. Baker, W.D. Pakela, and R. Parasuraman
1997   The effect of free flight on air traffic controller mental workload, monitoring and system performance. In *Proceedings of the 10th International CEAS Conference on Free Flight*, Amsterdam.

Hile, M.G., B.B. Ghobary, and D.M. Campbell
1995   Sources of expert advice: A comparison of peer-reviewed advice from the literature with that from an automated performance support system. *Behavior Research Methods, Instruments and Computers* 27(2):272-276.

Hockey, G.R.J.
1986   Changes in operator efficiency as a function of environmental stress, fatigue, and circadian rhythms. Pp. 441/44-49 in *Handbook of Perception and Human Performance: Vol. 11*, K.R. Boff, L. Kaufman, and J.P. Thomas, eds. New York: Wiley.

Hoffman, R.B., R.D. Kaye, B.H. Sacher, and L.S. Carlson
1995   TCAS II Resolution Advisory Downlink Evaluation Report. Technical Report MTR 95WO000080. MITRE Corporation, McLean, VA.

Honeywell
1989   *B747-400 Flight Management System Guide.* Phoenix, AZ: Honeywell, Inc.

Hopkin, V.D.
1989   Man-machine interface problems in designing air traffic control systems. *Proceedings of the IEEE* 77(11):1634-1642.
1991a   Automated flight strip usage: Lessons from the functions of paper strips. Pp. 62-64 in *Book of Abstracts of AIAA/NASA/FAA/HFS Symposium on Challenges in Aviation Human Factors: The National Plan.* Washington, DC.
1991b   The impact of automation on air traffic control systems. Pp. 3-19 in *Automation and Systems Issues in Air Traffic Control*, J.A. Wise, V.D. Hopkin, and M.L. Smith, eds. NATO ASI Series, Vol. F73. Berlin: Springer-Verlag.
1995   *Human Factors in Air Traffic Control.* London: Taylor and Francis.

Hughes Aircraft
1995   Virtual Controller (Air Traffic Control Simulator) and Virtual Tower (Next-Generation Visual Tower Simulators). Brochures. Hughes Training, Inc., Binghamton, NY.

Hughes, J., V. King, T. Rodden, and H. Andersen
1994   Moving out from the control room: Ethnography in system design. Pp. 429-446 in *Computer Supported Cooperative Work '94.* ACM 0-89791-689-1/94/0010. Cambridge, MA: ACM.

Hughes, J.A., D. Randall, and D. Shapiro
1993   Faltering from ethnography to design. Pp. 77-90 in *Verification and Validation of Complex Systems: Additional Human Factors Issues*, J.A.Wise, V.D. Hopkin, and P. Stager, eds. Daytona Beach, FL: Embry-Riddle Aeronautical University Press.

Hughes, D., and M.A. Dornheim
1995   Accidents direct focus on cockpit automation. *Aviation Week and Space Technology* (January 30):52-54. (Part of a two-issue series on cockpit automation.)

Hurn, J.
1989   *GPS: A Guide to the Next Utility.* Sunnyvale, CA: Trimble Nav., Ltd.

Hutchins, E.
1990   The technology of team navigation. In *Intellectual Teamwork*, J. Gallagher, R. Kraut, and C. Egido, eds. Hillsdale, NJ: Erlbaum.

Hutton, R.J.B.
1997   En route air traffic controller decision making and errors: An application of the recognition primed decision model to error analysis. In *Proceedings of the Ninth International Symposium on Aviation Psychology.* Columbus: Ohio State University.

Idaho National Engineering Laboratory
1997   Safety and risk evaluation. Internet: HTTP://WWW.INEL.gov/CGI-bin/highlights.prl?/
        www/TECHNOLOGY_transfer/FACT-HTM/
Idaszak, J.R.
1989   Human operators in automated systems: The impact of active participation and commu-
        nication. Pp. 778-782 in *Proceedings of the 33rd Annual Meeting of the Human Factors
        Society*. Santa Monica, CA: Human Factors and Ergonomics Society.
Irving, S.P., P. Polson, and J.E. Irving
1994   A GOMS analysis of the advanced automated cockpit. In *Proceedings of CMI*. New
        York: ACM, Inc.
Isaac, A.R.
1997   Situational awareness in air traffic control: Human cognition and advanced technology.
        In *Engineering Psychology and Cognitive Engineering*, D. Harris, ed. London: Ashgate.
Johnson, W.W., V. Battiste, S. Selzell, S. Holland, S. Belcher, and K. Jordan
1997   Development and demonstration of a prototype free flight cockpit display of traffic infor-
        mation. In *Proceedings of the SAE/AIAA World Aviation Congress*. Warrendale, PA:
        Society for Automotive Engineering.
Johannsen, G., and W.B. Rouse
1983   Studies of planning behavior of aircraft pilots in normal, abnormal, and emergency situa-
        tions. *IEEE Transactions on Systems, Man, and Cybernetics* SMC-13(3):267-278.
Jones, D., and S. Young
1996   Flight Demonstration of Integrated Airport Surface Automation Concepts. NASA Lan-
        gley Research Center.
Jones, P.M., C.M. Mitchell, and K.S. Rubin
1988   Intent inferencing with a model-based operator's associate. Report 88-2, Center for Hu-
        man-Machine Systems Research, School of Industrial and Systems Engineering, Georgia
        Institute of Technology, Atlanta. To appear in *Proceedings of the Sixth Symposium on
        Empirical Foundations of Information and Software Science*.
1990   Validation of intent inferencing by a model-based operator's associate. *International
        Journal of Man-Machine Studies* 33:177-202.
Jones, S.E.
1996   Human Error: The Role of Group Dynamics in Error Tolerant Systems. Unpublished
        doctoral dissertation, Department of Psychology, University of Texas at Austin.
Jorna, P.
1997   Human machine interactions with future flight deck and air traffic control systems. Pp.
        151-174 in *Engineering Psychology and Cognitive Ergonomics*, D. Harris, ed. Brookfield,
        VT: Ashgate Publishing.
Keeney, R.L., and H. Raiffa
1976   *Decisions with Multiple Objectives*. New York: Wiley.
Kerns, K.
1991   Data link communication between controllers and pilots: A review and synthesis of the
        simulation literature. *The International Journal of Aviation Psychology* 1(3):181-204.
1994   Human Factors in ATC/Flight Deck Integration: Implications of Data Link Simulation
        Research. MP 94W0000098. MITRE Corporation, McLean, VA.
Kerns, K., and D.W. Small
1995   Opportunities for Rapid Integration of Human Factors in Developing a Free Flight Capa-
        bility. Report 95W0305. MITRE Corporation, McLean, VA.
Kirwan, B., and L.K. Ainsworth
1992   *A Guide to Task Analysis*. London: Taylor and Francis.
Klass, P.J.
1997   New TCAS software to cut unneeded evasive actions. *Aviation Week and Space Technol-
        ogy* January 27:57-59.

Klingle-Wilson, D.L.
    1995   Integrated Terminal Weather System (ITWS). Demonstration and Validation Operational
            Test and Evaluation. Lincoln Laboratory Project Report ATC-234.
Knox, C.E., and C.H. Scanlon
    1991   Flight Tests with a Data Link Used for Air Traffic Control Information Exchange. NASA
            Technical Paper 3135. NASA Langley Research Center, Hampton, VA.
Kreifeldt, J.G.
    1980   Cockpit displayed traffic information and distributed management in air traffic control.
            Human Factors 22(6):671-691.
Krozel, J., and M. Peters
    1997   Conflict detection and resolution for freeflight. *Air Traffic Control Quarterly* 5(3).
Kuchar, J.K., and R.J. Hansman
    1995   A probabilistic methodology for the evaluation of alerting system performance. In *Pro-
            ceedings of the IFAC/IFIP/IFORS/IE Symposium*, Cambridge, MA.
Kyng, M.
    1995   Making representations work. *Communications of the ACM* 38(9):46-49.
Langer, H.A.
    1990   Keynote address at dedication of NASA Ames Human Performance Research Labora-
            tory. Operations Memorandum No. 90-40. Air Transport Association of America, Wash-
            ington, DC.
Lasswell, J.W., and C.D. Wickens
    1995   The Effects of Display Location and Dimensionality on Taxi-Way Navigation. Technical
            Report ARL-95-5/NASA-95-2. University of Illinois Aviation Research Laboratory, Sa-
            voy.
Lee, J.D., and N. Moray
    1992   Trust, control strategies, and allocation of function in human-machine systems. *Ergo-
            nomics* 35:1243-1270.
    1994   Trust, self-confidence, and operators' adaptation to automation. *International Journal of
            Human-Computer Studies* 40:153-184.
Lee, K.K., and T.J. Davis
    1995   *The Development of the Final Approach Spacing Tool (FAST): A Cooperative Control-
            ler-Engineer Design Approach*. NASA Technical Memorandum 110359. NASA Ames
            Research Center, Moffett Field, CA.
Lee, D., P.F. Kostiuk, B. Kaplan, M. Escobar, A. Odoni, and B. Malone
    1997   Technical and Economic Analysis of Air Transportation Management Issues Related to
            Free Flight. NS501T1. Logistics Management Institute, McLean, VA.
Lewandowsky, S., and D. Nikolic
    1995   A connectionist approach to modeling the effects of automation. In *Proceedings of the
            8th International Symposium on Aviation Psychology*. Columbus, OH: Ohio State Uni-
            versity.
Liang, T.-Y., and Y.-K. Teo
    1994   Implementing expert systems technology: A corporate-wide approach. *Behavior and
            Information Technology* 13(5):338-346.
Lind, A.T.
    1993   Two Simulation Studies of Precision Runway Monitoring of Independent Approaches to
            Closely Spaced Parallel Runways. DOT/FAA/NR-92/9. Lincoln Laboratory, Lexington,
            MA.
Liu, Y.R., R. Fuld, and C.D. Wickens
    1993   Monitoring behavior in manual and automated scheduling systems. *International Journal
            of Man-Machine Studies* 39:1015-1029.

Lozito, S., A. McGann, and K. Corker
   1993   Data link air traffic control and flight deck environments: Experiment in flight crew
           performance. Pp. 1009-1015 in *Proceedings of the Seventh International Symposium on
           Aviation Psychology*, R. Jensen and D. Neumeister, eds. Columbus, OH: Ohio State
           University.
Maignan, G.
   1994   What is PHARE? *Air Traffic Control Quarterly* 2(2):79-83.
Main Commission Aircraft Accident Investigation - WARSAW
   1994   *Report on the Accident to Airbus A320-211 Aircraft in Warsaw on 14 September 1993.*
           Warsaw: Main Commission Aircraft Accident Investigation - Warsaw.
Malone, T.W., and K. Crowston
   1990   What is coordination theory and how can it help design cooperative work systems? Pp.
           357-370 in *CSCW 90 Proceedings*. ACM 089791-402-3/90/0010/0370. Cambridge, MA:
           ACM.
Mankin, D., S.G. Cohen, and T.K. Bikson
   1996   *Teams and Technology*. Boston, MA: Harvard Business School Press.
Manning, C.A.
   1995   Empirical investigations of the utility of flight progress strips: A review of the Vortac
           studies. Pp. 404-409 in *Proceedings of the Eighth International Symposium on Aviation
           Psychology*, R.S. Jensen, ed. Department of Aviation. Columbus, OH: Ohio State
           University.
Manning, C.A., and D. Broach
   1992   Identifying Ability Requirements for Operators of Future Automated Air Traffic Control
           Systems: Final Report. DOT/FAA/AM-92/96. Federal Aviation Administration, Wash-
           ington, DC.
Marsh, G.
   1994   Conference explores differential GNSS policy and technology. *Avionics* (August):22-25.
Masson, M., and J. Paries
   1997   Team Resource Management Training for Air Traffic Controllers. Paper presented at the
           Second Eurocontrol Human Factors Workshop, Brussels, Belgium.
May, P.A., M. Campbell, and C.D. Wickens
   1996   Perspective displays for air traffic control: Display of terrain and weather. *Air Traffic
           Control Quarterly* 3(10):1-17.
McCann, R.S., D.C. Foyle, A.D. Andre, and V. Battiste
   1996   Advanced navigation aids in the flight deck: Effects on ground taxi performance under
           low visibility conditions. Paper 965552 in *Proceedings of the SAE/AIAA World Aviation
           Congress*, Los Angeles, California, October 21-24.
McCann, R.S., A.D. Andre, D. Begault, D.C. Foyle, and E. Wenzel
   1997   Enhancing taxi performance under low visibility: Are moving maps enough? Pp. 37-41
           in *Proceedings of the 41st Annual Meeting of the Human Factors and Ergonomics Soci-
           ety*. Santa Monica, CA: Human Factors and Ergonomics Society.
McClumpha, A.J., and M. James
   1994   Understanding automated aircraft. In *Human Performance in Automated Systems*, M.
           Mouloua and R. Parasuraman, eds. Hillsdale, NJ: Erlbaum.
McGreevy, M.W., and S.R. Ellis
   1986   The effect of perspective geometry on judged direction in spatial information instruments.
           Human Factors 28:439-456.
Mejdrich, E.
   1995   TAP/ASTA flight demo data analysis. Pp. 483-503 in *Langley Aerospace Research
           Summer Scholars, Volume 2.*

Mellone, V.J., and S.M. Frank
  1993   The behavioral impact of TCAS II on the National Air Traffic Control System. In *Proceedings of the 7th International Symposium on Aviation Psychology*, R. Jensen, ed. Department of Aviation. Columbus, OH: Ohio State University.

Merwin, D., J. O'Brien, and C.D. Wickens
  1997   Perspective and coplanar representation of air traffic: Implications for conflict and weather avoidance. In *Proceedings of the Ninth International Symposium on Aviation Psychology*. Department of Aerospace Engineering, Applied Mechanics, and Aviation. Columbus, OH: Ohio State University.

Merwin, D, J. Viera, and C.D. Wickens
  1997   Representation of air traffic: Implications for conflict and weather avoidance. In *Proceedings of the 9th International Symposium on Aviation Psychology*, R Jensen, ed.. Columbus, OH: Ohio State University.

Midkiff, A.H., and R.J. Hansman, Jr.
  1992   Identification of Important "Party Line" Information Elements and the Implications for Situational Awareness in the Datalink Environment. SAE Technical Paper 922023. Aerotech '92, Anaheim, California, October 5-8.

Miller, D., and A. Swain
  1987   Human reliability analysis. In *Handbook of Human Factors*, G. Salvendy, ed. New York: Wiley.

Miller, D.L., G.J. Wolfman, A.J. Volanth, and R.T. Mullins
  1996   Systems integration, user interface design, and tower air traffic control. *IEEE AES Systems Magazine* (April):22-25.

Ministère de l'équipement, des transports et du tourisme
  1993   *Rapport de la Commission d'enquête sur l'accident survenu le 20 janvier 1992 près du Mont Sainte Odile à l'Airbus A.320 immatricule F-GGED exploité par la Compagnie Air Inter*. Official English translation. Paris: Ministère de l'équipement, des transports et du tourisme.

Mitchell, C.M.
  1987   GT-MSOCC: A research domain for modeling human-computer interaction and aiding decision making in supervisory control systems. *IEEE Transactions on Systems, Man and Cybernetics* SMC-17:553-570.

MITRE Corporation
  1997   Internet: www.mitre.org/resources/labs/amass.html.

Molloy, R., and R. Parasuraman
  1996   Monitoring an automated system for a single failure: Vigilance and task complexity effects. *Human Factors* 38:311-322.

Monan, W.P.
  1986   *Human Factors in Aviation Operations: The Hearback Problem*. NASA Contractor Report 177398. Moffett Field, CA: NASA Ames Research Center.

Montgomery, P., H. Uematsu, and B. Parkinson
  1995   Full State Estimation and Control of a Large Model Aircraft Using Carrier Phase Differential GPS. Differential Satellite Navigation Systems Conference, Bergen, Norway. April.

Moray, N.
  1997   Mental models in theory and practice. In *Attention and Performance XVII*, D. Gopher and A. Koriat, eds. England: Oxford University Press.

Morrow, D., A. Lee, and A. Rodvold
  1993   Analysis of problems in routine controller-pilot communications. *International Journal of Aviation Psychology* 3:285-302.

Mosier, K., L.J. Skitka, and K.J. Korte
  1994   Cognitive and social psychological issues in flight crew/automation interaction. Pp. 191-
          197 in *Human Performance in Automated Systems: Current Research and Trends*, M.
          Mouloua and R. Parasuraman, eds. Hillsdale, NJ: Erlbaum.
Mosier, K., and L.J. Skita
  1996   Human decision makers and automated decision aids: Made for each other? In *Automa-
          tion and Human Performance: Theory and Applications*, R. Parasuraman, and M.
          Mouloua, eds. Mahwah, NJ: Erlbaum.
Muir, B.M.
  1988   Trust between humans and machines, and the design of decision aids. Pp. 71-83 in
          Cognitive Engineering in Complex Dynamic Worlds, E. Hollnagel, G. Mancini, and D.D.
          Woods, eds. London: Academic.
Mundra, A.
  1989   *A New Automation Aid to Air Traffic Controllers for Improving Airport Capacity.* MP-
          89W00034. The MITRE Corporation, McLean, VA.
Mundra, A., and K.M. Levin
  1990   *Developing Automation for Terminal Air Traffic Control: Case Study of the Imaging Aid.*
          MP90W0029. The MITRE Corporation, McLean, VA.
Mundra, A., J.J. Cieplak, D.A. Domino, O.B. Olmos, and H.P. Stgassen
  1997   Potential ADS-B/CDTI Capabilities for Near Term Deployment. MITRE Corporation,
          McLean, VA.
Nagel, D.C.
  1989   Human error in aviation operations. Chapter 9 in *Human Factors in Aviation*, E.L. Wiener
          and D.C. Nagel, eds. San Diego, CA: Academic Press.
National Aeronautics and Space Administration
  1995   Surface navigation in low visibility conditions. Internet: http://tag-www.larc.nasa.gov/
          tops/...ibits/inf/inf-144-95/inf14495.html.
  1996   What is SMA? Internet: http://sdtf.arc.nasa.gov/sma_public/whatis/whatis.html
  1997a   Technical areas productivity program. Internet: http://ast-server.larc.nasa.gov/tap/tap.html
  1997b   Three-dimensional aviation display. Internet: http://vision.arc.nasa.gov./afh/brief/
          auditory.s.t./3-d.a.t.html
  1997c   Pilot taxi innovations. Internet: http://www.nctn.hq.nasa.gov/nctn/sti/innovations 51/
          piltaxi.html
  1997d   SDTF. Internet: sdtf.arc.nasa.gov/pages/design.html
National Air Traffic Services Limited
  1996   *P/D 1 Final Report.* Document PHARE/NATS/PD-1-10.2/SSR.0.2. Brussels, Belgium:
          Eurocontrol.
National Transportation Safety Board
  1993   Safety Recommendations A-93-46 through A-93-48. March 23.
  1995a   Most Wanted Transportation Safety Improvements. Internet: http://www.ntsb.gov/Recs/
          runwinc/html.
  1995b   Memorandum. Safety Recommendation A-95-30 through -34. February 28.
  1997a   Grounding of the Panamanian Passenger Ship Royal Majesty on Rose and Crown Shoal
          Near Nantucket, Massachusetts, June 10, 1995. Report No. NTSB/MAR-97-01. Na-
          tional Transportation Safety Board, Washington, DC.
  1997b   Collision of Washington Metropolitan Transit Authority Train T111 with Standing Train
          at Shady Grove Station, near Gaithersburg, MD, January 6, 1996. Report No. NTSB-
          ATL-96-MR008). National Transportation Safety Board, Washington DC.
Navtech Seminars, Inc.
  1995   GPS for Charles S. Draper Laboratory. Course guide for course 301. Navtech Seminars,
          Inc., Arlington, VA.

Nii, H.P., and N. Aiello
1986   The blackboard model of problem solving. *Artificial Intelligence Magazine* 7(2):38-53.
Nirhjaus, H.B.
1993   Workload in Air Traffic Control Automation. NLR Technical Publication 93182L. National Aerospace Laboratory, Amsterdam, Netherlands.
Norman, D.A.
1993   *Things That Make Us Smart.* New York: Basic Books.
Odoni, A.
1996   Air Traffic Control Modeling. Presentation to the Panel on Human Factors in Air Traffic Control Automation, National Research Council.
Odoni, A.R., et al.
1997   Existing and Required Modeling Capabilities for Evaluating ATM Systems and Concepts: NASA AATT Program Final Report. Cambridge, MA: MIT International Center for Air Transportation.
Office of Technology Assessment
1988   *Safe Skies for Tomorrow: Aviation Safety in a Competitive Environment.* OTA-SET-381. Washington, DC: U.S. Government Printing Office, July.
Orasanu, J., E. McCoy, J. Davison, T. Owsley, M. Rodvold, R. Bullington, P. Smith, and L. France
in press Managing irregular operations in a free flight environment. In *Proceedings of the 9th International Symposium on Aviation Psychology.* Columbus, OH: Ohio State University.
Ozmore, R.E., and S.L. Morrow
1996   *Evaluation of Dual Simultaneous Instrument Landing System Approaches to Runways Spaced 3000 Feet Apart with One Localizer Offset Using a Precision Runway Monitor System.* DOT/FAA/CT-96/2. Atlantic City International Airport: Federal Aviation Administration.
Parasuraman, R.
1986   Vigilance, monitoring, and search. Pp. 43.1-43.49 in *Handbook of Perception: Volume 2. Cognitive Processes and Performance,* K. Boff, L. Kaufman, and J. Thomas, eds. New York: Wiley.
1987   Human-computer monitoring. *Human Factors* 29:695-706.
Parasuraman, R., T. Bahri, J. Deaton, J. Morrison, and M. Barnes
1990   Theory and Design of Adaptive Automation in Aviation Systems. Technical Report No. CSL-N90-1, Cognitive Science Laboratory. Catholic University of America, Washington, DC.
Parasuraman, R., P.A. Hancock, and O. Olofinboba
1997   Alarm effectiveness in driver-centered collision-warning systems. *Ergonomics* 40:390-399.
Parasuraman, R., R. Molloy, and I.L. Singh
1993   Performance consequences of automation-induced "complacency." *The International Journal of Aviation Psychology* 3:1-23.
Parasuraman, R., and M. Mouloua
1996   *Automation and Human Performance: Theory and Applications.* Mahwah, NJ: Erlbaum.
Parasuraman, R., M. Mouloua, and R. Molloy
1996   Effects of adaptive task allocation on monitoring of automated systems. *Human Factors* 38:665-679.
Parasuraman, R., M. Mouloua, R. Molloy, and B. Hilburn
1996   Monitoring automated systems. In *Automation and Human Performance: Theory and Applications,* R. Parasuraman and M. Mouloua, eds. Hillsdale, NJ: Erlbaum.

Parasuraman, R., and A. Riley
  1997 Humans and automation: Use, misuse, disuse, abuse. *Human Factors* 39:230-253.
Parkinson, B.W.
  1996 The Origins, Evolution and Future of Satellite Navigation. AIAA Von Karman Lecture. January 15.
Parnas, D.L., A. J. van Schouwen, and S.P. Kwan
  1990 Evaluation of safety-critical software. *Communications of the ACM* 33(6):636-648.
Patrick, N.J.M.
  1996 Decision-Aiding and Optimization for Vertical Navigation of Long-Haul Aircraft. Ph.D. thesis, Department of Mechanical Engineering, Massachusetts Institute of Technology.
Perry, T.S.
  1997 In search of the future of air traffic control. *IEEE Spectrum* (August):19-35.
Pew, R.W., and A. Mavor, eds.
  1997 *Representing Human Behavior in Military Simulations: Interim Report.* Panel on Modeling Human Behavior and Command Decision Making: Representations for Military Simulations, National Research Council. Washington, DC: National Academy Press.
Pisanich, G., E. Lee, and L. Beck
  1994 A part-task simulator for advanced automation and communications research. In *AIAA Flight Simulation Technologies.* Moffett Field, CA: NASA Ames Research Center.
Pisanich, G., and K. Corker
  1997 A Predictive Model of Flight Crew Performance in Automated Air Traffic Control and Flight Management Operations. Army/NASA Aircrew Aircraft Integration Program. Moffett Field, CA: NASA Ames Research Center.
Planzer, N.
  1997 Presentation to the Panel on Human Factors in Air Traffic Control Automation, National Research Council.
Planzer, N., and M.T. Jenny
  1995 Managing the evolution to free flight. *Journal of Air Traffic Control* (January-March):18-20.
Pritchett, A., and J.R. Hansman
  1997a Mismatches between human and automation decision making algorithms and their effects on the human's task and on system performance. Presentation at the Ninth International Symposium on Aviation Psychology, April.
  1997b Experimental studies of pilot performance at collision avoidance during closely spaced parallel approaches. Presentation at the Ninth International Symposium on Aviation Psychology, April.
Programme for Harmonised Air Traffic Management Research in Eurocontrol PD1
  1996 Evaluation of a Label Oriented HMI for Tactical Data Link Communication in ATC. Document 96-70-25. Brussels: Eurocontrol.
Prosser, M., and H. David
  1988 Real Time Simulation in Support of the ODID (Operational Displays and Input Development) Group. EEC Report No. 215. Eurocontrol Experimental Centre, Brétigny-sur-Orge, France.
  1989 Second Real Time Simulation for the Operational Displays and Input Development Group. EEC Report No. 226. Eurocontrol Experimental Centre, Brétigny-sur-Orge, France.
Prosser, M., H. David, and L. Clarke
  1991 ODID III Real-Time Simulation. EEC Report No. 242, Task AS02C. Eurocontrol Experimental Centre, Brétigny-sur-Orge, France.
RTCA (formerly known as Radio Technical Commission for Aeronautics)
  1995a Report of the RTCA Board of Director's Select Committee on Free Flight. RTCA Incorporated, Washington, DC.

1995b   Free Flight Implementation. RTCA Task Force 3 Report. RTCA Incorporated, Washington, DC.

Reason, J.T.
1990   *Human Error*. Cambridge, UK: Cambridge University Press.

Reason, J.T., and D. Zapf, eds.
1994   Errors, error detection and error recovery. *Applied Psychology: An International Review* 43(4):427-584 (special issue).

Rehmann, A.J.
1995   Airborne Data Link Program Plan. CSERIAC-FAA-TR-95-01. Federal Aviation Administration Technical Center, Atlantic City, NJ.

Reierson, J.D., W.R. Hershey, P.-Y. Ryberg
1990   The Human Role in AERA 3. MP-90W00061. Civil Systems Division, MITRE Corporation, McLean, VA, October.

Riley, V., C. Garg, and J. Adams
1996   Analyzing the Dynamics of a Next Generation Air Transportation Management System: Final Report. NASA Contract NASA2-14288. Honeywell Technology Center.

Robertson, G.G., S.K. Card, and J.D. Mackinlay
1993   Information visualization using 3D interactive animation. *Communications of the ACM* 36:56-71.

Rose, A. M.
1989   Acquisition and retention of skills. In *Application of Human Performance Models to System Design*, G. McMillan et al., eds. New York: Plenum Press.

Rosenberg, B.L., and T.E. Zurinskas
1983   Electronic tabular display subsystem (ETABS) study: A controller evaluation of an en route flight data entry and display system. FAA Technical Note. DOT/FAA/CT-TN83/09. Federal Aviation Administration Technical Center, Atlantic City, NJ.

Rouse, W.B.
1988   Adaptive aiding for human/computer control. *Human Factors* 30:431-438.

Rouse, W.B., N.D. Geddes, and J.M. Hammer
1990   Computer-aided fighter pilots. *IEEE Spectrum* 27:38-41.

Rudisil, M.
1996   Flight crew experience with automated technologies in commercial transport flight decks. In *Human Performance in Automated Systems*, M. Mouloua and R. Parasuraman, eds. Hillsdale, NJ: Erlbaum.

Runnels, M.H., ed.
1996   Concepts for Future NAS Operations. MITRE Report MITR 95W00107.

Sachs, P.
1995   Transforming work: Collaboration, learning, and design. *Communications of the ACM* 38(9):36-44.

SAE Aerospace Recommended Practice
1994   Human Engineering Recommendations for Data Link Systems. ARP-4791. SAE International, Warrendale, PA.

Sanderson, P., and J.M. Martagh
1989   Predicting fault performance: Why are some bugs hard to find? *IEEE Transactions on Systems, Man and Cybernetics* 1238-1243.

Sarter, N.
1997   Communication technologies, procedures, and strategies in support of future air traffic management (ATM) operations. In *Proceedings of the Ninth International Symposium on Aviation Psychology*. Columbus: Ohio State University.

Sarter, N.B., and D.D. Woods

1994   Pilot interaction with cockpit automation II: An experimental study of pilots' model and awareness of the flight management system. *International Journal of Aviation Psychology* 4(1):1-28.

1995a   How in the world did we get ever get into that mode? *Human Factors* 36.

1995b   "Strong, Silent, and Out-of-the-Loop": Properties of Advanced (Cockpit) Automation and Their Impact on Human-Automation Interaction. Technical Report CSEL 95-TR-01, Cognitive Systems Engineering Laboratory. Ohio State University, Columbus.

1997   New and envisioned communications technologies: How well can they support future air traffic management operations. Pp. 238-242 in *Proceedings of the 41st Meeting of the Human Factors and Ergonomics Society*. Santa Monica, CA: Human Factors and Ergonomics Society.

Scallen, S.F., P.A. Hancock, and J.A. Duley

1995   Pilot performance and preference for short cycles of automation in adaptive function allocation. *Applied Ergonomics* 26:397-403.

Scerbo, M.

1996   Theoretical perspectives on adaptive automation. In *Automation and Human Performance: Theory and Applications*, R. Parasuraman and M. Mouloua, eds. Mahwah, NJ: Erlbaum.

Schmidt, R.A., and D.E. Young

1987   Transfer of movement control in motor skill learning. Pp. 47-59 in *Transfer of Learning: Contemporary Research and Applications*, S.M. Cormier and J.D. Hagman, eds. San Diego, CA: Academic Press.

Schroter, H.

1996   A report of Eurocontrol's PHARE program. In *Proceedings of Airline Navigation '96-Flight International and Air Navigation International Conference*, October 9-11, Amsterdam, Netherlands.

Scott, W.B.

1994   CTAS tests confirm traffic flow benefits. *Aviation Week and Space Technology* October 17.

Seamster, T.L, R.E. Redding, and G.L. Kaempf

1997   *Applied Cognitive Task Analysis in Aviation*. Brookfield, VT: Avebury Aviation.

Segal, L.D.

1995   Designing team workstations: The choreography of teamwork. In *Local Applications of Ecological Approach to Human Machine Systems*, P. Hancock, J. Flach, J. Caird, and K. Vicente, eds. Hillsdale, NJ: Erlbaum.

Shallin, V.L., N.D. Geddes, D. Bertram, M.A. Szczepkowski, and D. DuBois

1993   Expertise in Dynamic, Physical Task Domains. Paper presented at the 3rd International Workshop on Human and Machine Cognition: Expertise in Context, Seaside, FL.

Shepherd, R., R. Cassell, R. Thapa, and D. Lee

1997   A Reduced Aircraft Separation Risk Assessment Model. Paper. American Institute of Aeronautics and Astronautics.

Sheridan, T.B.

1980   Computer control and human alienation. *Technology Review* 10:61-73.

1987   Supervisory control. In *Handbook of Human Factors*, G. Salvendy, ed. London: Wiley.

1988   Trustworthiness of command and control system. In *Proceedings of the IFAC Conference on Man Machine Systems*. Oulu, Finland.

1992   *Telerobotics, Automation, and Supervisory Control*. Cambridge, MA: MIT Press.

Sheridan, T.B., and R.T. Hennessy, eds.

1984   *Research and Modeling of Supervisory Control Behavior: Report of a Workshop*. Committee on Human Factors. Washington, DC: National Academy Press.

Sherman, P.J., R.L. Helmreich, and A.C. Merritt
 1997 National culture and flightdeck automation. Results of a multi-nation survey. *International Journal of Aviation Psychology.*
Shingledecker, C., and N.J. Talotta
 1993 Controller workload assessment in the development of data link air traffic control services. In *Proceedings of the Conference on Workload Assessment and Safety.* London: Royal Aeronautical Society.
Singh, I.L., R. Molloy, and R. Parasuraman, R.
 1993 Automation-induced "complacency": Development of the complacency-potential rating scale. *International Journal of Aviation Psychology* 3:111-121.
Skiles, T., P. Krois, R. Graham, and A. Marsden
 1997 Task and Workload Comparisons Between Air Traffic Control Systems. Poster presented at the 41st Annual Meeting of the Human Factors and Ergonomics Society.
Slameca, N.J., and P. Graf
 1978 The generation effect: Delineation of a phenomenon. *Journal of Experimental Psychology: Human Learning and Memory* 4:592-604.
Small, D.W.
 1994 Lessons Learned: Human Factors in the AAS Procurement. MP 94W0000088. MITRE Corporation, McLean, VA.
Smith, A., C. Evers, and R. Cassell
 1996 Evaluation of airport surface surveillance technologies. Rannoch Corporation, Alexandria, VA.
Smith, P., D. Woods, E. McCoy, C. Billings, N. Sarter, R. Denning, and S. Dekker
 1997 Human-Centered Technologies and Procedures for Future Air Traffic Management. 1996 Activities Report, Contract No. NAG2-995. Ohio State University Research Foundation, Columbus.
Smith, P.E., C. Billings, D. Woods, E. McCoy, N. Sarter, R. Denning, and S. Dekker
 1997 Can automation enable a cooperative future ATM system? In *Proceedings of the Ninth International Symposium on Aviation Psychology.* Columbus: Ohio State University.
Sollenberger, R.L., and P. Milgram
 1993 Effects of stereoscopic and rotational displays in a 3D path-tracing task. *Human Factors* 35(3):483-499.
Sorkin, R.D., B.H. Kantowitz, and S.C. Kantowitz
 1988 Likelihood alarm displays. *Human Factors* 30:445-459.
Stager, P.
 1991 The Canadian Automated Air Traffic Control System (CAATS): An overview. Pp. 39-45 in *Automation and Systems Issues in Air Traffic Control,* J.A. Wise, V.D. Hopkin, and M.L. Smith, eds. NATO ASI Series, Vol. F73. Berlin: Springer-Verlag.
 1993 Validation in complex systems: Behavioral issues. Pp. 99-114 in *Verification and Validation of Complex Systems: Human Factors Issues,* J.A. Wise, V.D. Hopkin, and P. Stager, eds. Daytona Beach, FL: Embry-Riddle Aeronautical University Press.
 1994 Achieving the objectives of certification through validation: Methodological issues. Pp. 401-411 in *Human Factors Certification of Advanced Aviation Technologies.* Daytona Beach, FL: Embry-Riddle Aeronautical University Press.
 1996 Automation in the Canadian Automated Air Traffic System (CAATS). Briefing presented to the Panel on Human Factors in Air Traffic Control Automation, National Research Council, December 6, 1996, Somers Point, NJ.
Steenblik, J.W.
 1996 Pilots complying with only half of TCAS RAs. *Airline Pilot* (September):5.

Stein, E.S., and D.J. Garland
   1993   Air traffic control working memory: Considerations in air traffic control tactical opera-
           tions. FAA Technical Note. DOT/FAA/CT-TN93/37. Federal Aviation Administration
           Technical Center, Atlantic City, NJ.
Stein, E.S., and D. Wagner
   1994   A psychologist's view of validating aviation systems. Pp. 45-52 in *Human Factors Cer-
           tification of Advanced Aviation Technologies*, J.A. Wise, V.D. Hopkin, and D.J. Garland,
           eds. Daytona Beach, FL: Embry-Riddle Aeronautical University Press.
Stix, G.
   1994   Aging airways. *Scientific American* (May):70-78.
Strain, R.C., E.C. Moody, B.E. Hahn, S. Dunbar, J.P. Kavoussi, and J.P. Mittelman
   1996   Airborne information initiatives: Capitalizing on a multi-purpose broadcast communica-
           tions architecture. *SPIE, 10th Annual International AeroSpace Symposium.*
Strasel, H.C., F.N. Dyer, J.T. Roth, I.N. Alderman, and D.L. Finley
   1988   Implementing Embedded Training (ET) (Volume 2 of 10): Embedded Training as a
           System Alternative (Research Product 88-22). AD A204 836. Army Research Institute
           for the Behavioral and Social Sciences, Alexandria, VA.
Strauch, B.
   1997   Automation and decision making: Lessons from the Cali accident. Pp. 195-199 in *Pro-
           ceedings of the 41st Annual Meeting of the Human Factors and Ergonomics Society.*
           Santa Monica, CA: Human Factors and Ergonomics Society.
Suchman, L.
   1995   Making work visible. *Communications of the ACM* 38(9):55-64.
Swain, A.
   1990   Human reliability analysis: Needs, status, trends and limitations. *Reliability Engineering
           and System Safety* 29:301-313.
Swain, A.D., and H.E. Guttman
   1983   *Handbook of Human Reliability Analysis with Emphasis on Nuclear Power Plant Appli-
           cations.* Pp. 294-298 in Report NUREG CR-1278. Sandia National Laboratories. Wash-
           ington, DC: U.S. Nuclear Regulatory Commission.
Swets, J.A.
   1992   The science of choosing the right decision threshold in high-stakes diagnostics. *American
           Psychologist* 47:522-532.
Swierenga, D.
   1994   Estimates of airline losses from ATC and airspace inefficiencies. Briefing documenta-
           tion. Air Transport Association.
Talotta, N.J., et al.
   1990   Operational Evaluation of Initial Data Link En Route Services, Volume 1. Report No.
           DOT/FAA/CT-90/1, I. Federal Aviation Administration, U.S. Department of Transporta-
           tion, Washington, DC.
   1992a   Controller Evaluation of Initial Data Link Terminal Air Traffic Control Services: Mini-
           Study 2, Volume I. Report No. DOT/FAA/CT-92/2, I. Federal Aviation Administration,
           U.S. Department of Transportation, Washington, DC.
   1992b   Controller Evaluation of Initial Data Link Terminal Air Traffic Control Services: Mini-
           Study 3, Volume I. Report No. DOT/FAA/CT-92/18, I. Federal Aviation Administra-
           tion, U.S. Department of Transportation, Washington, DC.
Tambe, M., W.L. Johnson, R.M. Jones, F. Koss, J.E. Laird, P.S. Rosenbloom, and K. Schwamb
   1995   Intelligent agents for interactive simulation environments. *AI Magazine* (Spring):15-39.
Thackray, R.I., and R.M. Touchstone
   1989   Detection efficiency on an air traffic control monitoring task with and without computer
           aiding. *Aviation, Space, and Environmental Medicine* 60:744-748.

Theisen, C.J., Jr., A. Salvador, and W.J. Hoffman
1987 Development of a system engineer workstation. Pp. 1421-1424 in *Proceedings of the Human Factors Society 31st Annual Meeting.*

Tobias, L., U. Völckers, and H. Erzberger
1989 Controller evaluations of the descent advisor automation aid. Pp. 1609-1618 in *AIAA Guidance, Navigation and Control Conference Proceedings.* Washington, DC: American Institute of Aeronautics and Astronautics.

Tulga, M.K., and T. Sheridan
1980 Dynamic decisions and workload in multi-task supervisory control. *IEEE Transactions on Systems, Man, and Cybernetics* SMC-10(5):217-231.

Twidale, M., D. Randall, and R. Bentley
1994 Situated evaluation for cooperative systems. Pp. 441-452 in *Computer Supported Cooperative Work '94.* ACM 0-89791-689-1/94/0010. Cambridge, MA: ACM, Inc.

U.S. Department of Transportation
1991 *Precision Runway Monitor Demonstration Report.* DOT/FAA/ RD-91/5. Washington, DC: Federal Aviation Administration.

Vakil, S.S., A.H. Midkiff, and R.J. Hansman
1995 Mode Awareness Problems in Advanced Autoflight Systems. MIT Aeronautical Systems Laboratory (abstract), Cambridge, MA.

Vicente, K., and J. Rasmussen
1992 Ecological interface design: Theoretical foundations. *IEEE Transactions on Systems, Man, and Cybernetics* 22:589-606.

Vickers, T.K.
1992 FAA's international TCAS symposium. *Journal of Air Traffic Control* (January-March):14.

Völckers, U.
1991 Applications of planning aids for Air Traffic Control: Design principles, solutions, results. In *Automation and Systems Issues in Air Traffic Control,* J. Wise, V.D. Hopkin, and M. Smith, eds. Berlin: Springer-Verlag.

Vortac, O.U., M.B. Edwards, J.P. Jones, C.A. Manning, and A.J. Rotter
1993 En route air traffic controllers' use of flight progress: A graph-theoretic analysis. *International Journal of Aviation Psychology* 3(4):327-343.

Vortac, O.U., and C.A. Manning
1994 Modular automation: Automating sub-tasks without disrupting task flow. Pp. 325-331 in *Human Performance in Automated Systems: Current Research and Trends,* M. Mouloua and R. Parasuraman, eds. Hillsdale, NJ: Lawrence Erlbaum Associates.

Waller, M.C.
1992 Flight Deck Benefits of Integrated Data Link Communication. NASA Technical Paper 3219. NASA Langley Research Center, Hampton, VA.

Waller, M.C., and G.W. Lohr
1989 A Piloted Simulation Study of Data Link ATC Message Exchange. NASA Technical Paper 2859. Hampton, VA.

Warm, J.S.
1984 *Sustained Attention in Human Performance.* London: Wiley.

Watts, J.C., D.D. Woods, J.M. Corban, E.S. Patterson, R.L. Kerr, and L.C. Hicks
1996 Voice loops as cooperative aids in space shuttle mission control. Pp. 48-56 in *Computer Supported Cooperative Work '96.* ACM 0-89791-765-0/96/11. Cambridge, MA: ACM, Inc.

Weick, K.E.
1988 Enacted sensemaking in crisis situations. *Journal of Management Studies* 25:305-317.

White House Commission on Aviation Safety and Security
1997   Final Report to President Clinton. Vice President Al Gore, Chairman. February 12.
Whitfield, D., and A. Jackson
1983   The air traffic controller's picture as an example of a mental model. In *Analysis, Design and Evaluation of Man-Machine Systems: Proceedings of the IFAC/IFIP/IFORS/IEA Conference*, G. Johannsen and J.E. Rijnsdorp, eds. Oxford: Pergamon.
Wickens, C.D.
1992   *Engineering Psychology and Human Performance* (2nd ed.). New York: HarperCollins.
1994   Designing for situation awareness and trust in automation. In *Proceedings of the IFAC Conference on Integrated Systems Engineering*. Laxenburg, Austria: International Federation of Automatic Control.
1996   Designing for stress. Pp. 279-295 in *Stress and Human Performance*, J. Driskell and E. Salas, eds. Mahwah, NJ: Lawrence Erlbaum.
1997   Frame of reference for navigation. In *Attention and Performance, Volume 16*, D. Gopher and A. Koriat, eds. Orlando, FL: Academic Press.
Wickens, C.D., and P. Baker
1995   Cognitive issues in virtual reality. Pp. 515-541 in *Virtual Environments and Advanced Interface Design*, W. Barfield and T.A. Furness III, eds. New York: Oxford University Press.
Wickens, C.D., and C.M. Carswell
1995   The proximity compatibility principle: Its psychological foundation and relevance to display design. *Human Factors* 37(3):473-494.
Wickens, C.D., and B. Huey, eds.
1993   *Workload Transition: Implications for Individual and Team Performance*. Panel on Workload Transition, National Research Council. Washington DC: National Academy Press.
Wickens, C.D., and C. Kessel
1979   The effects of participatory mode and task workload on the detection of dynamic system failures. *IEEE Transactions on Systems, Man, and Cybernetics* SMC-9:24-34.
1980   Processing resource demands of failure detection in dynamic systems. *Journal of Experimental Psychology: Human Perception and Performance* 6:564-577.
Wickens, C.D., D. Merwin, and E. Lin
1994   Implications of graphics enhancements for the visualization of scientific data: Dimensional integrality, stereopsis, motion, and mesh. *Human Factors* 36(1):44-61.
Wickens, C.D., and M. Yeh
1996   Attentional filtering and decluttering techniques in battlefield map interpretation. Pp. 2-55/2-42 in *Proceedings of Army Research Laboratory Advanced Displays and Interactive Displays Federated Laboratory First Annual Symposium*. Adelphi, MD: U.S. Army Research Laboratory.
Wickens, C.D., S. Miller, and M. Tham
1996   The implications of data-link for representing pilot request information on 2D and 3D air traffic control displays. *International Journal of Industrial Ergonomics* 18:283-293.
Wickens, C.D., S. Todd, and K. Seidler
1989   Three-Dimensional Displays: Perception, Implementation, and Applications. CSERIAC SOAR 89-001. Crew System Ergonomics Information Analysis Center. Wright-Patterson Air Force Base, Dayton, OH.
Wickens, C.D., C-C. Liang, T. Prevett, and O. Olmos
1996   Electronic maps for terminal area navigation: Effects of frame of reference and dimensionality. *The International Journal of Aviation Psychology* 6(3):241-271.
Wiener, E.L.
1985   Human Factors of Cockpit Automation: A Field Study of Flight Crew Transition. NASA CR 177333. NASA Ames Research Center, Moffett Field, CA.

1988   Cockpit automation. Pp. 433-461 in *Human Factors in Aviation*, E.L. Wiener and D.C. Nagel, eds. San Diego, CA: Academic Press.

1989   Human Factors of Advanced Technology ("Glass Cockpit") Transport Aircraft. NASA CR 177528. NASA Ames Research Center, Moffett Field, CA.

1993   Crew coordination and training in the advanced-technology cockpit. Pp. 199-229 in *Cockpit Resource Management*, E.L. Wiener, B.G. Kanki, and R.L. Helmreich, eds. San Diego, CA: Academic Press.

Wiener, E.L., and R.E. Curry
1980   Flight-deck automation: Promises and problems. *Ergonomics* 23:995-1011.

Wiener, E.L., T.R. Chidester, B.G. Kanki, E.A. Palmer, R.E. Curry, and S.A. Gregorich
1991   The Impact of Automation on Crew Coordination and Communication. I. Overview, LOFT Evaluations, Error Severity, and Questionnaire Data. NASA CR 177587. NASA Ames Research Center, Moffett Field, CA.

Wiener, E., and D. Nagel, eds.
1988   *Human Factors in Aviation*. New York: Academic Press.

Will, R.P.
1991   True and false dependence on technology: Valuation with an expert system. *Computers in Human Behavior* 7:171-183.

Wilson, M.A., and M.A. Zalewski
1994   An expert system for abilities-oriented job analysis. *Computers in Human Behavior* 10(2):199-207.

Winograd, T.
1994   Categories, disciplines and social coordination. *Computer Supported Cooperative Work* 2(3):191-197.

Wise, J.A., D. Hopkin, and D.J. Garland, eds.
1994   *Human Factors Certification of Advanced Aviation Technologies*. Daytona Beach, FL: Embry-Riddle Aeronautical University Press.

Wise, J.A., V.D. Hopkin, and M.L. Smith, eds.
1991   *Automation and Systems Issues in Air Traffic Control*. NATO ASI Series, Vol. F73. Berlin: Springer-Verlag.

Wise, J.A., V.D. Hopkin, and P. Stager, eds.
1993   *Verification and Validation of Complex Systems: Human Factors Issues*. NATO ASI Series, Vol. F110. Berlin: Springer-Verlag.

Woods, D.D.
1995   The alarm problem and directed attention in dynamic fault management. *Ergonomics* 38(11):2372-2393.

1996   Decomposing automation: Apparent simplicity, real complexity. Pp. 3-17 in *Automation and Human Performance: Theory and Applications*, R. Parasuraman and M. Mouloua, eds. Mahwah, NJ: Erlbaum.

Wreathall, J.
1990   Letter to the editor. *Reliability Engineering and System Safety* 29:383-385.

Wyndemere
1996   An Evaluation of Air Traffic Control Complexity: Final Report, Contract Number NAS 2-14284. Wyndemere, Boulder, CO.

Zingale, C., S. Gromelski, and E. Stein
1992   Preliminary studies of planning and flight strip use as air traffic controller memory aids. FAA Technical Note. DOT/FAA/CT-TN92/22. Federal Aviation Administration Technical Center, Atlantic City, NJ.

APPENDIXES

APPENDIX
A

Aviation and Related Acronyms

3-D	three-dimensional
4-D	four-dimensional
AAS	advanced automation system
AATT	advanced air transportation technology
ACARS	aircraft communication addressing and reporting system
ACT	adaptive control of thought
ADS	automatic dependent surveillance
ADS-B	automatic dependent surveillance - broadcast mode
AERA	automated en route air traffic control
AFSS	automated flight service station
AIDC	air traffic control interfacility data communication
AILS	airborne information for lateral spacing
AM	amplitude modulation, arrival manager
AMASS	airport movement area safety system
AOAS	advanced oceanic automation system
AOC	airline operations center
AOD	airline operations department
ARSR	air route surveillance radar
ARTCC	air route traffic control center
ARTS	automated radar terminal system
ASDE	automated surface detection equipment
ASOS	automated surface observing system
ASRS	aviation safety reporting system

ASP	arrival sequencing program
ASR	airport surveillance radar
ASTA	airport surface traffic automation
ATC	air traffic control
ATCSCC	air traffic control system command center
ATIDS	aircraft target identification system
ATIS	airport terminal information service
ATM	air traffic management
AWOS	automated weather observing system
CA	conflict alert
CAATS	Canadian automated air traffic system
CAMI	Civil Aeromedical Institute
CDC	computer display channel
CDTI	cockpit display of traffic information
CDU	control display unit
CENA	Centre D'études del la navigation aérienne
CMM	capacity maturity model
COMPAS	computer oriented metering planning and advisory system
COTS	commercial off-the-shelf
CP	conflict prediction tool (may include URET, AERA functions)
CPDL	controller to pilot data link
CR	conflict resolution advisor (may include URET, AERA functions)
CRDA	converging runway display aid
CRM	crew resource management
CRT	cathode ray tube
CSCW	computer-supported cooperative work
CT	cooperative tools
CTAS	center TRACON automation system
CWSU	center weather service unit
DA	descent advisor
DARC	direct access radar channel
DBRITE	digital bright radar indicator tower equipment
DCC	display channel complex
DGPS	differential global positioning system
DM	departure manager
DoD	Department of Defense
DOTS	dynamic ocean tracking system
DSR	display system replacement
DUATS	direct user access terminal system

EDARC	enhanced direct access radar channel
EEC	Eurocontrol experimental center
EFIS	electronic flight instrument system
EFMS	experimental flight management system
ERM	en route metering
ERT	emergency reaction time
ESP	en route spacing program
ETMS	enhanced traffic management system
FAA	Federal Aviation Administration
FAATC	Federal Aviation Administration Technical Center
FAR	Federal Aviation Regulations
FAST	final approach spacing aid
FDIO	flight data input output system
FDP	flight data processing
FM	frequency modulation
FMA	final monitor aid
FMC	flight management computer
FMS	flight management system
FPM	flight path monitor
FSS	flight service station
GPS	global positioning system
GPWS	ground proximity warning system
GSD	graphic situation display
GWDS	graphic weather display system
HIPS	highly integrated problem solver
HSI	horizontal situation indicator
IBLS	integrity beacon landing system
IFR	instrument flight rules
ILS	instrument landing system
IPT	integrated product team
ITWS	integrated terminal weather system
LAAS	local area augmentation system
LLWAS	low-level windshear alerting system
LOS	loss of separation
LVLAS	low-visibility landing and surface
MAMS	military airspace management system
MCC	maintenance control center

MLS   microwave landing system
MSAW   minimum safe altitude warning
MWP   meteorologist weather processor

NAS   national airspace system
NASA   National Aeronautics and Space Administration
NASA-TLX   National Aeronautics and Space Administration task load index
NARSIM   NLR air traffic control research simulator
NDI   non-developmental item
NEXRAD   next generation radar
NIMS   national airspace system infrastructure management system
NM   negotiations manager
NMAC   near-midair collision
NMCC   national maintenance coordination center
NOCC   national operations control center
NTSB   National Transportation Safety Board
NWS   National Weather Service

OAP   oceanic automation program
OASIS   operability and supportability implementation system
OCC   operations control center
ODAPS   oceanic display and planning system
ODID   operational display and input development
ODL   oceanic data link

PATS   PHARE advanced tool set
PFD   primary flight display
PGG   plan and goal graph
PHARE   program for harmonised air traffic management research in
             Eurocontrol
PIREPS   pilot reports
PRM   precision runway monitor
PS   problem solver
PVD   plan view display

R&D   research and development
RA   resolution advisory
RBDT   ribbon display terminal
RDP   radar data processing
RNAV   area navigation
RRT   recovery response time
RT   radiotelephone

RTCA	formerly the Radio Technical Committee on Aeronautics
RWSL	runway status lights
SAMS	special-use airspace management system
SATORI	situation assessment through recreation of incidents
SDTF	surface development and test facility
SIMMOD	airport and airspace simulation model
SIMNET	simulation network
SMA	surface movement advisor
STAR	studies, tests, and applied research
STARS	standard terminal automation replacement system
TACAN	tactical navigation
TAP	terminal area productivity
TCAS	traffic alert and collision avoidance system
TDWR	terminal Doppler weather radar
TLS	tactical load smoother
TMA	traffic management advisor
T-NASA	taxi navigation and situation awareness
TP	telecommunications processor, trajectory predictor
TRACON	terminal radar approach control
TTT	total transmission time
TVSR	terminal voice switch replacement
TWIP	terminal weather information for pilots
UAT	universal access transceiver
URET	user request evaluation tool
VFR	visual flight rules
VSCS	voice switching communication system
WAAS	wide area augmentation system
WARP	weather and radar processor
WSP	weather systems processor

APPENDIX

B

Contributors

Many individuals contributed to the panel's thinking and its drafting of various sections of the report by serving as presenters, advisors, and coordinators of sources of valuable information. The list below acknowledges these contributors and their affiliations.

Federal Aviation Administration Liaisons

David Cherry
Lawrence Cole
Mitchell Grossberg
Maureen Pettitt

Phyllis Kayten
Carol Manning
Mark Hofmann
Neil Planzer

Federal Aviation Administration Advisors and Presenters

William Griffith
Dyana Kelley
Michael McAnulty
Joseph Pointkowski
Richard Ridgeway

FAA Technical Center
FAA Technical Center
FAA Technical Center
FAA Technical Center
FAA Technical Center

Other Advisors and Presenters

Russell Benel	MITRE Corporation
Divya Chandra	Massachusetts Institute of Technology, Lincoln Laboratory
Charles Collins	Massachusetts Institute of Technology, Lincoln Laboratory
Mica Endsley	Massachusetts Institute of Technology
Karl Grundmann	National Air Traffic Controllers' Association
Brian Hilburn	NLR, the Netherlands
Charles Johnson	Massachusetts Institute of Technology, Lincoln Laboratory
Diana Klingle Wilson	Massachusetts Institute of Technology, Lincoln Laboratory
Anne Lind	Massachusetts Institute of Technology, Lincoln Laboratory
Anand Mundra	MITRE Corporation
Roderic V. Nemecek	NAV CANADA CAATS Project Team
Amedeo Odoni	Massachusetts Institute of Technology

Biographical Sketches

CHRISTOPHER D. WICKENS (*Chair*) is currently a professor of experimental psychology, head of the Aviation Research Laboratory, and associate director of the Institute of Aviation at the University of Illinois at Urbana-Champaign. He also holds an appointment in the Department of Mechanical and Industrial Engineering and the Beckman Institute of Science and Technology. He is currently involved in aviation research concerning principles of human attention, perception, and cognition and their relation to display processing, multitask performance, and navigation in complex systems. He received an A.B. degree from Harvard University in 1967 and a Ph.D. from the University of Michigan in 1974 and served as a commissioned officer in the U.S. Navy from 1969 to 1972. He is a member and fellow of the Human Factors Society and received the Society's Jerome H. Ely award in 1981 for the best article in the *Human Factors Journal*, as well as the Paul M. Fitts award in 1985 for outstanding contributions to the education and training of human factors specialists by the Human Factors Society. In 1993 he received the Franklin Taylor award from Division 21 of the American Psychological Association and is a fellow of the association. He has also served on the National Research Council's Committee on Human Factors.

CHARLES B. AALFS is a retired air traffic control specialist for the Federal Aviation Administration (FAA). He has over 30 years of experience as an air traffic controller for both the U.S. Navy and the FAA. While with the FAA, he served as an air traffic controller, air traffic automation specialist, air traffic facility officer, air traffic facility manager, air traffic regional office automation specialist and branch manager, and division manager of resource management.

When he retired, he was the manager of the new Southern California TRACON in San Diego, California. As an automation specialist, he was responsible for the software maintenance of the terminal automated radar system called ARTS III and IIIA. He is also the author of many design changes to the ARTS III program, one of which was the design to allow automated handoffs from one ARTS III site to another.

TORA K. BIKSON is a senior scientist in RAND Corporation's Behavioral Sciences Department. Since 1980, her research has investigated properties of advanced information technologies in varied user contexts. Her work emphasizes field research design, intensive case studies, and large-scale cross-sectional studies addressed to the use of computer-based tools in organizational settings. She received B.A., M.A., and Ph.D. (1969) degrees in philosophy from the University of Missouri at Columbia and M.A. and Ph.D. (1974) degrees in psychology from the University of California at Los Angeles. She is a member of Data for Development, a United Nations Secretariat providing scientific guidance on the use of information systems in developing countries, and a technical consultant to the United Nations Advisory Commission on the Coordination of Information Systems. She is a frequent reviewer for professional papers and has authored a number of journal articles, book chapters, and research reports on the implementation of new interactive media. She is a member of the American Academy of Arts and Sciences, the Association for Computing Machinery, the Computer Professionals for Social Responsibility, the Society for the Psychological Study of Social Issues, and a fellow of the American Psychological Association. She recently served on the committee of the National Research Council's Computer Science and Telecommunications Board that produced *Information Technology and the Service Society*.

MARVIN S. COHEN is founder and president of Cognitive Technologies, Inc. (CTI) in Arlington, Virginia. His professional interests include experimental research on human reasoning and decision making, elicitation and representation of expert knowledge, training cognitive skills in individuals and teams, development of decision support systems, human-computer interface design, and methods for representing and manipulating uncertainty. His current work at CTI includes experimental research on airline pilot decision-making processes, training decision-making skills under time stress in the ship-based anti-air-warfare environment, training for more effective distributed team decision making in naval air strike warfare, design of interfaces to enhance human performance with automatic target recognition devices, and modeling and training situation-assessment skills of Army battlefield commanders. He has an M.A. in philosophy from the University of Chicago and a Ph.D. in experimental psychology from Harvard University. For 11 years, he was at Decision Science Consortium, Inc., where he was vice president and director of cognitive science and decision systems. He has taught at George Washington University on the design of human-computer interfaces and has served on a committee of the National Research Council's Air Force Studies Board on tactical battle management.

DIANE DAMOS is president of Damos Research Associates. Until recently, she was an associate professor of human factors at the University of Southern California. After receiving her doctorate in aviation psychology from the University of Illinois, she became a member of the faculty of the Department of Industrial Engineering at the State University of New York at Buffalo. Prior to joining the University of Southern California, she was also a member of the faculty of the Department of Psychology at Arizona State University. Her research interests have focused on pilot selection and multiple-task performance, including workload management in advanced automation aircraft. She has authored numerous books and papers and edited *Multiple Task Performance*, which appeared in 1991. She is a member of the editorial board of the *International Journal of Aviation Psychology*.

JAMES DANAHER is the chief of the Operational Factors Division of the Office of Aviation Safety at the National Transportation Safety Board (NTSB) in Washington, D.C. He has more than 35 years work experience in the human factors and safety fields, in both industry and government. Since joining NTSB in 1970, he has served in various supervisory and managerial positions, with special emphasis on human performance issues in flight operations and air traffic control. He has participated in the on-scene phase of numerous accident investigations, in associated public hearings, and in the development of NTSB recommendations for the prevention of future accidents. He is a former naval aviator and holds a commercial pilot's license with single-engine, multi-engine, and instrument ratings. He has an M.S. degree in experimental psychology from Ohio State University and is a graduate of the Federal Executive Institute. He has represented the NTSB at numerous safety meetings, symposia, and seminars and is the author or coauthor of numerous publications.

ROBERT L. HELMREICH is professor of psychology at the University of Texas at Austin and director of the University of Texas Aerospace Crew Research Project. His research on team performance has included pilots, astronauts, aquanauts, air traffic controllers, and surgical teams. He has been involved with the definition and implementation of crew resource management training in aviation for nearly 20 years. He is author or editor of 5 books, including the forthcoming *Culture at Work in Aviation and Medicine: National, Organizational, and Professional Influences* (with Ashleigh Merritt). He has also published more than 190 chapters, monographs, and journal articles. Helmreich has B.A., M.S., and Ph.D. degrees from Yale University and served as an officer in the U.S. Navy. He is a fellow of the American Psychological Association and the American Psychological Society. He received the 1994 Flight Safety Foundation/ *Aviation Week and Space Technology* distinguished service award for 1994 for his contributions to the development of crew resource management and the 1997 David S. Sheridan award for distinguished service to mankind in the fields of science, medicine, and education.

V. DAVID HOPKIN is an independent human factors consultant who is based part time at Embry-Riddle Aeronautical University at Daytona Beach, Florida. He was formerly senior principal psychologist at the Royal Air Force Institute of Aviation Medicine at Farnborough and human factors consultant to the United Kingdom Civil Aviation Authority. He has also worked for the International Civil Aviation Organization, NATO, Eurocontrol, the Federal Aviation Administration, and numerous other international and national agencies. He has over 300 publications, including the 1995 *Human Factors in Air Traffic Control*. He has an M.A. in psychology from the University of Aberdeen, Scotland, and is a fellow of the Royal Institute of Navigation.

JERRY S. KIDD is senior adviser for the Committee on Human Factors and its various projects. He received a Ph.D. from Northwestern University in social psychology in 1956; he then joined RAND Corporation to help on a project to simulate air defense operations. He left RAND in late 1956 to join the staff at the Laboratory of Aviation Psychology at Ohio State University. There he worked under Paul Fitts and George Briggs until 1962, when he joined the staff of AAI, Incorporated, north of Baltimore, Maryland. In 1964, he moved to the National Science Foundation as program director for special projects. He joined the faculty of the College of Library and Information Services at the University of Maryland in 1967 and retired in 1992.

TODD R. LaPORTE is professor of political science and formerly associate director of the Institute of Governmental Studies at the University of California, Berkeley. He teaches and publishes in the areas of public administration, organization theory, and technology and politics, with emphasis on the decision-making dynamics of large, complex, and technologically intensive (and hazardous) organizations, and the problems of governance and political legitimacy in a technological society. He is a member of the National Academy of Public Administration, was a research fellow with the Woodrow Wilson International Center of Scholars, and has held visiting research appointments with the Science Center in Berlin and the Max Planck Institute for Social Research in Cologne, Germany, and recently with the Los Alamos National Laboratory. He has a Ph.D. in political science from Stanford University.

ANNE S. MAVOR is study director for the Panel on Human Factors in Air Traffic Control, the Panel on Modeling Human Behavior and Command Decision

Making, and the Committee on Human Factors. Her previous work as a National Research Council senior staff officer has included a study of the scientific and technological challenges of virtual reality, a study of emerging needs and opportunities for human factors research, a study of modeling cost and performance of military enlistment, a review of federally sponsored education research activities, and a study to evaluate performance appraisal for merit pay. She is currently directing a study of modeling human behavior and command decision making in military simulations. For the past 25 years her work has concentrated on human factors, cognitive psychology, and information system design. Prior to joining the National Research Council she worked for the Essex Corporation, a human factors research firm, and served as a consultant to the College Board. She has an M.S. in experimental psychology from Purdue University.

JAMES P. McGEE is a senior research associate supporting human factors and related activities in the Division on Education, Labor, and Human Performance of the Commission on Behavioral and Social Sciences and Education. Prior to joining the National Research Council in 1994, he held scientific, technical, and management positions in human factors psychology at IBM, RCA, General Electric, General Dynamics, and United Technologies corporations. He has also instructed courses in applied psychology and general psychology at several colleges. He is a member of the Potomac chapter of the Human Factors and Ergonomics Society and of the American Psychological Association. He has a Ph.D. in experimental psychology from Fordham University.

RAJA PARASURAMAN is professor of psychology and director of the Cognitive Science Laboratory at the Catholic University of America in Washington, D.C. Currently he is also a visiting scientist at the Laboratory of Brain and Cognition at the National Institute of Mental Health in Bethesda, Maryland. Since 1982 he has been at the Catholic University of America, where he has carried out research on attention, aging, automation, cognitive neuroscience, vigilance, and workload. He has a B.Sc. (Hons.) in electrical engineering from Imperial College, University of London (1972), and an M.Sc. in applied psychology (1973) and Ph.D. in psychology from the University of Aston, Birmingham (1976). He is a fellow of the Human Factors and Ergonomics Society and received the society's award for the best article in 1993 in the journal *Ergonomics in Design*, as well as the society's Jerome H. Ely Award for best article in 1996 in the journal *Human Factors*. He is also a fellow of the American Association for the Advancement of Science, the American Psychological Association (Division 21, Engineering Psychology), the American Psychological Society, and the Washington Academy of Sciences, and a member of the Association of Aviation Psychologists, the Psychonomics Society, the Society for Neuroscience, and the Society for Psychophysiological Research.

JOSEPH O. PITTS retired from the Federal Aviation Administration (FAA) in 1993, after more than 36 years of government service. He is currently employed by the VITRO Corporation, which supports the FAA through its surveillance technical assistance contract. He supports the integrated terminal weather system program and the air traffic weather division. While employed by the FAA, he held positions as air traffic manager, assistant air traffic manager, branch manager, area manager, and full-performance-level air traffic controller at several air traffic control facilities. In the last 10 years of his tenure with the FAA, he had the responsibility of managing several research engineering and development programs at FAA headquarters; he was very active in both the FAA's facilities and equipment and research engineering and development budgets.

THOMAS B. SHERIDAN is Ford professor emeritus of engineering and applied psychology in the Departments of Mechanical Engineering and Aeronautics and Astronautics and director of the Human-Machine Systems Laboratory at Massachusetts Institute of Technology (MIT). His research has been on mathematical models of human operator and socioeconomic systems, on man-computer interaction in piloting aircraft and in supervising undersea and industrial robotic systems, on computer graphic technology for information searching and group decision-making, and on arms control. He has an S.M. degree from the University of California, a Sc.D. from MIT, and an honorary doctorate from Delft University of Technology, the Netherlands. He has served as president of both the Human Factors and Ergonomics Society and the IEEE Systems, Man and Cybernetics Society and is a fellow of both organizations. He has chaired the National Research Council's Committee on Human Factors and has served on numerous other NRC committees. He is senior editor of the MIT Press journal *Presence: Teleoperators and Virtual Environments* and is a member of the National Academy of Engineering.

PAUL STAGER is professor of psychology at York University, where he has taught since receiving a Ph.D. from Princeton University in 1966. A licensed pilot, his research has been concerned with system evaluation, human error, computer-human interface design, and human performance assessment in complex operational systems, most often in the context of aviation. During the past 20 years, his research has addressed several human factors issues in air traffic control, including the potential impact of bilingual communications on instrument flight operations, the precipitating conditions for operational errors, and the human engineering specifications for an advanced workstation design. Since 1989, he has advised the federal government and, more recently, NAV CANADA on all human engineering associated with the development and evaluation of the Canadian automated air traffic system (CAATS). He was a lecturer at the 1990 NATO Advanced Study Institute on automation and systems issues in air traffic control and, as codirector of the 1992 Advanced Study Institute on the verification and validation of complex human-machine systems, he edited (with J. Wise and D. Hopkin) *Verification and Validation of Complex Systems: Human Factors Issues* (1993).

RICHARD B. STONE retired from Delta Airlines after almost 35 years as a pilot. He served as a line check airman and his last assignment was flying the B 767 extended range to Europe. During his years as an airline pilot, he also acted as an aircraft accident investigator, represented airline pilots in medical matters, and served as the president of the International Society of Air Safety Investigators. He currently acts as a safety consultant in aviation. He has a B.S. from the University of Illinois and an M.S. from the University of New Hampshire. He received his flight training from the U.S. Air Force.

EARL L. WIENER is a professor of management science at the University of Miami. He served as a pilot in the U.S. Air Force and the U.S. Army and is rated in fixed-wing and rotary-wing aircraft. Since 1979 he has been active in the aeronautics and cockpit automation research of the NASA Ames Research Center. He has a B.A. in psychology from Duke University and a Ph.D. in psychology and industrial engineering from Ohio State University. He is a fellow and former president of the Human Factors Society and a fellow of the American Psychological Association. He served two terms on the FAA's Research, Engineering, and Development Advisory Council and currently is a member of the National Research Council's Committee on Human Factors. He was the 1997 recipient of the Human Factors and Ergonomics Society Arnold Small Award. He is the editor (with D. Nagel) of *Human Factors in Aviation* (1988) and *Cockpit Resource Management* (with B. Kanki and R. Helmreich, 1993).

LAURENCE R. YOUNG is Apollo program professor of astronautics at the Massachusetts Institute of Technology (MIT). He is director of the newly established National Space Biomedical Research Institute, with headquarters in Houston. He is a member of both the National Academy of Engineering and the Institute of Medicine. His research is in the application of control theory to human-vehicle problems, particularly eye movements and spatial orientation, flight simulators, and space laboratory experimentation on vestibular function. He was a principal investigator of five Spacelab missions, and served as an alternate payload specialist astronaut for the 1993 Spacelab life sciences flight of the space shuttle. He is a consultant to various industrial and government organizations and has served on the Committee on Human Factors, the Committee on the Space Station, the Aeronautics and Space Engineering Board, and the Air Force Studies Board of the National Research Council. He has received the Franklin V. Taylor award in human factors from the Institute of Electrical and Electronics Engineers, the Dryden lectureship from the American Institute of

Aeronautics and Astronautics, the Hansen award of the Aerospace Human Factors Association, and the prestigious Koestler Foundation prize in Switzerland. He is a fellow of the Institute of Electrical and Electronics Engineers and former president and Alza lecturer of the Biomedical Engineering Society. He has an A.B. in physics from Amherst College, S.B. and S.M. degrees in electrical engineering from MIT, an Sc.D. in instrumentation from MIT, and a certificat de license in mathematics from the University of Paris.

Index